The Wounded Generation

Also by David Nasaw

The Last Million:
Europe's Displaced Persons from
World War to Cold War

The Patriarch: The Remarkable Life and
Turbulent Times of Joseph P. Kennedy

Andrew Carnegie

The Chief: The Life of William Randolph Hearst

Going Out: The Rise and Fall of Public Amusements

Children of the City: At Work and at Play

Schooled to Order: A Social History of
Public Schooling in the United States

The Wounded Generation

COMING HOME AFTER WORLD WAR II

David Nasaw

PENGUIN PRESS | NEW YORK | 2025

PENGUIN PRESS
An imprint of Penguin Random House LLC
1745 Broadway, New York, NY 10019
penguinrandomhouse.com

Copyright © 2025 by David Nasaw
Penguin Random House values and supports copyright. Copyright fuels creativity, encourages diverse voices, promotes free speech, and creates a vibrant culture. Thank you for buying an authorized edition of this book and for complying with copyright laws by not reproducing, scanning, or distributing any part of it in any form without permission. You are supporting writers and allowing Penguin Random House to continue to publish books for every reader. Please note that no part of this book may be used or reproduced in any manner for the purpose of training artificial intelligence technologies or systems.

PP colophon is a registered trademark of Penguin Random House LLC.

Illustration Credits:
Page 1: Copyright © 1947 by Bill Mauldin. Courtesy of Bill Mauldin Estate LLC; page 12: Copyright © 1944 by Bill Mauldin. Courtesy of Bill Mauldin Estate LLC; page 126: Courtesy of the National Archives, photo no. 80-G-377094; pages 133, 145, 204, 219, 251, 281, 351: Copyright © 1945 by Bill Mauldin. Courtesy of Bill Mauldin Estate LLC; page 155: Printed by permission of the Norman Rockwell Family Agency. Copyright © 1945 by the Norman Rockwell Family Entities;
pages 167, 180, 193, 235, 262, 361: Copyright © 1946 by Bill Mauldin. Courtesy of Bill Mauldin Estate LLC.

Designed by Amanda Dewey

LIBRARY OF CONGRESS CONTROL NUMBER: 2025023513
ISBN 9780593298695 (hardcover)
ISBN 9780593298701 (ebook)

Printed in the United States of America
1st Printing

The authorized representative in the EU for product safety and compliance is Penguin Random House Ireland, Morrison Chambers, 32 Nassau Street, Dublin D02 YH68, Ireland, https://eu-contact.penguin.ie.

*To the memory of my father, Joshua J. Nasaw,
who served in Eritrea in World War II as a second
lieutenant in the Medical Corps of the
United States Army*

Contents

Introduction   xi

Part 1
THE LONG ROAD HOME

Chapter 1. The Return of the Wounded   *3*

Chapter 2. War Stories   *22*

Chapter 3. Bad Habits   *41*

Chapter 4. Segregation in the Military   *59*

Chapter 5. The Last Bloody Year in Europe   *74*

Chapter 6. War Wives, Girlfriends, and Mothers   *82*

Chapter 7. Washington Prepares for the Veterans' Return   *93*

Chapter 8. Victory in Europe   *106*

Chapter 9. A "Slow Demobilization"   *128*

Chapter 10. Repatriated and Discharged   *142*

Part 2
HOME AT LAST

Chapter 11. Wounded Minds   *169*

Chapter 12. Violent Veterans   *192*

Chapter 13. Love and Marriage . . . and Divorce   202

Chapter 14. The Black Veterans Come Home   224

Chapter 15. The White Veterans' Vote   240

Part 3
READJUSTING TO CIVILIAN LIFE

Chapter 16. "Home, Sweet Home Is a Nightmare Crisis"   253

Chapter 17. Get a Job?   273

Chapter 18. The Veterans at College   291

Chapter 19. Vocational Schools and Job-Training Programs   310

Chapter 20. After Five Years   338

Part 4
LEGACIES

Chapter 21. The Veterans' Welfare State   353

Chapter 22. Aftermaths   364

Acknowledgments   387

Abbreviations   391

Notes   395

Bibliography   431

Index   461

Introduction

In its duration, geographical reach, and ferocity, World War II was unprecedented, and the effects on those who fought it and their loved ones at home, immeasurable. The veterans who returned home were not the ones who had left for war. "They are very different now," wrote the GI cartoonist Bill Mauldin in *Up Front*, published in June 1945. "Don't let anybody tell you they aren't. . . . Some say the American soldier is the same clean-cut young man who left his home. . . . They are wrong."[1]

Most returning veterans found it difficult, if not impossible, to get a full night's sleep. Many were troubled by recurring nightmares and flashbacks. They were irritable, angry, plagued by uncontrollable rages, feelings of social isolation, and fears of places and events that evoked memories of the war, their proximity to death, and the dead left behind. Large numbers sought relief by drinking to excess, as they had during the war and while awaiting repatriation. Those who sought professional help were told that they suffered from nothing more than battle fatigue that time would cure. It did not. The true cause of their distress, post-traumatic stress disorder (PTSD), would go undiagnosed and untreated for decades to come.

Nearly 16.4 million Americans, 12 percent of the total population, 32 percent of males between eighteen and forty-five, served in the armed forces of the United States in World War II. They left behind four million spouses, two million children, and tens of millions of parents, siblings, lovers, friends, and neighbors. The book that follows is an account of the aftereffects that lived on in the bodies, hearts, and minds of those who fought, those who awaited their return, and the nation that had won the war but had now to readjust to peace.

The war itself lasted nearly four years. The men and women who fought it on two oceans, in the air, and on the landmasses of Africa, Alaska, Asia, Europe, and the islands of the Pacific served an average of thirty-three months, three-quarters of them overseas for sixteen months on average, three times as long as their counterparts in World War I. Never before or since have so many been called away to war—and for so long.[2]

The brutality and carnage of a global war were brought home in graphic reports and visual images in the daily press, the weeklies, Hollywood films, and newsreels. The human costs were made manifest with the arrival stateside of troopships bearing cargoes of servicemen of no further use to the military. In 1943 alone, more than one million were sent home, half of them with disability discharges. The overall numbers were alarming, but more so the percentage of those disabled and discharged—40 percent for the army—with "neuropsychiatric defects."[3]

Why had so many hale and hearty young men broken down? In 1948, three years after the cessation of hostilities, Dr. William Menninger, chief consultant in neuropsychiatry to the army surgeon general, explained that the higher incidence of psychological breakdowns in World War II as compared with World War I was due in large part to the fact that the second world war was "a 'tougher' one.... It was nearly three times as long; it was fought on a rapidly moving and shifting basis instead of on fixed lines; it required many amphibious landings; it was fought in every extreme of climate; the lethal devices were far more devastating and nerve-racking than ever before; and more men were kept away from home for longer periods."[4]

There was a great deal of truth in Menninger's analysis, but his explanation brought neither solace nor relief to those who returned home with PTSD symptoms that could not be treated because they were not understood—by the veterans, their families, and the doctors and psychiatrists from whom they sought help.

The men and women at war—and their families on the home front—had anticipated that demobilization would follow soon after the enemy's surrender. But that was not to be. The occupation of enemy lands required millions of troops. And the repatriation of those not needed was delayed because there were not enough ships to bring them home. Soldiers and sailors marooned in foreign ports engaged in near mutinies; their wives and mothers organized Bring Back Daddy Clubs and protested, lobbied, and demanded immediate demobilization. The White House and the military responded by recalibrating their plans, reducing the numbers required for occupation duty, and accelerating the rate of discharge.

The nation to which the veterans returned was not the one they had left behind. There were shortages of every conceivable consumer item: white shirts and men's suits; meat and maple syrup; beef, bread, and barley; cars, used and new; and, most critically, affordable housing. What was most troubling was the lingering, inescapable fear that a return to economic depression was just around the corner, that the layoff of millions of war workers and the discharge of millions more servicemen would lead to massive unemployment.

Welcomed home and pleased to be there, the newly returned

veterans were moody, distant, easily distracted. No magic switch turned off the hurt, erased the memories, transported the veterans to the lives and homes they had left years before. The lost years were gone forever. Their homes might look the same at first, but they felt smaller, airless, near claustrophobic. Their loved ones were different too. The children had grown up; the adults were older, grayer, more wrinkled; their wives and girlfriends had a confidence and self-assurance that had not been there before or, if so, they had not noticed it.

Families that had been torn apart by war, those recently wed and those married before Pearl Harbor, tried to rebuild and revive their relationships. Their difficulties in doing so were exacerbated by a housing crisis unparalleled in the nation's history. War wives and girlfriends were cautioned that it was their responsibility to protect their relationships, to accept without recrimination husbands and boyfriends who might have been unfaithful during the war. Women who had worked and managed their households without the help of men were pressured to give up their jobs and return, with a smile, to their prewar status as full-time housewives, dependent on their husbands.

Returning GIs struggled to adjust to family life after months, often years, in male-only, hierarchical communities. Husbands and boyfriends who had lived in fear of receiving "Dear John" letters or hints from home that "their women" had strayed could not escape suspicions of betrayal. Fathers whose children had been born or raised while they were at war tried, but too often failed, to relate to their offspring, to be good parents, to hide their anger and visible disappointment when their infants and toddlers retreated, ignored them, preferring the company of mothers and grandparents.

The inevitable result of all this was broken families, separation, and divorce. Between 1940, the year before the declaration of war, and 1946, the first full year of peace, the divorce rate more than doubled. By 1950, a million returning veterans had left or been left by their wives.[5]

A greater proportion of Black servicemen than White served overseas during the war—and those who did were more than likely to be stationed in places where residential and workplace segregation were unknown. On their return, they were no longer willing or able to accept the racial status quo that deprived them of the rights and privileges of citizenship. Those who had lived in the South moved north and west, following the paths of family, friends, and neighbors who had, during the war, left their homes for well-paid war production work elsewhere. A small but significant portion remained behind and organized to secure the rights denied them and their families. Their efforts were repulsed by a White citizenry and elected officials who preemptively mobilized to beat back any challenge to the racial status quo. Black GIs who wore their uniforms because they could not afford a new suit of clothes were attacked for displaying evidence of their service. More African Americans were lynched in 1946 than in the preceding three years and from 1939 through 1941.[6]

To ease the veterans' readjustment to civilian life and the reconversion of the economy from war production, Congress passed the GI Bill, which was signed into law on June 22, 1944, and amended in December 1945. Billions of dollars were poured into a veterans' support system more generous than that designed by any other nation or for previous generations of American soldiers and sailors. The returning veterans were provided with health care and hospitalization, readjustment allowance checks for the unemployed, disability pensions, mortgage guarantees, business loans, job counseling and placement, college and vocational school tuition and living expenses. These funds not only rewarded the veterans for their service but forestalled mass unemployment by providing them with direct financial assistance until reconversion had been completed and decent-paying jobs were available.

Millions of veterans, so long as they were White, male, and married, were able to purchase homes. Those who had never dreamed of getting a college degree were able to do so. Large numbers attended vocational schools and job-training programs, some of them little more than scams that funneled money into the pockets of a new breed of businessmen/grifters; others, legitimate programs that enabled the returning veterans to study dance, theater, art, and music and energize a postwar cultural renaissance.

As victory in Europe came into sight, President Roosevelt declared in January 1945, as he had several times during his presidency, that "equality of opportunity remains one of the principal objectives of our national life." The nation at war had, in enrolling women and Black Americans in the armed forces and providing them with war production jobs, expanded the range of opportunities available to them. But these gains were not permanent. The GI Bill, for all the good it did for so many veterans and for the economy, retarded progress toward "equality of opportunity" by privileging a veterans' population that was more than 90 percent White and 98 percent male.

The bill could not have been passed without the active support and votes of southern Democrats and anti–New Deal Republicans who, to protect the social and racial status quo, restricted federal oversight and reserved for local and state officials control over decisions on how and to whom benefits were allocated. The result was that throughout the nation, but particularly in the southern states, Black veterans were deprived of their full share of benefits. Those who rejected menial work assignments at substandard wages were denied the readjustment allowance checks that were designed to support unemployed veterans on their return home. They were unable to use GI

Bill loan guarantees to purchase homes because local bankers rejected their mortgage applications and suburban developers like Levitt & Sons refused to sell to them. They were denied admission to southern colleges and universities that were segregated by law. Black veterans were not the only ones denied access to the benefits due them under the GI Bill. Service men and women who acknowledged or were suspected of engaging in same-sex relationships were saddled with "blue discharges," which barred them from benefits. Female veterans, restricted by law or custom from purchasing property or securing bank loans in their own names, were unable to make use of GI Bill mortgage guarantees. Women who had during the war been admitted to colleges and professional schools in larger and larger numbers were after 1945 turned away in favor of male veterans with tuition, fees, and living allowances guaranteed by the federal government.

This is a story of the generation that lived through World War II. The vast majority of men and boys ripped from their homes to fight a war abroad were not professional soldiers, airmen, or sailors, but a cross section of civilians for whom military service was not a calling, but an intrusion. Among them were those who would, on their return to civilian life, take their place in postwar America as poets, professors, playwrights, and novelists; comedians and singers; movie stars and directors; ballet dancers and baseball players; painters and jazz musicians; politicians and presidents. Their names may be recognizable. But there were many more whose names are not known and whose stories would be lost to history were it not for the oral histories collected by colleges, universities, libraries, and historical societies across the country in the closing decades of the twentieth century.

In writing this history, I have listened to the voices of the veterans and their wives and children in testimonies, interviews, memoirs, curated websites, and oral histories. I have read their letters in *The Stars and*

Stripes, Yank, home front newspapers, the NAACP Veterans Affairs Committee and the Southern Regional Council archives, and assorted published and unpublished collections. I have relied on first-person and reported stories about their experiences in war and on homecoming in mainstream, local, and African American newspapers; in general interest, veterans', news, and "glossy" weeklies and monthlies; in radio commentaries, commercial and government-sponsored newsreels and short films, Hollywood features, Broadway plays, novels, short stories, poems, drawings, and cartoons. Other primary sources consulted include congressional debates, documents, and committee reports; medical and psychiatry periodicals; memoranda and studies conducted by the Selective Service System, the War and Navy Departments, the Veterans Administration, the Office of the Army Surgeon General, the President's Commission on Veterans' Pensions, the Office of War Mobilization and Reconversion, the Center of Military History, and the surveys of soldiers' attitudes and beliefs conducted by the U.S. Army's Research Branch. The cartoons of Bill Mauldin, several of which are reproduced in the pages that follow, captured the veterans' experience as they struggled to adjust to civilian life on their return from war.

Our central focus is on the return of the World War II veterans and their diverse paths toward readjustment to family and civilian life. But we begin not with their homecoming, but with the war itself. If we are to understand the pain and hardships so many brought home with them, we must acknowledge their experience in war and of war, their wounds, injuries, and illnesses, their realization that they were expendable, that chance alone would determine whether they lived or died or returned home body and soul intact.

Part 1

The Long Road Home

"We ain't no lost generation. We just been mislaid."

Chapter 1.

THE RETURN OF THE WOUNDED

During the first two years of the war, close to one million American service members were returned to civilian life, almost half of them with disability discharges. These men and women, who had engaged in campaigns and battles in the Pacific, North African, Mediterranean, and European theaters of war, had suffered physical wounds and illnesses that would not heal. Not yet veterans, but of no further use to the military, they were transported to regional or specialty hospitals or VA facilities for further treatment or sent home to their families.

Among the first to be repatriated were the more than ten thousand marines who on August 7, 1942, had landed on Guadalcanal in the South Pacific to prevent the Japanese who had invaded the British protectorate in May 1942 from establishing a stronghold and cutting off communications and access to Australia, New Zealand, and the South Pacific.

The initial reports were celebratory; the American invasion had been uncontested. And then, on the evening of August 8 through the early hours of August 9, the Japanese navy attacked the ships that had supported the landing, sinking four cruisers and damaging a fifth and two destroyers. With the marines onshore deprived of air and sea support, the Japanese were able to reinforce the island with fresh troops. "All but abandoned by the vessels which brought them there," wrote the future bestselling author William Manchester in his 1980 war memoir, "reduced to eating roots and weeds, kept on the line though stricken by malaria unless their temperature reached 103 degrees, dependent for food and ammo on destroyers and fliers who broke through the enemy blockade, always at great risk, they fought the best soldiers Tokyo could send against them."[1]

The Japanese would be routed, but the cost of victory was steep—not only in the number of Americans and Japanese killed in battle, but in the daily suffering of those who survived the never-stilled, murderous discord of war. "Everyone was firing, every weapon was sounding voice; but this was no orchestration, no terribly beautiful symphony of death, as decadent rear-echelon observers write. Here was cacophony; here was dissonance; here was wildness . . . here was booming, sounding, shrieking, wailing, hissing, crashing, shaking, gibbering noise. Here was hell," Private Robert Leckie, 2nd Battalion, 1st Regiment, 1st Marine Division, recalled of his time on the island. It was impossible to escape the shelling from the sea, the detonating projectiles from the air, the dive-bombers and torpedo bombers and strafing fighters overhead.[2]

The Americans on Guadalcanal and elsewhere in the Pacific fought not only the Japanese but the unfamiliar jungle terrain and climate. "You looked at that island, and it was beautiful," the former marine Theodore "Ted" Cummings recalled in an oral history. "Once we were there, it was the most diseased place on earth, I think. Everything rotted, including your body. . . . And the heat and rain were constant. . . . And everything rotting. Jungle rot was the order of the day. . . . Every scratch was infected."[3]

The marines were attacked by flying and crawling centipedes, spiders, crabs, locusts, scorpions, leeches, and malaria-transmitting mosquitoes. Rare was the man who was not debilitated by malaria, which was regarded as a nuisance, not a cause for recall from the front lines. "The typical Marine on the island ran a fever," wrote William Manchester almost four decades later, "wore stinking dungarees, loathed twilight, and wondered whether the U.S. Navy still existed. He ate moldy rations and quinine. He alternately shivered and seared. If he were bivouacked near [the airfield taken from the Japanese], he spent his mornings filling in craters left by enemy bombers the night before. If he was on his way back to the line, he struggled through shattered, stunted coconut trees, scraggy bushes, and putrescent jungle, clawing up and down slopes ankle-deep in mud, hoping he would catch a few hours of uninterrupted sleep in his foxhole. Usually he was disappointed. Even when there were no Jap bayonet charges, every evening brought fireworks."[4]

Most painful of all for the marines trapped on Guadalcanal was the sense that you were surrounded by an enemy set on killing you and there was little you could do to escape; that in war, as Robert Leckie put it, "men are the most expendable of all. Hunger, the jungle, the Japanese, not one nor all of these could be quite as corrosive as the feeling of expendability."[5] For many, that "feeling" would follow them home and haunt them for the rest of their lives.

Following the initial landing on the island, home front newspapers, newsreels, and radio, advised and briefed by military public relations officers (PROs), reported only good news, ignoring the difficulties the marines encountered. On September 1, 1942, in an editorial titled "How We Licked the Japs," the *Chicago Daily Tribune* declared that "the successes achieved by the marines . . . have been magnificent both as an achievement and as a promise for the future." The newsreels broadcast the same message, amplified by rousing music in the background and illustrated with endless files of marines marching fearlessly toward the enemy. "Once the little men of Nippon were in complete control here," the voice-of-God narrator reports. "Now they are on the run. Plunging into malaria-infested jungles, the marines steadily, doggedly enlarge their hold on the island."[6]

Despite the early predictions of victory and abundant stories of dead "Japs" and heroic marines, Guadalcanal was not "liberated" from Japanese control until February 1943, six months after the landing. "The fighting itself," the military historian Gerhard Weinberg would write of Guadalcanal, "would be remembered by the survivors as one long nightmare; it took a full year's rehabilitation before the 1st Marine Division could again be committed to battle."[7]

The army and navy medical corps were totally unprepared for what they discovered at Guadalcanal—and would later encounter in every theater of war. They knew how to treat tropical and parasitic infections, repair fractures and dislocations, amputate limbs, treat burns, and tend to men and women with a variety of diseases. What they had not expected was that one-third or more of the casualties who appeared in their tents and hospitals were suffering from psychiatric disorders. The officers on the front lines had been assured that those under their command, having been approved for service by Selective Service System physicians and psychiatrists, were psychologically stable. Yet here they were, breaking down in large and growing numbers. With manpower in short supply, commanding officers demanded that those diagnosed as neuropsychiatric (NP) be returned to the front lines. The one psychiatrist on the island reluctantly agreed to do so, but predicted that "psychos" returned to duty "would soon break down again."[8]

When they did, they were transferred off the island to an army general hospital in Fiji where they were treated by Dr. Theodore Lidz, the only psychiatrist in residence there. "The sight of them remains unforgettable. They were bedraggled and emaciated youths with frozen expressions on their aged faces and a far-off stare in their eyes. The exhaustion had been relieved but not dissipated by the few days on the hospital ship. The stories they told, perhaps now commonplace by repetition and faded by time, were harrowing beyond all anticipation. Symptomatically the bulk of the patients suffered from anxiety and depression in varying proportions. Anxiety symptoms varied from tension symptoms to recurrent attacks of intense panic; depressive symptoms from preoccupation and hopelessness to complete disregard of the surroundings. Headaches, anorexia, frequency, tremors, insomnia, nightmares, palpitation, were individual symptoms or could all be present in one man. Aside from the few patients who were mutely inert, extreme restlessness prevailed. . . . The only patient who appeared moderately happy was obviously manic."[9]

The volume and intensity of the psychoneurotic cases from Guadalcanal and the other Solomon Islands was more than the general hospitals in Fiji, New Zealand, or Australia could handle. Many were evacuated to the United States. Lieutenant Commander E. Rogers Smith, a navy psychiatrist, examined and treated them at the naval hospital on Mare Island, outside San Francisco. He reported his preliminary findings at the July 1943 meeting of the American Psychiatric Association (APA). "We are not sure whether we are seeing a new disease entity. . . . We do believe, however, that never before in history has such a group of healthy, toughened, well-trained men been subjected to such conditions as the combat troops of the U.S. Marine Corps faced during the days following August 7, 1942. The strain and stress experienced by these men produced a group neurosis that has not been seen before and may never be seen again."[10]

Among those evacuated from Guadalcanal was Private First Class Leon Frank Jenkins. After six weeks on the island, with little to eat except barley and rice, under constant shelling, after killing his first and then several other Japanese in close combat, he found himself in a hospital in New Hebrides, with no memory of what had occurred or why he was there. Only after reading his medical chart—"Diagnosis-Psychoneurosis, War Nervous-Blast injury, Migraine Headaches"—did he conclude that "something must have happened the day the bomb hit close to me." After brief stays in hospitals in Auckland, New Zealand, and Sydney, Australia, Jenkins was transported by hospital ship to San Francisco and discharged with a diagnosis of psychoneurosis. According to his family, he never fully recovered. For the rest of his life he would be plagued by symptoms of post-traumatic stress disorder, which went unrecognized for more than four decades after his return to the United States.[11]

What happened to the troops on Guadalcanal prefigured what was to come. The conditions under which the marines and GIs lived and fought on Guadalcanal and in the Solomon Islands in 1942 and into 1943 were extreme by any measure. And yet the number and proportion who required treatment for psychoneurotic disorders were not dissimilar from those in subsequent campaigns in Africa, Europe, and the Pacific.

On November 8, 1942, three months after the marines first landed on Guadalcanal and ten thousand miles away, sixty-five thousand American and British troops disembarked on the beaches of Algeria and Morocco in North Africa, the first step toward an invasion of the European mainland. Though the climate, terrain, and enemy were different, the results were similar. As at Guadalcanal, "the early and adverse phase of the Tunisia Campaign produced a flood of psychiatric casualties. . . . From 20 to 34 percent of all nonfatal battle casualties were psychiatric."[12]

As Dr. Lidz on Fiji as well as the military psychiatrists in North Africa who treated the psychiatric casualties observed, those who were judged unfit for duty and removed from duty "were not . . . basically unstable." Their inability to continue in combat resulted from a mixture of hopelessness, sleeplessness, hunger, debilitating disease, lack of faith in their leadership, the long days and nights waiting for relief and replacement that never came, and the stench and reality of death.[13]

The army, navy, and VA doctors who encountered those with symptoms of what would later be diagnosed as post-traumatic stress disorder were unsure as to how to proceed and whether the men they treated would ever fully recover. "Our ideas are as yet vague," E. Rogers Smith wrote in an article for *The American Journal of Psychiatry* published in July 1943. Most of the GIs and marines evacuated from Guadalcanal with psychic disorders would, he hoped, "be able to return successfully to civilian life," but he could not "say as yet whether they will be as useful and successful as they were before their combat experience. It is possible that some may be more emotionally unstable, more irritable, more impulsively reactive to sudden stimuli." What that would mean for the veterans and their families, employers, and the society at large was yet to be determined.[14]

By the early spring of 1943, the defeat of the German and Italian armies in North Africa was complete and preparations for the invasion of Sicily and then mainland Italy were under way. Medical departments increased staff, supplies, and facilities to care for the wounded and evacuate those who were no longer fit for service; efforts were made to assure the folks back home that all troops, if wounded or injured, would be well cared for. A May 19, 1943, press release from the Office of War Information (OWI) in Washington declared boldly and unequivocally that "never before in the history of the world has the fighting man had available the medical care and equipment the United States now furnishes its defenders." To back up its claim, it provided a detailed thirteen-page description of the resources available to treat the wounded in the field, in evacuation hospitals, and, if necessary, at home. Newspapers across the country, large and small, from Salem, Oregon, to Freeport, Illinois, to Manchester, New Hampshire, to *The Washington Post* dutifully parroted the press release and emphasized its major theme, "the wounded don't die."[15]

On June 13, 1943, Waldemar Kaempffert summarized the OWI findings, without referencing his source, in a Sunday *New York Times Magazine* feature. "Never has there been a military organization quite like this; never have wounded and sick soldiers received such care. . . . Blood enough will be shed and cripples enough will limp to their work in the years to come. But the soldier of today who leaps into action or fires a machine gun in a foxhole has less reason to fear death from wounds or a crippling injury than ever before in history."[16]

Brigadier General Frank Hines, head of the Veterans Administration, acknowledged in an interview with Elizabeth Henney of *The Washington Post* in February 1944 that more veterans would be returning home with missing arms or legs than in previous wars. This, he added, was good news: The men were still alive. Rapid care, field amputations, drugs to prevent infection, and transfusions unavailable in World War I were saving lives.[17]

The daily press, the magazines, and the newsreels, encouraged by the OWI and the military public relations officers, featured story after story about recovering, smiling amputees and their loved ones. The February 1, 1944, edition of Fox Movietone News included a segment titled "Legless Heroes Get Artificial Limbs" that showed a sailor being fitted for his new leg, then dancing a jig, and sailors with artificial legs playing volleyball, kicking a ball around, and riding bicycles.[18]

To help the amputees adjust to civilian life, the War Department published *Helpful Hints to Those Who Have Lost Limbs* in March 1944 and followed it with a documentary, *Meet McGonegal*, about a World War I amputee who used his hooks to shave, tie his shoes, get dressed, feed himself, read the morning newspaper, drive to work, type, make a phone call, and sign his name to a document. The final shot was of McGonegal shooting pool.[19]

The prosthetic limbs were indeed better than those available for the World War I veterans, but far from perfect. They were, in fact, so uncomfortable, even after multiple operations to prepare the stump to receive them, that the veterans wore them only in public, removing them as soon as they returned home. Those who lost legs spent the last years of their lives in wheelchairs. They all suffered, some quietly, some angrily. And there was no relief from the pain.[20]

On July 10, 1943, 180,000 American and British troops landed in Sicily. After a week of heavy fighting, the Germans pulled back to their defensive lines and the Allies began their march northwest to Rome. On September 9, the Allies invaded the European continent at Salerno; on that same day, the Italian government that was formed after the Italian prime minister, Benito Mussolini, had been deposed surrendered. Naples was occupied on October 1. The expectation was that the liberation of Rome would follow within months. It did not. The Germans had retreated from southern Italy without major losses. They now dug in along a series of defensive lines that protected the southern approach to Rome.

"The war in Italy is tough," Ernie Pyle reported from the front lines on December 14, 1943. "The land and the weather are both against us. It rains and it rains. Vehicles bog down and temporary bridges wash out.... The fertile black valleys are knee-deep in mud. Thousands of the men have not been dry for weeks. Other thousands lie at night in the high mountains with the temperature below freezing and the thin snow sifting over them.... How they survive the winter misery at all is beyond us." Pyle ended on a hopeful note, not simply because that is what the army censors and public relations officers demanded of him, but because he did not want the folks back home to be discouraged by the news from the front. "Our men will get to Rome all right. There's no question about that. But the way is cruel."[21]

"Joe, yestiddy ya saved my life an' I swore I'd pay ya back. Here's my last pair of dry socks."

On the long slog north, thousands were wounded in battle or struck down by disease and noncombat injuries. Thousands more had to be removed from the front lines because of psychiatric breakdowns, which, following army protocol, were now identified as combat fatigue or exhaustion, a condition that, like "shell shock" in World War I, was so vague it was virtually useless as a diagnostic category. The primary treatment in Italy, as in the Pacific theater and North Africa, was sedation and rest. When "rest" and removal from the front lines didn't work or when, after a spell back on duty, symptoms recurred, the "combat fatigued" were evacuated to the nearest fully equipped medical hospital. Only when all hope was abandoned that they might be returned to the front were they discharged.

In December 1943, *Fortune* magazine, in a detailed, illustrated article titled "The Psychiatric Toll of Warfare," reported "that about one-third of all casualties now being returned to the U.S. from overseas are neuropsychiatric. . . . All told, around 10,000 men a month are now being discharged from the Army for psychiatric reasons. This rate of psychiatric breakdown is much greater than the armed forces were prepared for, but not greater than some psychiatrists expected." Regrettably, the writers concluded, "the chances are that once a psychiatric casualty lands in a U.S. convalescent hospital, his fate will be discharge. From the point of view of the armed forces, the release into civilian life of a stream of men whose nervous stability has been impaired in the service of their country is right and just. . . . From the human point of view, however, the situation is somewhat less justifiable." It was going to cost billions in future taxpayer dollars to provide those psychologically damaged with pensions and free medical care, but the financial costs were "negligible compared to the cost to our society of thousands of nervously misfitted human beings."[22]

They arrived home on converted troop transports and hospital ships. A smaller number were flown stateside on planes with special webbing installed to support several tiers of litters with wounded soldiers. From the debarkation hospitals, located at the port cities, the wounded were transported by train to one of the military's sixty-six general and convalescent hospitals. The volume of traffic by mid-1944 was so great that the military converted passenger trains into hospital trains by removing the seats so that the wounded in litters could be strapped in for the long ride home. After D-Day, the director of the Office of Defense Transportation warned civilians that travel plans, already booked, might "have to be canceled without notice as a result of increased military activity due to the invasion."[23]

Those who returned to their families were no doubt pleased to be home again. But there were downsides to early release, including the worry that their loved ones, neighbors, and past and future employers would question why anyone without obvious wounds had been discharged while the fighting still raged and others were dying overseas. Had they been released because they were too dumb, too soft, too frightened, too crazy, too weak to fight? "There was," Benjamin Bowker, a newspaper reporter and editor who served as chief of army orientation, observed, "real public suspicion [of those discharged early] except when men had obvious disabilities like an amputation. Discharged personnel bitterly resented implications that they were either 4F's or avoiding service."[24]

In late 1944, the Department of Agriculture interviewed 301 GIs who had been honorably discharged with medical disabilities and were now living in midwestern cities. What they found was that the men often felt guilty for being safely at home while their comrades remained in service. They worried that civilians would judge them to be cowards or psychotics. "'I don't feel right without a uniform,' says a veteran discharged with a neuropsychiatric disability. 'People look at me. It cuts me up. If I had my way, I would still be back with my buddies. . . . I don't feel right being a civilian.'"[25]

The army and navy stage-managed the homecoming of the physically and psychologically wounded, diverting attention from their pain and distress and emphasizing their heroism and perseverance. "As part of its campaign to steel the American public to sights ahead," Mary Hornaday reported for *The Christian Science Monitor*, "the War Department recently gave wide publicity to the landing of the hospital ship *Acadia*" and the 776 soldiers, sailors, and marines onboard. Fleets of ambulances and buses, doctors, nurses, litter bearers, orderlies, and two military bands welcomed the *Acadia* as it entered the port. "Scores of stretchers were photographed on Jersey docks waiting for the wounded. One fellow smiled broadly as he put his hand down to feel real American soil."[26]

The newspapers ran stories with photos of smiling soldiers awaiting disembarkation, playing cards and lying on their bunks, or waving from their stretchers as they were carried ashore. The *New York Herald Tribune* subhead read, "Blinded Soldier Exults: 'Even Air Smells Better'; Thrice-Wounded Man Says: 'Home Is Where People Understand You the First Time.'" The *Chicago Daily Tribune* subhead was more succinct: "Blind, Deaf, Burned, Glad to Be Home." The newsreel coverage, like that in the daily press, was dominated by photos of soldiers waving: soldiers on crutches, soldiers in traction, soldiers on stretchers.[27]

Lieutenant Colonel Thomas B. Protzman, commanding officer of the *Acadia*, interviewed by the reporters who greeted the ship, recounted how he "had supplemented his medical duties by helping organize the entertainment—bingo games, movies, a Christmas celebration with a Santa Claus and an evergreen tree 'we stole in Africa.'" He singled out by name one of his patients, Gilbert T. Wood, a seaman from New Jersey, who though he had "lost half his tattoos from the burn [was] hoping he'll 'be back in action soon, and in the Pacific.'"[28]

The breezy, upbeat story Protzman told the reporters was far different from the one he recorded in his private journal. "Just before daylight," in Oran, Algeria, "we took on our 150 NP [neuropsychiatric] cases; they were brought to the 'Acadia' heavily guarded. Two men came with each patient, and after boarding, they were taken to our security cages where we will only have 7 guards for the batch of them. If they really want to, one real wild guy can tear the place apart. I hope *Acadia*'s luck will hold this trip."

On the night of December 26, one of the "psychos got past the guard and it was several hours before we found him hiding. . . . Another one made a club out of tightly rolled paper and a small towel and nearly got one of the guards. Constant vigilance is our only safe guard."

Only a few days later, on December 31, there was a "riot in 'E4' where most of the mental cases are kept, and it was only with great difficulty that we succeeded in finally quieting them. . . . We are so heavily loaded with bad cases that we cannot separate them. . . . I spent the rest of the night patrolling the ship watching our NP cases with the other Officers. The only method is to watch each patient closely and the minute he gets into the excitement stage, and before he has a chance to become violent, grab him and give him sufficient sedation to keep him quiet for ten or twelve hours."

Protzman noted in his journal that almost all of the men on his ship were "so seriously wounded that they probably have seen their last battlefield. . . . Their greatest struggle lies ahead when they join the forgotten legions of war cripples that have years of suffering and hardship ahead of them. In one of my wards we have 19 young boys who have been shot through the spine. Totally paralyzed from the waist down, completely incontinent, they will become a care and hindrance to their loved ones until the good Lord takes them."[29]

Yank: The Army Weekly, written by GIs for GIs, offered its own homecoming narratives. Instead of larding its reporting, as the mainstream press did, with unstinting praise for the care the wounded received on the hospital ships, the joyous greetings and the brass bands that welcomed them home, and their delight on setting foot on American soil, *Yank* addressed the bewildering incongruity of celebrating with "swing music" the evacuation of wounded, injured, blinded, crippled, confused, and disoriented soldiers. "The swing music was as inappropriate, perhaps, as the marches for the men who couldn't walk—and none could walk very far." The men and boys who left the ship did not smile. "They were pretty solemn . . . those with an arm or a leg gone or the few who were blind, but there were no tears. Nobody bawled, no matter how much he felt like it."[30]

Unlike the *Yank* correspondents, reporters stateside were wary of writing anything that might hurt home front morale. But it was difficult, sometimes impossible to provide the spin the military encouraged. In early October 1944, Ralph McGill of *The Atlanta Constitution*, who would later win a Pulitzer as a crusading civil rights journalist and editor, drove the 350 miles from Atlanta to Charleston, South Carolina, to report on the arrival of a hospital ship. "Here is one of the places where you can see a part of the war. Here is where those newspaper headlines you read this morning connect up with the actual fighting of the war. . . . Here are the hospital ships that plow the seas bringing our wounded, and some of the enemy, too, to the hospitals we have built against such a day. . . . There are hundreds of men on each ship. This week three have arrived already and in the past week there were nine. . . . We are whipping the greatest army ever assembled in the long history of war, but it is not without its cost."[31]

In mid-January 1944, the Allies reached Cassino, ninety miles from Rome. "A more horrible place would have been hard to imagine," the novelist James Jones wrote in his war memoir/history. "The mud stuck like glue in the middle of the day, and was hard as iron at night. Cold wind and snow scourged the upper mountain slopes. Dead American bodies lay and froze in the valley the Americans had named Purple Heart Valley, their throats eaten out by packs of wild dogs."[32]

With ground forces stalled, the decision was made, after much debate and deliberation, to detour around the German defenses inland and land Allied troops by sea at Anzio. The landing was successful, but the Germans were able to seal off the beachhead to prevent Allied troops from breaking out and proceeding north toward Rome.

Soldiers who suffered through that winter in central Italy—and the rain and the mud, day after day after day—would find it difficult to forget what they had endured when they returned home. Fearing that no one would believe them or want to hear their complaints, they kept quiet. But the damage had been done. "Somewhere between my eyebrows and the back of my skull lurks the old, gray software of what I did or didn't do, what I endured, saw, heard or felt as a brash kid . . . thirty-five hundred miles from home sixty-four years ago," recalled the infantryman Joseph Garland. "To this day those neurons imprinted so long ago will not loosen their grip."[33]

From his base in Naples, Sergeant Bill Mauldin of the *45th Division News* drove his jeep to Anzio and the Cassino front. The GI bogged down in Italy, he would later write, was "living from minute to minute, wondering if each is his last. . . . He has changed. His sense of humor has changed. . . . Perhaps he will change back again when he returns, but never completely. If he is lucky, his memories of those sharp, bitter days will fade over the years into a hazy recollection of a period which was filled with homesickness and horror and dread and monotony, occasionally lifted and lighted by the gentle, humorous, and sometimes downright funny things that always go along with misery."[34]

By the winter of 1943–44, battle injuries, death, disease, and breakdown along the long march to Rome had exacerbated an already "critical shortage of infantrymen." In October 1943, the Selective Service System, having concluded that the only deferments the nation could afford were those based on occupation, not family status, eliminated automatic deferments for fathers. By April 1944, the percentage of inductees who were married had increased from 6.8 percent to 52.8 percent. By war's end, more than three million married men, 28 percent of all servicemen, had been called to service.[35]

The drafting of fathers, unfortunately, did not solve the replacement shortage that confronted the army as it prepared for the cross-channel invasion of the European mainland. In early 1944, the War Department cut back, then eliminated, the Army Specialized Training Program (ASTP), which had been introduced in the fall of 1942 to send GIs who had scored high on the army's intelligence tests to colleges and universities to take courses in engineering, mathematics, and languages, and acquire technical skills that would make them better officers. Unfortunately, by the spring of 1944, so many servicemen had been wounded, injured, taken ill, and separated from service that the program, with its 150,000 able-bodied men in college and university, had become a luxury that the military could no longer afford. Without warning, the young men who had been specially selected for their intelligence were pulled out of the training programs designed for them, the vast majority reassigned to infantry units as buck privates and fed into the maw of the military machine as replacements on the front lines.[36]

Among them was Franklin E. Kameny, who, rather than waiting to be drafted, had withdrawn from Queens College and enlisted in the army three days before his eighteenth birthday so that he could apply for the ASTP. He was accepted and sent to the University of Illinois, where he was put up "very nicely" and enrolled in a mechanical engineering program. And then—"it was vaguely February . . . the rug was just pulled out from under us, and I was on a troop train headed south, and the next day I was sleeping in a tent in a sodden field in Louisiana at what was then Camp Polk."[37]

Kurt Vonnegut, who had left Cornell University just before flunking out, enlisted in the army and was selected for the ASTP to study mechanical engineering first at the Carnegie Institute of Technology in Pittsburgh and later at the University of Tennessee in Knoxville. When the ASTP was shut down in the spring of 1944, he was transferred to Camp Atterbury, Indiana, to train with the "Battalion Intelligence" unit of the 106th Infantry Division.[38]

Henry Kissinger, a German-Jewish accounting major at the City

College of New York who lived with his parents in Washington Heights, had been drafted in early 1943. While the Selective Training and Service Act of 1940 required that all male residents register for the draft, the 1940 Alien Registration Act restricted German-born, non-naturalized residents from serving in the military. In March 1942, Congress resolved the contradiction with the Second War Powers Act, which authorized "accelerated naturalization" for "enemy aliens" like Kissinger who had served three months in the armed services. Kissinger received his citizenship papers at Camp Croft in South Carolina, where he had been sent for basic training. After scoring high on army aptitude tests, he was selected for the Army Specialized Training Program and assigned to Lafayette College to study engineering. He didn't stay long. When the program was disbanded, he was transferred with twenty-eight hundred other ASTP men to Camp Claiborne in Louisiana and reassigned to the 84th Infantry Division. In September, he sailed to England with his infantry division and in November crossed the channel to Omaha Beach.[39]

The drafting of fathers and the reassignment of men specially selected for their intellects for the ASTP was but one sign that the war was not yet won, the human costs not yet calculated. As the war entered its third year, with victory closer, but not yet in sight, it was increasingly difficult to ignore the news from abroad. Historically, war stories were recounted long after the hostilities had ceased. What was different in World War II was the simultaneity of event and narration and the immediate impact it had on the home front. While every parcel of information was managed by the military censors, enough got through to alert the home front to the escalating costs of war. The war was not a distraction from everyday life; it was a vital part of it. Rare was the person at home—man, woman, or child—who did not know and care for someone in uniform.

The immediate worry was the progress of the war itself. There was little doubt that the Allies would win, but no way of knowing when or how or at what cost. Would those on the front lines survive? What of those in the rear but still in range of enemy aircraft and artillery and those still stateside? How long before they were delivered into harm's way? As important as these immediate concerns were the longer-range anxieties about the toll of war on those fighting it. If they returned, when they returned, how would they readjust to civilian life? Would those who had been wounded, in body or mind, ever fully recover their equilibrium and return to where they had been before induction?

Chapter 2.

WAR STORIES

Those on the home front eagerly awaited letters from their loved ones abroad, though it was common knowledge among them all that every line in every letter had been heavily censored. Junior officers were authorized to read outgoing letters to friends, pen pals, parents, siblings, wives, girlfriends, and children to make sure no secrets, locations, or plans were divulged. Since GIs interacted daily with the officers reading their mail, they refrained from putting into writing anything personal or potentially embarrassing—or anything of substance that might cause their loved ones to worry. As Paul Fussell, a second lieutenant in the infantry and future bestselling author and critic, would later write, letters from abroad were "composed largely to sustain the morale of the folks at home, to hint as little as possible at the real, worrisome circumstance of the writer. No one wrote: 'Dear Mother, I am scared to death.'" The result was a syrupy blandness that was comforting, but almost entirely lacking in real-time information about what was going on.[1]

Shirley Hackett of Wallingford, Connecticut, whose husband was in Europe, recalled that "when the mail did come, often it was censored so much that you couldn't possibly figure out what he wanted to tell you in the letter."[2]

To save space on the ships and planes that carried the mail and speed delivery across the oceans, the War and Navy Departments implemented a postal system known as V-Mail, short for "Victory Mail." Anyone on the home front who wanted to write to a man or woman in uniform could visit the local post office once a day and get two special forms on which to write letters. The forms were microfilmed using Eastman Kodak Recordak machines, the films flown or shipped overseas to military post offices, censored, enlarged to four-by-six-inch size, addressed, and forwarded. By September 1944, 789,539,390 of these V-Mail letters had been delivered to soldiers abroad and correspondents on the home front. By war's end, "the total probably exceeded 1 billion."[3]

The letters and V-Mails were comforting, but empty of any real information about the progress of the war or the condition of the men and women fighting it. To find out more about what was going on overseas, those on the home front had no choice but to rely on the print media and the radio. The War and Navy Departments at home, Allied headquarters overseas, and the small armies of public relations officers attached to them provided the big-picture news in official reports and communiqués that were tedious, neutral in tone, with a positive twist at the end. Generals and admirals were regularly quoted; the men and boys in combat or support services, by and large, ignored.

It was left to the accredited war correspondents, 1,646 in all, 127 women, and 27 African Americans, all but 2 from African American newspapers, to deliver the news on what the enlisted men were doing, thinking, worrying about. The military and the government provided them with living quarters, transportation, rations, and telegraph, radio, and telephone connections to transmit their stories for broadcast or publication. And they censored every word they wrote. War correspondents were prohibited from divulging military secrets, spreading rumors, displaying photographs or newsreel images of dead or dying Americans, describing defeats in battle, discussing the sexual activities of men, boys, and women in uniform, or questioning the inevitability of victory, the courage of the fighting men, or the wisdom of their commanders.[4]

The rules were annoying, so too the military officers who enforced them, but they were not particularly burdensome, and the war correspondents cooperated for the most part. When General Dwight D. Eisenhower asked them not to write stories that might be bad for morale at home, they obliged. John Steinbeck refrained from writing about General George S. Patton Jr. slapping "a sick soldier in a hospital" or about the incidents when Americans mistakenly fired on, and sometimes killed, their own troops. "We edited ourselves much more than we were edited. We felt responsible to what was called the home front. There was a general feeling that unless the home front was carefully protected from the whole account of what war was like, it might panic. Also we felt we had to protect the armed services from criticism, or they might retire to their tents to sulk like Achilles."[5]

The pattern for wartime news gathering and reporting was established at Guadalcanal. Military PROs took the lead in declaring the marines' landing a success and posting celebratory communiqués of progress toward victory. Their official reports were augmented, at times artfully subverted, by the two accredited war correspondents on the island, Richard Tregaskis of Hearst's International News Service and Robert C. Miller of the United Press Service. From the moment they boarded the landing craft with the marines, they attempted, as best they could, to report the story of Guadalcanal from the marines' perspective. Their dispatches were censored by the marine PROs on the island, then transmitted to Pearl Harbor, where they were censored and edited again.[6]

Eyewitness accounts were, the newspapers alerted their readers, intended to provide a bit of color, to add human interest detail to the official war news. Tregaskis and his fellow correspondents focused their attention on writing about the daily life of the marines on the island, the drudgery alternating with moments of intense danger and death, the hunger, the loneliness, the fear, the wounds. The military censors pored over every word, but allowed the correspondents to describe the horrors of war so that the home front might understand what the men were enduring and appreciate their heroism. In one of his last dispatches, approved as they all were by the censors, Tregaskis, sparing the reader no bloody detail, described how two pharmacist's mates second class, one from McAndrews, Kentucky, the other from South Dartmouth, Massachusetts, "severed the pitiful remnants of the casualty's arm. . . . 'We had only a rusty scalpel to perform the operation with.' After the operation, the two corpsmen carried the casualty, under heavy sniper fire which came as close as two feet, to a foxhole, and there made him comfortable until he could be evacuated in a landing boat."[7]

Tregaskis kept a detailed diary in black ledger books at Guadalcanal. After seven weeks embedded with the marines, he was flown to Pearl Harbor, where he intended to write a full-length book, based on his diaries. Navy officials, worried that his diary might contain secrets that, if stolen by Japanese spies, would endanger American plans and lives, confiscated it. Tregaskis was allowed to consult his diary in the navy office, where it was kept under lock and key.[8]

Dozens of accredited war correspondents followed Tregaskis and Miller to Guadalcanal, among them John Hersey for *Life*. On

November 23, 1942, the magazine published Hersey's first dispatch, interrupted by dozens of gaudy advertisements for furniture, men's hats and garters, cigarettes, and liquors. While emphasizing the marines' heroism and courage, he too focused on the horrors of war, as experienced by the men on Guadalcanal. "I attached myself to a group who were wounded in a dreadful way.... They were shock and blast victims.... One man kept striking the sides of his befuddled skull with his fists. Another kept his hand over his ears. Several had badly battered legs." An officer who led the attack lay wounded, dying, as Hersey and the marine's comrades tried to ease his pain. "'Help me sit up, will you please, oh God my stomach.' ... Soon he said very softly: 'I wish I could sleep.' The wish was fulfilled: he dropped off in apparent peace. He gave a few short breaths and then just stopped breathing."[9]

The correspondents recognized that the travails of war would never be understood by the civilians who remained at home, but that did not deter them from publishing as much as they could about the suffering they had witnessed. The military and its censors gave them wide latitude to do so. The home front, it was agreed, had to be disabused of any notion that the war would be easily won and at minimal cost. "The first thing to do is to forget about the glorified fighting you have seen in the movies, and only too often read about," Herbert Matthews of *The New York Times* cautioned his readers from Italy in December 1943. "A battle is a long, slow process.... It takes youth and strength, and above all it takes 'guts'—not of the quick and exalted daring kind which are so much the easiest, but plodding, steady courage in the face of unutterable misery."[10]

During the war, 48 million copies of newspapers circulated every weekday, 40 million on Sundays to a population of 132 million. In addition to the newspapers, war news was featured in glossy photo journals like *Life*, *The Saturday Evening Post*, and *Look* and in the newsweeklies, the women's magazines, and "high-brow" but lower-circulation literary journals like *The New Yorker*. Paid circulation of the weeklies with war news soared. By 1944, *Life*'s circulation approached 4 million; *Time*'s, 1.2 million; *Newsweek*'s, 600,000; *The New Yorker*'s, 230,000.[11]

The war correspondents' audience multiplied when, often within months of initial publication, their dispatches were collected and published in hardcover books. "As our boys went into action," Lewis Gannett, the *New York Herald Tribune* book critic, recalled, "we were avid to read about them in books." It was, John Steinbeck would later call it, "the day of the Book by the War Correspondent."[12]

Tregaskis's book, *Guadalcanal Diary*, drawn from the accounts in his diary, was bought by Bennett Cerf at Random House, who knew a bestseller when he saw one. The reviews were enthusiastic. *The New York Times* recommended it as "tonic for the war weary on the homefront." It was selected by the Book of the Month Club, quickly climbed to the top of every bestseller list, and was, according to *Publishers Weekly*, the fifth-bestselling nonfiction book of the year.[13]

Hersey's articles were collected and published in *Into the Valley*, which came out only a few days after Tregaskis's *Guadalcanal Diary*. Hersey's prose was clearer, more dramatic, more polished than Tregaskis's, but told the same story: of brave but frightened men, lugging packs like donkeys, stumbling through the jungle and up jagged mountains, homesick, sleepless, weary beyond measure, and battered by an unforgiving climate, swarms of mosquitoes, and tropical diseases and wounds that would not heal. Every relative, friend, or acquaintance who had said goodbye to a man in uniform had to have come away heartsick at the images that exploded off the pages.

In 1943 and 1944, six of the ten *Publishers Weekly* nonfiction bestsellers were war related. Dozens made the bestseller lists, at *The New York Times* and elsewhere. A few were lighthearted and jokey, like Bob Hope's *I Never Left Home* and Marion Hargrove's *See Here, Private*

Hargrove. Others, like Hersey's and Tregaskis's, were dead serious first-person accounts. Among the most widely read were Ernie Pyle's two bestsellers, *Here Is Your War* and *Brave Men*, Captain Ted W. Lawson's *Thirty Seconds over Tokyo*, Robert Scott's *God Is My Co-pilot*, Quentin Reynolds's *Curtain Rises*, Robert Sherrod's *Tarawa*, and two collections of Bill Mauldin's syndicated cartoons, featuring disheveled, war-weary Willie and Joe. Almost every one of them would be refashioned into a feature film.

The newspapers provided readers on the home front with exhaustively detailed information about the course of the war, but their reports were published days after the events had taken place. Magazine articles appeared weeks later, and books months after that. To learn what was happening in as close to real time as possible, people turned to the radio, which, in addition to its other advantages, was free of charge to listen to and accessible. Eighty-seven percent of American households had at least one set in working order. "Everybody had a radio during the war," Emma Belle Petcher of Millry, Alabama, recalled in a later interview. "And three times a day, you got the national news and three times a day, you did not be far from that radio."[14]

The cousins Alpha and Carlis Burdine spent the war years in Orange, Texas, where their fathers and Carlis's mother worked in the shipyards. "We'd come in from school," Alpha Burdine remembered, "and we turned the radio on and listened to Jack Armstrong and the serials in the afternoon; but the moment it was time for the news we listened to the news, and I don't know any family that didn't, that didn't keep up daily." When the news was on, Carlis added, "you didn't play and make noise. . . . You sat down and shut up."[15]

Radio news was more concise than stories in the daily papers, and thus easier to absorb. Between 1939 and 1944, the hours of news broadcast on the four radio networks—NBC Red (which became NBC Radio in 1942), NBC Blue (which became ABC in 1945), CBS, and Mutual Broadcasting System—ballooned by more than 400 percent. When troops were landed, battles engaged, and victories won, regular programming was interrupted so bulletins could be read from studios in New York and Washington. The networks carried all the major, and too many minor, speeches by politicians, as well as regular fifteen-minute segments by celebrity "commentators" like Edward R. Murrow, Howard K. Smith, Charles Collingwood, Eric Sevareid, and Gabriel Heatter. Unlike the news announcers, the commentators conducted in-person interviews, provided eyewitness accounts, and voiced their opinions, so long as they were not too controversial.[16]

The war news was inescapable. Even listeners who switched the dial to comedy shows, big band music, sports parades, hit parades, Fred Waring, and *The Lone Ranger* were subjected to an endless array of "brief exhortations for military recruitment, the purchase of war bonds, contributions for the USO, and volunteer assistance in sundry defense programs."[17] Variety and comedy show hosts like Eddie Cantor, Jack Benny, Fred Waring, and Kate Smith promoted bond sales and made sure to include among their musical selections songs about the war and the brave boys fighting it. Daytime romances and dramas featured characters who were sent overseas and killed in action like Ma Perkins's son who had joined the infantry. Even Superman became an undercover Secret Service operative, battling enemy spies and soldiers at home and abroad.[18]

Like print media and the radio, picture shows were overloaded with reminders that a war was being fought overseas. Whether people bought tickets to see a war film, Bing Crosby's *Going My Way*, or Judy Garland's *Meet Me in St. Louis*, they were a captive audience for the newsreels, short films, and cartoons that preceded the feature and featured the war.

Five different newsreel companies, Fox Movietone News, Universal Newsreel, Hearst News of the Day, Paramount News, and Pathé News, produced and distributed two programs a week, each with multiple segments ranging from a minute to eight minutes in length. In 1942, 80 percent of newsreels included coverage of the war, rising to 90 percent in 1943.[19]

The newsreels did not break any news, but dramatized what had been previously reported in the newspapers and on the radio. "The attraction of the newsreel," Thomas Doherty has written, "was neither timeliness nor urgency but verification and coherence.... With maps and arrows, intertitles, capsule backgrounds, illustrative graphics, and sure narrative thrust, the newsreels explained bewildering events on remote atolls and taught geography, military strategy, and international politics to a public conscious of the importance but confused by the complexity. The newsreels made sense of the thing."[20]

Moviegoers were blasted with vivid, larger-than-life images of explosions, smoke and fire from air, land, and sea, sounds of rifles, bazookas, machine guns, artillery barrages. The effect was heightened by deep-voiced narrators and stirring orchestral music. Here was propaganda on a large scale. The only shortcoming of the commercial newsreels was that, compared to German propaganda films such as Leni Riefenstahl's documentary masterwork, *Triumph of the Will*, they were abbreviated and rather tame. Major Frank Capra, arguably the most influential and honored director in Hollywood, with five Academy Award Best Director nominations and three Oscars, recalled that the Riefenstahl film had "scared the hell out of me." But it also put pressure on him and other Hollywood filmmakers to produce films for the troops and the home front that carried the same visceral punch.[21]

Though the public was receiving a lot of information from letters, newspaper and magazine reports, newsreels, and radio broadcasts, the White House and the military recognized that more needed to be done. In 1941, Roosevelt appointed the journalist Lowell Mellett as coordinator of government films and then, in June 1942, established the Office of War Information under Elmer Davis to provide the press, radio, and motion pictures with stories intended to boost morale and explain in plain terms why the war had to continue until the nation's enemies surrendered unconditionally.

In its first year of operation, OWI produced propaganda pamphlets, films, and radio programs and pushed Hollywood to make movies that would reassure the public about the ongoing war. Barely a year after the office had been established, however, Republicans and southern Democrats, charging that it had become a publicity machine for the New Deal and Roosevelt, cut its funding to the bone.

Mellett's operation, meanwhile, which had been merged into the Office of War Information in mid-1942 and renamed the Bureau of Motion Pictures, went on to produce scores of inspirational, exhortatory, "victory" films and shorts that were distributed, at no charge, to nearly every movie house in the country. Customers who bought a ticket to see a lighthearted comedy or musical were compelled to sit not only through the commercial newsreels but through "community sings" of patriotic songs, "briefies" (one- or two-minute announcements from government officials or pleas from celebrities for war charities), and short government-made or -sanctioned films and cartoons urging them to conserve more scrap metal, eat healthier balanced meals, work harder in the war plants, and stop complaining about taxes.[22]

Washington and the military recruited the best talent Hollywood could offer to film, direct, and produce short and feature-length films. John Ford, who had between 1939 and 1941 directed *Stagecoach*, *Young Mr. Lincoln*, *Drums Along the Mohawk*, *The Grapes of Wrath*, and *How Green Was My Valley*, reported for active duty in the Naval Reserve in September 1941. On June 4, 1942, anticipating a Japanese attack on Midway Atoll, Admiral Chester Nimitz, Commander in Chief of the Pacific fleet, asked Ford to recommend a few cameramen to "document a mission in the Pacific." Ford "volunteered himself" and was transported to the atoll, 1,100 miles from Pearl Harbor. The morning of the attack, Ford positioned himself and his crew on the concrete roof of a major power plant and filmed Japanese planes bombing the nearby airfield. He returned to Los Angeles, had the raw film printed, directed his editor to avoid navy censors, and added a Hollywood-manufactured "soundtrack—music, narration, dialogue, and the sound effects of soaring planes, ocean waves, PT boat motors, gunfire, and falling and exploding bombs." Donald Crisp, who had worked on *How Green Was My Valley*, was recruited to do the voice-over and Henry Fonda and Jane Darwell from *The Grapes of Wrath* to record the voices of a young man and a mother. Alfred Newman composed the musical score.[23]

The Battle of Midway opens with a photograph of a navy plane landing on Midway, accompanied by a medley of patriotic songs. Japanese planes attack and are shot out of the sky. American guns roar. Navy officers look pleased. "The Battle of Midway is over. Our front yard is safe," the voice-over declares. The film ends with pictures of smiling American servicemen, introduced by name, interspersed with images of the wounded on their way to the hospital. The final shots are of the dead, draped in flags, placed on boats, and carried out to sea for burial, accompanied by a dirgelike fully orchestrated choral rendition of "My Country 'Tis of Thee." The last word sung is "Amen." There follows immediately a mélange of drumbeats and patriotic music as the screen is filled with printed cards, enumerating the Japanese planes and vessels destroyed in the battle.[24]

Ford's film presented the air war as a thrilling spectacle of machine against machine, man against machine, and, more chillingly, machine against man. It captured a moment of victory at a moment in time when they were in short supply. And it did so without pandering to the audience, without ignoring the costs of war in young men wounded, missing, dead. The finished film was distributed nationwide in September 1942. By the end of its run, it had played multiple times in three-quarters of America's theaters.[25]

The government and the military, in addition to making their own films, assisted the studios in the writing, production, and distribution of commercial features and newsreels. The studios didn't welcome the interference, but learned to live with it. "Hollywood went to war with gusto," Clayton Koppes and Gregory Black have written. "Blatant morale-building propaganda was a staple of its plots, speeches, and visual images.... Hollywood was trying to boost the war effort," and, in doing so, making money, lots of it. War films were big business. Of the 1,313 features released between December 7, 1941, and May 8, 1945, 30 percent could be characterized as war films, among them William Wyler's *Mrs. Miniver*, the top-grossing film of 1942, and *This Is the Army*, the top-grossing film of 1943.[26]

To satisfy and keep Washington and the military censors at arm's length, the war films, lighthearted and heavy-handed alike, were padded with images of wise, grizzled, unshaven generals; tough but fair officers who fought alongside their troops; dogfaces, sailors, marines, airmen, and angelic nurses who never flinched; wives, sweethearts, and children collecting old newspapers, selling war bonds, working in factories, doing whatever they could to help win the war. Some offered frivolous, near-scandalous looks on the brighter side, with singing and dancing, like *This Is the Army, Stage Door Canteen, Four Jills in a Jeep,* and *So Proudly We Hail,* with Claudette Colbert, Paulette Goddard, and Veronica Lake dressed up as nurses. But there were also serious dramas that did not hide the grim realities of war but instead attempted to depict the horrors of combat, reminding audiences that the wages of war included death.

Bataan, one of the first Hollywood war films, and one of the best and most popular, was released in the spring of 1943 after being vetted and revised in accordance with suggestions made by the Office of War Information and army censors. The producers, following the OWI recommendations, depicted a war fought by enlisted men from every class, region, and ethnicity: a deep-voiced Black private who hummed spirituals at his machine-gun post, a Jew named Feingold, a West Point graduate, a Pittsburgh son of the working classes, a sailor, a doctor, a man who spoke and prayed in Spanish played by Desi Arnaz, and two Filipinos. By the end, everyone, including the A-list male stars, Robert Taylor, Thomas Mitchell, and Robert Walker, was dead—blood- and sweat-drenched—killed by bombs, artillery barrages, sniper fire, swords, torture, malaria, knives, strangulation, and a burning beam. "This time, at least, a studio hasn't purposely 'prettified' facts," Bosley Crowther of *The New York Times* emphasized in his review. "This time it has made a picture about war in true and ugly detail. . . . There is sickening filth and bloodshed in it. Men die with marrow-chilling screams. Death is a grim inevitability."[27]

Even in the most treacly of home front war films, *Since You Went Away*, the good cheer exhibited by each of the characters is undercut by a sense of foreboding. Viewers know that someone, perhaps several among those who "went away," will not return. Hollywood studio heads did not relish having to remind their audiences that, as John Hersey would later put it, "the first postulate of the theorem of war is death." The nation was at war, and there was no disguising the growing number of dead and wounded. The studios—and their government and military advisers—walked a fine line. If they produced films that were too realistic, with too much pain, too much death, they might turn away audiences. But they also dared not risk having their feature films reviled and rejected as mindless, patriotic propaganda.[28]

The men and women in uniform would prove to be the severest critics of the Hollywood films. They were incensed by scenes of hard-nosed men thrown into battle, putting on their gear and marching toward the enemy, energized, courageous. The reality, they knew, was that only the demented and benumbed entered battle without fear. The "Mail Call" pages of *Yank* were filled with biting, often vicious commentaries on the distance between "The War" and "Hollywood's war." In the Memphis military hospital where he had been sent to recover from his wounds, James Jones and the other "retreads"* watched, with mounting irritation, the latest war movies from Hollywood. "They didn't understand anything about the war. And they didn't try to understand. Instead of trying to show the distressing complexity and puzzling diffusion of war, they pulled everything down to the level of good guy against bad guy. Instead of showing the terrifying impersonality of modern war, they invariably pulled it down to a one-on-one situation, a man-against-man, like a tennis match. At best they made it like a football game. But modern war was not a football game. And modern war was not man against man—if it ever had been. It was machine against machine. . . . Men had to die at the wheels or triggers of the machine. . . . But the movies never showed this, except only very occasionally and probably the movie-makers never did understand the tragedy or even the problem. And by extension, the great home public apparently never understood it either."[29]

During the first year and a half of the war, the American propaganda machine focused its efforts on emphasizing victories on land and sea, the superhuman heroism of U.S. servicemen and the

---

* The term, Jones explained, had been "originally coined by some soldier in World War II, when retread auto tires came into usage, to designate the used-up combat soldier who was sent back through the mill again."

sacrifices they were making to win the war, and the miracles wrought by military medicine. By the fall of 1943, this had begun to change as the president and his top political and military advisers grew more and more concerned that after the highly publicized landing at Salerno and the arrest of Mussolini, the public might come to believe that the war would soon be over, with no pressing need to draft replacement soldiers or recruit nurses, no compelling reason for war workers to work overtime, no necessity for rationing on the home front or the purchase of war bonds. It was time for a reality check, for a warning to those at home that the war was far from won.[30]

After conferring with the heads of OWI, the State, War, and Navy Departments, President Roosevelt in September 1943 recalibrated the boundaries of government censorship and propaganda to balance the celebration of victories abroad, even the most costly ones, with reports and images of casualties and the pain and hardship endured by the American forces as they pushed north in Italy and battled their way from island to island in the Pacific. Leo Cullinane of the *New York Herald Tribune* reported on September 4 that censorship restrictions were going to be loosened because the prevailing opinion in Washington was "that the public was being given the impression that the war was too easy for our side. The new policy, expected to be an effective weapon in combating home-front complacency, will show graphically that Americans have to receive hard blows as well as to give them." From this point on, *The New York Times* reported, the public would be presented with "a more realistic picture of the war."[31]

On September 20, 1943, *Life* magazine published an until-then-censored photograph of three dead soldiers that had been taken seven months earlier on Buna Beach in New Guinea. The photo was tasteful. No blood or wounds or bodily damage was evident, but it was clear that the three unnamed soldiers were dead. "Here lie three Americans. Why print this picture," read the editorial accompanying the photo, "of three American boys dead upon an alien shore? Is it to hurt people? To be morbid? These are not the reasons." There followed a long paean to America as "the symbol of freedom" around the world and the identification of these three anonymous Americans as "three units of freedom. . . . It is not just these boys who have fallen here, it is freedom that has fallen. . . . When these living units of freedom are extinguished we cannot bring them back to life. All we can do is to give meaning to their death."[32]

The newsreels, still crowded with pictures of ships and planes and bombs exploding in air, began to offer viewers more and more disturbing images of what the writer and broadcaster Lowell Thomas on October 1, 1943, referred to as the "terrifying spectacle and pandemonium of war": Americans pulled from downed aircraft, bandaged, placed on stretchers, lifted into ambulances, their faces blank or half smiling, some contorted with pain; airmen landing damaged planes; nurses bent over wounded soldiers; GIs and marines, impossibly filthy, digging trenches and foxholes under fire, trudging up and down ridges and mountains, into valleys and jungles and swamps, over swollen streams, straining, their backs swayed under the weight of their packs.[33]

"I'd sneak in the back of the theater and see these newsreels," Emma Belle Petcher remembered. "There were hand-to-hand battles, a lot of them. And, I mean, they weren't fiction. They were the real things. It was overwhelming in a sense. You would go to bed and dream about these battles, piercing people with knives and bayonets, you know. And they were very horrifying."[34]

Those who had cheered as their loved ones marched off to war recoiled now at the images presented across the media. And yet, despite the fears provoked, they could not look away. They had to know what was happening to the men and boys abroad and what effect all of this violence, this pain, this death would have on them.

Robert Sherrod, reporting for *Time* magazine, had accompanied the marines onto Tarawa, a tiny coral atoll in the Gilberts. *Tarawa*, the bestselling book based on his reporting, was released in early March 1944. "Now that it is light," Sherrod wrote of the morning of the second day of the battle, "the wounded go walking by, on the beach. Some are supported by corpsmen; others like this one coming now, walk alone, limping badly, their faces contorted with pain." The final thirty pages listed, in small type, the casualties from this one island in the Pacific. This was not the war the American public had anticipated, but this was the war their children, spouses, and fathers were fighting.[35]

The landing on Tarawa atoll that Sherrod described was filmed by a contingent of marine cameramen led by Louis Hayward, a Hollywood actor who on enlisting had been assigned to the 2nd Marine Division as a photographic officer. The film was filled with images of dead and dying Americans, Japanese, and Koreans. On December 28, President Roosevelt's press secretary asked Sherrod to stay behind after a press conference to speak with the president. "Have you seen those bloody films of the Tarawa battle?" Roosevelt asked Sherrod, who he knew had just returned from Tarawa. "I hear they are gruesome." Sherrod, who had viewed the rough unedited cuts, agreed. "Gruesome, yes, Mr. President, but that's the way the war is out there, and I think the people are going to have to get used to that idea."[36]

The final cut of the nineteen-minute film was released on March 2, 1944. (A longer documentary, with more disturbing images of Americans and Japanese dead and wounded, was shown to servicemen only.) *With the Marines at Tarawa*, *The Boston Globe* reported the day after its premiere in the city's first-run theaters, "is an amazing, spectacular, tragic, triumphant story of what our Marines went through in their fight against the Japanese. Amazing—because so far there have been no pictures taken of Americans fighting that have the authenticity, the power and the actual feeling of battle."[37]

Movie theater audiences witnessed images of corpses floating in water and burial ceremonies for those killed in action, all accompanied by a barrage of racist denunciations of their killers. "They're savage fighters," the narrator of the Tarawa film intones. "Their lives mean nothing to them."[38]

The Tarawa film, much like Sherrod's book, was loaded with the racist assaults on the Japanese that had become commonplace in print as well as in the films and cartoons produced by the studios, the government, and the military. In *Bataan*, the American GIs slaughter hundreds of Japanese in some of the worst choreographed fight scenes ever filmed. But the Japanese keep coming, advancing through the jungle intent on slaughtering every last American, which they succeed in doing. The moral of the story was clear: American boys and men, once peaceable and nonviolent souls, had to become merciless, pitiless killers in order to stay alive and defeat a merciless, pitiless enemy.

The Japanese were more hated than the Germans before as well as after Pearl Harbor, historian John Dower has written. Unlike the blue-eyed, blond, White Christian Germans who were represented as worthy foes, the Japanese were caricatured as vicious, conniving, beastly hordes of "monkeys" and "rats," unstoppable, demonic torturers and killers. The Germans, it was argued, fought by the rules, surrendered when they were beaten in battle, and treated their prisoners according to international conventions. That they were also engaging in genocidal warfare against the Jews was ignored. "I wish we were fighting against Germans," a marine told John Hersey on Guadalcanal. "They are human beings, like us. . . . The Japs are like animals. . . . They take to the jungle as if they had been bred there, and like some beasts you never see them until they are dead." Robert Sherrod alerted the American people, "There was no way to defeat the Japanese except by extermination."[39]

Characterizing the Japanese enemy as subhuman would do more

than give the home front an enemy to rally against; it also legitimized the domestic internment of Japanese Americans and might have prepared Americans to accept, if not applaud, the subsequent atomic bombing of innocent civilians.[40]

The news from abroad was both plentiful and meager. The war correspondents, radio commentators, newsreel cameramen, and filmmakers relayed abundant graphic images and descriptions of what service members were encountering at war. What was left unsaid was what would happen when they came home; what had the war done to those who had been immersed for months, if not years, in a male-only world, in which their only goals were survival and the deaths of men wearing enemy uniforms?

Chapter 3.

BAD HABITS

Men at war spend most of their time waiting for something to happen. Idleness wreaks almost as much havoc as combat. In an effort to boost morale, the military provided off-duty service men and women with magazines, movie screenings, books, sporting equipment, and live entertainment. Families and friends at home sent newspaper and magazine clippings, and letters—lots of letters. All of this was important in passing the time and reminding those overseas of what they were missing—and hoped to savor again.

On Bougainville in the northern Solomons, after the Allies had established a beachhead in November 1943 and constructed an airfield, the military built a "mini American city" for the marines and infantrymen, "a tropical representation of normal American life, with plentiful food and luxury," according to the historian John McManus. "Forty separate post exchanges (PX) soon came into being, selling a diverse array of goods, including beer, soda, watches, pens, lighters, cigarettes, dictionaries, alarm clocks, Whitman's chocolates, and even moccasins. . . . Phonograph records were common." There were film theaters featuring recent releases, live concerts, visiting performers, and regular USO shows; gyms, tennis and volleyball courts, boxing rings, and baseball fields; on-site instructors who offered courses for high school and college credit; chapels, a radio station, and a library.[1]

Thousands of copies of magazines and comics, from *Baseball Magazine* and *Collier's* to *Superman*, *Time*, and *Western Trails*, were available.* To save costs and shipping space, magazines were printed without advertisements on special lightweight paper. "*Newsweek* published a 'Battle Baby' edition, *Time* printed a 'Pony Edition,' and *The New Yorker*, *Science News Letter*, *The Saturday Evening Post*, and *Mc-Graw Overseas Digest* all printed special overseas editions."[2] Armed Services Editions paperbacks, produced by a consortium of American publishers and sold at cost to the army and navy, were distributed free of charge. These compact paperbacks, small enough to fit snugly into a back pocket, could be found wherever American service men and women were stationed. One hundred and twenty million free books were shipped overseas, a shipment of new titles every month. There were free books for every taste: war books; popular entertainment like *The Education of Hyman Kaplan* (the first book distributed), Booth Tarkington's *Penrod*, Betty Smith's *A Tree Grows in Brooklyn*, Zane Grey westerns; classics by Conrad, Dickens, Thackeray; short story collections, humor, biographies, histories, mysteries, poetry; in all, 1,322 titles.[3]

---

* In July 1944, the army had added 170 additional magazines to its list of those suitable for soldiers overseas. Included were the glossies, newsmagazines, women's magazines, and comic books. Excluded were *The New Republic*, *The Nation*, and the *New Masses*, not, according to the army, because of their politics, but because "no preference for these magazines was indicated by the troops." (Sidney Shalett, "189 Magazines Put on New Army List," *New York Times*, July 20, 1944, 8.)

Perhaps the most prized of the morale boosters supplied by the military were the cigarettes, distributed in their ration packs, which were omnipresent wherever GIs, soldiers, sailors, marines, airmen, WACs (Women's Army Corps) and WAVEs (Women Accepted for Volunteer Emergency Service) or Women's Reserve for the U.S. Navy gathered.

The GIs were not the only Americans who smoked through the war years, but they led the charge, smoking more than the general population and, after they returned home, afflicted at a higher rate by diseases associated with smoking. Cigarettes were regarded as military tools. They calmed nerves before and after battle, suppressed hunger, and kept men and women awake and alert long after they should have been asleep. From the moment they enlisted or were drafted, inductees were supplied with cigarettes. Draft boards gifted them with cartons on induction; Red Cross workers handed them out to the men as they boarded ship for service overseas; care packages from home included packs. GIs and marines were given extra rations as they went into battle. Those loaded into landing crafts for the journey across the English Channel on D-Day received cartons of cigarettes to ward off seasickness, reduce fear and shaking, and sustain them during the first days of the invasion. Ernie Pyle, who arrived in Normandy the day after the initial landing there, found thousands of discarded, water-soaked cartons all along the beach. After the beachhead was secured, the army delivered an additional sixty-three tons of cigarettes.[4]

To make sure there was no shortage for the men in uniform, tobacco farmers were exempted from the draft as "essential workers" and the Army Service Forces organized a division within the quartermaster corps to procure and distribute cigarettes. The need for "tailor mades," army slang for factory-made cigarettes, never slacked. Testifying before a Senate special committee, Colonel Fred C. Foy revealed that the army's request for 68 billion cigarettes in 1944 had "fallen woefully short" and it had raised the number projected for 1945 to 114 billion.[5]

"Anyone in the service," Paul Fussell has written, "who did not smoke cigarettes was looked on as a freak."[6]

On Guadalcanal, Private Robert Leckie recalled, keeping one's cigarettes dry was the first priority, ammunition came second. During the rainy season, when "a man was drenched in seconds, his teeth chattering . . . his hands [darted] swiftly to his precious cigarettes, transferring them to the safety of his helmet liner, cursing bitterly if he had waited too long before becoming conscious of their peril."[7]

The endless publicity, the subsidized cigarettes that the army made available, and the notion that to prove one was a real man, not a feckless boy or homosexual, you had to have a cigarette hanging from your lips like Bogart, contributed to the addiction of hundreds of thousands, probably millions, of American servicemen. Bob Dole, who arrived in Naples a few days after Christmas 1944, had not smoked a lot before the war. "Life in the army made many of us into smokers," he wrote in his wartime memoir, *One Soldier's Story*. "In every package of 'C' rations, I found some stew that had to be heated over a fire, some crackers and cookies, and at the bottom a package containing four cigarettes. At first, I wasn't too interested in smoking the cigarettes, so I gave them away to my friends. But after getting the cigarettes day after day, week after week, I finally thought, *I think I'll try these things. They must be okay. After all, the army is giving them to me every day. If the cigarettes weren't good for us, the army wouldn't put them in our food containers.* . . . Before long, I was smoking like a chimney."[8]

While the military did nothing to divert attention from the soldiers' reliance on cigarettes, alcohol was a different matter. "Army public relations," according to Paul Fussell, "labored to conceal the facts about military drinking from the public, stressing that the beer served at the training camps contained only 3.2 per cent alcohol and glossing over the ease with which you could get fighting drunk on it if you tried. Public relations omitted also to disclose the officers' two-bottle-a-month hard liquor issue, doled out whether wanted or not."[9]

"Alcohol was officially denied to boys on base," though, as the historian Michael C. C. Adams observes, it was the "ultimate act of willful naïveté to pretend that a man engaged in killing other men will be morally corrupted by a bottle of booze. Only the American army tried to keep its ranks dry (though, because of the military caste system, the prohibition excluded officers). The result was an army obsessed with obtaining liquor."[10]

Roy and John Spiegel, military psychiatrists in North Africa, were astounded by how much the airmen drank. "Their consumption of alcohol increases often to the point where it is limited only by the source of supply." In its 1955 study, *Preventive Medicine in World War II*, the army Office of the Surgeon General found that in the last six months of the war, "there were more deaths in the European theater due to a single agent, alcohol poisoning, than to acute communicable disease." "When beer and whiskey are not available, substitutes in the form of methyl alcohol, canned heat [small jars of liquid fuel used to sterilize medical instruments and heat up food], and antifreeze have been used, all with serious toxic hazards."[11]

The novelist James Jones, who served in the Pacific, recalled that in his unit, "we got blind asshole drunk every chance we got. About the only real genuine liquor we ever got hold of was when some plane flew up with some general from Australia, and the crew might sell us an English imperial quart of scotch. . . . So mainly we had to make our own. We made our 'swipe' by stealing a five-gallon tin of canned peaches or plums or pineapple from the nearest ration dump, and putting a double-handful of sugar in it to help it ferment, and then leaving it out in the sun in the jungle with a piece of cheesecloth or mosquito netting over it to keep out the bugs. It was the most godawful stuff to drink, sickly sweet and smelling very raunchy, but if you could get enough of it down and keep it down, it carried a wonderful wallop."[12]

As nation after nation was "liberated" from Nazi control, there was a dramatic increase in the amount of wine, beer, and whiskey available. "The GIs did not even have to search for alcohol. Wherever they passed on the Continent, Europeans flooded their liberators with liquor. In Normandy, people stood in the streets with pitchers and glasses to serve cider; from Marseilles to the Vosges, wine appeared to be the civilians' chief means of exchange; in the Walloons, Belgians gave away wine and champagne by the bottle; in Holland, bartenders handed out glasses of beer to paratroopers who had landed only hours ago."[13]

Leslie Moede, who served in Germany, recalled in his oral history the "time we liberated a lot of wine and champagne and cognac. Really a lot. Each of us had a locker, ammo locker, full. One had the champagne, one had the wine, and one had the cognac. . . . I never really drank until I got in the Service. I didn't smoke either until I got in the Service. I got all my bad habits in the Service."[14]

Dr. Eugene Eckstam, a senior medical officer on a landing ship during the Normandy invasion and later a doctor in the Philippines, recalled in his oral history that "there was alcohol all during the war, everywhere. . . . Every enlisted guy had a bottle of booze in his sea bag. . . . I took a whole case of cheap booze over with me." He and his roommate found "that our alcohol intake was going up precipitously. . . . It's easy to see why people who are in the military on a permanent basis become alcoholics. There is nothing to do on many stations after 5:00 p.m. You have no responsibilities; especially in wartime we all had the philosophy of live today because tomorrow you're going to get killed. So you drink and have a good time."[15]

John Bach served as a sonarman in the coast guard. "Every place you went, drinking was . . . horrible. I mean, I was drinking too and turned into an alcoholic I think. I'm a recovering alcoholic now . . . but I think that's where it started."[16]

As with nicotine addiction, drinking habits acquired during the war carried over into peacetime. Combat veterans were prone to alcoholism, but so too were servicemen in the rear who enjoyed ready and regular access to liquor. Loneliness, boredom, and frustrations, wrote Joseph Hirsh in his 1949 book, *The Problem Drinker*, "weighed especially heavily on men in the rear echelons of combat theatres and in isolated posts far from combat zones. Liquor was often their only escape. Indeed, it would have been strange under those circumstances to find troops not drinking more than had been their peacetime custom."[17]

It was inevitable, at least in retrospect, that the men and boys in uniform, separated from wives and girlfriends for months and years, bored, anxious, homesick, racked by fears that they would not survive the war or would return grievously wounded, would indulge near-insatiable sexual appetites. "If we are honest," wrote J. Glenn Gray, who served two years overseas in Europe and survived to become a professor of philosophy at Colorado College, "most of us who were civilian soldiers in recent wars will confess that we spent incomparably more time in the service of Eros during our military careers than ever before or again in our lives."[18]

The military establishment did its best to reassure the home front that it was doing all that was necessary to keep the men and boys in uniform pure and uncontaminated by foreign flesh. The reality was that there was little it could do to curb soldiers' sexual appetites. The commanders in the field and the higher-ups at headquarters recognized as much. The most they could do was to hand out condoms and organize an educational assault intended as much for the civilians at home as for soldiers overseas, replete with pamphlets, lectures, posters warning about venereal disease. "They're Both Destroyers: Avoid 'Venereal Disease'; Gonorrhea and Syphilis Aid the Axis," read the text of a garish, widely circulated poster with a tank firing in the background and the drawing of a curly-headed, unsmiling, overly made-up woman with a hat that read, "Venereal carrier."[19]

In retrospect, as the historian Jane Mersky Leder has written, "the military's wartime attempt to control prostitution and the 'promiscuous' woman problem seems both shortsighted and an exercise in hypocrisy. According to GIs, the first part of the 'sex talk' when they arrived in camp was delivered by the base chaplain and went something like: 'Remember your sisters and your mother and be good boys.' Then came the second message from the company commander: 'I know what the chaplain has told you. (*That's our way of covering our bases.*) But if you do go out (*and I suspect you will*), watch what you're doing (*protect yourself and use a condom*).'"[20]

Rather than attempt to prohibit sexual liaisons, local commands focused their attention on making sure that soldiers and sailors didn't contract venereal diseases that would render them incapable of fighting or infect women on the home front during furloughs or after discharge. Free condoms and chemical treatments were distributed, the law that prescribed loss of pay for men who acquired a venereal disease rescinded, and a special Venereal Disease Control Division within the army Office of the Surgeon General established. "'If you can't say no, take a pro,' was the oft-cited motto in the Army's campaign. 'Realizing that angels rightfully belong only in heaven,' as one medical officer explained, the Army established hundreds of stations in all theatres for chemical treatments after intercourse, as well as providing condoms *en masse*. For ten cents soldiers could obtain kits containing three condoms and a small tube of lubricating jelly; some units distributed these packets without charge. . . . As many as fifty million condoms were sold or freely distributed each month during the war.... This policy constituted an implicit recognition of the inability of officials to control the troops' sexual drives."[21]

Black soldiers took the same precautions as White soldiers, but because they were prohibited from visiting brothels or soliciting sex on streets or in public places where White soldiers might be found, they had no choice but to seek out the services of prostitutes who according to the U.S. Army Medical Department belonged to "a more highly infected civilian population." As a result, they contracted venereal disease at a higher rate than their White counterparts.[22]

The sexual rampage through Europe began in Naples with the Allied landings in the fall of 1943. According to a report by the army surgeon general's office, "women of all classes turned to prostitution as a means of support for themselves and their families. Small boys, little girls, and old men solicited on every street for their sisters, mothers, and daughters and escorted prospective customers to their homes." While some of the women bartered sex for food, cigarettes, or clothing, most needed American dollars for their own sustenance and that of their families, because inflation had rendered the lira nearly worthless. When 1,838 White and 847 African American servicemen were asked between January and June 1945 whether they had had "sexual intercourse since you have been in Italy," 80 percent answered in the affirmative.[23]

In *The Gallery*, John Horne Burns's brilliant novel of life in Naples in August 1944, Father Donovan of South Philadelphia observes the American GIs as they encounter scenes of poverty and destitution unlike any they have come across in the United States. "When an American has seen Naples and death and the wretchedness of the whole world, he may try to forget it when he goes back to the farm in Illinois. But he won't forget it completely." Father Donovan is most troubled by the sight of the "little children pimping. They'd learned a perfect and Saxon English for the pleasures they offered for sale, and their obscene phrases smote Father Donovan more brutally than the worst sins he'd heard in the confessional." He worries about the future lives of children robbed so early of whatever innocence they retained, but he worries as well about the soldiers who in debasing the local children—and women—have debased themselves.[24]

As a novelist writing in 1947 after the war was won, Burns could use a fictional character to explore and express his own fears for the future. Reporters who had to submit their copy to military censors and editors at home could not. They skirted past the squalor of poverty, the wives and young girls prostituting themselves, the small boys as pimps, the black marketeering and sexual adventures of American servicemen to report instead on the local women they portrayed as gleefully throwing themselves at their GI liberators.

In early June 1944, American troops finally reached Rome after their long struggle northward. "They felt some slight wonder and awe among the fabled monuments," Eric Sevareid observed in his 1946 war memoir, "but history was not their strong point, and they soon found their chief fascination in modern comforts and erotic pleasures. Rome might be eternal, but even in Rome a soldier felt that *his* life might be short. . . . The Eternal City became the unholiest pleasure palace in Europe. It is not likely that this war had seen anything to compare with the Hotel Excelsior, once the smartest in Rome, which developed into such a roaring, night-long brothel that decent girls were forbidden by their mothers even to be seen in the vicinity and the Vatican finally protested."[25]

Sex with the girls and women they had liberated was, the GIs convinced themselves, their reward for having won the war. Major General Albert W. Kenner, chief surgeon for U.S. forces in the European theater, reported in September 1945, "With the approach of the end of hostilities, there became apparent an unmistakable increase in the number of cases of venereal disease. Just prior to, and subsequent to, V-E Day, the rates mounted precipitously. . . . At the present time, an overall Theater annual rate of 190 per thousand has been reached.... Considering the present theater figure of approximately 2,000,000 men, there would thus occur 380,000 cases of venereal disease during the year if the present strength and the present rate were maintained."[26]

In the Pacific theater, as in Europe, American troops in "liberated" areas sought out young women and prostitutes who were prepared to exchange sexual favors for dollars or surplus cigarettes or rations they could cash in on the black market to support themselves and their families.

In Tsingtao,* China, Joseph Lanciotti recalled in his memoirs, there were "more bordellos than customers to use them." The marines stationed there were young, unsophisticated, and boiling with teenage testosterone. There was no type of sexual activity that could not be bought here for a price. There were bordellos with Chinese women only and higher-priced houses "run by Europeans who employed European and Eurasian women, and other variations of nationalities."[27]

In the Philippines, Dr. Eugene Eckstam, a navy surgeon whose tasks included treating officers with venereal diseases, recalled in an oral history the two officers who "had what they called emergency wives.... They went out and lived in these little grass shacks with their emergency wife and the father would solicit this because he wanted money.... You could live with any one of the daughters that you wanted to pick ... and live in the hut and she would do all your cooking for you and take care of anything that you wanted." The enlisted men, for the most part, "didn't bother with the formalities of emergency wives, they just visited the gals downtown all the time. The prostitute ring was just flourishing."[28]

---

* Now called Qingdao.

Unrestrained sexual adventurism, sometimes fueled by alcohol, too often led to sexual assault. Military leaders had to navigate their way along a taut tightrope. They had to keep these incidents hidden from the public back home while assuring local communities that the guilty would be punished. Fortunately for the officers in the field and the public back home, accusations made against the GIs were easily explained away. Reports of rape were quashed by blaming the victims. *Life* magazine, responding to charges that American GIs in Germany after V-E Day had become sexual predators, offered photos of winsome young women, "flimsily dressed" or in swimsuits, parading themselves "before GIs." If the GIs succumbed, the article implied, it was not their fault; they had been led on by German girls who knew what they were doing. The last photo in the article was of an army poster, "Hello ... Sucker!," which shows the "not uncommon sequence of willing girl, love-making, yells of 'Rape,' six months' hard labor."[29]

In an article titled "Nazi Girls' Rape Racket Fails to Fool U.S. Army: Fake Accusations Made to Harass Yanks," the *Chicago Daily Tribune* reported that high army officials were uncertain whether the accusations were the result of "an organized campaign of subtle sex sabotage or merely a sort of individual feminine guerrilla campaign." In either case they were unfounded.[30]

The provost marshal Lieutenant Colonel Gerald Beane was quoted in a dispatch from Berlin insisting that rape was not a problem for the American army. "A bit of food, a bar of chocolate, or a bar of soap seems to make rape unnecessary." The *Chicago Daily Tribune*, in an editorial, took umbrage at Beane's explanation. "There is some comfort, perhaps, to be found in the information that American soldiers are not raping German women, but the reason assigned for this happy state of affairs is insulting to our men and wholly and utterly discreditable to our government. . . . We don't believe that the American soldiers in Europe would engage in wholesale rape under any circumstances."[31]

It wasn't difficult to convince the folks back home that their men and boys were innocent. Overseas, particularly in France, charges of sexual assault by local women were taken seriously and presented the army with a serious problem. The solution, as Mary Louise Roberts has argued in *What Soldiers Do: Sex and the American GI in World War II France*, was to "racialize the crime of rape." Accusations leveled by French women against Black soldiers were given credence, while those targeting White GIs were dismissed. Rape in France was configured as a "Negro," not an American, crime. Black soldiers court-martialed and found guilty, often on flimsy evidence and questionable witness identification, were sentenced to death by public hanging. In Britain, 91 percent of the death sentences for rape were handed out to Black soldiers; in France, 92 percent. Twenty-five of the twenty-nine GIs publicly hanged in 1944 and 1945 were Black.[32]

Ollie Stewart in *The Afro-American*, published in Baltimore, recognized the dangers that lay ahead. "As soon as it can be told, the terrific rape record—that will attempt to prove black men absolute beasts—will be used against people here at home who strive for democracy. It's sure to come. Already the figures and facts are being marshaled for presentation—and they won't make pretty reading."[33]

Not every relationship between American servicemen and "liberated" local women was founded on the exchange of dollars or gifts for sex. A minority of soldiers, sailors, marines, and airmen, but a sizable one, young, unmarried, unattached to anyone in the States, and deployed for extended periods, formed lasting bonds with women they met overseas. Well over 125,000 of these relationships led to marriage, often to children.

In June 1942, already anticipating the upcoming "overseas marriage boom," the War Department established new regulations governing soldier marriages. Members of the armed forces who wished to marry non-Americans were obligated to notify their commanding officers at least two months in advance of the wedding. (This waiting period was often waived when the affianced was pregnant.) The officer would then write a letter to whoever had been selected to officiate and interview the prospective bride. So long as the intended bride was English speaking, not an obvious "gold-digger," and groom and bride were ethnically and racially matched, permission was usually granted, though often with delay and the usual army snafus. Black servicemen who sought to marry White women were discouraged if not prohibited from doing so. Marriage to former enemy women, German or Japanese, was forbidden.[34]

Large numbers of marriages took place in Great Britain, where millions of GIs and airmen were stationed, and in Australia, where GIs congregated in large numbers on furlough and rest leaves. Marie Houtz, an Englishwoman, and her future husband, Earl, a staff sergeant in the air force, met in April 1943, were engaged in May 1944, and married in September. The marriage had been held up at first because the army refused to grant them permission to marry, Marie thought, because she was sixteen and had lied about her age. "I was in tears," she recalled in her oral history. "I thought I'd never be able to marry this wonderful man. And a few months later we got a letter from the Air Force to say that yes, they had given us permission. . . . We had a small, quiet wedding . . . in the St. Mary's Church in Hemsby where my husband was stationed. . . . We went to London for our honeymoon and spent our honeymoon in an air raid shelter with I don't know how many neighbors."[35]

While heterosexual servicemen, with the exception of those Black soldiers charged with rape, were able to feed their sexual appetites almost with impunity, gay men and lesbians recognized from the moment they enlisted or were drafted that they would have to disguise their sexual preferences to avoid being called out, court-martialed, imprisoned, or released with a blue discharge, which barred them from receiving veterans' benefits when they returned home.

Blue discharges were neither honorable nor dishonorable. The *War Department Technical Manual* listed the reasons for granting them as "misconduct" ("AWOL and desertion" and "conviction by civil court") or "undesirable habits or traits of character." Homosexuality was regarded as an undesirable habit or trait.[36]

To avoid suspicion or identification as homosexuals—and the blue discharges that came with it—gay service members tried to limit their liaisons with same-sex partners to time spent at liberty and on furlough, in hotels, boardinghouses, bars, parks, and other locations where they would be left alone by military police and shore patrols. For the most part, they succeeded. William Menninger, who served as chief neuropsychiatry consultant to the army surgeon general, estimated that "for every homosexual who was referred or came to the Medical Department there were 5 or 10 who never were detected. Those men must have performed their duty satisfactorily, whether assigned to combat or to some other type of service." Menninger's estimates were, according to Allan Bérubé, author of *Coming Out Under Fire*, far too low. "If Alfred Kinsey's wartime surveys were accurate and applied as much to the military as to the civilian population, at least 650,000 and as many as 1.6 million male soldiers were homosexual."[37]

Franklin E. Kameny, who in the postwar period became an influential gay activist and cofounder of the D.C. branch of the Mattachine Society, answered no when asked before induction if he had any "homosexual tendencies." For his three years in the military, he let "opportunities" for liaisons with other gay soldiers pass him by—"And, oh, there were so many!"—because he feared being identified as homosexual. "It was generally known . . . that you would be thrown out," which at that time was a "kind of stigmatizing disaster."[38]

Eddie Fuller and Tyler Carpenter, two successful Broadway actors, had lived together for only four months when Ty received his draft notice. "'Well, there are options,' Eddie responded between tears. 'You can declare your homosexuality, and you'll automatically be disqualified from service.' 'Never,' [Ty] retorted. 'I may be as queer as Oscar Wilde, but I'm a man. I won't give the bigots the satisfaction of saying that the sissy did not serve his country.'"[39]

Merle Miller, who in 1971 authored one of the first and most influential articles about "what it means to be a homosexual," disguised his homosexuality in the army and encountered no trouble receiving an honorable discharge. "I was afraid I would never get into the army, but after the psychiatrist tapped me on the knee with a little hammer and asked how I felt about girls, before I really had a chance to answer, he said, 'Next,' and I was being sworn in. For the next four years as an editor of *Yank* . . . I continued to use my deepest city-editor's–radio-announcer's voice, ordered reporters and photographers around and kept my evenings to myself, especially in Paris."[40]

Miller chose to remain in the closet during his service, as did most gay men and lesbians. The consequences for those who did not or could not were blue discharges and the denial of postwar benefits. John Hall from Sonoma County, who served stateside in San Francisco, recalled in his oral history that he had gone out with boys since grade school and "got along beautifully in the service. I had no problems. Everybody was pleasant, nobody gossiped or talked or tattled. Everything was strictly private," until, one night, at a military camp in Arizona, a soldier who had been stalking Hall returned from town drunk and marched through the barracks, bellowing, "Where is that queer cocksucker? I want to kill him." After another soldier outed him, Hall was called into the captain's office. "Of course he knew I was gay—and he said I had better report to the medical doctor and have a talk with him." Called before a board of officers, Hall denied everything at first, "but finally got to the point where I just thought,

'Oh well, to hell with it.' I said, 'Yes, I am a homosexual. I suck cock. I sucked every air force boy's cock on the grounds.' . . . That is what they wanted to know so I told them." Hall was confined to a hospital for ten weeks and then discharged.[41]

Others had it much worse. "John McPherson"* was hospitalized after admitting "being homosexual. . . . Without hesitation, I was driven handcuffed from town to camp, and spent a night in solitary confinement. I also spent three days in a stockade" and three weeks in "a 'sane nuts' neuropsychiatric ward in the station hospital," after which he "was unceremoniously dumped outside the main gate of camp in civilian clothes" and discharged.[42]

Lesbians appeared, at least at first, to have an easier time avoiding surveillance and punishment. The WAC leadership had, from the outset, grappled with the all-too-common assumption that women who volunteered for military service had, in doing so, renounced "feminine values for the embrace of the masculine." Removing WACs from service because they were lesbians would only confirm this presumption. Instead, those accused or suspected of being homosexuals were given every opportunity to explain away or renounce their behavior and, in doing so, avoid dishonorable or blue discharges.[43]

Lesbians in the military built their own subculture, founded clubs and bars and hotels where they could be together, and avoided doing anything that might force their officers to discipline or discharge them. What they feared most—and rightly—were the investigations of suspected homosexual activity that increased dramatically after V-J Day and the possibility that they would be presented with the choice of either informing on others or being dishonorably discharged.

"After the war, when we were no longer needed, they decided to get rid of the dykes," recalled Pat Bond, who served in occupied Japan with the medical corps. "They were throwing us out of the army

---

* The pseudonym of a veteran interviewed by Mary Ann Humphrey.

with dishonorable discharges. One woman killed herself, for God's sake." A friend of Bond's was told by investigators "that unless she gave them the names of ten of her friends," she would be dishonorably discharged. Every woman in the company was called in for investigation. In an earlier bid to protect herself, Pat had married Paul Bond, a gay male soldier. Fearing now that someone would inform on her and her lover, she told her commanding officer that she was married and wanted to "go home.... So I got sent back to San Francisco."[44]

There was a rather sharp disconnect during the war between the experience of servicemen who were homosexual and/or Black and those who were White and heterosexual. While homosexuals and Black GIs had to watch their steps lest they be accused of sexual misconduct, called out, and punished, White heterosexuals enjoyed nearly free rein to indulge in what would, when they returned home, be denounced as bad habits if not crimes.

The misbehavior of the men in uniform, despite the best efforts of the armed forces, was never entirely hidden from the folks back home. It was not a secret that they drank too much, smoked too much, used foul language, and had sexual relations with prostitutes. Those who would have condemned such behaviors had they occurred on the home front were likely to forgive and try to forget what happened abroad or in camps stateside, with the simple disclaimer that men at war, if they were not Black or rapists or confirmed homosexuals, deserved a bit of moral leeway. What those on the home front, particularly the war wives and girlfriends, feared most was that the veterans would bring home with them bad habits, tolerated in wartime but destructive and dangerous in civilian and family life.

Chapter 4.

SEGREGATION IN THE MILITARY

The American military remained, from training camp to service overseas, divided into two discrete, segregated armies: a Black or "colored" one, which "included anyone who had any discernible trace of 'Negro' descent," and a White one, which "at its most inclusive . . . corralled everyone *not* colored." Americans of Mexican, Puerto Rican, Filipino, Chinese, Samoan, Hawaiian, Korean, or Native American descent were, with few exceptions, designated as White and integrated into "White" units.[1]

Japanese Americans occupied a category all their own. They were classified after Pearl Harbor as "enemy aliens," made ineligible for the draft, permitted to enlist, but barred from serving in combat units, the air corps, and the signal corps. Only in mid-1943, as the need for replacement troops escalated, was that policy changed and Japanese Americans sent into combat. The 100th Infantry Battalion, made up of fourteen hundred second-generation, American-born men from Hawaii, was shipped in August 1943 to Italy, where it fought at Cassino and Anzio and then joined the campaign to drive the Germans north of Rome. A second all-Japanese combat unit made up of volunteers, the 442nd Regimental Combat Team, arrived in Italy in June 1944. Japanese Americans were also assigned to integrated service units and, in the Pacific, to military intelligence units. The "extraordinary performance" of Japanese Americans, as Assistant Secretary of War John McCloy characterized it, coupled with the growing troop shortage, persuaded the War Department in early 1944 to change the status of second-generation Japanese Americans from draft ineligible to draft eligible.[2]

Black Americans were the only American citizens who, with no ambiguity, no exceptions, no regard for longevity of family residence in the United States, no attention to skin color or mixed parentage, were locked into segregated units and barred from combat roles.

The War and Navy Departments, after World War I, convinced that Blacks made poor soldiers and that White morale would be damaged by serving alongside them, had deliberately barred or limited enlistment in every branch of the peacetime armed forces. By June 1940, African Americans constituted 1.5 percent of the army, 1.5 percent of the navy, and 0 percent of the army air force and marines.[3]

In the fall of 1940, in response to pressure for an increase in the number of African Americans and the integration of the military, and to forestall any defection to the Republican nominee for president, Wendell Willkie, who was actively campaigning for Black votes, President Roosevelt directed the War Department to put into immediate effect "a policy providing that the services of Negroes will be utilized on 'a fair and equitable basis.'" The army agreed to increase the number of African American troops in uniform, but categorically refused to permit them to serve in integrated units. "The policy of the War Department is not to intermingle colored and white enlisted personnel in the same regimental organizations. This policy has been proved satisfactory over a long period of years and to make changes would produce situations destructive to morale and detrimental to the preparations for national defense."[4]

There was no mistaking the army's intentions. As U.S. Army Chief of Staff General George C. Marshall wrote in a December 1, 1941, memorandum to Secretary of War Henry L. Stimson, the military should not be tasked with solving or ameliorating a "social problem which has perplexed the American people throughout the history of this nation. The army cannot accomplish such a solution, and should not be charged with the undertaking. . . . Experiments within the Army in the solution of social problems are fraught with danger to efficiency, discipline, and morale."[5]

The War Department would enroll Blacks in every branch of service, but they would be trained and serve in strictly segregated units; the only exceptions permitted were the White officers who would command them. Because there were as yet no Blacks in the army air corps, the War Department announced in January 1941 plans to organize the 99th Pursuit Squadron, which would undergo training at a new segregated facility in Tuskegee, Alabama. Though military officials were convinced that Blacks were not fit for combat, the Tuskegee Airmen were deployed in the spring of 1943, first to North Africa, then to Sicily and mainland Italy. In the two years between their deployment overseas and V-E Day, May 8, 1945, Black airmen would fly more than fifteen thousand sorties.

While the War Department had responded positively to the president's request that it increase the participation of Blacks in the military, the navy had not, and Roosevelt, an old navy hand, refused to do anything about it. The navy, which got its personnel not from the draft but from enlistment, would continue to accept Black volunteers, but only a portion of them and only for positions in the "Messman Branch, where they shined shoes, washed dishes, prepared meals, and ironed clothes as stewards, cooks, and mess attendants." It would take until April 1942 before Secretary of the Navy Frank Knox agreed to expand Black enlistments for general service, but only in the reserves.[6]

The historian John Hope Franklin, like other young men with low draft numbers who feared being conscripted into the infantry, attempted to voluntarily enlist in the navy after seeing an ad in the local paper seeking recruits to do office work. Franklin, who could type, take shorthand, and handle business machines, had studied accounting in high school and had a PhD from Harvard, reeled off his qualifications to the navy recruiter, who, at the end of the interview, told him that he "was lacking in *one* qualification and that was color." Franklin tried again to be of service to his country and applied to the War Department, which was recruiting historians to write a history of the war. He received no response. Having been rebuffed twice, Franklin concluded "that the United States did not need me and did not deserve me. Consequently, I spent the remainder of the war years successfully and with malice aforethought outwitting my draft board."[7]

The underrepresentation of African Americans among the nation's armed forces did not go unnoticed. By early 1943, more than a year after Pearl Harbor, the army had inducted 375,000 Black soldiers; an additional 300,000 had been classified 1-A, but the army delayed their induction. The navy, which was now part of the draft system, had taken 19,790; the marines, only 639; the WACs, 2,500. Though African Americans made up 10 percent of the population, they accounted for only 5.9 percent of the men and women in uniform.[8]

In a September 1943 hearing of the Senate Committee on Military Affairs on the married men exemption, Senator Burton Wheeler of Montana questioned whether the manpower shortage that had led to the enlistment of fathers could have been remedied by inducting more African Americans, including the 500,000 Negroes in the southern states who were "otherwise willing and available for active combat services" but had been turned down because they were illiterate. "They certainly could be taught to read and write in a comparatively short time, and if they were otherwise unfit, physically unfit, they could be used for the guarding of bridges and buildings and other things. Here is a lot of colored people who want to get into the service but who are turned down because of the fact they cannot read and write.... What about using some of those?"[9]

As the war ground on and injuries mounted, manpower shortages overseas compelled the army to reconsider its racial policies. "The demand for new service units," in which Blacks were clustered, "soared as the size of the overseas armies grew." By September 1944, Black servicemen accounted for 9.6 percent of the army.[10]

Nine hundred thousand African Americans would by war's end serve in every campaign and every theater of war, the overwhelming majority in army noncombat units. They supplied GIs, marines, sailors, and airmen with cigarettes and liquor; prepared and cooked their meals, cleaned up after them, and did the laundry; built the bridges and roads they crossed and blew up those the enemy might use; removed mines, repaired railroad tracks, treated and evacuated the injured, and buried the corpses.

Black GIs constructed airfields on Pacific islands and built roads in Alaska, the jungles of Burma, the Pacific islands, and the Philippines. Black engineer, chemical, and quartermaster units landed with and worked alongside White GIs at Salerno and Anzio; a Black barrage balloon unit, the only one, protected White invading troops on D-Day from German air attacks; ordnance ammunition companies handled and distributed ammunition to the troops at the front. Black service companies at ports in North Africa, Europe, the Pacific, and

Asia unloaded the supplies the troops required; quartermaster truckers like those of the Red Ball Express in Europe and their counterparts elsewhere sped them to the front lines. Black WACs performed clerical work at headquarters and the post office and were stationed at motor pools and hospitals.

Thirty-eight thousand Black sailors served as mess stewards, cooks, and bakers, another twelve thousand as stevedores, construction workers, and manual laborers overseas.

Seventeen thousand Black marines served in the war, most as messmen, stewards, or laborers. In the Pacific, they loaded, unloaded, and stockpiled ammunition and other supplies and landed cargo onshore. A small minority was attached to combat units, "assigned to the hazardous duty of unloading ammunition and hauling supplies, sometimes under fire, on captured shores."[11]

The contribution of African American men and women to the war effort, in service and in combat, was, with the exception of the Black press, "unsung," ignored, and, when mentioned, done so in a condescending, dismissive tone. National and local newspapers and radio commentators focused attention on White GIs, sailors, airmen, and marines in combat; war correspondents paid little or no attention to Black messmen, stewards, truckers, construction workers, stevedores, and medics.[12]

The Office of War Information and the military, worried that Black morale had fallen to the point where it might disturb active if not enthusiastic participation of African Americans in the war effort, pressured Hollywood to do more to present the war as a democratic exercise that required the contribution of all Americans, White and Black. Lowell Mellett, the OWI's man in Hollywood, urged producers, directors, and writers "to increase the visibility of Black people in their movies; . . . to put them in crowd scenes, in the stands of ball games, in stores, restaurants, and hotels, and on sidewalks as background presences." When MGM shared the script of *Bataan* with

OWI, the government officers in Hollywood were overjoyed at the democratic mix of GIs. While in real life Black soldiers were kept out of combat and units with White soldiers, *Bataan* was applauded for its make-believe insertion of a Black soldier into an integrated combat unit.[13]

Another attempt to distract Black soldiers and the public from the reality that they were trapped in a Jim Crow army was the propaganda documentary *The Negro Soldier*, produced by Frank Capra's unit, which highlighted "the contribution of black Americans to the war effort." The film was shown to Black troops and some White, and eventually released to commercial theaters in the United States. The film might have succeeded in raising morale on the home front, but it is doubtful that it did much for the soldiers assigned to pick and shovel duty in service units overseas, or those stateside who were discriminated against and humiliated on a daily basis in training camps in the South.[14] A documentary praising their contribution to the war effort was not going to salve their wounds nor was it going to magically grant them the rights and privileges enjoyed by their White comrades. When asked by army researchers whether they thought most African Americans were "being given a fair chance to do as much as they want to do to help win the war," only 35 percent of Black enlisted men answered in the affirmative. The corresponding figure for White GIs was 76 percent.[15]

From the moment Black servicemen arrived in basic training or boarded Jim Crow railway cars for southern training camps, they were kept apart from White enlisted men. They slept in separate barracks, used separate latrines, ate in separate mess halls, and trained on separate rifle ranges and parade grounds. They prayed in segregated churches; spent their free time in segregated swimming pools, service clubs, post exchanges, movie theaters, and gymnasiums; were transported in Jim Crow buses; and, when punished, were jailed in separate stockades. In some camps, Blacks protested and mutinied, and complained to the Black press, Black leaders, and Washington. Their rebellions were, for the most part, quickly put down, and the rebels punished.[16]

"In the army," the future senator Edward Brooke recalled in his autobiography, "I felt racial discrimination more keenly than ever before. . . . The segregation was total. In every regard, we were treated as second-class soldiers, if not worse, and we were angry. I felt a personal frustration and bitterness I had not known before in my life."[17]

While Black inductees from the South were accustomed to discrimination in almost every facet of daily life, those from the North, like Brooke, had a particularly difficult, sometimes impossible time accepting, then adjusting to, the Jim Crow laws and customs. Clemon Jones of Jackson, Mississippi, recalled in an oral history that the "guys from California" who trained with him at Camp Rucker in Alabama "couldn't understand how come we was segregated here. . . . A lot of them got in trouble. A whole lot of trouble. . . . They just didn't want to put up with it, with what was happening. . . . We was here, we understood what it took. . . . They didn't take what we would take."[18]

Senator John Bankhead of Alabama, concerned that Black soldiers from outside the South might pose a challenge to White supremacy, petitioned the army chief of staff, George Marshall, to station and train "northern colored troops . . . only in the North." Marshall refused to do so, citing the need to "station our troops in accordance with the dictates of military necessity."[19]

Afraid that southerners would pick up bad habits—and worse—from Blacks from the North and West, White southerners doubled and redoubled their efforts to enforce segregation outside the military camps and on the trains and buses the Black service men and women rode to and from their bases. Corporal Marguerite Nicholson, an African American WAC from Philadelphia stationed at Fort Jackson in South Carolina, was arrested for refusing "to move forward from where she was sitting to the coach reserved for colored. . . . Special officers boarded the train and placed her under arrest. . . . The young woman soldier claims that an officer abused, cursed, and struck her before committing her to a cell."[20]

Jackie Robinson, raised in Pasadena, California, an All-American halfback at UCLA and future Hall of Fame baseball player, was in 1944 stationed at Camp Hood, Texas. On a military bus transporting him from his army post to the hospital where he was being examined to see if he was fit to go overseas, he took a seat next to a fellow Black officer's wife. "We sat down together in the bus, neither of us conscious of the fact that it made any difference where we were sitting. The driver glanced into his rear-view mirror and saw what he thought was a White woman talking with a Black second lieutenant. He became visibly upset, stopped the bus, and came back to order me to move to the rear." Robinson refused. He was court-martialed not for his refusal to ride in the back of the bus but for talking back and being insolent when questioned by superior officers. Eventually acquitted of all charges, but "pretty much fed up with the service," Robinson requested and was granted an honorable discharge.[21]

Because he was a famous athlete and had a good lawyer and the Black press behind him, Robinson was not punished for his transgressions. He was one of the lucky few. According to the law professor Margaret A. Burnham, author of *By Hands Now Known*, "Between 1941 and 1946 at least twenty-eight active-duty soldiers lost their lives in the US for refusing to submit silently to the humiliations of Jim Crow. Hundreds more suffered nonfatal gunshot wounds, imprisonment in civilian jails, chain-gang sentences, and military sanctions."[22]

While segregation remained near inviolable in the southern states where the majority of troops were stationed, it was a different matter overseas. Timuel Black recalled in his oral history that the French people he encountered in Paris and elsewhere were bewildered and bothered by "the division on the race lines. That really disturbed them.... They just couldn't handle it.... They'd never seen people of color; it was amazing." So was their "cordiality.... You felt comfortable."[23]

"The English people," Ollie Stewart cabled home to Baltimore's *Afro-American* in the fall of 1942, "show our lads every possible courtesy and some of them [the Black troops] accustomed to ill will, harsh words, and artificial barriers, seem slightly bewildered. They never had a chance to leave their Southern homes before, and therefore never realized there was a part of the world which was willing to forget a man's color and welcome him as a brother." While White southern MPs, enlisted men, and officers spread malicious rumors about Black soldiers and did all they could to keep them out of pubs, bars, restaurants, and movie houses and restrict them from eating, dancing, laughing, or, God forbid, dating White women, the local population, with some exceptions, paid them little heed. "There is a certain stubbornness about the British people which makes them unwilling to have others form their opinions for them," George Goodman, former secretary of the Washington Urban League, reported to the Black reporters gathered at the Capital Press Club[*] in May 1944. "They have formed their own opinion about the colored soldier, whose sense of humor, good nature and friendly attitude have won the hearts of the British people."[24]

This "breakdown of strict segregation overseas," according to the

---

[*] The Capital Press Club was formed by Black reporters who were excluded from the National Press Club.

historian Jason Morgan Ward, "alarmed many white southerners, and they could do little to stop it," other than complaining to their officers overseas and alerting politicians at home to what was going on. "It was nothing strange in Australia," a White South Carolinian wrote home, "to see a negro walking proudly down a street with a beautiful 'Aussie' girl. . . . What's to happen when those fellows get back, after having been with white girls?"[25]

While the leadership of the American military had, somewhat reluctantly, agreed to increase the number of Black servicemen in uniform, it remained committed to restricting them to segregated service units and barring them from combat roles. By early 1944, with the need for replacement infantrymen critical, it had become increasingly obvious that these policies made less and less sense. In March 1944, Assistant Secretary of War John McCloy, who chaired the Advisory Committee on Negro Troop Policy, recommended to Secretary of War Stimson, "With so large a portion of our population colored, with the example of the effective use of colored troops . . . by other nations, and with the many imponderables that are connected with the situation, we must, I think, be more affirmative about the use of our Negro troops." Stimson and Chief of Staff Marshall agreed to commit Black troops to combat, but only on a experimental basis.[26]

The 92nd Infantry Division, which had been organized during World War I and nicknamed the Buffalo Soldiers after its divisional insignia, was transported to Naples in July 1944, and entered combat in central Italy and, after the liberation of Rome, in the Italian Alps. Like every other combat division, the 92nd experienced defeats in battle; unlike every other division, these defeats were attributed to the inferior martial qualities and the inherent cowardice of Black soldiers. A second combat unit in Europe, the 761st "Black Panther"

Tank Battalion, had been organized in April 1942, but did not arrive in France until October 1944, where it too was thrown into almost continuous combat, "serving for 183 consecutive days, fighting in six countries and four major Allied campaigns." Black infantrymen were also sent to the Pacific "as reinforcements on Bougainville Island."[27]

The Black combat troops sent to Italy and the Pacific might have helped build Black morale and reduce racial tensions, but in the end they offered little relief for already overstressed troops and did not solve, in the slightest, the replacement shortages in the European theater, which mounted during and after the Battle of the Bulge.

On December 26, 1944, Lieutenant General John C. H. Lee, commander of the Communications Zone in the European theater, suggested to General Eisenhower that additional Black troops already stationed in the European theater be trained for and committed to infantry combat. General Eisenhower agreed and issued a call for volunteers. More than forty-five hundred African American soldiers volunteered, though only twenty-five hundred could be accommodated. Because only privates were eligible to volunteer, a considerable number of African Americans agreed to a demotion in order to join infantry combat units. The volunteers were divided up into segregated platoons led by White officers and trained and sent into battle in previously all-White combat divisions. The army carefully monitored their performance. In May and June, the Army Research Branch surveyed White officers, platoon sergeants, and enlisted men and found that more than 80 percent of White officers interviewed "reported that the Negroes had performed 'very well.' . . . Nearly all the officers questioned admitted that the camaraderie between white and black troops was far better than they had expected." Notably, the results of the survey were not made public for fear that it would encourage Black leaders to push for full integration and alienate those opposed.[28]

The experiment in the integration of combat units, compelled by infantry and riflemen manpower shortages, lasted only so long as the Black volunteers were needed on the front lines in the European theater. That ended with V-E Day. Some of the Black GIs who had seen combat were sent home—for discharge or reassignment to the Pacific. Others were reassigned to segregated service units in the occupation army.[29]

Large numbers of Black servicemen were, in fact, left behind in the European and Pacific theaters and assigned to occupation duty. "They will send the white ones home first," Langston Hughes's Simple Minded Friend* explained in February 1946, "and leave the colored soldiers over there in Germany and Japan and Manila to do the dirty work the white folks have done got tired of doing. They always give us colored men all the jobs that white folks don't want. . . . When every last white GI that wants to come home is home—and every last good job in the USA is taken—they still gonna have the colored soldiers patrolling the natives way over yonder in Guam or somewhere, and unloading ships, and digging drains around air-bases. . . . The white man does not want that kind of work, and that is what they are going to give to colored."[30]

Whatever camaraderie between Black and White soldiers in combat might have existed vanished with the cessation of hostilities and the reassignment of troops for occupation duty. The future historian David Brion Davis, who served in the security police in occupied Germany, recalled years later that "the most traumatic and shocking events [I encountered] had nothing to do with our pursuit of escaped SS officers, my watching Hermann Göring at Nuremberg, or my arrest of a Polish soldier who had raped and given gonorrhea to a

---

* Simple Minded Friend was a character Hughes used in several of his *Chicago Defender* columns.

six-year-old German girl named Maria. The most disturbing reality was American racial conflict.... A high command summoned our police unit to the Mannheim railroad station in order to keep a trainload of contemptuously termed 'jigaboos' from 'acting up,' as they passed through on their way back to the United States." In a "pep talk" to Davis's unit, Major Commander Ernest Harmon declared that "America's stupidest mistake ... was to send colored soldiers to Europe. He [Commander Harmon] had warned the government not to send any Niggers. Now they were a much bigger problem than the Germans."[31]

There was a perverse truth, at least for those who hoped to sustain the racial status quo after the war, to complaints, like Major Commander Harmon's, that Black soldiers should never have been sent overseas. For those who honored, respected, and hoped to sustain the racial status quo in the southern states, World War II would prove to be somewhat of a disaster. By placing Black GIs, airmen, marines, sailors, WACs, and WAVEs among peoples who did not discriminate against them because of their race and could not understand why White Americans did, the military undermined White supremacy. Large numbers of Blacks recognized, some for the first time, that racial discrimination was neither natural nor inevitable. "Service overseas," as the historian Christopher Parker has written, "stimulated a racial awareness that peeled away the veil of white supremacy that many black Southerners had reluctantly come to accept as a fact of life. Coming into contact with more tolerant cultures and observing the tenacity of white supremacy among some white troops pushed black GIs to question the legitimacy of Jim Crow more than they would have had they remained in the South."[32]

The future civil rights activist Medgar Evers was discharged from the army on April 16, 1946, nearly a year after V-E Day. While overseas, he had "met a local French family and fell for their daughter. In

Mississippi," his brother Charles later recalled, "Medgar could never have touched her. In France, he walked with her, kissed her in public.... To a Mississippi Negro, this was amazing.... Going with this French girl made Medgar even more sure the racism we'd grown up with in Mississippi was unnatural and could be changed."[33]

As the nation prepared for what it hoped would be the last push toward victory in Europe, with American troops landing in France on D-Day, it was left to the writer Langston Hughes to remind his readers that despite their having been rendered virtually invisible in the press, in the newsreels, and on the radio, "American Negroes are a part of that Invasion moving in blood and death and determination into Europe.... We are there on the French Coast today—you and I.... Are you ashamed that some of us are Jim Crowed into not fighting—only working? The shame is not ours.... This is our War because we are dying in it. This is our country because we are dying for it. This is our Invasion."[34]

Chapter 5.

THE LAST BLOODY YEAR IN EUROPE

The job will be the toughest American soldiers have ever taken on," *Life* magazine proclaimed in its photo essay "American Invaders Mass in England," published three weeks and a day before D-Day. "The expectations are that they will do the job, but some will die doing it. Before they have died they will have confronted the Nazi with the qualities of the man America produces in the year 1944." The story included photographs of General Eisenhower, Field Marshal Bernard Montgomery, and Prime Minister Winston Churchill inspecting the troops, an M4 Sherman tank on maneuvers, paratroopers practicing a landing, infantrymen mock invading a beach, and hundreds of troops marching in formation on the docks alongside the ships that would ferry them across the Channel.[1]

News of the invasion was managed as carefully as the invasion itself. The few war correspondents chosen by the military to accompany the troops were collected, housed, and sworn to secrecy. An enormous contingent of British and American film directors, including the Hollywood titans John Ford and George Stevens, dozens of cameramen with their heavy equipment, and two hundred still photographers, were commissioned to photograph every element of the invasion. The first reports would come from headquarters; the war correspondents, photographers, and newsreel and film producers would be kept on a tight leash until the military thought the time had come to give the home front their eyewitness accounts.

The filmed record of the invasion would not be released for decades. "Apparently the government was afraid to show so many casualties on screen," John Ford later recalled.[2]

Listening to their radios, Americans stateside learned in the early morning hours of June 6, 1944, that the invasion had begun. Bells rang, churches opened their doors for prayer services, major- and minor-league baseball games, boxing matches, and racing at Aqueduct racetrack were canceled. At 9:57 p.m., President Roosevelt addressed the nation. "My fellow Americans: Last night, when I spoke with you about the fall of Rome, I knew at that moment that troops of the United States and our allies were crossing the Channel in another and greater operation. It has come to pass with success thus far."[3]

Initial reports from the front were tightly censored and uniformly positive. "This was D-day and it has gone well," Raymond Daniell of *The New York Times* reported from London. The *Los Angeles Times*, citing German sources, declared that the Allies had advanced ten miles into France with "losses surprisingly low."[4]

For several days after the invasion, the only news to reach the home front was that relayed by the military to the press. Ernie Pyle, one of thirty correspondents authorized to cross the Channel with the troops, arrived on June 7, the morning after the beaches had been secured. His account of the human cost of the invasion would not appear in print for several days. "Here in a jumbled row for mile on mile are soldiers' packs. Here are socks and shoe polish, sewing kits, diaries, Bibles and hand grenades," letters and snapshots from home, toothbrushes and razors and extra trousers and first-aid kits, abandoned shoes, cartons of cigarettes, writing paper and envelopes. "I walked around what seemed to be a couple of pieces of driftwood sticking out of the sand. But they weren't driftwood. They were a soldier's two feet. He was completely covered by the shifting sands except for his feet. The toes of his GI shoes pointed toward the land he had come so far to see, and which he saw so briefly."[5]

The cost of the invasion in matériel and lives lost was enormous, but Allied troops were now planted on French soil. To guard against undue optimism that the war in Europe would soon be over, the war correspondents stressed the difficulties that lay ahead. "On the German side in Western Europe," Ernie Pyle told his readers on June 22, "we face an opponent who had been building his defenses and his forces for four years. A great army of men were here waiting for us, well prepared and well equipped."[6]

The Americans pushed inland through the bocage, a landscape of fields or pastures, divided by immense hedgerows, weeds, bushes, and trees. It was difficult for tanks to move forward and for infantrymen to get past or detour around German machine-gun positions and snipers in the trees. It would take until the end of July to break through. The total number of U.S. Army casualties from June 6 to July 24, 1944, reached 63,360, with 16,293 deaths. These figures did not include the additional 25 percent to 33 percent of men who were removed from the front lines with "combat fatigue" and sent off to "exhaustion centers" established by "divisional neuropsychiatrists."[7]

J. D. Salinger landed on Utah Beach and then moved northward with his unit. In "The Magic Foxhole," he tells the story of Lewis Gardner, the company point man, who, looking for shelter, jumps from foxhole to foxhole, finding in each of them a ghostlike soldier.

The story was never published, perhaps because it was too grim for the home front to bear.[8]

Years later, Salinger's daughter, Margaret, recalled that her father, remembering his time in Normandy, "spoke to me, or perhaps just out loud to no one in particular, 'All those big strong boys'—he shook his head—'always on the front line, always the first to be killed, wave after wave of them,' he said, his hand flat, palm out, pushing arc-like waves away from him."[9]

Allied troops continued to meet heavy and often unexpected resistance from the Germans as they extended their front lines. Still, their progress, made easier by supremacy in the air, appeared inexorable. By the end of August, Paris was liberated. Fifty-five percent of Americans surveyed now believed victory would come before the year was over.[10]

On September 5, 1944, in preparation for the arrival of peace in Europe, but not in the Pacific, the War Department released the preliminary plans for demobilization it had been working on for almost two years. "Prior to the defeat of Japan," demobilization would be "partial." Only soldiers considered "non-essential" would be released to civilian life.[11] Governor Thomas E. Dewey of New York, the Republican nominee for president, criticized the administration for planning a delayed, gradual, and partial demobilization, instead of bringing the troops home "at the earliest practical moment." The Democrats, he warned, were "afraid to let men out of the Army," because they feared that the rapid demobilization of millions would result in mass unemployment. To prevent this impending disaster, Dewey asked voters to elect him, instead of giving Roosevelt a fourth term.[12]

The president did not respond to Dewey's charges, but cabinet members and chief aides did. "There are only two things that will affect the speed of demobilization," Secretary of War Henry Stimson, a Republican, declared at a Washington press conference. "One is the military necessity of retaining sufficient troops in service to quickly and permanently defeat Japan. The other is available shipping. Except for those limitations, the Army is arranging to return those eligible for demobilization as quickly as possible. No economic or political factors enter into that planning."[13]

In early September," General Omar Bradley recalled in his memoirs, "most men in the Allied high command believed that victory over Germany was imminent." They were quickly proved wrong.[14] In September, on their way into Germany, the Allies were defeated in Operation Market Garden in Holland, with seventeen thousand battle losses in nine days, then bogged down in the Hürtgen Forest, just east of the Belgian-German border, for a full three months. "The enemy had all the advantages of strong defensive country," Eisenhower would later write in his war memoir. "The weather was abominable and the German garrison was particularly stubborn." Of the 120,000 Allied troops who entered the forest, more than 30,000 would be killed, wounded, or captured. Thousands more, exhausted, panicked, disoriented, not knowing if replacements were on the way or how long they would remain under enemy fire, broke down and had to be pulled off the front lines.[15]

On September 27, Joseph C. Harsch reported in *The Christian Science Monitor* that "all the news of events on the Western Front and all the estimates, official and semiofficial, of their meaning combine today into a conclusion that the early defeat of Germany has ceased to be a reasonable expectation and that in all probability victory is to be achieved not this autumn, but next spring and summer."[16]

The toll of German resistance and counterattack on the Allied combat units was enormous. General George Marshall, army chief of staff, was so disturbed by the growing number of men who had to be withdrawn from the front lines that in late September he forwarded to Generals Eisenhower, Douglas MacArthur, and Mark Clark a memorandum from the army surgeon general which suggested that the longer men remained at the front, the greater their susceptibility to psychiatric breakdown. Eisenhower distributed the memorandum "to all commanding officers down to the regimental level in the European Theater." Secretary of War Stimson, on reading the memorandum, confided to his diary that it "gave a rather appalling analysis of what our infantrymen are confronting in the present war in the way of psychosis."[17]

The report highlighted what the enlisted men and officers in the field already knew. "There is no such thing as 'getting used to combat.' . . . Each moment of combat imposes a strain so great that men will break down in direct relation to the intensity and duration of their exposure. Thus psychiatric casualties are as inevitable as gunshot and shrapnel wounds in warfare." The number of casualties could, however, be reduced by providing soldiers with "a break" from combat and the "promise of an honorable release . . . at a definite time."[18]

Recommendations that limits be put on the number of days GIs and marines spent in combat were eminently sensible; none of the commanding generals in the field disagreed with them. Unfortunately, it was too late in the war—and replacements in too short supply—to make any substantial change in rotation policies.[*]

The consequences were far-reaching. Overburdened infantrymen who had been on the front lines for months, some since the Normandy landings, remained there for weeks and months on end. Their effectiveness declined the longer they were in the field; they became irritable or unresponsive, unable to sleep or communicate, angry, snappish,

---

[*] The recommendations would be implemented in Korea and Vietnam with strict limits set on the amount of time soldiers would remain in combat.

tearful, sometimes violent. The need for replacements was extreme and exacerbated as battle casualties in the European theater increased from 31,617 in October 1944 to 77,726 in December and non-battle casualties from 28,364 to 56,695. In mid-October, Roosevelt, in a message to Churchill, acknowledged what was now obvious. "All of us are now faced with an unanticipated shortage of manpower." By mid-December, even before the German counterattack at the Battle of the Bulge, General Omar Bradley would recall in his memoir that he was most "preoccupied" not by the "possibility of an enemy attack through the Ardennes but rather an alarming crisis in manpower. Not only were we short of divisions, we were also critically short of manpower *within* the divisions. Particularly riflemen."[19]

The manpower shortages compelled the War Department not only to rethink its policy of barring Black GIs from combat, but to cut back the number of servicemen stationed stateside, retaining only those disqualified for overseas duty by age or physical condition. Privates and noncommissioned officers were culled from stateside divisions, trained as riflemen, and sent overseas. Dave Brubeck, already an accomplished jazz pianist, serving in a military band at a Riverside, California, base, was reassigned, trained, then shipped overseas as a replacement infantry rifleman. The Army Specialized Training Program recruits, among them Henry Kissinger and Kurt Vonnegut, were reassigned to infantry divisions bound for Germany. Because he spoke perfect German, Kissinger was attached to an intelligence unit. Vonnegut was not so fortunate. He was thrown into combat in the Battle of the Bulge and taken prisoner on December 19, 1944.[20]

The Allies had been caught by surprise by the German counteroffensive. In little more than a month of combat, nineteen thousand Americans had been killed, forty-eight thousand wounded, more than some twenty-three thousand taken prisoner in the Battle of the Bulge.[21]

There were 550,089 young men wounded or killed in battle in the last and bloodiest year of the war in Europe. Many more were removed from duty, sent off to receive medical care, and evacuated with non-battle injuries and illnesses. Those who returned home having come close to death would find it difficult, if not impossible, to leave the war behind them and readjust to civilian life.[22]

It was not only the soldiers who would find it difficult to adjust; those on the home front had also been changed by the war. Wives, girlfriends, and mothers, whose lives had been turned upside down when their husbands, boyfriends, and sons were inducted and sent into harm's way, would face their own struggles when their loved ones returned from overseas.

Chapter 6.

WAR WIVES, GIRLFRIENDS, AND MOTHERS

"It was very difficult when he went overseas," recalled Shirley Hackett, who had traveled to North Carolina to live with her husband, "until he was shipped to Europe. I did everything I could to stay busy.... Being by yourself was very lonely. You couldn't plan from one day to the next, because life was very precarious. Death was always around you. Everybody dreaded a telegram."[1]

The author and journalist Paul Hendrickson's mother, with her babies in tow, spent thirty months following her husband to "fourteen towns and cities, one field or base or depot after another," until, in September 1944, they said goodbye in Amarillo, Texas. He would soon be sent overseas to Iwo Jima.[2]

The women who chose to accompany their husbands to training camp packed their belongings and boarded buses or trains for places they had never been. On arriving, they squatted in cheap rented rooms in strangers' homes and hoped and prayed that their husbands would get leave to visit and, if possible, spend the night. And they supported themselves and their children by going to work.

"You'd go to live with your husband, far from home," Dellie

Hahne told Studs Terkel. "You'd work in a factory or a restaurant.... The townspeople were accommodating because they needed us. But you never got the feeling that you were welcome. It was an armed truce."[3]

Lena Sanchez followed her husband, Emiliano, from Los Angeles to Salem, Oregon, where she rented a room in a boardinghouse and got a job plucking chickens for a butcher. It was her first time away from home. When Emiliano was shipped to Missouri, Lena followed, and when he was transferred to Pennsylvania, she once again followed him and rented an apartment from a war widow and her mother.[4]

By February 1944, almost 6.7 million war wives, those who had left home to be with their husbands and those who had stayed behind, worked outside the home, a quarter of them mothers with children under ten. They did so for a variety of reasons, some because they were bored at home and believed war work was a patriotic duty they could not skirt; the majority because they needed a regular paycheck to supplement their family allowance checks. Some had worked before; others were entering the workplace for the first time. Most found their entry into the war industries or as replacements for the men overseas much less difficult than they had imagined. A June 1944 survey in the *Ladies' Home Journal* found that 70 percent of married women with children and 83 percent without children "enjoyed working more than they enjoyed staying at home." They recognized nonetheless that their work lives would be disrupted, if not discontinued, when their spouses returned. Sixty-eight percent of war wives with children and 76 percent without acknowledged in the *Ladies' Home Journal* survey that their husbands "wanted them to give up their jobs at war's end."[5]

Though most of the war wives with children had taken jobs out of necessity, they were castigated for leaving the little ones at home and inciting what the press and the politicians decried as an epidemic of juvenile delinquency. "Wayward," unsupervised girls, it was claimed, were offering themselves to servicemen; young boys were smoking marijuana cigarettes, going on joyrides in stolen cars, indulging in every variety of criminal behavior; Mexican American and African American teenagers were running wild in the streets, dressed in outlandish, provocative zoot suits. None of this would have happened, the child-rearing experts declared, had the mothers not abandoned their responsibilities at home and taken jobs.[6]

Even though the rising tide of delinquency was largely illusory, someone had to be held accountable for the disruptions of life on the home front, and it was far easier to indict working mothers than the federal government for insufficient family allotments or the local schools, churches, and governments that offered neither after-school nor day-care programs. "The federal government's child-care program," the historian Susan Hartmann has written, "at its peak in July 1944 . . . enrolled only 130,000" of the 4.5 million children whose mothers were at work.[7]

In the last year of the war, as the GIs liberated Paris and much of France, the war wives, those at work and those who remained at home, were confronted by a new source of worry. The newsreels and glossy magazines had begun to alternate grisly images of wounded and ill servicemen with photos of the beautiful young women who, a *Life* magazine caption exulted, "hugged and kissed their liberators" as they rode their jeeps and tanks into newly "liberated" towns and cities. "What the girls lacked in virtue they made up in enthusiasm," William Walton, a correspondent for *Time* and *Life* magazines, reported from Paris.[8]

Wives and sweethearts might not have known exactly what their loved ones were up to, but they had more than sufficient grounds for suspicion. "From the moment Allied occupation troops entered Axis territory, two things became apparent," Susan Carruthers has written in *The Good Occupation*: "first, that GIs would waste little time in finding new sexual partners; and second, that with just as much gusto, American reporters and photographers would alert stateside audiences to these liaisons."[9]

The same sexual adventurism occurred in the Pacific theater. "Marines Find Pin-Ups and Glamour on Guam," *Life* magazine reported in a June 1945 photo essay. Letters home were filled with references to Asian women, including geisha girls and Okinawans who worked in the fields naked from the waist up. None of the letter writers admitted to any liaisons with the women, though several reported on comrades who had visited prostitutes and contracted VD.[10]

Women on the home front were confronted with hints that their boyfriends and husbands were sexually active overseas, but admonished to accept this as a by-product of wartime service, not to be condemned. "What is more natural than that they find themselves with exaggerated mating desire?" Grace Sloan Overton, a well-known, well-traveled Christian counselor and commentator on youth, marriage, and the family, instructed military wives in *Marriage in War and Peace*, published in the summer of 1945. "Women become more and more important to many of them. This needs to be added to other factors in understanding the sex delinquency which is as much a part of war as are 'the wounded,' 'the missing,' and 'the killed.'"[11]

The men abroad were not the only ones whose sexual lives were thrown into turmoil by the war. The women in the home front also had sexual needs and desires, but while the men and boys in uniform were permitted if not encouraged to let off steam, visit brothels, and solicit sex on the street, their wives, fiancées, and girlfriends were supposed to remain faithful. To protect the men at war from possible betrayal, neighbors, parents and in-laws, and patriotic busybodies policed their comings and goings. "The wives were," Robert Havighurst and a team of sociologists at the University of Chicago reported in *The American Veteran Back Home*, "vividly aware that the dictum 'Be faithful' was enforced by an alert, community-wide network of gossip and informal espionage." They were under continual surveillance. "'It doesn't matter what time it is,'" one of the wives reported, "'the people upstairs jump up to peek whenever I go out or come in.' The few wives who did 'run around' quickly brought down upon themselves the censure of the community."[12]

And still, despite the warnings, surveillance, and national pressures, opportunities arose for flirtations, one-night stands, and longer relationships that the war wives could not and did not deny themselves. "You had a war situation," Shirley Hackett remembered, "in which the women didn't know when or if the men were coming back. The men didn't know when they'd be coming home. Inevitably you wound up with a lot of cheating on each other."[13]

Ernest Groves, a University of North Carolina sociologist, marriage counselor, and contributor to *Parents* magazine, conceded as much in *Conserving Marriage and the Family*, widely read and excerpted in, among other publications, *Better Homes & Gardens*. "It will surprise some of my readers, and shock many more, to be told that . . . a considerable number of wives who under ordinary circumstances undoubtedly would be faithful to their husbands have had intercourse with other men." The war, Groves explained to readers, had "sexual consequences" for the women at home, as for the boys and men in uniform. "Greater sex license is a product of war just as are wounds and deaths." Groves was attempting here to normalize the abnormal, to excuse behavior that before the war would have been denounced if not criminalized.[14]

In the April 1945 issue of *Harper's*, Margaret Mead tried to calm the waters by explaining, patiently, that marriage and the family were not static institutions, but changeable, adaptable ones. In peacetime, "gentle, continuous, unremitting social pressure" exerted by parents and in-laws, the surrounding community, and religious institutions governed sexual relationships by confining them to the marriage bed. In wartime, there were no such "social pressures," and men sought the outlets available: casual sex with women. "With new freedom, with unusual hours and opportunities, with long absences, both men and women find new sex partners," but these "temporary alliances" posed no "real threat" to the survival of the family. Men at war and wives at home "know that they face new problems. No illusions blind their eyes to the fact that the old patterns cannot be relied upon." It would take a "concerted effort" to put husband and wife and children back together again, but it would be done, because that is what family members wanted and would work toward.[15]

News and rumors traveled in two directions in wartime. While wives and girlfriends at home were, in the final year of the war, besieged with images of GIs being hugged and kissed by French, Italian, British, Australian, and other women overseas, the men in service received similar reports on the wanton behavior of women stateside. Armed forces radio and newsreels, *Yank* and *The Stars and Stripes*, local newspapers and national magazines, and letters from friends and family provided vivid images of life on the home front. Every soldier, sailor, airman, and marine knew that there were plenty of available and attractive men still at home: able-bodied civilians with 4-F or work-related deferments, men in uniform on leave or stateside duty.

Once set in motion, the soldier's anxieties about sexual betrayal were limitless. *Yank* tried to make light of the matter in a story titled "Jilted GIs in India Organize First Brush-Off Club" about a group of GIs "whose gals back home have decided 'a few years is too long to wait.'" The "jilted" met "weekly to exchange condolences and cry in their beer while telling each other the mournful story of how 'she wouldn't wait.' The club has a 'chief crier,' a 'chief sweater' and a 'chief consoler.' Initiation fee is one broken heart or a reasonable facsimile thereof."[16]

The *Yank* story was written with tongue firmly in cheek and intended to reassure GIs that there was life after being "jilted." Similar lighthearted stories appeared in print stateside. According to Susan Carruthers, the first mention of what would soon be known as "Dear John" letters appeared in an October 1943 article by Milton Bracker of *The New York Times*. "The dourest dogfaces in Africa these days are strictly non-dues-paying members of the 'Dear John' club. . . . 'Dear John' clubs are composed of G.I.'s—and officers, too—who have received letters from home running something like this: 'Dear John: I don't know quite how to begin but I just want to say that Joe Doakes came to town on furlough the other night and he looked very handsome in his uniform, so when he asked me for a date—'"[17]

The "Dear John" stories bemoaned the plight of the "jilted" men overseas while castigating the "jilters" at home. "In the press, popular culture, and private letters," Ann Elizabeth Pfau has written, "American women were bombarded with the message that it was their duty to be true to the soldiers (even though their husbands and boyfriends might not have been so faithful)." The outcome of the war, the wives were warned, depended in part on their remaining faithful. Suspicious or jilted boyfriends and husbands made bad, sometimes near-suicidal soldiers who endangered themselves and their comrades in arms.[18]

The most notorious of the "Dear John" letters was the one received by Corporal Samuel Kramer, stationed in England, from Anne Gudis of Newark, New Jersey. Kramer forwarded the letter to *Yank*, claiming that it might be "the shortest V-Mail ever received in the E.T.O. [European Theater of Operations]":

> Mr. Kramer:
>> Go To Hell!
>
>> With love,
>> Anne Gudis

After her V-Mail was published in *Yank*, Anne was besieged by letters, including one from Corporal Kramer's executive officer, denouncing her for being so cruel to a man in uniform. No one knew—or cared—that she had told her boyfriend, "Go To Hell!" only after he had sent her several letters about the women he had met overseas. Anne eventually apologized for her outburst: "The past was yours to do with as you pleased and the future remains to be seen." Anne and Mr. Kramer were, after her apology, reunited by mail and engaged.[19]

The burdens placed on the war wives and girlfriends were multiple. They were not only expected to remain faithful and forgive their husbands' infidelities, but were advised as well that they would be responsible for nursing the wounded back to health. In its May 15 pre-invasion issue, *Life* included "A Manual on How to Treat the Disabled of This War When They Return to Civilian Life." The advice offered was simply put but not always easy to follow: look upon the wounded as men, not cripples; "be casual"; do not worry if he "goes through a period of lethargy and apathy"; "never help him unless he shows that he wants your help"; "be natural and considerate in your conversation"; "don't stare." The final rule was directed at the women in the veterans' lives: wives, girlfriends, and mothers. "Never forget that a man's own family can make him more irritable than anyone else. You may be fond of him but you do not serve that fondness well if you coddle him . . . if you show any anxiety for his future."[20]

In the fall of 1944, Army Surgeon General Norman Kirk elaborated on the advice offered in the *Life* magazine "Manual." "Parents, relatives and friends," he warned, "must be realistic and honest. They should not tell [the wounded veteran] he looks fine, when he doesn't. But they can tell him he will soon be as good as new." [21]

The surgeon general's instructions were repeated and reinforced in the women's magazines, the glossies, and the newspapers, on the radio, and in the movies. No matter what the returning veteran's problem, be it amputation, malaria, tuberculosis, blindness, or psychiatric disorder, the onus on restoring him to normalcy would fall on the women in his life, whose task it was to project their confidence, no matter how far-fetched, that recovery was just around the corner.

In the October 1943 radio broadcast of *Double Furlough* on the NBC Blue network, James Cagney played the role of a psychoneurotic soldier on holiday furlough from a military hospital who meets and falls in love with a woman, also on furlough, but from a prison where she is serving a sentence for manslaughter. The radio drama was subsequently made into a film and renamed *I'll Be Seeing You*, which opened Christmas week 1944, with Joseph Cotten starring in the role of the soldier being treated for symptoms of what was at the time referred to as psychoneurosis but would decades later be known as PTSD. Alone in his YMCA furnished room, with a copy of a glossy magazine on the coffee table opened to "The Problem of the Neuro-psychiatric Soldier," Cotten fights his demons, sweats, and stumbles, his heart beats faster and faster, he hears planes and guns and sounds of battle and imagines bombs falling everywhere. "The wound on your mind is going to take a little more time. . . . You'll get well," he repeats to himself over and over again, drawing whatever sustenance he can from the doctors at the military hospital who had assured him that he would recover. In the end, it is not the doctors alone who will save him, but the women he encounters on his Christmas furlough: his girlfriend, Mary, played by Ginger Rogers, Mary's little cousin, Shirley Temple, and her aunt, Spring Byington, each of whom, in her own way, quietly reassures him he'll be okay. With their help, Cotten learns how to calm himself, to pull out of his anxiety/panic attack. He returns to the hospital not fully cured but hopeful that he will be. "Mary, I know I'm going to get well . . . because you figure in all my plans. . . . Without you, I'm back where I started. I'm sunk."[22]

In the immediate postwar years, this plot would be employed again and again, with the wounded veteran saved by loving, reassuring, sympathetic women who rather than pitying the wounded reassured them that they would recover. In *Pride of the Marines*, Al Schmid, a real-life hero at Guadalcanal, played by John Garfield, returns home blind. He attempts to break up with his girlfriend, Ruth, played by Eleanor Parker, but she refuses to abandon him. At film's end, with Ruth beside him, Al begins to see again.

In *The Men*, Ken, the paraplegic veteran, played by Marlon Brando, also tries to break up with his fiancée, played by Teresa Wright, who he is convinced stays by him out of pity. In the film's final scenes, Ken realizes he cannot live without her, returns to her side, and accepts her love and assistance. The last shot is of Wright pushing Brando in his wheelchair as they enter her house.

The most moving and well crafted of these love-of-women-saves-wounded-veteran films is undoubtedly *The Best Years of Our Lives*, in which Harold Russell plays a character not unlike himself who has lost both arms in the war and returns home with hooks in their place. He too pushes away his girlfriend, Wilma, until she proves to his satisfaction that she loves but does not pity him. He agrees to marry her.

The message of these films was that the military medical establishment would do its best—and it was plenty good—but full recovery depended on the love, support, and faith of the women in the veteran's life.

It is hard to imagine how the war wives, girlfriends, and mothers reacted to the advice offered them. They were being warned, almost threatened, that if the soldier on his return was unable to readjust to civilian life, it would be their fault, not the army's or the navy's or the war's. They awaited his homecoming with a complicated, confused, unstable mixture of emotions, foremost among them the realization that they had no idea who was going to appear at the front door. "Will he be changed?" Franklin Reck asked in the December 1944 issue of *Better Homes & Gardens*. "'Yes,' Colonel William Menninger, famous psychiatrist in the Surgeon General's office, assures you. 'He'll be changed. No man can live thru the experiences your boy has undergone without being changed. Every soldier will be a reconversion problem. It took time to turn Bill into a soldier, and it will take time to make him a civilian.'"[23]

Chapter 7.

WASHINGTON PREPARES FOR THE VETERANS' RETURN

No one in Washington and few among the general public had forgotten what had happened in 1932, when world war veterans thrown out of work by the Depression marched on Washington to demand the payment of bonuses that were due in 1945 but that they needed now to support their families. The so-called Bonus Army camped out in abandoned buildings, built shacks in a vacant plot of land on Anacostia Flats, and vowed to stay until they received their cash bonuses. President Hoover called on the army to remove them. General Douglas MacArthur, with four companies of infantry, four of cavalry, and six tanks, routed the veterans, chased them from government buildings, and burned down their shacks. Images of the violence meted out to this ragtag, poorly organized army of aging, infirm, impoverished, unemployed veterans were captured by newsreel cameras and played back on a seemingly endless loop to theatergoers across the land. Recurring memories of the protesting veterans, destitute and desperate, would haunt the public and the politicians for years to come.

Franklin Delano Roosevelt's victory in November 1932 had been secured, in part, by revulsion at Hoover's cold-blooded response to the Bonus Army's march. Once in office, however, he not only rejected the demand for immediate payment of the bonuses, as had his predecessor, but days after his March 4, 1933, inauguration called for a $400 million cut in benefits for "disabled" World War I veterans. Seven months later, on October 2, 1933, in a speech at the American Legion's annual convention, he revealed the principles that would govern his administration's policy on veterans' benefits. "The first principle," he declared, "is that the Government has a responsibility for and toward those who suffered injury or contracted disease while serving in its defense. The second principle is that no person, because he wore a uniform, must thereafter be placed in a special class of beneficiaries over and above all other citizens. The fact of wearing a uniform does not mean that he can demand and receive from his Government a benefit which no other citizen receives."[1]

Roosevelt was in favor of expanding social welfare benefits—and would do so in his first two terms in office—but the welfare state he envisioned was going to accommodate all citizens, not just the veterans.

Immediately after Pearl Harbor, Paul McNutt, head of the Federal Security Agency and a former national commander of the American Legion, suggested to the president that a new federal "vocational rehabilitation program" be organized to assist servicemen disabled in war and civilians disabled in work accidents in "a war industry." Congressman Graham Barden of North Carolina and Senator Robert La Follette Jr. of Wisconsin were enlisted to introduce legislation creating and funding "a single rehabilitation program for all citizens" to be administered by the Federal Security Agency. The major veterans' groups, joined by anti–New Deal Republicans and southern Democrats, opposed the bill because it provided no special provisions for veterans and would be administered by a New Deal agency, not the Veterans Administration. The bill was, they protested, not only an insult to veterans but a blatant ploy to create new and expensive social welfare programs by cloaking them in the political armor of veterans' benefits.[2]

Congressman John Rankin, Democrat of Mississippi, and Senator Bennett Champ Clark, Democrat of Missouri, sponsored an alternative bill establishing a veterans-only rehabilitation program administered by the VA. Veterans, Rankin maintained, were "in a class by themselves" and should have their own federally funded program. "Whereas the civilian . . . was not taken away from his home for foreign service and did not suffer any physical handicap as a result of anything he did for the Government; and therefore he is in an entirely different category, as I see the matter, from the veteran. Besides, I do not want to make the World War veterans the common carriers for the enormous appropriations that I can see in the distance for all the social uplifting that we will have and all the social and physical rehabilitation that may be undertaken."[3]

Roosevelt was fighting a losing battle. The Congress that convened in January 1943 was ruled by a coalition of Republicans (they had gained forty-seven seats in the House and three in the Senate in the 1942 midterms) and southern Democrats with no appetite for approving any New Deal–type social programs other than those that benefited veterans—and veterans only. After a rather perfunctory debate, both houses passed, and on March 24, 1943, the president signed into law, the veterans-only rehabilitation bill introduced by Rankin and Clark.

Public Law 16 proved to be a godsend for disabled veterans. Hundreds of thousands would enroll in vocational rehabilitation programs at a cost of $1.6 billion. Willis Allen was one of them. His right leg had been severed in combat and his left so damaged it had to be amputated. Discharged after long stints in military hospitals, he returned to his wife and children in Cleveland, Ohio, with two artificial limbs and a disability allowance. Four years after his discharge, he applied for Public Law 16 benefits and was able to enroll in the National Business School in Cleveland to study bookkeeping and accounting. After completing his coursework and receiving his certificate, he took a job as a bookkeeper at the Cleveland Chair Company and was soon promoted to head accountant. "The salary was good," and he was able to support his family and save enough to buy his parents' house.[4]

Senator Robert Dole, in his autobiography and speeches, credits the GI Bill for paying for his undergraduate education and law school, but it was Public Law 16 that did so. Dole had been struck by a German shell in Italy in mid-April 1945 and transported to an evacuation hospital with spinal damage and paralysis from the neck down, severe and lasting damage to his right shoulder and arm, and a full body cast. In June 1945, he was repatriated to Winter General Hospital in Topeka, Kansas. He would spend a total of thirty-nine months in this and other military hospitals. He never regained use of his right arm and hand, but learned to write with his left and carry a pen in his right to ward off friends, family, and well-wishers who wanted to shake hands. Before the war, he had been a star athlete at the University of Kansas and dreamed of becoming a doctor. But neither collegiate sports nor a career in medicine was possible now. When his doctors told him he "would likely do better living in a warmer climate for a while," he applied to the VA and was granted Public Law 16 funds to enroll at the University of Arizona. After a year at Arizona, he transferred to Washburn Municipal University in Kansas and, again with Public Law 16 assistance, completed an undergraduate major in history and a graduate degree in law.[5]

As in other areas, disabled African American veterans found it more difficult than Whites to get the benefits they were due under

Public Law 16. VA physicians who determined whether veterans were truly disabled, how disabled, and what benefits they were eligible to receive disallowed the claims of many Black servicemen, who, they charged, were faking their disabilities or had inherited racial characteristics that rendered them more susceptible to what appeared to be, but were not, service-connected disabilities.[6]

Joseph H. Maddox of Boston, a Black disabled veteran and college graduate, had used Public Law 16 to enroll at Boston University for a master's degree in sociology. After a dispute with his faculty adviser, he applied for transfer to Harvard and was accepted for the 1945–46 school year. When the VA vocational rehabilitation officer in Boston refused to authorize tuition payments to Harvard, Maddox sought help from Jesse Dedmon Jr., secretary of the NAACP's Veterans Affairs Committee. Dedmon met with the director of vocational rehabilitation in D.C., who reviewed the case, reversed the adverse local decision, and certified Maddox as eligible to study at Harvard.[7]

This particular case of discrimination was resolved, but only because Maddox knew what he was doing, had a college degree and written several articles for the Black press, and was able to contact an attorney who contacted the NAACP. There is no telling how many Black veterans, without Maddox's contacts or the wherewithal to get in touch with the NAACP, were deprived of benefits rightfully due them.

Public Law 16 was the first of the special benefits laws enacted for World War II veterans. On March 10, 1943, days before he signed the bill, President Roosevelt presented Congress with an ambitious program authored by the National Resources Planning Board (NRPB) to provide all Americans, veterans and nonveterans, with the assistance they were going to require "to meet the problems of the transition period from war to peace." The government, the NRPB declared in its "Post-war Plan and Program," should "underwrite full employment for the employables; . . . guarantee a job for every man released from the armed forces and the war industries . . . ; [and] guarantee and, when necessary, underwrite: Equal access to security, Equal access to education for all, Equal access to health and nutrition for all, and Wholesome housing conditions for all." The only provision explicitly designed for future veterans was a "special unemployment compensation program" that would provide up to twenty-six weeks of benefits.[8]

Once again, Senate Republicans and southern Democrats, fearful that Roosevelt was attempting to extend the New Deal into the postwar period, scuttled the plan and slashed the NRPB's budget to the point where it "had no choice but to dismantle its operations." *The New Republic* saw only disaster ahead. "Congress is not making adequate advance plans for demobilization and full employment. . . . When demobilization day comes we are going to suffer another Pearl Harbor, a Pearl Harbor perfectly foreseeable—now. . . . Peace will catch Congress as much by surprise as did war."[9]

The president, disinclined to expend political capital to save a doomed plan and preoccupied, as he should have been, with waging war, did nothing to protect the NRPB or support the comprehensive postwar welfare program it had proposed for civilians and veterans alike. In his July 28, 1943, fireside chat, he declared instead, echoing John Rankin, that because the veterans had made greater sacrifices "than the rest of us," they deserved to be specially rewarded. In late October, he asked Congress to authorize education benefits for the returning veterans. A month later, he outlined the package of veterans' assistance he supported, including mustering-out pay on discharge.[10]

While the president's proposals were slowly wending their way through congressional committees, the number of servicemen arriving home disabled in body or mind and requiring medical care and financial assistance continued to grow. The Veterans of Foreign Wars (VFW) had, in the spring of 1943, begun to call attention to the plight of the disabled veterans. Warren Atherton, who was elected national commander of the American Legion in September 1943, attempting to reassert the Legion's primacy as chief veteran watchdog and advocate, focused his and the Legion's attention on the plight of the returning disabled veterans. He directed officers in thirty-four states to collect information on the number and condition of disabled GIs who, the Legion claimed, had to rely on public charity because of government neglect.[11]

"More than 100,000 young men and women," he charged in a radio speech in mid-December 1943, "have already made the long trek from the front line to the evacuation hospital, to the general hospital and then across the sea to the hospitals of this country; more thousands are arriving every week; an attack on northern Europe will crowd the hospital ships with new victims of Hun frightfulness." Atherton demanded that the VA construct more hospitals, that the army and navy quickly resolve claims for disability assistance, and that Congress move beyond "thinking and talking" and do something for the "war wounded."[12]

Recognizing that a major cause of Washington's failure to act was institutional (there were too many bills languishing in committee), Atherton organized a small American Legion subcommittee chaired by John Stelle, the former governor of Illinois, to draft an omnibus veterans' benefits bill, which would be brilliantly nicknamed "a bill of rights for GI Joe and GI Jane." To build support for the bill, Atherton enlisted the help of William Randolph Hearst and his chain of newspapers and provided detailed instructions to every Legion post in the country on how to pressure elected representatives to support the bill. The benefits enumerated in the Legion bill were more generous than those recommended by the president in his messages to Congress. Roosevelt had proposed to "make it financially feasible for every man and woman who has served honorably . . . to spend a period up to one calendar year in a school, a college, a technical institution, or in actual training in industry." Only those with "special aptitudes" would get federal assistance "to carry on their general, technical, or professional education for a further period of one, two, or three years." The Legion bill also offered a year of education to all veterans, and an additional three years for those whose education had been interrupted by military service, but did not limit this assistance to those with "special aptitudes." It provided loans for homes, businesses, and farms at low interest rates; an employment agency to help veterans find jobs; unemployment compensation, known as readjustment allowances, to tide them over until there were jobs available; and increased funding for veterans' hospitals.* The benefits were to be administered by the Veterans Administration.[13]

On January 11, the day the American Legion's "Bill of Rights for GI Joe and GI Jane" was introduced in the Senate by Clark of Missouri and a day after it was introduced in the House by Rankin of Mississippi, President Roosevelt, in his 1944 State of the Union address, offered Congress his proposal for a "second Bill of Rights." The differences between the Legion's and the president's "bills of rights" were striking. The president's was directed toward all citizens, "regardless of station, race, or creed." The Legion's was for veterans only, 98 percent of whom were male, more than 90 percent White. The president's was aspirational, transformative. If implemented, it would have leveled the playing fields providing rich and poor, Black and White, veteran and citizen with new economic rights. The Legion's bill was, on the contrary, a conservative measure intended to preserve, not alter, the social status quo. It was to be centralized and administered by the VA "to insure that the returning servicemen," and only

---

* A separate provision authorized mustering-out pay or bonuses, but when the president in early February 1944 signed legislation providing $200 for all personnel, $300 for those who had served overseas, the Legion withdrew the mustering-out section from its omnibus bill.

the returning veterans, "could resume their civilian status right at the point at which the war had disrupted their lives."[14]

Congress took no action to implement or seriously consider the president's "second Bill of Rights." The Legion's bill, on the contrary, was vigorously debated, revised, and on March 24, 1944, unanimously passed by the full Senate. Passage in the House was delayed by Congressman Rankin, who had earlier introduced it. When asked why the bill had not been reported out of his committee, Rankin declared that it was not only "probably the most explosive and most far-reaching measure of its kind ever proposed in Congress . . . [but it] has some provisions in it that are very disturbing to a large number of Members of the House." For Rankin, the most "disturbing" of these was the promise of readjustment allowances for unemployed veterans "for 12 months after discharge [which] . . . would cost probably five or six billion dollars," and discriminate "against the man who does go back to work [while] encouraging other men to stay on the unemployment rolls." In a letter to a constituent he identified the reason for his opposition to readjustment allowances for unemployed veterans. "We have 50,000 negroes in the service from our state, and in my opinion, if the bill should pass in its present form, a vast majority of them would remain unemployed for at least another year, and a great many white men would do the same."[15]

National Commander Atherton, who had not expected any pushback from Rankin, was outraged at his opposition to the readjustment allowance provisions of the bill. "If Mr. Rankin means that he wants to deny unemployment insurance to the men now carrying a bayonet for Uncle Sam, the veterans of the American Legion intend to fight him right down the line and take the issue to every voter in the country. . . . It isn't going to help the morale of those men for Congress to show an attitude of neglect toward a bill to protect service men against unemployment and provide them with aid during the critical demobilization period."[16]

On May 6, Senator Clark, who had shepherded the Legion's bill through the Senate, joined the attack on Rankin and his committee for holding up passage in the House. The delay, he claimed, was "based entirely upon the hatred of certain congressmen for the colored portion of our armed forces. They are so unwilling to allow the colored troops to have the unemployment insurance to which they are entitled that they would be desirous of withholding absolutely deserved benefits from all of our troops."[17]

Rankin, recognizing that he would not be able to eliminate unemployment benefits for the returning soldiers, sought instead to limit them to twenty-six weeks instead of the year provided by the Senate bill. Charley Cherokee, writing in *The Chicago Defender* on May 27, explained to his readers that reducing the time frame for unemployment benefits was "intended to keep darklings from benefiting too much. Conference between two Houses will straighten it out a bit, but not enough."[18]

As Cherokee predicted, the conference committee restored the unemployment benefits to fifty-two weeks, but in almost every other area Rankin got his way. State and local officials were given near carte blanche to administer the bill. There would be no federal oversight to guarantee that Black servicemen in the South received the benefits to which they were entitled, no provisions that would disturb the racial status quo in the Jim Crow South. On June 22, 1944, the president signed the bill into law. Directly behind him stood Congressman Rankin, arms crossed over his stomach, with a stifled but noticeable half grin on his face.[19]

The GI Bill was designed, in large part, to bind the veterans' wounds and ease their adjustment to civilian life. But it was not altruism or obligation alone that precipitated its passage. It was fear as well, fear that the veterans, if not cared for, would follow the example of the Bonus Marchers twelve years earlier and wreak havoc on the nation, its institutions, and its economy.

"If the man in uniform would go from the battle line to the breadline, the common theme ran, he probably would demand radical economic and political changes," the historian Keith Olson has written. "The fear of unemployed veterans, not the fear of maladjusted veterans motivated the persons who enacted the G.I. Bill." A surge of wartime spending had rescued the nation from the Depression; a comparable outpouring of postwar spending on veterans' benefits would protect it from backsliding. "The economy needed federal help; the veterans served as a convenient, traditional, and popular means to provide that assistance."[20]

The historian Kathleen Frydl reached similar conclusions in her book on the GI Bill. "The Great Depression still haunted the nation, and many feared a return to a contracted labor market and curtailed production following the war's conclusion. How could the labor market absorb millions of returning soldiers and still remain stable? Perhaps, war planners suggested, diverting some number of these veterans to a school or job training would ease the transition to a peacetime economy. Thus the GI Bill was born from fear—fear of veteran activism, and fear of economic recession."[21]

Mustering-out pay would get the veterans safely home with a bit of money in their pockets; readjustment allowances would support those unready or unprepared to return to work or school; vocational training and educational programs would remove them from employment lines until there were more jobs available; housing loans would provide them with shelter; business and farm loans would assist the self-employed; counseling and job placement programs would ease those ready for work into jobs suitable for them; VA hospitals and clinics would care for the physically wounded, the ill, and those afflicted by psychoneurotic disorders.

"The idea behind the GI Bill," Dave Camelon would explain in the semiofficial American Legion history, was "to give the men who were fighting the opportunity they deserved—to restore them, as nearly as possible, to the position they might have held if they had not been called to serve America."[22] As its formal title made explicit, the Servicemen's Readjustment Act of 1944 was designed to put "a broad constituency of middle-class and upper working-class Americans" back on the educational and career paths they were on before they were drafted or enlisted. It was not intended to provide the veterans with opportunities to advance beyond the social and class status they had enjoyed before the war. "College stipends were of little use to veterans disproportionately poor and Black, who had not completed high school. . . . Even under the bill's generous terms, home buying was out of reach for many poorer veterans, and the bill offered little to those who needed to rent." The bill was both revolutionary in establishing a new social welfare state for veterans more generous that anything that had preceded it—or anything offered by the other Allied nations—and conservative in protecting class, gender, and racial status quos.[23]

"The war years," writes Ira Katznelson in *Fear Itself*, had "witnessed the growth of an ever-more-obsessive anxiety about race by vigilant southern legislators." The bill could not have been passed without the support of southern congressmen whose numbers and strength within the Democratic Party had increased as a result of the 1942 midterm elections. Twenty-six of 57 Democratic senators and 110 of 222 Democratic House members who voted for the bill were from the former states of the Confederacy. These Democrats, allied with anti–New Deal Republicans, made sure that while the provisions of the bill would be fully funded by the federal government, decisions on how and for whom the money would be spent would be made by state governments, local banks, and educational institutions. The bill, declared Thomas Abernethy of Mississippi, who introduced it on the House floor, was "a States' rights bill. It is not a Federal bill."[24]

In the final analysis, the GI Bill and the amendments that soon followed established an elaborate and generous social welfare program that rewarded the veterans for their service and pumped needed dollars into the economy. Because the World War II veteran population was more than 90 percent White and 98 percent male, the benefits extended to veterans only would, in the decades to come, serve to preserve and extend racial and gender inequities that had begun to narrow during the war.

Chapter 8.

VICTORY IN EUROPE

On April 30, 1945, Adolf Hitler committed suicide. On May 7, Germany surrendered to the Western Allies.

Paul Fussell was in a military hospital in France, recovering from wounds, when the little radio in the officers' ward brought "news of the German surrender. To the infantry, that meant not the end of their travail but merely a shift of venue from Germany to the mainland of Japan, and more of the same, but this time with an enemy even more resolute than the one we knew, who should have quit but chose to tear up our bodies instead. . . . When V.E. Day was announced, I did celebrate by consuming a can of warm beer I'd been saving. But there was no pleasure in it."[1]

In another hospital in France, Sergeant Ralph Martin, a reporter for *Yank*, asked Private Junior H. Powell for his reactions to the announcement. "'It's a great thing all right,' he said, 'but I kinda wish it'd all happened a month ago.' Then he pointed to his missing leg."[2]

Eugene Sledge was on Okinawa. "We were told this momentous news, but considering our own peril and misery, no one cared much. 'So what' was typical of the remarks I heard around me. We were resigned only to the fact that the Japanese would fight to total extinction on Okinawa, as they had elsewhere, and that Japan would have to be invaded with the same gruesome prospects. Nazi Germany might as well have been on the moon."[3]

Staff Sergeant J. D. Salinger was, on V-E Day, stationed outside Nuremberg with a counterintelligence corps (CIC) detachment. "It's been a mess," he wrote to his friend Elizabeth Murray. "Wonder if you have any idea. . . . I celebrated the day wondering what close relatives would think if I fired a .45 slug neatly, but effectively through the palm of my left hand, and how long it would take me to learn to type with what was left of my hand. . . . I have three battle participation stars and am due a fourth, and I intend to have them all grafted onto my nostrils, two on each side. What a tricky, dreary farce, and how many men are dead."[4]

To give the GIs overseas some idea of how the home front was greeting V-E Day, "YANK asked civilian newspapermen and staff writers in various parts of the country to send in eye-witness reports. . . . Dallas was quiet, Des Moines was sober, Seattle was calm, Boston was staid. In some towns crowds gathered and tried to think of something to do to celebrate. Mostly, they didn't seem able to focus their thoughts. . . . From Portland, Ore., came a report of a conversation between a Broadway street car conductor and a young woman passenger wearing a service star. 'So this is VE-day,' the motorman said, 'but we'll have to lick the little yellow men before I go on a toot.' The young woman said, 'And my husband will have to come home before I go on a toot.'"[5]

In her syndicated column, published two days after V-E Day, Eleanor Roosevelt confessed that she could not "feel a spirit of celebration today. I am glad that our men are no longer going to be shot at and killed in Europe, but the war in the Pacific still goes on. Men are dying there, even as I write. . . . Some of my own sons, with millions of others, are still in danger."[6]

On May 10, the War Department announced that 3.1 million of the 3.5 million GIs in Europe were coming home; 400,000 would remain as an occupying force. That was the good news. The bad news was that most of the GIs in Europe would be shipped to the Pacific after a thirty-day stateside furlough (ninety days if they agreed to reenlist) to fight another war.[7]

Demobilization would be gradual, extended, and based on the point system,* which the War Department had determined earlier and now released. GIs with 85 points would be the first to be discharged, though those with "special skills required for the war against Japan" would, because of "military necessity," be retained on duty until suitable replacements could be found.[8]

As *Yank*'s Washington bureau explained, "Nobody in the Army, no matter how many points he has, will get out unless the Army says that he is not necessary. As a matter of fact, the only enlisted men in the Army right now who are eligible to be discharged without their commanding officers deciding first whether they are essential are men who have been awarded the Congressional Medal of Honor or who are over 42 years old."[9]

The bitter truth, as every GI knew, was that the army could not be trusted. "Despite my high discharge points and my five years in stir," Bill Mauldin worried, "all the army had to do was shift my classification papers around to something 'essential,' and I would wait an awful long time for discharge."[10]

For GIs with fewer than the required 85 points, there was no uncertainty. They were going to be sent to the Pacific. Paul Fussell, after recovering from his wounds, was transferred to a division bound for

---

* One point toward discharge would be awarded for each month in service; 1 point for each month overseas; 5 points for decorations and awards for combat service (including participation stars); 12 points for each dependent child under eighteen (up to a maximum of 36 points for three children).

the Pacific. "Morale could not be said to have been very high. Most of us were sick of the war by now.... The way we dealt with the coming hell of further and doubtless much more savage fighting was to ignore its inexorable approach and to solace ourselves with images of the great times (meaning drink and sex) we were going to enjoy on our magic thirty days [furlough]. I think none of us had the courage to face openly the grave unlikelihood of our survival. Instead, we repressed it below consciousness, where it festered and broke out in nameless angers, quarrels, and fistfights. We spent the hot days of early August bitching, eating, and sleeping."[11]

The GIs in Europe and their loved ones were grateful that the war on the continent had been won and they had escaped relatively unharmed. But would their luck hold out? Carolyn Bridgforth, whose husband was scheduled for transport to the Pacific, worried that he would never make it back home. "I knew that that was a death warrant if he went on to the Pacific and fought in Japan. I knew he would never survive that."[12]

Yank magazine was positively schizophrenic in its coverage. Week after week, from June through mid-August, its pages were filled with cheerful tidbits and cartoons about gaiety and girls in "Paree," juxtaposed with articles, photographs, and drawings about "the ordeal at Okinawa." For the 70 percent of the GIs in Europe scheduled for redeployment to the Pacific it outlined what lay in store: the "weather and the combat methods . . . and the fancy Far Eastern diseases that don't grow in Brooklyn. . . . Here are a few of the diseases that GIs who wind up on Formosa or Japan will have to be on their guard against: dysentery, typhoid, malaria, tapeworm, scrub typhus, filariasis, dengue, schistosomiasis and hepatitis."[13]

The redeployment from Europe began within days of the German surrender. "Columns streamed westward on the first leg of the road to Japan (or for some the road back to civilian life)," *The New*

York Times* reported on May 20. "They come by plane from recent battlefields deep in Germany and by jeep and truck from points nearer the French border to a staging area near Le Havre, France—where some of the most bitter fighting of the Normandy campaign took place almost a year ago."[14]

They were housed in tent cities named for American cigarettes: Old Gold, Twenty Grand, Philip Morris, Herbert Tareyton, Home Run, Wings, Pall Mall, and, the largest of them all, Camp Lucky Strike. The first to arrive and the first to be sent home were former prisoners of war, RAMPs (Recovered American Military Personnel) in military parlance. "Many were wounded or sick, malnourished, suffering from dysentery and rotten teeth, gums as pale as watermelon rinds. They would be given medical treatment and prepared for demobilization."[15]

Kurt Vonnegut, a former POW in Dresden, was flown into Camp Lucky Strike. "I'm being wonderfully well fed and entertained," he wrote to his family on arriving. "The state-bound ships are jammed, naturally, so I'll have to be patient. I hope to be home in a month. Once home I'll be given twenty-one days recuperation at Atterbury [the camp in Indiana closest to his home], about $600 back pay and—get this—sixty (60) days furlough!" Vonnegut would have preferred a discharge rather than a furlough, but he didn't have enough points. "85 are needed. I have something like 43."[16]

In the cigarette camps, as everywhere else during the war, African American servicemen awaiting embarkation were segregated and policed by White officers and MPs. "There was an almost psychotic terror on the part of white commanders" that Black GIs were going to associate with White women, Alfred Duckett, a freelance journalist for African American newspapers, recalled in his interview with

Studs Terkel. "One night in a Red Cross tent, a member of our regiment, Allen Leftridge, was talking to a French woman who was serving doughnuts and coffee. When a white MP ordered him not to stand there talking to this woman, Allen turned his back on him. He was shot in the back and killed. Another black, Frank Glenn, was also killed during this incident." The Black soldiers, "determined to avenge the deaths even if they got wiped out," broke into the supply room, grabbed their guns, and started to march. Fortunately for everyone, a few White officers whom the Blacks respected intervened to defuse the situation. The next day the Black outfit was relocated. The White soldiers who had murdered the two Blacks were court-martialed and acquitted. The widow of one of the Black GIs was later denied military benefits because her husband's death was ruled as "due to his own misconduct."[17]

A large part of the racial tension in the cigarette camps and elsewhere was prompted by the Black troops' realization that they were being discriminated against in peace as they had been during the war. The point system that determined who would be discharged— and when—might not have been intentionally designed to keep Blacks in service longer than Whites, but in operation it represented, as Edgar Brown, director of the National Negro Council, charged a week after V-E Day, "the rankest kind of discrimination against Negro troops because most were segregated into work and noncombat units and could not receive points for combat work." *The Chicago Defender* reported in a front-page story on May 26, 1945, that only seventy-five of the twenty-five hundred soldiers discharged from the army the day the point system went into effect were Black. As *The Pittsburgh Courier*, an African American weekly, pointed out, the army's ongoing need for laborers, stevedores, and airfield workers "definitely leaves the colored soldiers holding the bag. . . . Negro soldiers will be among the last to be discharged, no matter when the war ends."[18]

Even for the minority of Black GIs who had accumulated sufficient points to be discharged, there were inordinate delays in demobilization. By June 30, Charles H. Loeb of Baltimore's *Afro-American* reported from Saipan that "hundreds of high-point soldiers are still out here. . . . So when a GI writes you enthusiastically that he has counted up 119 points, restrain yourself, and look not too eagerly towards the happy day you shall meet him at the station. It may be a long time before he arrives. If he is a member of a service outfit in Europe, there's an excellent chance that he may find himself out here in the Central Pacific long before he gets a chance to show off his arithmetic."[19]

The situation was no better in Europe. Timuel Black of Chicago had served with a quartermaster unit in Europe after D-Day and accumulated enough points to be sent home, but he and other Black GIs were bumped from the boat they were scheduled to return on in favor of White troops with less service time. "And a young white guy says to me, 'You mean to tell me that you've been over here all this time and I just got here, and you're going to let them take you off that boat so I can get home?' . . . I said, 'But see, the difference is you're white and I'm a Negro.'"[20]

On September 22, 1945, *The Chicago Defender* reported that "high point men throughout this area have started a campaign of protest by wearing large signs on their backs, which read, 'I Am a Forgotten Bastard with 112 Points and Can't Go Home.' And another one was, 'I Have a Wife and Child That I Haven't Seen in Three Years,' etc. The boys are carrying their gripes on their backs." In Camp Lucky Strike, "some 12,000 colored troops of several port battalions" were waiting for transportation home. "The gripes are many, which are gaining momentum every day. Higher headquarters have sensed the low state of morale among the colored troops." Brigadier General Benjamin O. Davis, former commander of the Tuskegee Airmen, was brought in to urge the Black GIs to be patient, but according to the *Defender*, his advice "had little effect on these war-beaten troops, many of whom have been away from home for three years."[21]

In mid-December, the situation worsened when the officers of the aircraft carrier USS *Croatan*, which had arrived at Le Havre with space for more than 1,200 passengers, refused to board 123 Black soldiers because, as *The Chicago Defender* put it, "they had no facilities to Jim Crow them." Congressman Adam Clayton Powell Jr. protested to Secretary of the Navy James V. Forrestal, who agreed to investigate the case while insisting, "Navy policy . . . is one of no segregation." Roy Wilkins of the NAACP, in a letter to the Navy Department, demanded that in the future "all Navy commanders be ordered to return veterans to the United States regardless of race or color. . . . If the United States Navy is to leave as a final memory in the minds of Negro American soldiers the bitter thought that because they are not white they cannot receive at the hands of their country's Navy the same treatment as other veterans who fought the good fight, then the war against Hitlerism had not been won."[22]

Army officers and MPs did their best to keep the men in the cigarette camps safe, sound, and segregated. There were churches, barbershops, auditoriums where films were shown nightly, American Red Cross Java Junctions where coffee was served, a doughnut shop, boxing rings, libraries, volleyball and basketball courts, softball and hardball diamonds, a horseshoe-pitching area, and a track equipped for pole vaulting.[23] The amenities offered the GIs were generous, but not enough to keep large numbers from looking for excitement elsewhere. The war was over—at least in Europe—and men in uniform were ready to let loose; to indulge appetites suppressed; to eat, drink, and be merry.

"Inevitably," Dana Adams Schmidt of *The New York Times* reported from Reims, France, "the waiting on this bleak plain, over which chalk dust storms sweep at least one day in five, is wrought with boredom and frustration. The Red Cross, United Service Organization and public relations must try to make it as tolerable as possible and prevent the restless Americans from swarming en masse into French towns. The latter eventuality, with its potentialities of friction, has been feared for a long time by Paris government circles as one of the great dangers of American redeployment through France."[24]

Large numbers of GIs left their camps and barracks, many on leave, some without passes, to seek adventure in nearby port cities and Paris. "The people of Le Havre," according to Mary Louise Roberts in *What Soldiers Do*, her study of sex and the American GI in World War II France, "were not ungrateful, but they now found their city virtually occupied by their liberators. Le Havre was in a state of siege, bemoaned the mayor Pierre Voisin in a letter to Colonel [Thomas] Weed, the American regional commander." Still recovering from the British carpet-bombing campaign in September 1944, which had been directed against German forces in the city but had resulted in the deaths of two thousand French civilians, the city was less than a year later overrun by American GIs looking for a good time. As the mayor wrote to Colonel Weed, "The good citizens of his city were unable to take a walk in the park or visit the grave of a loved one without coming across a GI engaged in sex with a prostitute. At night, drunken soldiers roamed the street looking for sex, and as a result 'respectable' women could not walk alone." The city had become home to hundreds of prostitutes who had arrived to service the GIs. "There were too many of them and not enough police or medical personnel to ensure the safety of the community" or prevent an epidemic of venereal disease.[25]

It was just as bad, if not worse, in Paris, which was besieged by GIs on furlough, on the way somewhere else, or AWOL, an invasive horde of unmannered, drunken, rambunctious, sex-starved Americans who wandered the streets, the bars, the nightclubs, and the cafés, as if they owned them. "The violent incidents in Paris, Reims and Le Havre in the past week," Schmidt reported on November 11, "that provoked a reminder from Gen. Dwight D. Eisenhower to the soldiers to mind their manners are symptoms of a thing that had been quietly getting worse since very shortly after the liberation." The Americans had been greeted and celebrated on their arrival, but they had overstayed their welcome. "Frenchmen see them swinging into bars and say, 'They act like conquerors in an occupied country.' The incidents are too numerous to detail. There are fights in the Pigalle district of Paris [the red-light district the soldiers referred to as Pig Alley] and elsewhere nightly. The French police fear to interfere unless accompanied by M.P.'s. The most serious incidents, such as hold-ups, are committed by AWOL soldiers who need money."[26]

"Every night," wrote Mel Most of *The Atlanta Constitution*, "a 'lost regiment' of perhaps 2,000 men pours into the soldier-congested areas of Paris, swells the wave of postwar petty crime, and disappears into its secret dwellings before dawn. They are American soldiers, but they obey no orders. They are the 'AWOLs.' More than one-fifth of them in the European theater are believed to have drifted to Paris."[27]

Michael Gold, one of the GIs in the historian Thomas Childers's *Soldier from the War Returning*, after spending much of the war in a German POW camp, had, like Vonnegut, been relocated to Camp Lucky Strike near Le Havre to await repatriation. When he had recuperated enough to leave the camp, he visited Rouen on a twenty-four-hour pass, then hitchhiked to Paris, where he joined the army of AWOLs. "He met women with ease: dark-eyed, thick, and worldly. He spent nights in their cluttered rooms, sometimes in student hostels or pensions. . . . Glorious, unhurried days unfolded. . . . He was overdue at Lucky Strike, but he was not much concerned. With GIs crowding the boulevards and brasseries, the military police were overmatched. No one asked for papers."[28]

Gold was left alone, in large part, because he was a White man and the MPs tasked with keeping order concentrated their limited resources on locating and arresting Black GIs. "Any colored GI . . . seen on the streets was," Ollie Stewart reported for *The Afro-American* from Paris, "immediately suspected of being AWOL—and in many cases he was. Almost every night I was stopped by MP's who held a flashlight in my face and a .45 automatic in my stomach until they were satisfied with my right to be in Paris." One of the cabarets that the Black servicemen patronized was raided regularly by "the riot squad of M.P.s [who] barged in every night about 12 and shook the place down. . . . Dancing couples were halted on the floor while MP's shoved through swinging sticks and demanding passes." The MPs claimed that they were looking for AWOLs, but "any night club in Paris at that time harbored its share of AWOLs, and though I visited dozens, I never saw any other club raided every single night [except] the one frequented by colored soldiers. This seemed to have been Army policy."[29]

The American military gave the GIs, so long as they were White, virtual carte blanche to consort with citizens of Allied nations, enjoy meals at their homes, dance, cavort, even have sexual relations. The exception was Germany, where fraternization with the enemy, which was defined as any social engagement of any sort, was strictly forbidden. When, in the fall of 1944, American troops first entered and occupied "a small corner of western Germany . . . and the press photographers . . . filed pictures showing German civilians, generally women and small children, greeting U.S. soldiers," Chief of Staff George C. Marshall cabled General Eisenhower with a message from the president. "There have appeared in the press photographs of American soldiers fraternizing with Germans in Germany. These photographs are considered objectionable by a number of our people.

It is desired that steps be taken to discourage fraternization by our troops with the inhabitants of Germany and that publication of such photos be effectively prohibited." In a vain attempt to prevent fraternization, fines were levied against GIs: "$10 for conversing with a German in the open, $25 for unauthorized presence in a German dwelling, and $65 for cohabitation with a German woman." The fines were a warning, never heeded, because seldom enforced.[30]

"In Germany," Percy Knauth reported for *Life* magazine on July 2, 1945, "fraternization is officially a matter of high policy. But for the GI it is not a case of policy or of politics or of going out with girls who used to go out with the guys who killed your buddies. You don't talk politics when you fraternize. It's more a matter of bicycles and skirts waving in the breeze and a lonesome, combat-weary soldier looking warily around the corner to see if a policeman is in sight."[31]

"I'm shacking with the sweetest thing this side of a PW cage," one GI wrote to his buddy after V-E Day. "All Germany is just one big Whore House. They don't even preach fraternization to us any more because it is a big joke."[32]

Mass demobilization would have to await the defeat of the Japanese. That much was clear. Still, in the weeks after V-E Day, there were increasing complaints by the GIs and their loved ones at the pace of demobilization and calls for an adjustment in the age at which servicemen would be automatically discharged: from forty to thirty-eight, thirty-five, even thirty. The army dismissed these complaints out of hand. At a May 31 press conference, Undersecretary of War Robert P. Patterson "pointed to the Pacific war map, where gains are being made after bitter, costly fighting, and declared: 'We will not ask any American soldier to lay down his life in order that another American soldier may return home a few days sooner. . . . Those now slated for discharge are all whom the Army thinks it is safe to discharge.'"[33]

"The $64 question now," Sergeant Barrett McGurn reported for *Yank* on June 3, 1945, "is: 'How long will we have to fight the Japanese?' The War Department has no official answer to it, other than that neither the Army nor the Navy is basing future plans on the idea that the complete defeat of Japan will be a pushover. Unofficially, however, a lot of guesses are being made. The predictions most often heard in the handsomely tiled latrines of the Pentagon, the War Department's giant doughnut-shaped headquarters, run from 1 to 2 years—and up." In the Treasury Department, Secretary Henry Morgenthau Jr., who had two sons overseas, warned his aides, as Eleanor Roosevelt had warned her readers, that it was not yet time to celebrate. "We have got another very tough one ahead of us."[34]

James Bartelt of Wausau, Wisconsin, who served with a radio intelligence unit, recalled in his oral history that troops in the Pacific feared that the war would not be over until Japan was invaded. "We expected it to be very tough because of the defense that they'd thrown up on Okinawa would be repeated. So there was fright, I guess you would say." He feared that he would have to remain in the Pacific for a long time to come. "Well at that time there was a saying about the 'Golden Gate in '48.'"[35]

On August 6, 1945, at 8:15 in the morning, the first atomic bomb, Little Boy, was dropped and exploded on the city of Hiroshima. An estimated sixty-six thousand men, women, and children were killed, with sixty-nine thousand wounded. Almost everything, humans, plants, animals, and inanimate objects within a mile of the blast center, was destroyed.[36]

President Truman, who had taken office on April 12, after FDR's death, released a statement sixteen hours after the bomb was dropped, claiming falsely that Hiroshima was "an important Japanese Army base." He then boasted, correctly this time, that the bomb which had been detonated "had more power than 20,000 tons of T.N.T. . . . With this bomb we have now added a new and revolutionary increase in destruction to supplement the growing power of our armed forces. . . . It is an atomic bomb. It is a harnessing of the basic power of the universe. The force from which the sun draws its power has been loosed against those who brought war to the Far East." Neither the president nor Secretary of War Stimson offered any estimate of the casualties.[37]

On August 7, the morning papers described the awesome power unleashed by the bomb, as reporters and editorial writers struggled to make sense of what it meant. "If the imagination was numbed by the story of the German rocket bombs, it is utterly paralyzed by President Truman's revelations concerning the new 'atomic bomb,'" read the *Washington Post* editorial on August 7. "It is probably correct to say that most Americans received this news not with exultation but with a kind of bewildered awe."[38]

The *New York Herald Tribune* editorial that same day declared that Truman's statement was "not only the most important single announcement in the course of the war; it is an announcement more fateful for human history than the whole war itself. . . . The statement is weird, incredible and somehow disturbing; one forgets the effect on Japan or on the course of the war as one senses the foundations of one's own universe trembling a little. It is as if we had put our hands upon the levers of a power too strange, too terrible, too unpredictable in all its possible consequences for any rejoicing over the immediate consequences of its employment."[39]

"Yesterday we cinched victory in the Pacific," Hanson Baldwin reported in *The New York Times*. The bomb's "use will probably save American lives, may shorten the war materially, may even compel

Japanese surrender. Yet when this is said, we have sowed the whirlwind.... We have been the first to introduce a new weapon of unknowable effects which may bring us victory quickly but which will sow the seeds of hate more widely than ever."[40]

On August 8, the Soviet Union declared war on Japan. The journalist John Bartlow Martin, at the time an army corporal at home on furlough, heard the news from a captain who stopped him on the street. "'Have you heard the news, Corporal?' I didn't know what he was talking about. He told me Russia had come in. It was incredibly wonderful news."[41]

On August 9, a second atomic bomb, Fat Man, was detonated over Nagasaki. Again, there were no casualty or damage figures provided, though it was later estimated that thirty-nine thousand had died, with twenty-five thousand wounded. The press was told that the bombing crew had reported "good results," that the city "was completely covered with smoke rising to 20,000 feet," and, a few days later, "that 30 percent of Nagasaki had been destroyed in the mission of devastation."[42]

On August 10, at 7:30 in the morning, Eastern Time, CBS Radio interrupted its regularly scheduled program with a bulletin from San Francisco. A Japanese news agency had "broadcast reports that the Japanese will accept the Allied terms if the sovereignty of the Emperor is not compromised." The following morning, at 11:21, CBS announced that the four powers, the United States, the U.K., China, and the Soviet Union, had agreed on the surrender terms. And then, on August 14, 1945, at 7:00 p.m., Robert Trout declared triumphantly from the CBS studios in New York that "the Japanese have accepted our terms fully. That is the word we have received from the White House in Washington.... Our last great enemy is defeated."[43]

"When word was flashed that peace had come to the world again," Eleanor Roosevelt wrote in her August 15, 1945, "My Day" column, "I found myself filled with very curious sensations. I had no desire to go out and celebrate.... There is quiet rejoicing that men are no longer bringing death to each other throughout the world. There is great happiness, too, in the knowledge that some day, soon, many of those we love will be at home again.... In every community, if we have eyes to see and hearts to feel, we will for many years see evidence of the period of war which we have been through. There will be men among us who all their lives, both physically and mentally, will carry the marks of war; and there will be women who mourn all the days of their lives. Yet there must be an undercurrent of deep joy in every human heart, and great thankfulness that we have world peace again."[44]

Prompted, in part, by racist propaganda that portrayed the Japanese as other-than-human belligerents, the consensus shared by politicians, military leaders, journalists, the servicemen, and civilians on the home front was that the bomb was a military necessity. Without it, the war might go on for years at a cost of untold numbers of American casualties. In wartime, the commander in chief's first duty was to secure victory and save American lives. To refuse to do so was an impeachable offense. Signs that the Japanese were contemplating negotiating for an end to the war were ignored. "Policymakers," Martin J. Sherwin concluded in *A World Destroyed*, "never seriously questioned the assumption that the bomb should be used."[45]

On August 26, 1945, an American Institute of Public Opinion poll found that 85 percent of Americans approved of "using the new atomic bomb on Japanese cities," and only 10 percent disapproved. Second-guessing might come later, but for now Americans everywhere, with few exceptions, could only smile with delight at the knowledge there would be no further fighting in the Pacific, no invasion of the Japanese homeland.[46]

James Bartelt was in Okinawa when "we got the news about the atomic bomb.... And it was beyond comprehension ... that one bomb could destroy an entire city.... The other feeling, of course, was one of immense relief that there may not be an invasion after all."[47]

Benerito Seferino Archuleta, who had fought with the 99th Infantry Division in northern France, Belgium, and Germany, had been designated for transfer to the Pacific, but was home on furlough and had already been "given tropical-weight uniforms to replace the winter clothing he had worn in battle in Europe. Three or four days before Archuleta was to report in San Francisco to be sent to Japan, he received news the war in the South Pacific had ended. 'I was getting a haircut and getting ready to go when all the bells and sirens cut loose. The war had ended in Japan.... The guy didn't even finish cutting my hair.'"[48]

Eugene Sledge was in Okinawa, setting up a tent camp in the north after the mop-up in the south was completed, the bodies buried, and the eighty-two-day campaign for the island finally over. "We received the news with quiet disbelief coupled with an indescribable sense of relief. We thought the Japanese would never surrender.... Sitting in stunned silence, we remembered our dead. So many dead. So many maimed. So many bright futures consigned to the ashes of the past. So many dreams lost in the madness that had engulfed us. Except for a few widely scattered shouts of joy, the survivors of the abyss sat hollow-eyed and silent, trying to comprehend a world without war."[49]

Carolyn Bridgforth heard the news at Camp Shelby in Hattiesburg, Mississippi, where she had been briefly reunited with her husband, who was on furlough on his way to the Pacific. "It was a reprieve from death. I was ecstatic. He would not have to go to Japan."[50]

No one cheered the dropping of the atomic bomb with more joy and abandon than the soldiers and sailors awaiting redeployment.

In San Francisco, jammed with servicemen who had, until the atomic bombs detonated, expected to be shipped to the Pacific, the celebrations quickly turned violent. "People all around are yelling and shrieking, hollering, crying, kissing and hugging," Josette Dermody Wingo, a WAVE stationed at nearby Treasure Island, recalled. "It's still fairly early, like nine or ten o'clock but the paddywagons are making their way through the crowds, trying to clear the way for the immobilized firewagons. By an overturned taxicab, shore patrol are knocking guys out with their truncheons and stacking them into the paddywagons like cords of wood, sober or drunk, but it seems like almost everybody is drunk.... Somehow there is a change in the atmosphere. What had been celebrating crowds, grabbing ladies to kiss them in exuberance, has turned into marauding bands. They start smashing the windows of the liquor stores and passing out the bottles to the crowd.... I'm really just plain scared."[51]

Life magazine, in its report on the celebrations, published a photograph of sailors breaking into a liquor store in San Francisco. "Revel turned into a riot as tense servicemen, reprieved from impending war-zone duty, defaced statues, overturned street cars, ripped down bond booths, attacked girls." A hostess at the Fairmont Hotel officers' club recalled that "guys were kissing, and practically raping, everybody on Market Street.... They were pulling girls' pants off and sailing them down the street." The riots went on for three days with "at least eleven deaths, over a thousand injuries, and tens of thousands of dollars in property damage."[52]

"News of Japan's unconditional surrender turned Boston into a joyous madhouse within minutes last night," Seymour R. Linscott reported for *The Boston Globe*. Pent-up tension, which had been mounting since the first surrender hint, "exploded like a giant firecracker . . . and sent deliriously happy crowds pouring into the downtown area.... It was a perfect evening, warm and clear. People were keyed up to the breaking point by days of uncertainty. The city was filled with servicemen." Thousands flooded the city's streets; the bars and liquor stores stayed open all night. "On the streets, it seemed that everyone had a bottle containing his favorite beverage.... When the excitement really got under way, servicemen—and again sailors seemed to dominate the picture—began the interesting game of trying to kiss every pretty girl they saw."[53]

The celebrations roared on into and beyond the next day. "Boston Keeps Up Victory Whoopee: Sailors Still Kissing Girls as Holiday Roars On," read the next day's *Boston Globe* headline. "During the orgy of kissing that went on in the crowds near the corner of Tremont and Boylston sts., a sailor in catching a girl in his arms grabbed at her skirt and it came off in his hand. The tar began waving it around his head like a flag, but was finally prevailed upon to return it to its owner. She retired, blushing to a doorway."[54]

"Street Kisses and Embraces to Servicemen Order of the Day," the *Los Angeles Times* reported. "The Men of War Kiss from Coast to Coast," *Life* magazine declared with a photo montage of kisses. "When peace news was confirmed, Americans, full of the same high spirits they had displayed abroad, put on a spirited display of public kissing at home.... From city to city and block to block the purpose was the same but the techniques varied. They ran the osculatory gamut from mob-assault ... to indiscriminate chain-kissing. Some servicemen just made it a practice to buss everyone in skirts that happened along, regardless of age, looks or inclination."[55]

Richard Milhous Nixon, who, after serving fourteen months in the South Pacific as an Air Transport Command officer, was in New York City when the Japanese surrendered, visited Times Square with his wife, Pat. "It was the largest, happiest mob I ever saw," he wrote to his parents. "Service men were kissing all the unescorted girls and the girls didn't mind a bit."[56]

The New York Times reported in a front-page feature that kissing had become "a popular and a public pastime.... One sailor firmly took hold of a girl and as he gave her a longer-than-movie kiss a shipmate jokingly fanned him. It was evident that formal introductions were definitely non-essential. As always there were exceptions. One girl, her lipstick smeared, marched down the street, indignant. 'They don't ask a girl's permission—can I kiss you? They just grab,' she said."[57]

Some of those "girls" might have surrendered peaceably to the soldiers who grabbed them; some might even have initiated or welcomed the kisses. But there were many who were disturbed or frightened by the "kissing" assaults that swept through every city. The sailors and soldiers were out of control, drunken, unwilling to take no for an answer to the questions they never asked.

Victor Jorgensen, a navy photojournalist in Times Square on V-E Day, took a photograph of a sailor kissing a woman in white. Alfred Eisenstaedt, working for *Life*, shot the same scene. In a later interview, he recalled watching "a sailor running along the street grabbing any and every girl in sight. Whether she was a grandmother, stout, thin, old, didn't make a difference. . . . Then suddenly, in a flash, I saw something white being grabbed. I turned around and clicked the moment the sailor kissed the nurse." George Mendonsa was the sailor. "I saw the nurse," he told an interviewer. "It was the uniform that did it. I believe if that girl did not have a nurse's uniform on, that I never would have grabbed her."[58]

The woman Mendonsa "grabbed" was not a nurse and didn't want to be kissed. Her name was Greta Zimmer. She was Jewish and had escaped Austria in 1939, at age fifteen; her parents had died at Auschwitz. Zimmer was working at the time as a dental assistant in a Times Square office, hence the white uniform. Aware that the Japanese were about to surrender, she had left her office to look at the giant Times Square news ticker at Broadway and Seventh Avenue and was returning to the office when she was grabbed. Decades later, Zimmer told an interviewer that it "wasn't her choice to be kissed. . . . The

*Taken by Victor Jorgensen in
Times Square on August 14, 1945*

guy just came over and grabbed. . . . He was very strong. He was just holding me tight." When another reporter asked what had gone through her head at that moment, she responded that she worried about breathing. "'I couldn't speak,' she explained. 'I mean somebody much bigger than you and much stronger, when you've lost control of yourself, I'm not sure that makes you happy.'"[59]

Eisenstaedt's photo was published in *Life* magazine in the August 27, 1945, issue and for decades to come reprinted in posters, featured on book covers, and memorialized in life-size statues. The photo is an integral part of the postwar narrative, a visual marker of the servicemen's triumph and the women who stood behind them from the moment they went off to war to the moment they returned. But the almost universally accepted interpretation is deeply flawed. A careful look at the photographs of the girls and women embraced and kissed shows many of them resisting, arms or elbows pushing back against the men who had grabbed them.[60]

"If Mendonsa had been in civilian clothing," the historian Brooke Blower has written, "police might well have been called. . . . If he had been black, he may have been beaten or killed." But protected by his uniform and his white skin, he was allowed, encouraged, and cheered on as he grabbed and kissed young Greta Zimmer in her dental assistant's white uniform.[61]

Greta Zimmer, like so many women, young and older, wives, sweethearts, sisters, mothers, and daughters, did not push back and did not complain. It was common knowledge that the men who had fought a war abroad were not the same ones who had left years before. They had been hardened by the years spent abroad in a males-only environment, by witnessing friends killed or wounded, by learning to kill and, for many, having killed themselves. They had been wounded, physically and psychically. There was no place now, as they returned from war, for recrimination or criticism of the bad behaviors they had acquired in wartime.

Chapter 9.

A "SLOW DEMOBILIZATION"

With Germany's unconditional surrender followed within three months by the atomic bombing of Japan and its surrender, the military's demobilization plans were thrown into total disarray. Three days after the bombs had fallen on Hiroshima, the *Los Angeles Times* alerted its readers in large headlines that V-J Day was not going to result in a "mass release of servicemen." The War Department planned to keep 3 million men in uniform: 1 million to occupy and police Japan, 400,000 in Germany, 500,000 in Alaska, Greenland, the Caribbean, North Africa, and elsewhere, and another million or so "assigned to army centers in this country to operate the supply system, hospitals, ports and similar installations."[1]

News of the military's plans for a slow, measured demobilization resulted in an outburst of angry questions. Why was it going to take a year or more to bring home the five million scheduled for discharge? Did the United States really require a peacetime military of three million? Why were so many American men and boys who had fought and won a war now going to be consigned to policing duties overseas? Why weren't the French and British in Europe and the Chinese and Koreans and Filipinos in Asia going to share occupation duty?

Congressmen were besieged by protests that projections for a peacetime army and occupation forces were bloated and demands that they be scaled back; that fathers be immediately discharged; that more ships be made available and discharge procedures sped up. On September 14, Albert "Happy" Chandler, Democrat from Kentucky, took to the Senate floor to read a letter he had received "from a little mother at Maysville, Ky. She sent me the pictures of her three children pasted on a sheet of paper, and on the same sheet is a poem":

> I'm Johnny, jr. I go to school.
> And I know all the answers to things as a rule.
> The war's over now. I heard people cheer.
> Can somebody tell me why Daddy's not here?
>
> I'm Dianne; and I tell my Mommy all day
> "I want my Daddy. Why he go away?"
> Mommy say he at sea, and I say, "You go get him!"
> Why she say, "He can't come home because they won't
>   let him."[2]

In the House, Congressman Clare Hoffman of Michigan called attention to a letter from a farmer whose son was on occupation duty in Germany. "His dad tells me that there is plenty of work at home on the farm. Buildings and fences are out of repair, soil erosion is depleting the fertility of the land, and the farmer and his wife—both of whom are well past 50—just cannot do the necessary work. But the boy, their son, their only son, their only child, is kept in Europe to tidy up the streets and the public squares, to aid in rebuilding the homes of those he fought."[3]

D emobilization—getting the boys back home—is obviously whipping up into an explosive issue," Thomas L. Stokes, a political columnist for *The Atlanta Constitution*, concluded on September 23, 1945. "It is ready-made for political exploitation. It's easy, it's simple, it's understandable. Everybody wants the boys back home. It's like being against sin."[4]

President Truman and the War Department were caught in the crosshairs between demands for immediate demobilization and the need to maintain a sizable army of occupation "to expand America's diplomatic, economic, and military presence throughout the world, especially in Europe and Asia."[5] The home front's hunger to get their loved ones home now, not later, fueled by endless Republican scolding, could not be ignored. The White House and the military rather quickly arrived at the conclusion that they had no choice but to bow to public opinion, reconfigure their immediate postwar plans, and reduce the size of the occupation army. In mid-August, the War Department estimated that it would require an army of 3 million to win and maintain the peace. By September 12, that number was reduced to 2.5 million, and then two weeks later to 1.95 million, which *The New York Times* noted was "550,000 below the last previous estimate given by the War Department." At his swearing-in ceremony as secretary of war, Robert Patterson, on September 27, announced that "'if future events permit it,' the size of the army would be reduced even lower."[6]

T he administration's strategic recalibration of the size of the postwar army did not still the dissent or address the demands of a growing protest movement for immediate and total demobilization. War wives and parents organized dozens of local and national letter-writing and lobbying groups, including the Service Fathers' Release Association, the Parents Selectee Legion, the United Parents of Veterans, the Wives in Waiting Club, the Gold Star Mothers, the Blue Star Mothers, and more than three hundred Bring Back Daddy Clubs. As Christmas 1945 approached, their campaign intensified. The five hundred members of the Chicago Bring Back Daddy Club sent ten thousand letters to congressmen urging them to speed up demobilization. More than thirty members of the Maryland chapter "threatened to put on slacks and picket the Capitol unless Congress soon orders the release of all fathers from the armed services." In St. Paul, Minnesota, a hundred mothers marched on the state capital "in five below zero weather . . . to enlist the aid of the Governor in their efforts to get fathers released from military service." Club members wrote, petitioned, visited their congressmen, and vowed that they would never, ever vote for candidates who ignored their demands.[7]

Foreign-born war wives simultaneously organized GI Bride Clubs in Europe and Asia and demanded that the War Department provide them with ships to transport them to the United States to join their husbands. "Several thousand wives picketed the U.S. embassy in London near the end of October. Shouting, 'We want our husbands!' they demanded immediate family reunification." *Life* magazine in November 1945 featured these GI "brides and their babies" in an article illustrated with photographs of toddlers with American flags and a young woman carrying two infants, one of them newborn, in front of a sign, WHO'LL FEED G.I. BABIES? "Many of the British brides are short of money and burdened with children. Most undoubtedly feel that every day spent apart puts additional strain on a hasty and long-sundered wartime marriage."[8]

Responding to pressure from veterans to reunite them with wives stranded overseas, the American Legion in November 1945 passed a resolution urging the government "to facilitate the admission to this country of such nationals of other countries—married abroad to members of our armed forces." While the Legion and its supporters in Congress opposed granting visas to displaced persons in Europe, they were willing to make an exception for women who had married or were betrothed to American servicemen. Senator Richard Russell declared that it was "the least we can do for the men who fought our wars overseas, who have married aliens, and who now wish to have their wives join them in this country." On December 28, Truman signed into law the War Brides Act, which had been approved by both houses of Congress. Foreign war brides and the children of servicemen were now eligible to receive visas on a nonquota basis if they were "otherwise admissible under the immigration laws." Asian war brides who remained inadmissible under current immigration laws were denied entry under the War Brides Act.[9]

The campaigns to swiftly and without delay repatriate overseas war wives and servicemen made for strange bedfellows. The Congress of Industrial Organizations (CIO) and its National Maritime Union (NMU) joined with the mothers' clubs, Republican congressmen, and the veterans' organizations in blasting the Truman White House and the military for not doing nearly enough to hasten the return of the men and women still overseas. The CIO and NMU, denying charges that longshoremen's strikes had delayed demobilization, called on the "War Department and the War Shipping administration [to] round up every available ship to bring home all servicemen not needed in the occupation forces." Union activists claimed that 20 troopships were lying idle in San Francisco Bay; another 175 merchant ships in New York City, Baltimore, Philadelphia, Camden, and Boston were available for conversion to troop carriers, which spokesmen for the

"I don't remember no delays gittin' us overseas."

NMU insisted could be completed in just eight days. In mid-November, the Greater New York CIO claimed it had distributed "a million leaflets urging the public to send President Truman letters and postcards calling on him to 'ship the boys home by Christmas.'"[10]

In episode 15 of *Decision: The Conflicts of Harry S. Truman*, the television documentary that appeared in late 1964 and early 1965, Truman, according to a summary of the "takes" cut from the episode, "discussed the tremendous pressure he was under from parents and other relatives to bring the troops home. At one point in his discussion, Mr. Truman imitates a childish voice asking to go home." The White House was getting more than a thousand letters a day, but Truman proudly declared that he had refused to let this "pressure rule him."[11]

The soldiers, sailors, and marines still overseas swore that they were slowly going mad. "For six months when there was no war," Karl Kleemann of Wisconsin, an anti-aircraft gunner in the South Pacific, recalled in his oral history that he and the others marooned in the Pacific did "basically nothing, just twiddled our thumbs." The idleness bred discontent, which, in its turn, led to a breakdown in discipline. With the war now won, enlisted men rebelled against the privileges and prerogatives of rank, the striking, grating inequalities between the food, the housing, the liquor, and the "women" available to them and to their officers. Officers' clubs served hard liquor; the enlisted men got watered-down beer. Nurses and WACs were off-limits for enlisted men, but not for officers.[12]

> Differences between rich and poor, king and queen,
> Cat and dog, hot and cold, day and night, now and then,
> Are less clearly distinct than all those between
> Officers and us: enlisted men.

So wrote the future ballet impresario Lincoln Kirstein, who served with the army in northwest Europe.[13]

When, in November 1945, the Army Research Branch, in a survey of "attitudes towards army life," asked whether "too many officers take unfair advantage of their rank and privileges," an astounding 91 percent answered in the affirmative; 77 percent believed that "most officers" put their own welfare above those of the enlisted men.[14]

GIs on occupation duty rebelled against the military discipline they had accepted while the war was being fought. "Getting drunk, and brawling with civilians or rear-echelon types, remained a problem," wrote Harold P. Leinbaugh and John D. Campbell, in their history of K Company, which had been assigned to a town near Heidelberg. Enlisted men had begun to routinely disobey orders. "When a newly promoted sergeant ordered a private to clean, shine, then lace up his boots, the private barked back, 'If you want my goddam boots shined you'll have to shine them yourself.'"[15]

The future Arkansas governor Orval Faubus, who was, in fall 1945, at Camp Pittsburgh near Reims, France, was horrified by the near-mutinous behavior of his troops. "By now the high discipline and good order for which the American army up to then had been noted, had disappeared. Gone was the unit loyalty and the excellent 'espret [sic] de corps.' Everyone was bitching, including doctors and Red Cross personnel, even the chaplains. . . . Agitation and complaints, fanned by editorials and news in the official publication, 'Stars and Stripes,' became rife. Open and defiant demonstrations broke out. Officers were uneasy and often uncertain how to handle them. Some were frightened at the possible consequences."[16]

"I wanted to go back home. We all did. Wasn't the war over?" the navy reserve lieutenant Robert Edson Lee recalled in his memoir. "We saw no reason why we should not, each of us, return to the States not only immediately, but also before anyone else."[17]

There were exceptions of course. Henry Kissinger, now a special agent with the counterintelligence corps, was eligible for discharge in November 1945, but chose to remain in Germany as a civilian and accepted a job as an instructor in the army's "intelligence school" in Bavaria. J. D. Salinger, like Kissinger a CIC special agent, also stayed on in Germany as a civilian contract worker for the occupation government. He did not return home until April 1946, when his contract with the government expired.[18]

By early December 1945, seven months after the cessation of hostilities in Europe and four months after Japan's surrender, service men and women still overseas, frustrated and furious that they had not yet been repatriated, took matters into their own hands. They joined together in No Boats, No Votes, Get Us Home Clubs, organized petition drives, and bombarded their congressmen with urgent, angry letters. In Manila, where more than twenty-five thousand GIs had been cleared for discharge and were awaiting transportation that never arrived, *The Stars and Stripes* Pacific editions and the *Daily Pacifican* were flooded with threats against politicians who refused to heed the warnings. "The United States Army veteran in the Pacific is raising a terrific howl in the attempt to get himself home by Christmas," wrote Lindesay Parrott for *The New York Times* on December 5, 1945, "or, failing that, at the earliest possible moment. He is not impressed by such 'excuses' as the vast complexity of the operation or the lack of shipping to move millions of men over the long distances of the Far East."[19]

"The clamor to bring the boys home," *Time* magazine reported on December 17, 1945, "grew louder & louder. Millions complained that demobilization was a scandal.... Some servicemen overseas were almost psychopathic in their anxiety to get home."[20] On Christmas Day 1945, four thousand men in Manila marched on "replacement depot headquarters ... in protest against cancellation of a scheduled transport sailing for home. The soldiers carried banners proclaiming, 'We want ships.' They were met by Col. J. C. Campbell, depot commander. He ordered them to return to their barracks," behave like soldiers, and cease their griping. "You men forget you're not working for General Motors. You're still in the army," a not very subtle reference to the United Auto Workers (UAW) strikers in Detroit.[21]

The discontent at the slow pace of demobilization boiled over on January 6, 1946, when the army announced that it could no longer guarantee, as General Marshall had promised in September 1945, that all two-year men would be home by March 20, 1946. Discharges, which had been averaging 1 million a month for the last three months of 1945, were going to be reduced to 800,000 in January and 500,000 from February through July.[22]

The reaction to the now official announcement that the army was not going to keep its promises was immediate. The boredom, the feeling of being pawns or suckers in a high-stakes game they did not understand, the fear that by the time they returned available jobs would be taken, and the seething resentment of officers who were enjoying themselves with wine, women, and first-class accommodations while the enlisted men were expected to wait on them and dine on the scraps precipitated near-mutinous protests, marches, and demonstrations almost everywhere American troops were stationed.

In Manila, twelve thousand GIs "jammed into the shell-battered ruins of the Philippines Hall of Congress for a noisy but orderly mass protest . . . and thundered approval of a resolution calling for a congressional investigation. . . . Earlier, thousands of milling enlisted men had marched to . . . headquarters" to demand that General W. D. Styer, commander of western Pacific forces, explain why demobilization had been slowed down and departure delayed. "Morale of American armed forces now in the Pacific," *The Christian Science Monitor* reported, "is at its lowest ebb since Pearl Harbor. It has reached a point where efficiency and discipline are being undermined seriously. Officers as well as men are being affected by slowly-corroding resentment against the War Department and top Army commanders for demobilization mix-ups. . . . 'Going home' has developed into a service-wide obsession that is threatening to turn the remnants of what five months ago was the world's most powerful army into a stranded mob. Even though the mass protest parades and meetings have been orderly, the situation is serious. Soldiers do not demonstrate idly against their commanders."[23]

In Yokohama, Colonel Charles A. Mahoney broke up "what he described as a 'near mutiny' [of the troops] who greeted Secretary of War Patterson with cries, 'We want to go home.'"[24] Fourteen thousand officers and men participated in mass meetings on Guam. Ten thousand soldiers protested in Honolulu. Forty-five hundred GIs in Calcutta joined committees to plan ongoing protests.[25]

The unrest spread to the European theater. In its final issue on December 28, 1945, *Yank* described how "all over Europe the people faced a winter of cold and death, and the GIs left behind to clean up loose ends, to work with Military Government, to route luckier soldiers home, to wait endlessly for their own turn to board a liberty ship or a transport or a C-47 are an unhappy body of men."[26]

There were demonstrations at General Joseph T. McNarney's headquarters in Frankfurt, and in Berlin, Paris, Le Havre, and Vienna. In London, five hundred GIs protesting outside army redeployment headquarters "shouted for Eleanor [Roosevelt] to help them." Nine delegates were invited to meet with her at Claridge's, after which she promised that "she will carry our message personally to the United States and promised she would do what she could."[27]

President Truman, asked at a January 8 press conference about the soldiers' demonstrations, responded that he didn't "know all the facts . . . [and] would prefer not to comment on it." At the conclusion of the conference, the columnist Drew Pearson, who had taken on the role of GIs' champion, presented the president with a petition signed by thirty thousand GIs in Manila demanding that they be brought home at once. Truman was near apoplectic. Two hours later, he issued a statement defending the army and navy. "There were two major reasons members of the armed forces could not be discharged immediately upon the close of the war: One was the enormous job of getting them home, and the other was the nation's commitment to share the task of preserving peace and destroying the war-making potential of the former enemy nations." The president's remarks did nothing to quell the unrest. On the contrary, his acknowledgment of the nation's commitment to the task of "preserving peace" overseas only stoked the anger of those who wanted an immediate disengagement.[28]

It was left to General Eisenhower, named army chief of staff in November 1945, to put out the fires. On January 15, he acknowledged, at a mass meeting with members of the House and Senate in the auditorium of the Library of Congress, that the slowdown in demobilization had caused a great deal of confusion that might have been avoided had military planners paid closer attention to the "emotional wave to get men out of the army." That wave of emotion was, he believed, "wholly understandable. It was to be expected. But I am frank to say that I had never anticipated this emotional wave would reach proportions of near-hysteria. I am confident that Members of the Congress are as anxious as I that straight thinking be substituted for emotion in this matter." His references to "emotion" and "near-hysteria" were clearly directed at the protesting, letter-writing wives and mothers whose interference in manly, military matters, he seemed to suggest, was uncalled-for and counterproductive. Demobilization, he insisted, was proceeding apace and ahead of schedule.[29]

On January 18, 1946, Eisenhower delivered an address over the CBS and associated radio networks in which he offered the same reassurances. "Tonight I should like to speak to every man and woman in the service, and also I hope that my words go straight to the fireside of every family at home with a loved one overseas. It is my purpose to tell you the facts about the demobilization situation, which has suffered much from misunderstanding." Taking his cue and borrowing his folksy tone from FDR's fireside chats, he declared, passionately but patiently, that "the army has really put its heart into returning war-weary men to their homes." The slowdown had been necessary because of a shortage of volunteer replacements, but it was only temporary. "The men who received the Army's pledge to be released by June 30, 1946, will be released by that time or be on a ship coming home." The army was going to be reduced in size from the 1.95 million, previously announced, to 1.5 million, and that number was now set in stone.[30]

The next stop on Eisenhower's public relations tour was the House

Committee on Military Affairs. On his way to the hearing room, he was confronted by a group of women who demanded a word with him. As *The Washington Post* reported on January 23, 1946, "the man whose military genius brought the Wehrmacht to its knees was routed yesterday by a shrill task force of women. . . . Unable to cope with them, he retreated into the office of [committee] Chairman [Andrew] May (D., Ky.) . . . , where he listened" as the spokeswoman for the Bring Back Daddy Clubs, Mrs. Dorothy Galemb of Wilkinsburg, Pennsylvania, explained that the mothers' protests were prompted by fears that their marriages could not survive any further delay. "One marriage out of three is ending in divorce. . . . 'How do you think we mothers feel?' she asked. 'Marriage won't stand this isolation.'" Eisenhower replied that 500,000 of the 700,000 fathers still in the army were scheduled to be home by July 1. He sympathized with the mothers and "wished he could get their husbands home at once. At the same time, he added, he sympathized with unmarried men overseas who wanted to come home, get married and start families. Mopping his brow, Eisenhower finally escaped and made his way to the committee room. The hearing opened ten minutes late."[31]

Though President Truman and General Eisenhower would not say so publicly, stateside protests and near mutinies by GIs overseas had played a large part in the decision to reduce the size of the postwar army from the 3 million projected in August 1945 to 1.95 million in September 1945, and 1.55 million in January 1946.[32]

Neither the military nor Secretary of State James F. Byrnes nor Secretary of War Robert Patterson were pleased with this turn of events, but they recognized that there was little they could do about it. General Eisenhower, answering a letter from the wife of a young lieutenant who was "alarmed" by the rapid demobilization—"We made that mistake in the last war and should not be making it again"—replied that he appreciated the "soundness of your thinking" and agreed with "your point of view," but added that it was incumbent on both of them to "recognize that the present rate of demobilization, while it may have been accelerated beyond that degree desirable for security, still represents the spontaneous expression of the will of the American people."[33]

Chapter 10.

REPATRIATED AND DISCHARGED

Johnny Came Marching Home, not all at once, but in starts and stops and pauses. Two million three hundred thousand soldiers, sailors, marines, airmen, WACs, and WAVEs returned before the cessation of hostilities; 1.4 million between V-E Day and September 1945; 3.3 million between October 1945 and April 1946. It would take until September 1946, a year after V-J Day, for demobilization to be completed.[1]

While in later years "greatest generation" narratives accentuated the positive experiences, growth, and maturity the World War II veterans experienced in service, the men returning from war did not see it this way. When a representative sample of army enlisted men (excluding those who had served less than a year) was asked in November 1945 if the army had hurt them more than it had helped, 58 percent answered "hurt"; 61 percent that they were more "bitter and cynical" than they had been before induction; 76 percent that they were more "nervous and restless"; 41 percent that they were now "less self-confident and less sure" of themselves; 47 percent that they had acquired "a lot of bad habits"; 54 percent got "angry more quickly"; 49 percent drank more.[2]

Fifteen months later, surveyed by the National Opinion Research Center, another sample of veterans displayed the same appraisal of their time in the military. Seventy-eight percent "answered—often in bitterness, cynicism, or discouragement, sometimes hopefully or even thankfully—that the war had been responsible for major changes in their lives." When asked if the war had made their lives "generally better or worse," 48 percent of that 78 percent—or almost two-thirds—answered "worse."[3]

The final steps in the journey home were marked by delays, disruptions, intrusive interviews, physical examinations, officers to be saluted, and "chickenshit" rules. Before boarding their ships, those cleared for discharge filled out mountains of paperwork, submitted their luggage for inspection, received certificates authorizing them to bring home no more than twenty-five pounds of "captured enemy weapons, binoculars, cameras, or other souvenirs." They got booster shots, were sprayed with DDT, converted their foreign currency to dollars, and waited.[4]

Some were flown home, the vast majority transported on civilian vessels, including luxury liners that had been commandeered by the War Shipping Administration. After the Japanese surrender the navy launched Operation Magic Carpet, the slick name provided by public relations officers, and deployed its full fleet of cruisers, troop carriers, destroyers, battleships, and aircraft carriers to bring the boys home. The aircraft carriers provided the most amenities. The hangar decks were converted to mess halls and movie theaters; flight decks to open-air dormitories with stacks of four or five cots, one on top of another, welded or bolted in place. Additional oceangoing vessels were borrowed or leased from allies whose troops had already been repatriated. The four great ocean liners, the RMS *Queen Mary*, RMS *Queen Elizabeth*, SS *Île de France*, and RMS *Aquitania*, which had transported 60 percent of American troops eastward during the war, were now deployed to bring them home.

The early arrivals got the most attention. Army and navy PROs managed their homecoming with consummate skill, making sure that the press focused its attention on the waving, smiling men onboard—and the women there to greet them with a kiss. Still, the *New York Herald Tribune,* reporting on August 16, 1945, could not help but notice that the troops "marched soberly ashore . . . apparently intent on the problems of a civilian future, in sharp contrast to civilian surrender jubilation. They whistled at WACs and listened to the Camp Shanks Negro band. . . . But they were thinking about jobs and adjustment to civilian life. . . . 'And maybe we're quiet because we're thinking of the fellows who aren't coming back,' said Private First Class Thomas J. Quirk, of 13 Church Street, Woburn, Mass."[5]

The lucky ones were greeted by family as they disembarked. "I pulled into New York harbor and my mother and father met the ship," Joseph Argenzio of Bay Ridge, Brooklyn, recalled in his oral history. "I had sunglasses on and if your parents were there to meet you they let you off the ship first ahead of the bulk of them. I came down the gangway and my mother is yelling 'He's blind, he's blind. I knew it.' I said 'Mom, I'm not blind. I just have a pair of cheap sunglasses on.'"[6]

On disembarking, the soon-to-be veterans were bused to staging areas where they spent the next twenty-four hours. Some were given a few days' leave, for one final bender; others were dispatched directly to separation centers. All they wanted at this point was to be discharged, but there was a long way yet to go. Between May and October 1945, almost 760,000 GIs arrived in New York. There were too

"He thinks the food over there was swell. He's glad to be home, but he misses the thrill and excitement of battle. You may quote him."

many to process and too few filing clerks, typists, payroll clerks, and counselors to do the interviewing and paperwork.[7]

"Even the most stolid and patient among us," the army airman Louis Falstein wrote in *The New Republic*, "considered one day's delay in our discharge as an irreparable blow to the progress of mankind. We were in a hurry.... No golden promises awaited us outside, and many looked with fear and uncertainty to the future. But now, getting *out* was the important thing."[8]

"On our arrival at [Fort Dix in New Jersey]," Merle Miller wrote in the final issue of *Yank*, "we were hurried into a cluttered barracks marked 'Incoming Personnel' where a captain, apparently anxious to prove that we were still EM [enlisted men] and not civilians, treated us with a studied rudeness, ordered a sergeant to take our records, pointed disdainfully at a bench on which we were to sit and, in a speech of welcome to ourselves and a hundred other prospective dischargees who soon gathered, several times screamed at us to 'pipe down, dammit, or I'll keep you here all day.'"[9]

The newly arrived were given white tags and directed to print name, rank, and serial number, then tie the tag to their left pocket. When their names were called, they stepped up to a counter where they were handed their clothing records and directed down a long corridor to hand in excess clothing. When they had completed this task, they were handed a blue card and instructed to write their name, rank, and serial number on it. They were then marched or bused to the barracks that would be their home for the next few days, assigned bunks, given a sheet, pillowcase, and blanket, and told to make up their beds. "Most of us stayed near our bunks, just in case something turned up," wrote Milton Lehman in *The Saturday Evening Post*. "We stayed there waiting, not wanting to challenge luck, not wanting to talk about it. We smoked. We got up and walked around. We sat down. We looked at our watches." Some men started a poker game, others went to watch the boxing matches at the gymnasium, most stayed in the barracks and chatted with GIs they had never met before, but who were now "brothers." Whatever they had done in the war, wherever they had been, they were in the same fix, hoping that the final steps to discharge would go smoothly, worried they would not.[10]

"Anything might happen," said a sergeant in the barracks with Merle Miller. "I had malaria once; they might keep me in for that." A corporal appeared, and the men asked him how long it would be until they were discharged. "'Forty-eight hours,' he answered, 'after you get on a roster. But it might be a week before you get on one. Might be longer.'"[11]

Three men in Louis Falstein's barracks had been waiting to get on a roster for four days. "One of the men, tall, flabby, with six overseas bars on his shirt-sleeve, talked with the bitterness and cynicism one finds so frequently in the Army among those who feel trapped. 'Four days I been here!' he said. 'I ain't no dischargee. If you ask me, I'm a retainee.'" The men who talked the most were those who worried the most. "Suppose we flunked the physical test and the Army refused to release us? Suppose Finance snafu-ed the works? We built a thousand pessimistic suppositions. A former paratrooper in dirty uniform and sparkling jump-boots summed up our feelings: 'You ain't out of the Army till you got that white piece of paper.'"[12]

At the mess halls, they were startled by the sound of German as they were served army chow, and large portions of it, by POWs who, after capture, had been transported to prison camps stateside. Outside meals, there was little to do but follow orders and sweep and mop under their beds, then lounge around, try to make phone calls, maybe play some poker or see what movie was at the camp theater. Twice a day, a disembodied voice called over the loudspeaker that rosters were being posted, and the GIs made a mad rush and pushed and shoved to get a look at the bulletin board near the mess hall. Each roster was numbered, and the men who were on it were marched to the theater where "the chaplain, a huge hearty man," greeted them with a joke and a lieutenant told them about their discharge pay and the GI Bill and explained that the next step in the process was a meeting with a counselor in another building. They were given cards to check off the questions they wanted to ask and directed to cubbyholes where the counselors answered their questions, asked their own, and filled out Form 100, listing the work and skills they had acquired in service that might be of use in civilian employment. "'It might come in handy sometime,'" Merle Miller's counselor told him. "'I doubt it, but it might.' Then, quite brusquely, he asked: 'You don't want to join the Enlisted Reserve, do you? . . . I once had a man who did. . . . But he was the only one, and I've talked to a lot of guys.'"[13]

One of the last steps—and it was the one the GIs feared most—was the physical examination. "We opened our mouths, had our lungs checked by the X-ray specialist, our blood drawn and examined by a corporal who had trouble finding the right vein. We were weighed, measured, prodded and ordered to jump up and down on one foot. 'This time,' said a gray-haired soldier with a slight paunch, 'you don't want to flunk. If there's anything wrong, they can hold you at the hospital. This time you want to be One-A.' 'Even if my leg was missing, I'd tell them everything was okay,' a rifleman remarked. 'I just want out of here.'"[14]

The doctors warned the GIs to report whatever ailed them, that telling the truth about wounds, illness, nightmares, insomnia wouldn't delay their discharge, but might come in handy later if they had to file for disability. Dentists offered to fill cavities for free. Some men asked if they could delay their discharge long enough "to complete treatments for venereal disease at Army rapid treatment centers, rather than risk the stigma which they felt would result from reporting to local health authorities."[15] GIs with health problems were advised "to file claims with the Veterans Administration for service-connected disabilities. One fellow with large, feverish eyes who suffered from recurrent malaria, asked: 'If I file a claim, will it hold up my discharge?' He was assured it would take only an additional ten minutes to file a claim. . . . There were many men who did not file claims because they feared it might create another obstacle in their path to liberation."[16]

Those who passed their physicals were marched haphazardly into the supply room, where they dumped the last of their army gear, except for the two uniforms they were allowed to take home with them, and then into a small room where they took off their shirts and handed them to one of the dozen soldiers who "sewed on discharge patches over our right pockets and handed the shirts back." They were then directed to sign three copies of their discharge papers, fingerprinted, and marched into the finance office, where they lined up at cashier's cages and were given "government checks for our back pay, plus $100 as the first installment of our mustering out pay, plus enough funds to buy our railroad tickets home. The cashier gave us each a small envelope containing the gold lapel button with the spread-eagle wings,* the honorable-discharge insigne from the Army of the United States. Then we stopped at a second window to buy our railroad tickets home."[17]

"It was all downhill now," Walter Bernstein wrote in *The New Yorker*. "We lined up outside and marched off to the chapel. . . . The chaplain waited for absolute quiet, then rose. We rose with him, and he said a prayer. . . . Then he nodded to the colonel, who stood up and began to talk. An organ started to play softly, making a bed for his words. The colonel told us what an honor it was to have served and how proud we should be. . . . After a while I couldn't listen to the colonel any longer. . . . The organ was playing 'Oh, What a Beautiful Morning.' . . . The colonel was still talking, but it didn't matter what he said." When the colonel finished, a private rose and began reading off names, one after another. As each name was spoken, the soldier saluted, was handed an envelope with his discharge papers, "shook hands with the colonel, saluted again, and walked out the door." Bernstein waited for the other men in his outfit, and together they walked "in silence," broken only when one of the men declared, "'You know, I feel just the same.' But he didn't. None of us felt the same. I knew that something very important had happened to me, but I didn't know exactly when or where it had happened."[18]

Most headed straight home after receiving their papers. But many, how many we will never know, hesitated, unwilling to return just yet. They stopped off for one last party, one last fling; they wandered the streets or camped out in train station lobbies, trying to keep busy, delaying their homecoming as long as they could. In Chicago, a major transportation hub for veterans, volunteers at the Travelers Aid

---

* The gold lapel button or pin would subsequently be known as the ruptured duck, the sign that the man wearing the pin was formally discharged, not AWOL.

Society were struck by the numbers loitering in the lobbies. Many appeared to be "emotionally disturbed," alone, unmoored, with no place to go.[19]

As demobilization accelerated through the summer and fall of 1945, the problems getting home intensified. There were simply not enough railroad cars to accommodate the returning servicemen and civilian traffic. Earlier in the year, the Office of Defense Transportation had ordered the railroads "to discontinue seasonal services to resort areas"; in July it directed them "to withdraw sleeping cars from regular services in order that they might be available for troops returning from overseas."[20]

Train problems were most acute on the West Coast. In Los Angeles, more than two thousand servicemen, mostly sailors, were stranded in Union Station for twenty-four hours on December 15. "During the long, weary wait, the servicemen sprawled on every available bench, piece of luggage, on the tiled floor, and even on top of lockers—everywhere but on the chandeliers." Eighty-two thousand GIs recently arrived from the Pacific would spend their first Christmas stateside in West Coast port cities, awaiting transportation home. In San Francisco, the "situation has become so serious that troops had to remain aboard troop ships . . . because there was no room for them in the staging areas." Unable to get train tickets, some took to the roads with their thumbs in the air. "Throughout the land nowadays," L. H. Robbins wrote in the April 7, 1946, *New York Times*, "hundreds of GI Joes are homing in that fashion when ticket offices turn them away. . . . The most familiar figure in the American scene this winter is probably the chap in olive drab thumbing a ride."[21]

They did not expect to be greeted as heroes when they returned. They had done the job they were asked to do, no more, no less. Sixty-one percent had been drafted; the remainder had enlisted, many because they knew they were about to be drafted into the army and preferred the navy or marines. Contrary to the patriotic homilies conceived and delivered by the OWI, the War Department, and the politicians, they had gone off to war because they had no choice in the matter and because, as they told army researchers, their country had been attacked at Pearl Harbor and "once in the war the United States had to win." Only a handful, when questioned by army researchers, replied that they had joined the war effort to protect the four freedoms* at home—or extend them abroad.[22]

There were ticker-tape parades for the generals and the admirals and war heroes like Audie Murphy, but not for the vast majority of veterans, and that was fine with them. "Every time I hear these Vietnam era veterans talk about 'we weren't welcomed back,' my god, I don't know," Calvin Hewitt, who had served in France and Germany, told an interviewer. "I suppose in World War II, the first ones in 1945 maybe after the war was over . . . may have had some bands or something, but I'll bet there were several million that had my experience of it. Just nothing. I mean, nobody was looking for that. Who needed it?"[23]

Clinton Riddle, a radioman in North Africa, Italy, and then, after D-Day, in France, Holland, Germany, and the Battle of the Bulge, was discharged in Boston in the fall of 1945. "Got on the Greyhound bus, traveled all night, and arrived in Sweetwater [Tennessee] in the afternoon. There wasn't any band there; there wasn't anybody greeting me except the girl that I had [written] to while I was overseas that worked in the office across from where I got off. She come out and greeted me. . . . That was my homecoming."[24]

Private Dennis Baca, who had served with the infantry in New Caledonia, the Solomon Islands, Guadalcanal, and the Philippines, was discharged on December 3, 1945, and returned to his home in

---

* The "four freedoms," as identified by President Roosevelt in his 1941 State of the Union address, were freedom of speech, freedom to worship, freedom from want, freedom from fear.

Albuquerque, New Mexico. "When he arrived, there were no ticker-tape parades, no grand celebrations planned. . . . 'My folks didn't recognize me because I was yellow from malaria. It took me years and years to get over it.'"[25]

The veterans knew that the world they were returning to was not going to be the one they had left. The news from the home front had warned them to expect shortages and rationing. Still, they could not help but be surprised, shocked might be the better term, to discover that the basic commodities they needed to reenter civilian life were not available at a price they could afford. And would not be for some time after their return.

In June 1946, a full year after V-E Day, "the country," according to *Fortune,* was still "short of meat, maple syrup, lemons, bread, butter, cheese, milk, barley, ice cream, candy, pie, cake, fruit syrups, onions, bacon, sugar, fats, doughnuts, molasses, coconut oil, olive oil, cottonseed oil, . . . lumber, coal, steel, tin, lead, antimony, textile piece goods, shellac, glass, lead pipe, paint, copper, . . . men's suits, children's clothing, film, cameras, lenses, towels, sheets, pillowcases, automobiles, trucks, tractors, tires, bourbon, Scotch, rye, beer, chewing gum, soft drinks, white shirts, pianos, radios, washing machines, refrigerators, work clothing, maple for high heels, shoe tacks, telephones. The list of shortages is endless, almost."[26]

Their introduction to this world of shortages came when they went shopping for clothes. "To be a civilian you first must look like one," the former army captain, now veteran Harold L. Elfenbein had warned them in *The American Legion Magazine.* The captain recommended that they take off and put away their uniforms as soon as they could. He was preaching to the choir. Only those unable to find or afford new clothes wore them after their discharge.[27]

William J. Heath's first stop on returning home to Jackson, Mississippi, was a "little men's store. . . . Bought me a suit. And when I got to my aunt's house I changed clothes. . . . My folks never saw me in uniform. . . . I just resented being in the Army that much." When asked by an interviewer about his priorities on returning home, the former infantryman Raymond Ray listed them in order: sleep, "getting out of the GI clothing . . . getting some new fancy clothes, seeing some of the girlfriends, going out dancing."[28]

On July 30, 1945, *Life* published a lighthearted pictorial on the veterans' plight. "Hunt for Clothes" followed the path of Sergeant Paul Steffens of East Orange, New Jersey, who, on his return home, "like most veterans . . . found that his old suits and shirts either did not fit or had been given away. What he wanted to buy was tropical-worsted suits, white broadcloth shirts, striped pajamas, lounging robe and underwear. What he found was practically bare racks and shelves."[29]

"What irks all the men, poor or not," Agnes Meyer reported for *The Washington Post* in the spring of 1946, a year after V-E Day, "is inability to buy clothes. Those who have a number of old suits, usually have grown too thin or too stout to wear them. The average lad has none to fall back on."[30]

Next to the suit shortage—and even more serious—was the lack of dress shirts for special occasions and job interviews. "Demand . . . during the first year after the war . . . was estimated at about 26,000,000 dozen," but only 5.4 million were manufactured. By November, production had increased to 770,000 dozen, but that accounted for only one-third of the total demand.[31]

"One of the things a returning veteran wants most is a white shirt," *Newsweek* reported in January 1946, "but the white shirt is the shortest item in all the men's wear shortage." In Beloit, Wisconsin, Sam Meister, who couldn't find a white shirt in the stores, "advertised that he would swap a pint of whiskey" for one.[32]

The vets found ways around the shortages. They had their prewar clothes refitted until they looked almost presentable. Betty Baker, who had served with the WACs in Karachi, India (now Pakistan), was discharged in January 1946 and "dyed my uniform kind of a brownish because I was going to have to wear it for a long time."[33]

The shortage that caused the most trouble was of the automobiles they were going to need to get to work or school. The manufacture of motor vehicles for civilian use had been halted on February 22, 1942, when Detroit factories were refitted for the production of tanks, planes, guns, ammunition, heavy-duty trucks, and other military hardware. "Factory sales of passenger cars dropped to a mere 139 units in 1943 and 610 units in 1944."[34]

The new-car shortage forced the veterans to look for used ones they could afford. One young soldier who had sold his 1941 model for $750 to a defense worker when he went off to war found, to his disgust, that "on my return, this same fellow asks me $1,500 for the same car, which he had used these three years and some odd months."[35]

The cartoonist and veteran Bill Mauldin devoted an entire chapter of his memoir *Back Home* to his and his fellow veterans' difficulties buying used cars, then getting them repaired when they broke down. "The term 'highway robber' was never used in a more literal sense than when applied to America's present-day used-car shysters, and within a few hours after I started shopping I became painfully aware of it.... I saw 1937 Pontiacs—cars that had cost around a thousand dollars when new and were now eight-year-old jalopies—priced at $1500.... The prize package in the first establishment I visited was a 1942 Cadillac convertible that had cost about $2000 when new, and had nearly fifty thousand miles registered on the speedometer.... The salesman said the car was available for $5000."[36]

REPATRIATED AND DISCHARGED

For the 70 percent of veterans who were unmarried, the first stop after discharge was their parents' house. There was joy at the veteran's return and more still if he had survived without illness, injury, or visible wound. But that joy was accompanied by uneasiness, uncertainty as to whether or how long it would take before the veteran would truly feel at home again.

Homecoming GI, the iconic Norman Rockwell painting published on the cover of *The Saturday Evening Post* on May 26, 1945, has been hailed as a celebratory portrait of this joyous moment. On closer examination, however, art historian Alexander Nemerov notes, the "sadness" and "awkwardness of coming home" becomes all too evident. "The veteran has returned, glum and changed, to the place where he grew up." We do not see his face or his expression, only the smiles of those greeting him, energy surging through them, while the soldier is motionless. "His heavy bag and large army boots emphasize his downward, burdened posture." He is suspended in limbo, separated from his mother, his siblings, his girlfriend, his neighbors, unable to breach the distance in space and time, "different, changed, not himself," not the boy who left, but a man weighed down by the recent past, unable as yet to cross the threshold into the present.[37]

"I knew that at twenty six I was a different person from the naïve boy who had gone straight from his cocoon into a world war," Edward Brooke, the future senator from Massachusetts, recalled in his memoirs. "My parents were alarmed by this son they did not entirely know. Sometimes, I would catch them observing me, and I would wonder if I really was acting strangely. In truth, my thoughts were often on the uncertainties of the future . . . and dark memories from my past in Italy."[38]

The future poet Frank O'Hara, who had enlisted in the navy at age eighteen, gently but firmly warned his parents via letters that he was a different man now, "on the whole, more independent, freer, more confident, happier, and more at ease . . . because I've found I can rely on myself. . . . The trouble is that I may have trouble readjusting myself when I do get home . . . but I imagine our mutual affection will take care of most of the obstacles." It didn't. At home on leave for Christmas 1945, he and his father fought as they had never fought before the war. In a 1950 letter to a friend, O'Hara "described the disorienting experience of returning home. . . . 'It upset me terribly because I first in the Navy managed to establish my identity with real people and situations . . . and upon discharge I had to return home like a prodigal who has done many evil things only to find that his parents didn't even hear about them!'"[39]

The actor Ossie Davis, who had spent thirty-two months in Africa in charge of a medical ward in a Liberian hospital, returned to his parents' home in Valdosta, Georgia. Homecoming "provided me with no sense of joy at all.... I was sullen, moody, hostile, filled to the brim with self-pity and despair, and wanted only to be left severely alone. The family obliged.... I was often drunk and smoked a lot.... I remember that Mama was very concerned about me, but said nothing. I remember Daddy, sensing my need for silence and for privacy, also said nothing. I don't remember the rest of the family at all."[40]

Women veterans experienced similar tensions on returning from war. They were no longer the same "girls" they had been. An ex-WAC told Nancy McInerny, a *New York Times* reporter, that "Mamma loved me best the way I was before I went into the Army." When she returned after three years away, "Mamma" found it difficult to get along with her because she now refused "to admit that Mamma knows best."[41]

Some veterans stayed where they were, in their parents' home for a while, then elsewhere in the communities they had grown up in. Many left forever.

The largest exodus was of Black veterans from the southern states. The mass departure of African Americans had begun during the war as they moved north and west to work in the war industries. It continued in force as hundreds of thousands of returning veterans made the decision to leave the Jim Crow South. When, in August 1944, the army's research department conducted a survey, "Post-war Plans of Negro Soldiers," it found that only 33 percent of the 72 percent who had been born in a southern state planned to return there after the war. By 1950, according to John Modell and his associates, in their study "World War II in the Lives of Black Americans," more than half of the Black veterans who had been in their twenties when they served had left the South, compared with one-third of Black nonveterans and less than a quarter of White veterans.[42]

Henry Kirksey of Tupelo, Mississippi, left home soon after his discharge in August 1946 and did not return until 1961. "Many veterans in the South came back determined that they were going to use whatever they achieved in terms of resources out of World War II to—not so much change things, but to get the hell out of here. And that was one of the most often expressed intents for those veterans that I talked to. 'I've got to get out of the South because I can't stand it anymore,' and 'I'm going to wind up in prison if I don't get out.' ... So it was ... a commitment, in effect, to the belief that changing things was just a hopeless thought, that you just get the heck on out and do the best you can in some other place, where you didn't run into all the discrimination that you ran into, and you had always run into, in your life in the South."[43]

Douglas Conner returned to Mississippi in May 1946 with no intention of remaining there. The local Whites were "much touchier than usual. In fact, there seemed to have been just a fear that blacks coming back from the service were going to take over Mississippi, especially since, at that time, I guess the population was 50-50—maybe a few more blacks than whites at that. There seemed to have a real fear that, 'We've got to find ways to keep the black in their places even more so than we did before the war.'" Conner spent the first summer after his discharge working in a Chicago steel mill and then, in the fall, entered medical school at Howard University, in D.C.[44]

Edward Brooke's parents hoped he would stay in D.C. and attend law school at Howard, but Brooke felt he had to get away to a northern city, perhaps Boston, where he had been told "life was better for Negroes."[45]

Many gay and lesbian veterans left their hometowns to return to one of the cities, San Francisco, New York, San Diego, Chicago, Seattle, Boston, Los Angeles, where they had found a more welcoming and open gay community than they had encountered anywhere else. In interviews with the historian Allan Bérubé, the veteran Maxwell Gordon (a pseudonym) spoke about his experiences in New York City after being discharged. "'When I got there ... I found out that literally there were hundreds and thousands of people just like me, who'd been in either Europe or the Pacific,' veterans who had gone home but discovered they just didn't fit in. 'So they all ended up in New York City for one more party.'" Gordon's friends were honorably discharged veterans, as he was, "trying to come to terms with their homosexuality. They ate meals together, went out to the gay bars together, and slept on each other's sofas when it was too late or too expensive to take the subway home." Some tried to return home, "get married, have kids, start a home. . . . Then they'd come back to New York. We would say, 'Well, you can go back all you want, but it won't work. Because you're gay.'"[46]

The former WAC Pat Bond, who had served in occupied Japan, remained in San Francisco after being discharged in 1947 rather than return to Iowa. She moved into a house with other lesbians, got a job, and joined the extended lesbian and gay family that gathered in the gay bars. "We certainly knew everyone. If you went to the gay bars in San Francisco, you knew everybody who was gay in San Francisco. . . . The bars were really family. There was no community at all outside the bars."[47]

Every returning veteran had problems of one sort or another navigating the transition from war to peace. For most, these problems would be sorted out and solved in time, with the help of their GI benefits. This was not the case for the veterans who returned home with blue discharges, which barred them from receiving GI Bill benefits.

Black servicemen were disproportionately issued blue discharges and barred from receiving the benefits due them under the GI Bill. It was easier for commanding officers to get rid of troublemakers by giving them blue discharges than bringing them up for court-martials, which required more time and effort and afforded the accused the chance to defend themselves. By June 1, 1945, Black GIs had received almost eleven thousand, or 22 percent, of blue discharges, though they comprised less than 10 percent of military personnel. *The Pittsburgh Courier*, an African American weekly, charged that the army had been "handing out the blue ticket with reckless abandon [and] allowing prejudiced white officers to use it as a means of punishing Negro soldiers who do not like specifically unbearable conditions growing out of the Army's doctrine of white supremacy." In a follow-up editorial, the paper decried what it referred to as "a widespread conspiracy to give blue discharges to as many colored soldiers and sailors as possible. Eager to get out of the services, many colored boys are gladly accepting these blue discharges. They do not realize what such a discharge means to their future, and their commanding officers know it. . . . Soldiers and sailors presented with blue discharges should refuse to accept them."[48]

Gladys Pace, a Black schoolteacher who had enlisted in the WACs, complained to her superior officer at Fort Des Moines that a White officer had "used the word 'nigger.'" The officer to whom she complained "stated that where she came from, namely Texas, that was the accepted term as far as Negroes were concerned." As a result of her complaint, Pace received "an unsatisfactory efficiency report," was "coerced" into resigning "for the good of the service," and given a blue discharge, which she accepted. Other Black GIs accepted blue discharges to avoid court-martials or because they were told, misleadingly, that they were equivalent to medical discharges. Only later would they learn that blue discharges might render them ineligible for GI readjustment benefits on their return to civilian life.[49]

Like Black service men and women, suspected and self-identified homosexuals—some nine thousand of them—were disproportionately charged with misconduct and "undesirable traits and character," hauled before boards of officers, given blue discharges, and sent home. During the first year of the war, "sodomists," as they were referred to, had been court-martialed and, if found guilty, imprisoned. Army and navy psychiatrists objected to the policy, arguing that homosexuality was a mental disease, not a crime. By late 1943, as it became apparent that the army and navy could ill afford to lose trained and effective personnel whose sexual preferences posed no danger to themselves or others, the War Department acceded to the psychiatrists' recommendations to hospitalize accused "sodomists" rather than bring them up on formal charges. Commanding officers were directed to remove suspected homosexuals from duty, place them on sick call, and admit them to hospitals for observation and diagnosis. Those who were considered reclaimable would receive medical treatment and, when possible, be returned to active duty. Those "who [were] not deemed reclaimable" were separated from the armed forces with blue discharges.[50]

The GI Bill, as drafted and passed, had not barred all veterans with blue or bad conduct* discharges from receiving benefits. As Bennett Champ Clark, who had sponsored the bill, explained on the floor of the Senate, men who had been given blue discharges because they had "not shown sufficient aptitude towards military service" or "lied a little about [their] age, in order to get into the service" or committed some minor offense should not be denied "the benefits which soldiers generally are entitled to." Only those who had received blue discharges under "dishonorable conditions," those who were "goldbrickers" or "habitual dead beats" or guilty of crimes, should be refused their benefits. The decision on whether a soldier with a blue

---

* "Bad conduct" discharges were the navy equivalent of the army "blue" discharge.

discharge should be barred from receiving benefits because his "service has been dishonorable" was delegated to the VA.[51]

The VA did not put into writing the criteria to be used in determining whether a blue discharge had been issued under honorable or dishonorable conditions. These decisions were left to local officials, which, as *The Pittsburgh Courier* observed, meant that "many holders of the blue discharge will be subject to the whims and prejudices of local officers of VA. To the Negro in the South holding a blue discharge, this constitutes a menace of serious proportions." On April 21, 1945, ten months after the GI Bill had become law, Frank Hines, VA administrator, responded to the confusion about honorable versus dishonorable conditions by declaring that a "blue discharge issued because of homosexual acts or tendencies generally will be considered as under dishonorable conditions and a bar to entitlement" of benefits authorized by the GI Bill. As historian Margot Canaday has written, while blue discharges were given "for a variety of traits or behaviors, only the discharge for homosexuality led to a separate policy statement from the central office."[52]

The economic effects of receiving a blue discharge as a homosexual were immediate and long-lasting. To apply for a GI mortgage or business loan, education benefits, or unemployment compensation, the veteran had to produce his discharge papers. The same was true when seeking employment. "The ex-soldier, looking for a job and seeking to rehabilitate himself in some civilian sphere of life," the House Committee on Military Affairs observed in January 1946, "must approach a prospective employer with a large sheet of striking color in his hand instead of the customary white one. He meets with instantaneous suspicion. It is a vague suspicion of something mysteriously but dreadfully wrong."[53]

Marty Klausner had received a blue discharge after admitting he was a homosexual. He returned to Pittsburgh in June 1945, Allan Bérubé tells us in *Coming Out Under Fire*, "to live with his parents and find work. He reported to the local VA office with his blue discharge, where he was 'more or less interviewed and made out an application for schooling. I then casually asked whether I would have any trouble getting it and they said I would.' . . . He called his friend Tony who had also received a blue discharge" and found that he too had been denied his education benefits. When Klausner "applied for 'a terrific job at the largest hotel in P[ittsburgh]' . . . the personnel officer 'asked to see my discharge—she studied it for a while . . . and sent me to see another man who after about two words sent me back to the woman who said she was terribly [sorry] but I simply wouldn't do because she had called the Vets Ad and had of course found out that I was an undesirable.'" Klausner subsequently got a job at a department store. When he was laid off, he applied for his unemployment allowance checks, but was told that because he had a blue discharge, he was not eligible to receive them.[54]

"Legally, I'm only partially a veteran," John McPherson, who had received a blue discharge after admitting to being a homosexual, recalled in his oral history. "The first time I went into a Veterans' Reemployment Office, I practically got thrown out and was told I had no right to set foot inside the door. . . . For civil service, I had no five-points credit, was ineligible for any federal job until a year from my discharge date. . . . My three and a half years of wearing a uniform was just a simple tailor's error. I was entitled neither to muster-out pay nor to a discharge pin."[55]

A WAC who had served more than three years as an officer with "excellent" efficiency before being sent home with a blue discharge wrote to *Yank* on November 16, 1946, that when she looked for work, she was asked to "show my discharge. . . . The result is—I am still hunting for a job."[56]

Blue-discharged veterans could appeal to the War or Navy Department for a review of their status, but the review process was cumbersome and required an appearance in person in D.C. "Many gay veterans made their discharge appeals on their own, afraid to reveal their homosexuality to anyone, including veterans' groups or their families." Large numbers "traveled from all over the country. . . . They 'accumulated in little groups' in Washington, explained Navy psychiatric consultant Dr. Francis Braceland, 'attempting to get their discharges changed because they were afraid to return to their homes'" with pieces of paper that indicated that they had been discharged because they were homosexuals.[57]

Jesse Dedmon Jr., NAACP secretary of veterans' affairs, encouraged Black holders of blue discharges to appeal and offered assistance and legal representation in Washington. Most of those who responded to his request had been given blue discharges not because they were identified as homosexuals, but because they were Black and had protested discriminatory treatment. Samuel R. Cassius, who was represented by an NAACP attorney, had while he was still in the navy publicly denounced "naval policy which confined Negroes to menial assignments." His commander requested that he be given a blue discharge because he had "openly expressed dissatisfaction with the Naval services and policies . . . fomented unrest, discontent and malcontent among the mess attendants." Upon appeal, he was granted "a certificate of discharge Under Honorable Conditions [making] the ex-sailor eligible for educational, job and other G.I. benefits."[58]

By mid-June 1946, twelve of the fourteen African American servicemen the NAACP represented before the Army Board of Review and all ten of the sailors who appealed to the Naval Discharge Review Board had their blue discharges changed to honorable ones. Several more would be granted honorable discharges on review in the years to come. Unfortunately, they represented only a small minority of blue-discharged veterans. The majority, lacking the will or the wherewithal to appeal, had to make do in civilian life without the benefits promised to other veterans.[59]

No two homecomings were the same. The veterans returned with different expectations under strikingly different conditions. Those with blue discharges would have the most difficulty reentering civilian life without the benefits the GI Bill had authorized. But they were not the only ones who had trouble readjusting.

The veterans brought the war home with them. The physically wounded or afflicted by disease carried it on their bodies. Millions more returned encumbered by invisible, undiagnosed, and untreated psychic wounds that would haunt them on their homecoming and for years to come.

Part 2

Home at Last

"There's Jack O'Malley on his way home from the Pacific."

Chapter 11.

WOUNDED MINDS

By the end of the war, more than 312,000 servicemen had been discharged for "neuropsychiatric disorders."[1] Many more should have been but had disguised their symptoms or stayed clear of military doctors.

A "psych" discharge was a liability, and the servicemen knew it all too well. After V-E Day, J. D. Salinger committed himself to a civilian hospital, instead of a military one, because he did not want to be sent home on a psych discharge. He confessed as much in a letter to Ernest Hemingway, whom he had met in Paris. "I'd give my right arm to get out of the Army, but not on a psychiatric, this-man-is-not-fit-for-the-Army-life ticket. I have a very sensitive novel in mind, and I won't have the author called a jerk in 1950. I am a jerk, but the wrong people mustn't know it."[2]

The number of GIs who had been treated for psychoneurosis during the war and would need further treatment on their return was so great that the War Department brought out a special pamphlet, *What's the Score . . . in a Case Like Mine?*, to reassure them that they were going to get better. Psychoneurosis was not a permanent condition. "What happens to you in the future will depend, to a large extent, on your own efforts and your attitude."[3]

In large part to "convince business owners . . . that they had nothing to fear in hiring war veterans," the army commissioned the film director and now major John Huston to make a documentary about the rehabilitation of GIs who had been psychologically damaged by the war. In preparation for the film, Huston visited several military hospitals before deciding to shoot at Mason General Hospital in Brentwood, Long Island. He and his crew spent ten weeks on location, filming a group of soldiers from the moment they arrived until they were ready to leave the facility. While none of the scenes was staged, the film was edited to create the impression that no matter how disturbed, how nonfunctional, how seemingly "crazy" the GIs might have been on entering the hospital, they would exit it cured and prepared to return to civilian life as fit as, probably more fit than, they had been on entering the service.[4]

The voice-over narration, by the director's father, Walter Huston, sets the scene, as a group of injured soldiers struggle and stumble down a gangplank, accompanied by nurses and orderlies. "Here is human salvage, the final result of all that metal and fire could do to violate mortal flesh. . . . These are the casualties of the spirit, the troubled mind, men who are damaged emotionally. . . . Here are men who tremble; men who cannot sleep; men with pains that are nonetheless real because they are of a mental origin. Men who cannot remember; paralyzed men, whose paralysis is dictated by the mind. However different the symptoms, these things they have in common: unceasing fear and apprehension, a sense of impending disaster, a feeling of hopelessness and utter isolation."[5]

The military psychiatrists in Huston's film, like those who treated veterans elsewhere, operated under the Freudian presumption that the underlying causes of the soldiers' ailments were childhood traumas that had been triggered by wartime events. "They asked me," Salinger had written to Hemingway from the army hospital in Nuremberg, "about my sex life (which couldn't be normaler—gracious!) and about my childhood (Normal. My Mother took me to school till I was twenty-four—but you know New York streets)."[6]

In a scene from *Let There Be Light*, the final title Huston gave his film, a psychiatrist stands at the front of a classroom, lecturing twenty or so veterans sitting at desks. He gently but firmly suggests that their distress is due to the "lack of safety" they live with and that their feelings of not being "safe" stem from childhood. The veterans, on the psychiatrist's prompt, recall stories that validate his supposition.[7]

In the course of the film, we watch grown men unable to walk or talk, staring blankly into space, sobbing, stuttering, shaking uncontrollably. The camera is unflinching; the scenes of distraught, agitated GIs difficult to watch. And then, miraculously, they are cured. The speechless speak, the stuttering and shaking cease, the paralyzed walk, sobbing is replaced by smiles. The final scenes are of patients, now healed, enjoying a friendly game of baseball and waving to the nurses as the bus that will take them back to civilian life leaves the hospital. The psychiatrists had worked miracles—or so it appears. We do not know what happened when the men returned home, but the evidence we do have on soldiers hospitalized for psychiatric disorders suggests that most would require further treatment.[8]

Huston's artfully contrived propaganda piece exaggerated not only the effectiveness of the army psychiatrists' treatment but the extent of the damage to the veterans' psyches on entering Mason General. "Huston slobbered over the patients," Dr. Herbert Spiegel, who worked at the hospital, told Ben Shephard, who reviewed the film after a 1998 screening at the London Film Festival. "He encouraged them to act like cry-babies. He wanted to sentimentalize how the poor boys suffered."[9]

Let There Be Light was scheduled for debut in April 1946 at the

Museum of Modern Art as one of the "spotlight attractions" in an upcoming documentary film series. Afterward, it was to be released for public viewing. The army had already given permission for stills to be inserted in *Harper's Bazaar* and a *Life* magazine story by John Hersey. All was proceeding according to schedule when, with no advance warning, the army informed Huston in March that it was not going to release his film to the public or screen it for new recruits. The army's embargo would remain in place until December 1980.[10]

In his autobiography, Huston argued that the army blocked distribution of the film it had commissioned and funded because it violated "the 'warrior' myth, which said that our American soldiers went to war and came back all the stronger for the experience, standing tall and proud for having served their country well. Only a few weaklings fell by the wayside. Everyone was a hero, and had medals and ribbons to prove it. They might die, or they might be wounded, but their spirit remained unbroken." The images of broken GIs were, the army had concluded, too disturbing for the public to see. The war was over now; it was time to celebrate victory, not mourn the damage it had inflicted.[11]

The men Huston filmed were but a small minority of those who returned with psychological problems. "Virtually all the men who come back from the war have trigger tempers that are set off at the slightest provocation," observed Herbert I. Kupper, a psychiatrist at the marine hospital on Ellis Island. They were angry at their wives and girlfriends whom they suspected of cheating on them, at their children for growing up without them, at the 4-Fs who had stayed home and made piles of money, at the officers who had sneered, insulted, and humiliated them for months on end, and at the government and the military that had robbed them of years.[12]

"I felt kind of cheated—two years out of my life—I had education, things to do," recalled Jack Dunn, who had served as a medic with the 82nd Airborne Division in Europe. "I think I might have been a quite difficult person to get along with at that particular time."[13]

Psychiatrists advised the veterans to exercise patience and counseled their wives, girlfriends, and parents to refrain from admonishing them for their drinking, violent outbursts, and alternating bouts of inertia and near-hyperactive restlessness. "They may be nervous, explosive and impatient, chain-smokers, seekers after stimulants and diversions," the VA psychiatrist Alexander G. Dumas and his coauthor, Grace Keen, warned in *A Psychiatric Primer for the Veteran's Family and Friends*, published in August 1945. "None of this means that they have become misfits. It simply means that they need time to get back into the swing of things." The memories of war would fade, their "restlessness gradually subside."[14]

They suffered in silence. Talking about the war only brought to the surface memories they wanted to bury. And what would be gained by burdening those who hadn't been to war with the images they needed to erase? They did not want to be pitied.

They did not speak of the deaths that haunted them. "When we got out, you couldn't talk about things like that," the veteran Otis Mackey recalled. "You held it all in. I didn't want to take it to my family. If you'd say anything, people wouldn't believe half of what you say, anyway."[15]

The death toll was more than 400,000, far fewer than the Soviets or the Germans, but enough that most surviving servicemen carried with them, as baggage never to be unloaded, names, images, remembrances of those who would not return. In combat or in the rear, at Anzio or the Hürtgen Forest, at Tarawa or Iwo, at sea, in the air, on the ground; driving tanks or trucks or building barracks or repairing roads or unloading cargo or dishing out grub or lifting the wounded onto stretchers, they had passed by, stepped over, detoured around dead putrefying bodies; they had smelled the stink, borne witness to the decomposition of the flesh. Memories of the dead generated guilt and shame and puzzlement. Why had they returned and not their comrades, their buddies, the men they had encountered at the depots, onboard the ships, in the airplanes, on the ground, in the foxholes, at the first-aid stations and evacuation hospitals and hospital ships? These were unanswerable questions and, because unanswerable, they could not be dismissed or laid to rest.

"Before we'd finished in Europe," wrote Paul Fussell in *Doing Battle: The Making of a Skeptic*, "we'd seen hundreds of dead bodies, GIs as well as Germans, civilians as well as soldiers, officers as well as enlisted men, together with ample children. We learned that no infantryman can survive psychologically very long unless he's mastered the principle that the dead don't *know* what they look like. The soldier smiling is *not* smiling, the man whose mouth drips blood doesn't know what he's doing, the man with half his skull blown away and his brain oozing into the ground thinks he still looks OK. And the man whose cold eyes stare at you as if expressing a grievance is not doing that. He is elsewhere."[16]

The returning veterans had accepted the possibility of death as a commonplace of war. "All over the ship, all through the convoy, there was a knowledge that in a few hours some of them were going to be dead," Norman Mailer, who had seen combat in the battle for Luzon, in the Philippines, wrote in the first paragraph of *The Naked and the Dead*.[17]

In J. D. Salinger's short story "The Stranger," Babe Gladwaller, the author's fictional stand-in, is haunted by the memory of his dead buddy Vincent Caulfield. The week after his return home, Babe decides to take his young sister out for lunch at a chop suey joint and then to a matinee. He finds himself instead in Vincent's girlfriend's apartment. "I thought you might want to know a little about it all. . . . I can't tell you he was happy or anything when he died. I'm sorry—I can't think of anything good—Yet I want to tell you the whole business.... I didn't come here to torture you. I just thought... that you'd want to hear this stuff. I'm sorry I have to be a stranger.... It seems lousy. Everything seems lousy. I didn't think it would be any good, but I came anyway. I don't know what's wrong with me since I'm back."[18]

John Ciardi had enlisted in the army air force and become a gunner on B-29s, flying some twenty missions over Japan before he was transferred to desk duty in early 1945. "I found myself writing a lot of elegies for friends of mine who did not make it. Then it occurred to me that the way things were going, I might not make it. So I decided to write my own: 'Elegy Just in Case.'"[19]

> Here lie Ciardi's pearly bones
> In their ripe organic mess.
> Jungle blown, his chromosomes
> Breed to a new address.

Ciardi's war poems, published after his return to the United States in October 1945, were packed with images of the dead left behind. In "First Summer After a War," he writes "of dead men closed / Under the softening linen of the grass"; in "I Meet the Motion of Summer Thinking Guns," of "the flowerless dead"; in "Poem for My Thirtieth Birthday," of the "boys that went / Like tinsel into wind and blew like flame."[20]

Jack Brukman, who served with a B-29 ground crew in the Pacific, brought home with him the memory of the nineteen-year-old who took a direct hit that "blew his arm off... and he was bleeding out.... I said, 'Mike,' [and all Mike said in return was] 'I want my mama, I want my mama.' And his eyes rolled over and he was gone." The dying soldier's voice haunted Brukman for the rest of his life. "But you learn to handle these things. You have to live with it."[21]

Norman Gordon, a medic in Italy, never talked about the wounded and dead. But his stepdaughter was struck by "his stoicism in facing his own death. He truly was not afraid; he had seen it over and over and he had more time he knew than so many of his friends and fellow soldiers. I've seen people die before and after Norman but no one whose passing, in my experience, could be considered graceful. His was."[22]

The GIs who had liberated the concentration and death camps or come into contact with the survivors returned burdened by images of the horrors they had witnessed and could not forget. J. D. Salinger visited a slave labor camp that was a satellite of Dachau on April 27, 1945, within days of the German surrender. According to Stephen B. Shepard, author of *Salinger's Soul*, it was a "traumatic experience" for Salinger and the other GIs. His daughter recalled her father telling her that "you never really get the smell of burning flesh out of your nose entirely, no matter how long you live."[23]

"It's a hell of a load for a young fellow to bear," Herman Josephs, a Jewish GI from San Antonio, recalled of his visit to Dachau. "We had been through four battles already, and we thought we were immune from being shocked. . . . There were dead people lying in the gas chambers. They had a ravine there, and they had piled the bodies in the ravine and put lye on them." Josephs kept silent about his experiences in war—and his visit to Dachau—for forty years. "I just didn't mention it. It was too horrible to dredge up my memory."[24]

Wilson Canafax of Dallas, a chaplain with the 110th Engineer Combat Group in Germany, visited Buchenwald soon after D-Day. Afterward, he prepared sermons, organized a worship service for the Jewish survivors, performed his duties as an army chaplain. "For a long time, you wouldn't let it affect you. You almost wanted to eliminate that period of time in your life that was there, and just get back in to where you had been and what you were doing. . . . Eventually I came to terms with it. . . . And I accepted the fact that it happened. That was the only way I could do it. I couldn't deny the fact."[25]

William Dippo was one of the GIs who liberated Mauthausen. Six and a half decades later, he still gets "emotional" when he recalls his visit to the camp or "even think[s] about it. . . . I can't help it. Because it's there, it'll never go away."[26]

It was easier during the daylight hours to banish the memories, to stop time traveling back to the war, to forget the dead and the wounded left behind. After dark, the nightmares arrived. Some of the veterans suffered only sporadically or for the first few years. Others would never again have a sound night's sleep. Eugene Sledge, a marine veteran who had served in the Pacific, awakened for years after his return "either crying or yelling, always sweating, and with a pounding heart. Some nights I delayed going to bed, dreading the inevitable nightmares. Old comrades wrote me that similar troubles drove many of them to drink and to the ensuing misery of alcoholism."[27]

Nightmares shook the bed and the house. The content was private; the disruption, public. Family members tried but failed to screen out the sounds, the screams, the cries. "He'd be sleeping, his eyes closed," Betty Bradley recalled of her husband, John, who had served on Iwo Jima.* "But he'd be whimpering. His body would shake, and tears would stream out of his eyes, down his face."[28]

Clayton Chipman, a marine wounded on Iwo Jima, had trouble sleeping for the six years he lived at home after his discharge. "Whatever took

---

* Bradley was initially thought to have been one of the marines in the iconic photo of the flag raising, but the Marine Corps, after a 2016 investigation, found that he was not.

place psychologically or maybe even physically in your body just didn't go away. We didn't say anything. We thought it was normal."[29]

The poet Louis Simpson saw combat from D-Day through the end of the war. He returned stateside, he told the author Tom Mathews, "with what the medics were beginning to call combat fatigue.... He heard voices. He was hallucinating." His relatives committed him to Kings Park State Hospital on Long Island, where he was given shock therapy, which, he later wrote, "brought me out of the fog in which I had been walking." But he was not cured. "I relived the war almost every night in my dreams. This continued for years.... I dreamed of encounters with the Germans that I never had.... Or I dreamed about horrors.... I used to think that having such dreams was a thing to be ashamed of. For what had I suffered in comparison with others? When I thought of them, the dead, and those who were in wheelchairs, or blinded, or insane, had I really known war at all?"[30]

The veterans who were most likely afflicted by what would later be diagnosed as PTSD symptoms were those who had been in combat, like Simpson. But soldiers, sailors, airmen, WACs, WAVEs, and Red Cross volunteers who had cared for the wounded or spent time within earshot of the front lines were also beset by traumatic memories on their return from war. Phyllis McLaughlin, one of the thousands of Red Cross volunteers who as a "Donut Dolly" served GIs coffee and doughnuts on their way to or from the front lines, was injured in a jeep accident in Germany. Her son, who was born ten years after his mother's return, recalled how "her nightmares woke us nearly every night, leaving her hoarse. She had inexplicable outbursts of anger during the day.... I now recognize my mother was tortured by PTSD, her nightmares and outbursts classic symptoms of something she would never understand: After all, 'battle fatigue' was for the boys."[31]

Alcohol offered the most effective palliative, or so the veterans believed, for the restlessness, the sleeplessness, the recurrent flashbacks, the anger they lived with on their return home. Many had begun drinking or drinking to excess while in the service. They found it difficult, if not impossible, to quit on their return. "The veterans all want to drink," one young woman told researchers from the University of Chicago. "My husband, he wouldn't sit at a table—he'd sit at a bar, because he hadn't got over his war-jitters or whatever you call it, and at a table the drinks didn't come fast enough."[32]

"There is all too much truth," the psychiatrist Herbert I. Kupper observed, "in the familiar story-book and Hollywood tale of the homecoming service man who joins 'the boys' at night, instead of remaining with his faithful spouse."[33]

In the dry states and cities, veterans paid dues to veterans' associations because, as private clubs, they were exempt from blue laws. John Bidwell returned from war an alcoholic and "joined the VFW so I could drink on Sunday."[34]

Ossie Davis started drinking heavily—a fifth of whiskey a day—in Liberia, where he served in the surgical ward of a military hospital, and kept drinking after his return home. By late 1946, early 1947, in Los Angeles starring in *Anna Lucasta* with his soon-to-be-wife Ruby Dee, Davis got drunk after every performance. "Slowly, behind a smoke screen of laughing, singing calypso, and spouting everything from dirty jokes to high iambic pentameter, I was becoming a drunk," he wrote in his joint autobiography with Ruby Dee. "It wasn't so much a love of whiskey to which I was responding; it was rather my way of finding a deeper place within myself to hide." Davis was rescued, he claimed, by Dee, who refused to let him wallow in self-pity and alcohol or to think that such was his inevitable future. "The fact is," she told him, "one day, you're going to get as sick of all this puking and

"Bottle fatigue."

whining, this po'-colored-soldier-begging-for-pity shit as I am. And that will be the end of that."[35]

In 2010, Marcus Brotherton interviewed the children of twenty-six members of Easy Company, the subject of the historian Stephen Ambrose's 1992 book, *Band of Brothers*, and the ten-part 2001 HBO series created by Tom Hanks and Steven Spielberg. Albert Blithe, an Easy Company veteran, was, according to his son, "a chronic alcoholic, probably due to the war." George Potter Jr.'s son recalled that his father, "like many of his generation, chose to self-medicate with alcohol. . . . I don't ever remember a time when alcohol wasn't an issue with him"; Gordon Carson's son remembered that his father "drank a lot. . . . That was that generation's drug of choice"; Robert Marsh's daughter told Brotherton that her father "drank from the time he returned from the war until the day he died"; Lavon Reese, according to his daughter, was always drinking; Joe Toye, his son remembered, "when he wasn't drinking . . . was really a great guy, but, yes, the drinking was always there."[36]

Joshua J. Nasaw,[*] who returned from Eritrea with a medical discharge, later told his younger son, Jonathan, that he began drinking when he woke up and continued through the day, consuming a fifth of J&B scotch daily. He stopped only when his wife bundled up his two children to take them to her parents' home. To stop her leaving, he swore that he would never drink again—and miraculously, kept his word. He was unusual in this regard.[37]

Alcohol abuse fueled near-violent bouts of rage among veterans who were already having difficulty adjusting to family and civilian life. "Until the war he never drank," one war wife told Studs Terkel. "When he came back he was an absolute drunkard. . . . He started slapping me around and slapped the kids around. He became a brute."[38]

The veterans drank to wash away their anger, nervousness, restlessness, loss of purpose, inertia, nightmares, flashbacks: all symptoms of what would later be diagnosed as post-traumatic stress disorder. Their wives drank to keep up with them and keep them at home. The children cowered in their bedrooms trying to hide from the verbal abuse and physical violence that too often followed a night of drinking.

Marilyn Tittle was three years old when her father returned from war, an alcoholic, at times a violent one. "One time he was drunk and tore up our house badly." Marilyn begged her mother "to leave Dad and get us [she had two younger siblings] out of there, but she kept saying that she wanted us kids to grow up first."[39]

"There were about fifteen really rough years when the drinking took hold of him completely," Marcia Reese Rood, the daughter of

---

[*] The author's father.

Lavon Reese, remembered. "Daddy could get so mad, so mean, when he was drinking.... He went and sat on the back porch with his rifle, mumbling and yelling and shooting into the woods behind our house.... Daddy never threatened us with his gun.... But when somebody's drinking and holding a rifle, you never know what kind of damage he might do."[40]

The veterans were not the only Americans with drinking problems, and this was one of the reasons why their alcoholism caused less concern than it should have. The nation, during and after the war, was awash in beer, whiskey, cocktails, and wine. Between 1940 and 1948, the number of male alcoholics in the United States increased by a million, with the largest increase occurring after 1945 when the veterans returned. "The year following V-E Day," Joseph Hirsh wrote in *The Problem Drinker*, published in 1949, "boasted an expenditure of $9,500,000,000 for alcoholic beverages, and ... saw more ballyhoo for and against alcohol, more newspaper and magazine articles, books, and films than the previous ten years added together." The wave of veteran alcohol abuse energized temperance crusaders, who proposed legislation that was adopted in a number of states.[41]

Those who sought help from local or VA doctors for their drinking or for their wildly alternating bouts of inertia and hyperactivity, their sleeping problems and nightmares, their agitation, restlessness, and uncontrollable tempers were reassured that there was nothing dangerously wrong with them, that they were suffering from battle fatigue, shell shock, war neurosis, or other forms of psychoneurotic disturbances that were temporary and would, in time, disappear without a trace.

"No one had heard yet of post-traumatic stress disorder," Paul Fussell would later write, "but for the first couple of years after the war I experienced something close to it. Emotionally, I was very shaky, given to tears at late-night parties, not all attributable to drink. I remember sometimes lying under the furniture crying my eyes out, just as I had at the evacuation hospital. So avid were most Americans to resume without any change their prewar lives that it was assumed that once the war was over, and gloriously and victoriously over, such midnight behavior as mine must be the result of affectation or simple drunkenness."[42]

"In those days we didn't have this 'post-traumatic stress syndrome,'" Don Dondero, a navy pilot, recalled in his oral history. "Looking back, I realize I wasn't quite right. We got drunk a lot and raised hell, and slowly that helped you come back. When you've been putting your can on the line every day, you adopt a 'don't give a damn' attitude, and I had to get over that. It was like we had been driving a jeep a hundred miles an hour, and everybody said that's the right way to do it; then suddenly the war's over, and you want us to put on the brakes and change. But you can't just change right off and become a solid citizen."[43]

Staff Sergeant J. D. Salinger returned home without disfiguring or noticeable wounds, but scarred emotionally, physically, psychologically. He wrote no war novel or memoirs, granted no interviews about his time in service, said little, if anything, to friends and family. He hid his pain inside his fictional characters, transmuted autobiography into fiction, and wrote short stories about soldiers and veterans tortured by symptoms that would later be associated with post-traumatic stress disorder.

"A Perfect Day for Bananafish," published in *The New Yorker* on January 31, 1948, recounts the last days of Seymour Glass, a veteran who never recovered his psychic balance. On vacation with his wife in Florida, Seymour meets a young child, Sybil, and tells her a story about "bananafish." They have a grand time together—no mention of the war or soldiers or anything other than bananafish and "Little Black Sambo." Sybil says goodbye and Seymour returns to his hotel room, opens his luggage, retrieves a pistol, and surrenders to the living horrors of war still raging within him. "He released the magazine, looked at it, then reinserted it. He cocked the piece. Then he went over and sat down on the unoccupied twin bed, looked at the girl [his wife sleeping on the other twin bed], aimed the pistol, and fired a bullet through his right temple."[44]

Seymour Glass, a fictional character, represented an extreme example of what a psychiatric disorder, triggered or worsened by the war, but unrecognized and untreated during or afterward, might lead to. Most veterans did not commit suicide, but learned to live with nightmares and flashbacks they could not erase. They found ways to distract themselves, by focusing on their careers, working excessive hours. Some, pushed to the edge, reached out for help. Twenty-eight percent of the veterans admitted to Kings Park State Hospital on Long Island between August 1, 1945, and June 19, 1946, including the poet Louis Simpson, were treated for "mental conditions" that had developed after their discharge. William Menninger, chief consultant in neuropsychiatry to the army surgeon general, reported that "as of December 1946, 54 percent of the patients in veterans' hospitals were neuropsychiatric." Psychiatrists at the VA Mental Hygiene Clinic in Los Angeles were in 1950, five years after the war had ended, encountering "fresh cases that have never sought treatment until the present time." In 1955, ten years after the war, 90 percent of army and navy personnel who had been treated in 1944 complained of psychiatric symptoms, 49 percent of irritability, 45 percent of anxiety, 45 percent of restlessness, 43 percent of headaches, 42 percent of psychogenic gastrointestinal complaints, 32 percent of insomnia, 30 percent of depression. Forty percent felt the need for additional treatment.[45]

Many of the veterans tormented by what would later be diagnosed as PTSD had sustained traumatic brain injuries (TBIs) after being struck or being in the vicinity of loud, concussive explosions from grenades, land mines, bazookas, mortar rounds, artillery barrages, and anti-tank, anti-aircraft, and machine guns. "There was nothing subtle or intimate about the approach and explosion of an artillery shell," Eugene Sledge recalled from his time with the marines in the Pacific. "When I heard the whistle of an approaching one in the distance, every muscle in my body contracted.... As the fiendish whistle grew louder, my teeth ground against each other, my heart pounded, my mouth dried, my eyes narrowed, sweat poured over me, my breath came in short irregular gasps, and I was afraid to swallow lest I choke. I also prayed, sometimes out loud.... To me artillery was an invention of hell."[46]

As the historian John Ellis has written, "Soldiers' fear of weapons seems, in fact, to have been related much more to the noise they made than to their lethality." And with good reason. One didn't have to be hit directly to suffer the consequences of these attacks.[47]

Military doctors in the field and stateside did not consider these injuries serious or potentially chronic, in large part because unlike head wounds caused by incoming artillery or shrapnel, TBIs left no visible traces on the body: no lacerations, swelling, bleeding. "Socalled blast injury," doctors in the European theater concluded, was a "psychoneurosis." Psychiatrists stateside who treated patients diagnosed the primary source of the symptoms as "an antecedent emotional unrest." That being the case, the most effective treatment was psychotherapy. "This often produced encouraging results." If psychotherapy did not restore the veteran to normalcy, the passage of time would.[48]

Audie Murphy, the baby-faced GI who became the most decorated of America's war heroes, was tormented by insomnia, nightmares, poor health, and ulcers on his return to Texas after the war. He was irritable, angry, demanding, and rather brutal toward his first wife, Wanda Hendrix, a teenage aspiring movie star whom he married in

January 1949 and divorced fifteen months later. Only after his death did she talk about the man she had loved and feared. "The war had taken its toll on him. He was an ancient young man," seized by "unpredictable rages. . . . She never knew when he was going to blow up over something. . . . Always there was the threat of violence."[49]

The cause of his suffering was PTSD, aggravated or triggered by TBIs. In Sicily, he sustained a concussion from "a high-impact 20mm round [that] knocked him unconscious, provoking nose bleeds that lasted a decade. . . . Twice in January 1945 he sustained concussions, from a mortar round . . . and from a shell blast that knocked him flat. Conventional medical wisdom held that the effects of these blows to the brain would go away with time. Murphy's postwar behavior," the historian Michael C. C. Adams concluded, "suggests otherwise."[50]

Steve Maharidge, a marine veteran who had fought in the Pacific theater, was, like Audie Murphy, a victim of TBIs and PTSD. After Steve died, his son Dale Maharidge, a journalist, author, and professor at the Columbia Journalism School, interviewed marines who were with his father on May 30, 1945, when he suffered a blast concussion on a ridge near a concrete tomb built into Hill 27 on Okinawa. When one of the marines threw a grenade into the tomb, which contained a ton of stored explosives, the hillside exploded. "It went *ZOOM!*" Frank Palmasani told Maharidge. "You'd swore it was like they had dropped the atomic bomb there. God-darn smoke and you could see arms and legs and everything going up in the air. . . . There must have been seven or eight that got shell-shocked. They didn't even know where they were. Their eyes—they weren't straight out. They went in this direction, that direction. They looked goofy."[51]

Some of marines on that ridge in Okinawa would, on their return, have little or no problems adjusting to civilian life. But others had enormous difficulties staying sober, finding work, establishing stable, loving relationships with wife and children, sleeping through the night, controlling their uncontrollable rages, erasing memories.

Jim Laughridge, asked if he thought much about the war, told Dale Maharidge that after he watched "World War II stuff" on the History Channel, he'd "have nightmares. Now this is after sixty-years. . . . Somehow or other I believe you don't ever get over something like that. Okinawa—I think it's done something to my mind. . . . When I dream about the war, it's realistic. And I wake up and, shit, I'm just washed out, man."[52]

VA doctors and psychiatrists, overwhelmed by admissions and readmissions of veterans with undiagnosed PTSD and TBIs, made use of every method available, including shock treatments, to reduce hospital stays and send their patients home, better if not cured. As early as March 22, 1945, according to the VA administrator, Frank Hines, every VA "neuropsychiatric hospital" was either "giving electric shock therapy or preparing to institute this form of treatment." Two and a half months later, on June 6, 1945, Colonel John Baird, the assistant medical director of the VA in charge of the Neuropsychiatry Division, reported that 70 percent of psychotic veterans who had received shock treatments had "improved" as a result of the therapy.[53] A course of treatment that consisted "of eight to 15 shocks, averaging 12 grand mal convulsions," had become the go-to therapy for veterans who were not progressing sufficiently to be released from hospital.[54]

Willie Garcia, a Mexican American from Marfa, Texas, served in North Africa and then Italy, where he moved ammunition to the front lines at night. He was supposed to sleep during the day, but couldn't. After six months or so, the stress got to him and he was brought back to the States. "He couldn't eat. He couldn't walk," his wife, Elizabeth Ruiz Garcia, recalled. He heard voices and train whistles and couldn't stop scratching himself. He was moved from hospital to hospital and ended up in Waco, where "they started giving him electric shocks." The shock treatments had the desired effect, and he was released from the hospital after a year, though the doctors warned his wife not to live alone with him because he might have violent episodes. The Garcias moved in with her parents, where they stayed for five years while Willie recovered and trained as a tailor under the GI Bill.[55]

Willie Garcia was one of the lucky ones who was helped by shock therapy. Despite the VA's enthusiasm, the results were not nearly as positive nor as long-lasting as had been hoped, in part because shock therapy was prescribed indiscriminately and inappropriately for a variety of psychiatric ailments and the treatments were discontinued before they had had optimal effect.[56] A 1949 study by two VA psychiatrists at the Kennedy Veterans Hospital in Memphis found that while 49 percent of the psychotic veterans who had received electroshock treatments had improved, only 12 percent could be considered "recovered," with a large number relapsing "following the termination of treatment."[57]

Many of those who showed no improvement after shock therapy treatments were scheduled for lobotomies. The VA medical establishment, which prided itself on providing the best possible treatment for its patients, had been swept up in the enthusiasm for the psychiatric profession's grand new experiment. "The surgical operation known as leukotomy, sometimes called prefrontal lobotomy, is being used more and more in Veterans' hospitals, and with decided success," Daniel Blain, chief of the Neuropsychiatry Division of the VA, informed fellow military surgeons at their November 1947 convention. "The operation borders on the miraculous."[58]

The earliest lobotomies were surgical procedures performed by licensed neurosurgeons. To pick up the pace and lower the cost for state and VA hospitals, Dr. Walter J. Freeman, the nation's primary advocate and publicist for the operation, introduced a new procedure that did not require the presence of a neurosurgeon and was much less expensive than a surgical lobotomy, with a faster recovery and results just as good. An ice-pick-like instrument was inserted into the brain through the thin bone above the eye socket and swiveled to cut loose prefrontal brain tissue. After its 1946 introduction, 56 percent of lobotomies performed in state hospitals used this method. In 1948, the VA hospital in Tuskegee invited Freeman to demonstrate the new procedure "on 15 or 20 veterans." VA headquarters initially approved the invitation, then, after opposition from a few of its neurosurgical consultants, withdrew it. A few years later, however, the VA reversed itself and allowed each hospital to decide for itself whether to lobotomize its patients surgically or with ice picks.[59]

The veterans who returned home with psychological problems, large and small, worried that their families, friends, and future employers would look on them as flawed, volatile, potentially violent, and incapable of adjusting to civilian life. In preparation for his own homecoming, Henry Kissinger felt obliged to assure his parents that they need not "worry so much about re-adjustment. After all, not everybody came out of this war a psycho-neurotic."[60]

John Bratton of Noroton, Connecticut, in a June 1945 letter to the editor of the *Ladies' Home Journal*, responded less casually and with considerable anger to the solemn, hand-wringing sermon the Barnard College sociologist Willard Waller had offered mothers and wives in a February article that prescribed how they should treat their damaged sons and husbands. Bratton's son, like the vast majority of veterans, was not, his father virtually shouted in print, a "neurotic wreck, and in need of the kid-glove treatment and psychological handling that your article implies." He had endured "the worst that war has to offer," but like other veterans was "taking it in stride." Insinuations about the mental health of returning veterans, Bratton maintained, were both unfounded and damaging. "They will surely resent it, and it will confuse and annoy them if they are treated as quasi–mental cases."[61]

Technical Sergeant David Dempsey, who had worked at *Reader's Digest* before joining the marines, was bewildered and bothered by the presumption that he was so damaged by war that he required extra sympathy and care from friends and strangers. He was confused when, on disembarking at San Francisco, a retired navy officer insisted on paying for his meal, a barber refused a tip, and Red Cross workers "encumbered me with help."

"It was not until an old friend of mine—a woman—looked at me sceptically [sic] and said, 'But are you all right?' that a glimmer of what was happening dawned on me.

"'Of course,' I replied, 'why shouldn't I be?'

"'But what you've been through—it must be terrible.'"

His "friend's attitude," Dempsey discovered, was "typically that of too many mothers and wives who expect the worst of their men when they come home. The advice they are getting from various magazine and newspaper 'authorities' on the subject of adjusting returning servicemen is in danger of turning them into kitchen psychologists determined to 'cure' the veteran—even at the cost of his sanity." The veteran, Dempsey explained, had indeed changed. But he had not, as the experts charged, become "rude and overbearing," so "overcome with boredom" that he craved "coarse entertainment," or "addicted to violence." He recognized the difficulties that lay ahead, but was prepared to meet them, to get on with his life without being smothered with sympathy or coddled by family, friends, and strangers because he had been damaged in war.[62]

John Bratton and David Dempsey were perhaps protesting a bit too much about the ease with which the veterans would be able to readjust to civilian life. The reality was that large numbers had come home with psychological problems, and these problems were not going to cure themselves with the passage of time.

Chapter 12.

VIOLENT VETERANS

Immediately after the war ended, there was joy at imminent homecoming, but there followed a period of uncertainty in both soldier and civilian," the military psychiatrists Norman Q. Brill and Herbert I. Kupper concluded in "Problems of Adjustment in Return to Civilian Life," published by the Historical Unit of the Army Medical Service. "Slowly, anxiety mounted about the possible emotional and psychological problems of demobilization. Families and communities became worried over how much their men had changed, and the public press with a hue and a cry began to publish 'scare articles.'" It was impossible to suppress or dismiss "the fear that the man who had been taught to kill by the Army would return to civilian life without the restraints society had, previously, so carefully built into him. Possibilities of 'epidemics' of crime and violence were predicted by some who believed that the hostile aggressive forces which had been released by war could not be suddenly turned off."[1]

"This prevailing tendency to regard a man who has been in uniform as a potential criminal lunatic is probably the most depressing

"I can't tell whether he's a war-embittered young radical or a typical, sound, 100 percent American fighting man."

phase of a veteran's homecoming or thoughts of home," the veteran and author Charles Bolté observed in the fall of 1945.[2]

Police chiefs, law enforcement experts, and local and national FBI officials fed the home front fears and offered themselves up as the best, perhaps the only bulwark of defense.

Vigilance was called for, demanded. "That German pistol or Jap sword sought by servicemen as souvenirs can easily, on the return to peace, bring to America a wave of crime," California's attorney general, Robert Kenny, warned in late March 1944 at the fiftieth annual convention of the California State Sheriffs' Association. "Innocent souvenir-collecting practice may result in an unprecedented wave of crime after the war. . . . Resources of peace officers will be taxed to the utmost in the postwar era when 11,000,000 veterans of the war . . . begin a period of readjustment."[3]

Every soldier who had been in combat or in harm's way, the public was warned, posed a potential danger to the community. In a powerful December 1944 article in *The Saturday Evening Post*, Arch Soutar, who had served "as a foot soldier in the Tunisian campaign," told the story of a veteran who, while working in the woods, saw a neighbor's dog stealing his lunch. "Now, to the normal boy, this wouldn't be a crisis, but to the returned man it was. There was the sharp ax in his hands.... The soldier didn't think. He reacted. And the woodsman's ax became a familiar combat weapon, catching the beast squarely between the shoulders.... He was reacting like an emotionally disturbed veteran in a crisis. Before he went to war, his mother told me later, he couldn't kill a chicken for dinner, much less see a dog in distress." The soldier, brought before a judge for killing the dog, explained that he was a different man because of the war. "'Now that I've been trained to kill, it's different. And when I saw something taking my food—and I didn't know exactly what—the ax left my hands by itself.' ... Well, this time, it chanced to be a dog," Soutar concluded, but "what if the thief had been a man? ... You've got to help us prevent this thing ... prevent it from becoming shocking fact. But I can't tell you how."[4]

Recurring and spectacular news stories about violent, senseless crimes committed by veterans who had been trained to kill, and solemn treatises on the threat of a postwar crime wave, had a rather chilling effect on the home front. The civilian population was called on to prepare itself for an invasion of damaged and demented GIs and sailors. "In approved military jargon," reporter Benjamin Bowker wrote in prose soaked in sarcasm, "the enemy established a beachhead during 1944–5," when the first two million veterans returned. "The 'enemy' consisted of United States soldiers, sailors, marines, and coastguardmen.... Armchair strategists shifted their talents from suggestions for confounding the Germans and Japanese into expedients for defense against invading veterans."[5]

"During a period when veterans were big news," Bill Mauldin noted in *Back Home*, "every time an ex-soldier got himself in a jam the fact that he was a vet was pointed out in the headline. An ordinary killing or assault seldom rated the front page, but if it involved a jealous veteran or a battle-fatigue case, it could be sure of a prominent play. . . . The sad fact was that such headlines gave added impetus to the rumor that always appears in every country after a war—that the returning soldiers are trained in killing and assault and are potential menaces to society."[6]

"We knew from our pony editions [special editions of books and magazines published for the servicemen overseas]," author William Manchester later wrote, "that there was some concern at home over how to handle trained killers like us when the war ended. One prominent New York clubwoman suggested that we be sent to a reorientation camp outside the States (she suggested the Panama Canal Zone) and that when we were released there, we be required to wear an identification patch warning of our lethal instincts, sort of like a yellow star."[7]

Noir crime films and fiction featuring veterans who brought home the war and its violence became a staple of postwar culture. Sometimes, as in *The Best Years of Our Lives*, in which the Dana Andrews character, Fred Derry, cannot control his temper and punches a customer, the violence is peripheral to the main plot. More often, it is central to it. "The most commercially successful kind of veterans' stories," historian Richard Lingeman has written, "were those that took the form of a violent crime film." They expressed, embellished, and heightened the home front's "fear that vets would commit acts of violence."[8]

The disaffected, hardened, world-weary veteran takes center stage in postwar noir films and fiction as hero or villain or both, his violence a result of the anger he experiences on returning home and discovering that the wholesome, ordered society he had left behind has gone to hell in his absence. Women have become more sexually adventuresome, children more rebellious, businessmen more avaricious and corrupt, government and crime-fighting institutions more ineffective. The veteran has to take the law into his own hands because the courts and police, through incompetence or corruption, were letting the bad guys get away. Having defeated evil abroad, he is honorbound to do the same at home. "Typically, in the postwar movie and fiction plot," Paula Rabinowitz writes in *American Pulp*, "the domestic front appears almost as violent and unstable as the combat zone."[9]

The men's adventure magazines *Argosy* and *Blue Book*, according to Timothy Shuker-Haines, published dozens of stories between 1944 and 1947 in which "the home front, deprived of its fighting young men, has become deeply corrupted and must be purified by the vet." Criminals, hustlers, drug pushers, pimps, Nazi spies, hedonists, perverts, and rapacious dames run roughshod, barely contained by the nation's police forces and moral guardians, compelling the returning veterans to deploy their masculinized authority to restore the idealized postwar world they had left behind.[10]

The temporary loosening of the Motion Picture Production Code during the war made it possible to produce veteran crime films soaked in violence. "Of late," wrote Lloyd Shearer in *The New York Times* in early August 1945, "there has been a trend in Hollywood toward the wholesale production of lusty, hard-boiled, gat-and-gore crime stories.... Every studio in town has at least two or three similar blood-freezers before the cameras right now, which means that within the next year or so movie murder—particularly with a psychological twist—will become almost as common as the weekly newsreel or musical.... The war has made us psychologically and emotionally ripe for motion pictures of this sort."[11]

Because moviegoers appeared ready to accept violent acts committed by veterans more readily than those perpetrated by common criminals, screenwriters transformed novels that had nothing to do with ex-GIs into veteran return films. In the film version of Dorothy Hughes's novel *Ride the Pink Horse*, adapted by Ben Hecht and Charles Lederer for the screen, the low-life Chicago street thug known as Sailor becomes Gagin, a handsome veteran in suit and tie, played by Robert Montgomery, who travels to a New Mexico border town to avenge the murder of Shorty, with whom he had served in New Guinea. Gagin is tailed by a law enforcement officer who urges him not to take the law into his own hands. "You're like the rest of the boys, all cussed up because you fought a war for three years and got nothing out of it but a dangle of ribbons. Why don't you let your Uncle Sam take care of him?" This being a Hollywood film that needed a happy ending, Gagin steps aside and instead of killing the bad guy hands him over to the authorities.[12]

The most violent of the fictional veterans was Mike Hammer, the detective created by the bestselling crime writer and World War II airman Mickey Spillane. In *I, the Jury*, Spillane's first novel, Hammer sets out to avenge the brutal death of his one-armed army buddy, "the guy that shared the same mud bed with me through two years of warfare in the stinking slime of the jungle . . . who said he'd give his right arm for a friend and did when he stopped a bastard of a Jap from slitting me in two." Hammer makes it clear to the police detective investigating the case that he wants "the killer for myself. . . . You have a job to do, but so have I. . . . The law is fine. But this time I'm the law." As a veteran, Spillane implies, Hammer has the right to take the law into his own hands, to serve as jury and executioner. "After the war I've been almost anxious to get to some of the rats that make up the section of humanity that prey on people. . . . I shoot them like the mad dogs they are."[13]

Ken Millar, who had served in the navy through the spring of

1946, became, under the pen name Ross Macdonald, another fixture of the postwar crime fiction scene. Millar's early novels had featured three different veteran heroes: Ensign Sam Drake, who chases a spy ring led by a female temptress; John Weather Jr., a twenty-two-year-old veteran who battles corruption in his hometown on his return from service; and a naval lieutenant with amnesia who hunts down his wife's killer. In large part because, as Tom Nolan, Millar's biographer notes, "private eyes were having a boom year in 1947," his fourth veteran protagonist was Lew Archer, a former army intelligence officer, now a private investigator. Millar's next seventeen novels would feature Archer, who returned home "to find himself operating in a world altered by war. . . . Almost all the Archer novels allude in one way or another to the war's cataclysm, and to the way it left Americans greedy and hard."[14]

In multiple novels and films, like Spillane's *I, the Jury* and the film version of Dorothy Hughes's *Ride the Pink Horse*, the plot revolves around a veteran who deploys violence to avenge the murder of a war buddy. In the 1947 film *Dead Reckoning*, the former paratrooper Rip Murdock, played by Humphrey Bogart, discovers that his friend Johnny has been murdered and goes AWOL in search of the killer. In *Act of Violence*, Joe Parkson, a disabled and violent veteran, played by Robert Ryan, travels to Santa Lisa, California, to murder Frank Enley, played by Van Heflin, and avenge the American POWs who had been slaughtered when Enley informed the Nazis of their escape plan. In *Key Largo*, another ex-veteran, again played by Bogart, visits the family of a soldier who had served under him in Italy, only to find them menaced by a gang of violent criminals led by Johnny Rocco, portrayed menacingly and brilliantly by Edward G. Robinson. Despite his wish for peace and quiet, the veteran is honor-bound to protect his fellow veteran's sister and her family because the police have proved incapable of doing so.

Not every postwar noir film provided the violent veteran with a righteous motive for his actions. In *The Brick Foxhole*, written by the former marine corps sergeant Richard Brooks, a veteran, played by Robert Ryan, who has spent the war years stateside in a "brick foxhole" just outside Washington, D.C., murders an innocent homosexual for no apparent reason. In the film adaptation, renamed *Crossfire*, the murdered man is transformed from a homosexual to a kindly Jew who, just before his death, explains to the veteran who will kill him that the postwar world and the veterans who inhabit it have been overwhelmed by hatred, carried over from the war. "We're too used to fightin'. But we just don't know what to fight. You can feel the tension in the air. A whole lot of fight and hate that doesn't know where to go."[15]

In a Lonely Place, Dorothy Hughes's brilliant 1947 novel, the reader is forced to ponder whether the serial-killer veteran is a born killer or has been turned into one by war. Dix Steele learned to kill as an army air force pilot in England—and was entranced and entrapped by the ease and thrill of doing so. On his discharge and return to civilian life, he stalks, rapes, and murders young women. Hollywood, unwilling to leave viewers with the inference that wartime service had created a serial killer, turned the plot upside down. The film version of Hughes's novel, starring Humphrey Bogart, portrays the veteran as angry, with a propensity for violence, but not as the serial killer.

Brutal, sometimes murderous veterans also took center stage as the major protagonists on Broadway. *Truckline Cafe*, written by Maxwell Anderson and produced and directed by Harold Clurman and Elia Kazan, featured Marlon Brando as a veteran who on his return to Southern California discovers that his wife has had an affair, shoots her, and dumps her body into the ocean. Elia Kazan, impressed by Brando's performance, cast him as Stanley Kowalski, the lead character in Tennessee Williams's *Streetcar Named Desire*. Violence and the threat of violence infuse Brando's speech, his swagger, and his relationship with his friends, his wife, whom he beats, and his sister-in-law, whom he rapes. *Streetcar* had been written by Williams while he was living with Amado "Pancho" Rodriguez y Gonzalez, a veteran who like Kowalski had "served two and a half years in the South Pacific, right in the thick of it, and then was let out of the army without an honorable discharge." Elia Kazan was convinced that the real-life Pancho was the model for Stanley Kowalski.[16]

The public's fear of the returning veteran was so pervasive that it spawned a noir subgenre in which innocent men are accused of murder, simply because they are veterans. The falsely accused veteran was so serviceable a character that when 20th Century Fox adapted a true story from 1922 about a wandering tramp charged with the murder of a priest, it turned the tramp into a veteran. In *Boomerang*, directed by Kazan, seven eyewitnesses finger the veteran, played by Arthur Kennedy, as the murderer. A psychiatrist is brought in to interview him. Asked by the state attorney, played by Dana Andrews, if the veteran sounds "like a murderer or not," the psychiatrist replies, "Well . . . he's frightened and he seems to be more than usually bitter and resentful. . . . He's just out of the Army. That might account for his bitterness a little. The difficulty of readjustment or possibly . . . it's something else." Because this is a Hollywood film and because the fear of veterans was matched by sympathy for their plight, the accused veteran is found innocent. In the end, he is left where he was when the film began: angry, homeless, jobless.[17]

These films, plays, short stories, and novels presented their audiences with a nightmarish vision of a world that bore little if any resemblance to the real one. Despite the warnings, the threats, the images of dangerous men in dark suits and trench coats, there was no veteran crime wave. The returning GIs, sailors, airmen, and marines did not use their souvenir weapons to wreak havoc; they did not engage in violent cleansing operations to rid their communities of crime and corruption; they did not become criminals or con men. Still, the fears of what the veterans might do, stoked by the films and novels that portrayed them as broken, damaged, and dangerous, persisted. While the returning veterans were not violence-prone killers and criminals, they were unpredictable and consumed by a discontent and anger that had an immediate, visceral, and sometimes frightening effect on their families.

Chapter 13.

LOVE AND MARRIAGE...
AND DIVORCE

The war ripped families apart, but the hope had always been that when it was over, those families would be reunited and resume life as they had known it—or imagined it—before the war. For large numbers of veterans, their wives, and children, this was not to be. Between 1940 and 1946, the overall divorce rate more than doubled. Leading the surge were the veterans. By 1950, a million had been divorced.[1]

The "divorce muddle" that had begun "well before the war was over," *Life* magazine reported on September 3, "is gathering momentum as more servicemen come home and rid themselves of unfaithful or incompatible or simply unwanted wives, and as service wives do some discarding of their own. Already Reno, the national capital for quick, painless divorce, resembles a California mining town during the days of '49."[2]

In mid-November 1945, *The Washington Post* reported that the offices of two of Washington's busiest divorce attorneys were swamped with returning veterans. The rate of filings had "shot upward 60 percent during the fiscal year of 1945 over the fiscal year of 1939, and is increasing monthly.... Many Washington veterans were using terminal leaves to start actions, often going to Reno or other jurisdictions where the procedure is less difficult than in the District."[3]

The University of Chicago researchers who authored *The American Veteran Back Home* found that five of the twenty-four veterans in the small midwestern city they studied "had been divorced or separated during or directly after the war period," compared with only two in the nonveteran control group.[4]

It was assumed, wrongly, that the vets getting divorced were youngsters who had rushed into marriage. Sociologists Eliza Pavalko and Glen Elder Jr., in a 1990 study, found, to the contrary, that while more veterans than nonveterans had been "divorced by 1955," those most likely to dissolve their marriages were over thirty and had been married before the war. They divorced not because they preferred the single life but because they could not put their prewar marriages back together again. Most remarried quickly, boosting the marriage rate simultaneously with the divorce rate.[5]

The "divorce boom" fed on itself. As the number of marriages broke up, the stigma of separating from one's spouse dissipated. "For growing numbers of men and women," as Steven Mintz and Susan Kellogg have written, "divorce was no longer seen as a symbol of disgrace. Said one divorced woman in 1946: 'I used to think that I'd cut off my head before I ... admitted that I made a bust of marriage. But now, so what? Of the first five girlfriends I made in New York, three are divorced, and I'm on my way. I'm not blasé about it, because it hurt. But I'm not wearing sackcloth and ashes either.'"[6]

Hollywood, looking to capitalize on the divorce trend, released *Divorce*, starring Kay Francis, in late summer 1945. The film opens with an ominous scroll accompanied by ominous music.

"Hullo, Suzy ... I wondered why ya broke off our engagement while I wuz in Sicily."

"MARRIAGE—entered into with such high hopes—such promise of happiness. Then—too often—DIVORCE—which solves no problems—merely creating new ones—And—in its wake, leaves disillusionment, heartbreak, despair—Of such is our story." The four-time divorcée Dianne Carter returns to her hometown, where she sets out to seduce a former boyfriend and veteran who is now married and the father of two Hollywood-perfect sons. The veteran appears normal, but when a neighbor asks his wife about him, she replies that "he's still restless. And takes an awful lot of humoring. But he'll get adjusted." He also drinks too much, has a temper, is bored, and, as such, is easy prey for Dianne Carter, who offers him glamour, money, "big things," and an escape from his humdrum existence as husband and father. Fortunately for all, this being a Hollywood production, the veteran, in the end, leaves the divorcée who had seduced him and returns home to wife and children. The plotting was predictable, at times laughable, the characters stick figures: a loving wife, a weak veteran, and a femme fatale who wreaks havoc. Still, what the film portrays rather accurately—and this may have helped its box office appeal—was the suffering that precedes and follows divorce.[7]

As the end of the war came into sight, psychiatrists, social workers, counselors, and a host of individuals and organizations stepped forward to offer their services to wives awaiting the return of their husbands. Their goal was to reduce the possibility of divorce, which, they proclaimed, posed a danger not only to the family but to the social fabric.

In the three-week period between November 12 and December 3, 1944, the Child Study Association held a benefit for "its program of counseling families confronted with wartime problems"; the Kiwanis Club in Huntington Park, California, opened a "new counseling center . . . to aid local residents in solving personal and family problems caused or accentuated by the war"; the Division of Rehabilitation of the National Committee for Mental Hygiene released a pamphlet with advice for "the families of returning servicemen"; the Board of Managers of the National Congress of Parents and Teachers directed its eighteen thousand local chapters to set up counseling centers; and the Association for Family Living held an all-day institute at the Standard Club in Chicago on "how wives may assist in bridging smoothly the years and miles of separation between G.I. Joes and their families." Each of these organizations, and their publications, emphasized—and not very subtly—that it was the wives, not their husbands, who would be responsible for rescuing endangered marriages.[8]

The women's magazines were the chief vehicle for persuading the war wives to take back their husbands. Article after article was published warning them to put aside their doubts, their fears, their uncertainties, to welcome home their men and do whatever it took to preserve the marriage. "As the wife of an American fighting man," Toni Taylor warned other war wives in *Redbook* in December 1944, "the future of your own marriage and of the institution of marriage is largely in your hands." Irene Stokes Culman in *Good Housekeeping* in May 1945 warned those who might have been contemplating divorce to refrain from doing so at all costs. "These coming months and years are going to be full of problems that will call for the learning of life's two hardest lessons: patience and compromise. Learn them, if occasion arises, for the sake of yourself and your husband and your marriage," Culman urged the war wives. "You took your soldier, young woman: he's yours. In heaven's name stick with him."[9]

Eleanor Stevenson, who had received a Bronze Star for her work with the Red Cross during the war and become a traveling lecturer on veterans' marriages and families afterward, summed up the prevailing wisdom in a speech delivered for Planned Parenthood over the CBS network between 5:45 and 6:00 p.m., when, it was assumed, America's wives were preparing dinner and listening to the radio. "Because of his long absence, the trying conditions of war and his dreams," the veteran, on returning home, was deeply insecure. "The wives of America have a big responsibility and must give their husbands the necessary emotional security through the marriage relationship without making him over-dependent. Their job is to help him become the strong independent man he actually is." Stevenson acknowledged that this was no easy task and suggested outside help and counseling. Planned Parenthood, she announced, had already risen to the challenge and "expanded its program into the field of Family Living and Education for Marriage."[10]

To support the war wives in their struggle to save their marriages, the nation's YWCAs, colleges and universities, the Red Cross, community centers, veterans' organizations, and religious groups established educational programs for young marrieds. The YWCA opened a "brides' school" in Brooklyn. Universities offered newly created courses in "Marriage and the Family." The Central Conference of American (Reform) Rabbis recommended at its 1946 annual meeting "that a 'major portion of the 1947 summer institutes be devoted to the divorce problem.'" The Federal Council of Churches of Christ in America, an ecumenical association of Protestant congregations, urged "churches and communities to provide skilled educational and counseling help . . . which will enable people better to understand marriage. . . . When a couple in difficulty takes pains to gain the best human guidance and at the same time pray together often and persistently they can win their way back to a satisfying relationship."[11]

The veterans and their wives were inundated with advice that was so intense, exaggerated, and patronizing that Robert M. Yoder, a newspaperman and editor who had spent the war on the home front, feared that they would be paralyzed by it. "Such is the interest in welcoming the returning soldier into civilian society," he wrote in *Woman's Day*, "that every conceivable authority on human relations, from child psychologists to [the actress] Katharine Cornell, has written or spoken on this subject, and a more doleful collection of predictions rarely has been accumulated. . . . The nonfiction articles come in one distinctive flavor—they adopt a low-voiced, resigned tone such as you might hear in a hospital corridor. . . . The fiction writers join in this head-shaking, and it is an exceptional month when the magazines don't present a story telling how Don and Cecilia came near to busting up just at the moment of their reunion."[12]

What was missing in all this advice literature was sympathy for the women whose lives had now been disrupted twice: once when their husbands were called away and now again on their return. "What about the wives?" Mary Barr, whose husband had just returned, asked Mona Gardner in the rather ominously titled article "Has Your Husband Come Home to the Right Woman?," published in the December 1945 *Ladies' Home Journal*. "Everybody's talking about how to treat your soldier and help him reconvert to civilian life! Well, what about wives? They've got a job of reconverting too. They've got to stop being independent and get used to having a full-time boss around the house. They've got to adapt themselves to the male ego after being comfortably female for several years. It isn't so easy! . . . People are always writing manuals these days—about how to treat the Arabs, how to treat the British or the Greeks! Why doesn't somebody write one about how to behave toward a wife when she's reconverting into a clinging vine?"[13]

The wives who had worked outside the home during the war and were fired as soon as it was over might have had the most difficult time adjusting to the changes in their lives. "By September 1945," the sociologist Ruth Milkman has written, "one-fourth of the women who had been employed in factories three months before had lost their war jobs, and by the year's end more than a million women had been claimed by layoffs. In manufacturing, the post–V-J Day layoffs affected women at a rate nearly double that for men."[14] Frankie Cooper was "working in the Kaiser shipyards in Oregon, as a welder, doing an important job, and doing it well, and then all at once here comes V-J Day, the end of the war, and I'm back making homemade bread."[15]

Some of those abruptly laid off were more than ready, after the stress of wartime work, to return to being full-time wives and mothers. Others voluntarily resigned because that was what their husbands wanted, if not demanded. *Parents' Magazine* reported in September 1945 that many of the women working outside the home while waiting for their husbands to return intended to quit their jobs to avoid "conflicts which may grow out of their increasing independence.... Many men sound very proud when they tell what their wives are able to accomplish—household, children, earning a wage and all. But many of the soldiers say, 'That is only until I get home.' Sometimes this statement may express sympathy for the wife who is overworked.... But at other times the same statement represents a threat. It does not express sympathy for the wife but fear of her, since her capacity to be self-sufficient seems to threaten his position in the family and shakes his belief in his own masculinity."[16]

The war wives had taken on a host of new responsibilities while the men were absent. They had paid the bills, run the errands, shoveled the snow, called the plumber or electrician, seen to repairs of the car, the roof, and the kitchen sink. The experts who wrote for the newspapers and women's magazines warned them now to downplay or disguise their newfound abilities so that their husbands could resume their rightful positions as heads of household. For the sake of domestic stability, they were advised to defer to the men and follow their lead when it came to jobs outside the home, having company over, sexual relations, and what to eat for dinner. Wives were directed to wear dresses and not slacks, indulge their husbands' wanderlusts and restlessness, let them go out with their buddies and drink late into the night, refrain from correcting them when they used foul language, resist nagging them to get a job, try not to call attention to their nightmares or troubled sleep, and nod in earnest agreement when they criticized 4-Fs and others for not doing their duty, while they had risked their lives.

"I was so grateful that he was back that I wanted to please him and do what he wanted me to do," Shirley Hackett recalled in her oral history. "All of us went back into the syndrome with which we were brought up—the quiet wife.... I reverted to the role of housewife and mother."[17]

"After the war fashions changed drastically, you were supposed to become a feminine person," Frankie Cooper recalled. "We laid aside our slacks, our checkered shirts, and we went in for ostrich feathers, ruffles, high-heeled shoes. All this was part of the propaganda in magazines and newspapers to put a woman back in her 'rightful place' in the home. . . . My husband would have been happy if I had gone back to the kind of girl I was when he married me—a little homebody there on the farm, in the kitchen, straining the milk. But I wasn't that person anymore."[18]

The difficulties in putting a marriage back together were many and intertwined. Sexual dysfunction among veterans was a serious problem, "a major tragedy," warned the psychologist Dorothy W. Baruch and her coauthor, Lee Edward Travis, who interviewed hundreds of returning veterans and consulted with psychiatrists and officers at VA facilities. "Many men . . . come home and find themselves either unable to get an erection or unable to maintain it. Many find themselves unable to last as long as they want. . . . For some unfathomable and strange reason, and in utterly mysterious fashion, they are not able to manage their sexual impulses in a way that makes them feel virile and proud." Wives were counseled to ignore what Mona Gardner delicately referred to in the *Ladies' Home Journal* as the returning veteran's reluctance "to express himself in any physical tenderness toward his wife" and to reject the notion that their husbands were sexually unresponsive because they were still in love with the women they had consorted with overseas.[19]

It was far easier for the experts to offer advice than it was for the wives to accept and live by it. The historian Thomas Childers recounted how his mother, Mildred Childers, found a letter her husband had written, but not yet sent, to a woman named Marjorie in England. "She took the letter to him. Who is Marjorie? she asked casually. . . . His answers seemed evasive, pried out of him like an impacted tooth. . . . It was nothing special, [her husband] Tom insisted, nothing unusual at all." Mildred contemplated divorce. "No one in the family or in her circle of friends had ever gotten a divorce. But now divorce was everywhere she turned—in newspapers and magazines, on the radio." In the end, she decided, despite the evidence, to try to accept her husband's denial. "They remained together; they struggled on," their son would later write. And they were able to do so because they were never honest with each other. Mildred never acknowledged the degree to which she suffered. Tom never confessed his infidelities.[20]

Honesty appeared not to be the best policy when it came to sexual betrayal. One of the veterans interviewed for *Father Relations of War-Born Children*, written by a team of Stanford psychologists led by Lois Meek Stolz, had had an affair overseas and believed that his sexual failures at home were caused by guilt at his infidelity. He said nothing about this to his wife. "The only way is to start all over again when you get back, push your experiences back into the unconscious. Forget about them. The thing is not to talk about your war experiences to your wife, for they include dirt, filth, infidelity."[21]

It was different in the movies, where the veteran's confession only strengthened the marriage. Sloan Wilson's bestselling novel *The Man in the Gray Flannel Suit* and the film that followed starring Gregory Peck and Jennifer Jones were popular with audiences because they soothed the still-festering fears of adulterous veterans and betrayed wives with a happy ending and a strengthened marriage. The novel and film's hero, Captain Tom Rath, though married, had moved in with Maria, a young Italian woman, while on furlough in Rome awaiting reassignment to the Pacific. Years later, when he learns that Maria had given birth to his baby, he confesses to his wife that he had had an affair in Rome, has a child, intends to support him, and asks for her blessing.

"I'm not the only man to leave a child behind during the war.

There are hundreds of thousands of war children in Japan and Italy and Germany. There are more in France and England and Australia. Anywhere the men were sent out to fight, quite a few ended up becoming fathers. . . . That's a dirty thing, I suppose. Wars are full of dirt. . . . I find it hard to be really ashamed."

In the fairy-tale ending tacked onto the novel and film, Tom's wife responds with fury. And then she forgives him. "I don't know anything about war. All I know is the wife's side of it—four years of sitting around waiting, believing that faithfulness is part of what you call love. . . ."

"Stop it," he says. "We're going to have a good life together."[22]

The resolution of *The Man in the Gray Flannel Suit*, with a war wife forgiving her unfaithful veteran husband, provided the ending the public wanted. Had the transgressor, however, been the wife, no such forgiveness would have been expected or tolerated, much less applauded. Over and over again, in newspapers and magazines, radio dramas and films, errant veterans were exonerated for their unfaithfulness, unfaithful war wives and girlfriends condemned.

The different sexual standards to which the servicemen and their wives were held were, on face value, preposterous, and a handful of commentators took note of this. The University of North Carolina sociologist Ernest Groves implored the returning veterans not to hide behind the age-old but no longer meaningful double standard. "If a man returns from the conflict and knows beyond doubt that his wife has been sexually unfaithful it seems fair that before he rushes for a divorce he should scrutinize his own conduct. If his conduct has been the same, he has no greater grievance than has his wife."[23]

James L. Hicks, a staff writer for the Negro Newspaper Publishers Association,[*] founded in 1940, was outraged by the behavior of

---

[*] In 1956, the name would be changed to the National Newspaper Publishers Association.

veterans who sought refuge from their own misdeeds by taking revenge on their wives. "The courts are crowded these days with cases of returned veterans who are . . . seeking divorces because some busybodies said their wives were cutting up while they were away. It's no doubt true that many of the wives of soldiers strayed from the straight and narrow path and yielded to the pressure of the war-worker-wolves but in comparison with the number of their husbands who went wrong with mademoiselles, frauleins and other foreign ladies, the wife still looks like the image of your patron saint."[24]

The veterans' suspicions, which had been aroused while they were abroad, were fed on their return by recurring newspaper reports of the epidemic of adultery that had broken out in their absence. On August 1, 1945, the *Baltimore Sun* reported on its front page that Corporal Stanley Heck, who had lost his legs in Germany and might have to have his left arm amputated, had from his hospital bed in Texas filed charges against his wife for "desertion and adultery" and against the man she had been seeing for "love theft." The *Chicago Daily Tribune* informed its readers, also in a front-page story, that State Attorney William J. Tuohy had assigned an assistant state's attorney to canvass the divorce courts and prosecute "wives shown to be guilty of adultery." In October came the news from Los Angeles, widely covered in newspapers across the country, that the baby-faced American cartoonist Sergeant Bill Mauldin was seeking divorce on grounds of adultery. His wife, he charged, had, while he was overseas, engaged in an affair with Elmer Gaines, a civilian.[25]

Hollywood, like the newspapers and the pulp fiction paperbacks, confirmed, in exaggerated fashion, the worst fears of the returning veterans. "The end of the war in Europe," Fred Stanley wrote for *The New York Times* on May 20, 1945, "had given added impetus to Hollywood's year-long interest in stories with post-war themes. . . . In some of the proposed films even such delicate themes as marital unfaithfulness are to be treated."[26]

In *The Best Years of Our Lives*, Fred Derry, played by Dana Andrews, discovers his wife with another man. He asks if she had known him while he was away, to which she answers, cruelly, brazenly, that she had known "lots of people. What do you think I was doing all those years?" The scene ends with her announcing she's going to get a divorce.[27]

The same scene is played out, with much less subtlety, in *The Blue Dahlia*, with a screenplay by Raymond Chandler. Johnny Morrison, portrayed by Alan Ladd, returns home from the navy and finds his wife hosting a raucous, booze-filled party and then kissing one of the guests. He slugs the guy, and the guests leave the apartment. When he asks his wife if they can "talk this out" and could she stop drinking, she snarls at him, "I take all the drinks I like any time, any place, I go where I want to with anybody I want. I just happen to be that kind of girl." She then confesses that their son, Dickie, had died not from diphtheria, as she had written him, but in a car accident because she had been driving drunk after a party. Johnny pulls a gun on her, then walks out. When she is murdered, that same evening, he becomes the prime suspect.[28]

Because both *The Best Years of Our Lives* and *The Blue Dahlia* were Hollywood productions, the films conclude with the betrayed veterans finding girlfriends to replace their adulterous wives: the cloyingly innocent Teresa Wright for Dana Andrews; the gorgeous, glamorous, and mysterious Veronica Lake for Alan Ladd.

Similar stories populated the pages of postwar fiction. In Ann Petry's *Country Place*, published in 1947, the veteran Johnnie Roane returns from war to find his wife, Glory, in love with Ed, an older man who owns a gas station and has been kept out of war by age and a weak heart. Unlike the Hollywood films, there were no happy endings in Petry's novel.[29]

In real life, as in the movies and fiction, the veterans' suspicions were too often confirmed. Joseph Goulden, the author of *The Best*

Years, 1945–1950, interviewed E. V. Faber, an airman who, on returning to Chicago and his wife, mistakenly, "out of boredom if nothing else," told her about "the women and the parties and the drinking.... She listened for a couple of days.... Then one morning, she said, 'I guess you realize that we can't stay married, not after what you've done.' Without thinking much of what I was saying, I answered, 'I suppose you're right.'" Years later, after their divorce, Faber called his ex-wife to say hello on Christmas. "Friendly conversation, sort of bringing ourselves up to date on what we'd been doing. And then she blurted out this thing that she felt awful about making me take all the guilt, because she deserved some too.... She said she'd had a lover too, a naval lieutenant.... Then he was sent overseas, and she got tied up with one of his friends, and so on."[30]

Staff Sergeant Robert Minch, an army truck driver in New Guinea and the Philippines, didn't return home until two or three months after V-J Day. He had been away from home and his wife for almost four years. "When I left, I had an apartment with the wife. When I got home, my wife had found somebody else.... We stayed together a little while. My wife was almost an instant stranger. She was a beautiful girl. But, so I ended up living with the folks. I was thirty years old, and I had to start my whole life all over again."[31]

While the veterans and their wives struggled to resume and rekindle their marriages, the children looked on, confused, bewildered, anxious. The historian William M. Tuttle Jr., in researching his book *Daddy's Gone to War*, solicited and received more than twenty-five hundred letters from the children of World War II veterans. Those that "detailed troubled reunions when fathers returned ... outnumber by four to one those that describe happy reunions with fathers, or tell of postwar bonding and warm friendship."[32]

Cheryl Kolb, whose father had left for the war when she was three and returned when she was seven, traveled with her mother and sister to meet him in New York City. Her father called from the lobby of the hotel they were staying in to say he was on his way up in the elevator, "but when the elevator door opened, 'Oh, oh, here was a whole group of men, all in uniform, all with aviator glasses on—I couldn't recognize my own father.'" Preschoolers hid in fear, frightened of the men who entered their homes. "A four-year-old watched 'the stranger with the big white teeth' come toward her and as he did, she 'ran upstairs in terror & hid under a bed.'"[33]

Two-year-old Tom Mathews climbed onto the roof of the garage behind the apartment house in Salt Lake City to "get a good look" at the father who had "left a few months after my first birthday." When his father saw him, he commanded him to jump down, but the two-year-old was afraid and stayed where he was. His father asked again, then turned his back on his son and stormed into the house. "'No son of mine is a coward.' . . . From that first day, my father thought—not without reason—that he was looking at a soft little pain in the neck, and I thought, on balance, that my life would be off to a better start if only the Germans had killed him."[34]

The veterans too were distressed by their sons' and daughters' reluctance to recognize them or show them the love and respect they desired and deserved. George Cordier, a marine veteran of the Pacific theater, returned home in late 1945, and after being separated from his son for two years "wanted to pick him up, but he wouldn't come to me. He didn't know who I was. He thought I was some stranger. And I had that hardest problem for a while, until I finally got him to realize that I was his father."[35]

"When my husband came back from the Navy," Barbara De Nike recalled in her oral history, "he had a difficult time adjusting to our daughter and realizing that she was a person and part of our family. She was fifteen months old when we started living together again, and it became clear to me how much of her early development he had missed, and the effect that it had on him. . . . She was at the stage where she was trying desperately to get her spoon from the cereal dish to her mouth and landing it on her ear. To me this was progress. . . . But he got very impatient with her over little things like that, and I realized how much he had missed."[36]

Lois Meek Stolz and her collaborators at Stanford University found that less than a third of the veterans interviewed for *Father Relations of War-Born Children*, funded by the National Institute of Mental Health of the U.S. Public Health Service,* were, on their return from war, "ready to accept the child immediately and wholeheartedly." The others had difficulties from the moment they set eyes on their firstborn. They knew something was wrong, something missing, but did not know how to correct it.[37]

Veterans who were trying desperately to reconnect with their wives found the kids in the way—and there was nothing they could do about it. "Under the most favorable circumstances," the psychiatrist Alexander Dumas and his coauthor, Grace Keen, declared, in their 1945 book, "a first child raises new problems in marriage, and if the child is two years old when the father first makes its acquaintance, these problems are likely to be aggravated." Eighteen of the nineteen veteran fathers in the Stanford study complained that their wives spent more time with the child than with them. "Every time I sat down beside my wife, our daughter would want something and my wife would get up and leave me and do it. That irked me—especially when it seemed to me the baby was just doing it to be a nuisance."[38]

The veteran who had not been around to cuddle, feed, comfort, or read to his firstborn felt superfluous, an interloper. The only role in which he felt comfortable—and needed—was that of disciplinarian.

---

* While the Stanford study is the best—in many ways, the only—study we have of the effect of the father's return on children born and raised in his absence, it included only a handful of preschoolers, all of them White, disproportionately middle class.

One returning father confessed to interviewers that while his "wife didn't believe in spanking, I felt it was the only way to make Allen conform. . . . I felt he was my son and it was up to me to straighten him out—instinctively I felt that. . . . I wasn't going to let him have his own way and that caused conflict."[39]

The army air force pilot Joe Hendrickson, who, on his return, got a job as a commercial pilot, when told by his wife that his boys had misbehaved while he was away, took off his belt and whipped them so viciously that a neighbor, hearing the screams, intervened. For the rest of his life, his son, now grown, would shiver whenever he saw "a belt out of its belt loops."[40]

"I came home very much the 'sergeant' in the Marine Corps," George Peabody recounted in his oral history. "Everybody had to do everything I said and do it now, not just for convenience but because it was supposed to be done now. . . . It was a very uncomfortable situation for my family, having this marine intruder come into the house. And then, being disabled, I had to be waited on quite a bit [and that] was very difficult for an undisciplined young wife to swallow along with caring for our two children. And it was difficult for the children because sometimes I was unnecessarily violent with them . . . when they weren't responsive to my demands. The violence was not necessarily physical but vocal; and sudden surges of anger occasionally caused me to jerk them or act in ways toward them that a father normally wouldn't."[41]

Fathers returned convinced that they had to take control, to discipline unruly infants and youngsters, to restore order in the household. There were perpetual, acrimonious fights over child-rearing. Mothers and in-laws, the returning fathers complained, had been too lenient, too forgiving. They had let babies spit out their food, refuse toilet training, make too much noise.

In the Stanford study, sixteen of the nineteen veterans "thought their child was 'spoiled.'" The study, which compared the attitudes of

"He behaved beautifully until you came home."

returning veterans toward their firstborn children with those of non-veterans, found that the veterans complained much more about their children's eating habits, toilet training, sleeping behaviors, and relations with other children. Their major complaint, regarding their sons, was what the investigators referred to as "sex-inappropriate" behaviors. Because the boys had been brought up and were intensely close to their mothers and grandmothers, their fathers feared they lacked "'manly' attributes." More than half of the veterans in the Stolz study reported problems like this. Their boys played only with girls or younger children; they were bullied but refused to defend themselves or fight back; they cried too much, sucked their thumbs, whined. They were sissies.[42]

The veterans who rejected, complained about, or severely punished their firstborn children were not brutes or sadists or incapable of paternal love. Their failures as fathers were confined to the child who had been born and raised while they were away. They had no such problems bonding with children who were born after their return. All but two of the veterans in the Stanford study admitted to interviewers "that they love the second child better than the first. . . . In the family constellation for the war-separated group the first-born is the mother's child and the second-born is the father's child." Their father's disapproval and disdain took its toll. Queried by the Stanford investigators, both parents "described their first-borns as having fairly severe developmental problems." Compared with a control group of children whose fathers had not gone to war, the veterans' children had "more serious problems" with toilet training and sleeping; were "less independent in eating and dressing"; were more fearful and more anxious and had more trouble "getting along with adults and with other children."[43]

The ex-servicemen and their foreign brides, separated from one another at war's end, had perhaps the most difficult time holding their marriages and families intact. The War Brides Act, enacted on December 28, 1945, authorized visas and free transportation to the United States for foreign war brides, with the exception of those who were Asian and "inadmissible," but the delay in reuniting the veterans and their wives was interminable. Ray Ostroff, a Jewish GI from Philadelphia, had married Bella Lewkowicz, a French Jew who had survived the war in hiding. When, in January 1946, he learned that the waiting list for "war bride ships" was six to nine months, he spent $500 of his own money, equivalent to $8,000 in 2023, to buy a plane ticket to bring Bella home.[44]

Roy Duff married his wife, Norma, while stationed in Australia and, after the wedding and a honeymoon in Brisbane, was shipped off with his unit. Norma stayed behind, working and living with her parents. She did not gain passage on a ship to the States until April 11, 1946, when she departed Brisbane with six hundred other war brides for San Francisco. After she disembarked in San Francisco, the Red Cross put her on a train to Montana. When a girl asked what her husband looked like, "I said, 'How do I know what he looks like? I haven't seen him in two years.' . . . We were both scared of each other. . . . We hadn't seen each other and we didn't know how to react to each other. All we'd done is write letters." She spent her first year with her husband in Whitefish, Montana, living, somewhat uncomfortably, with his family. At the time of her interview with the Montana Historical Society in 2002, she and Roy had been married for fifty-eight years.[45]

For Asian brides of American GIs, reunification with their husbands was near impossible. Asians were not "racially admissible" under the 1924 immigration laws. Only the Chinese, who became U.S. allies in 1943, were allowed into the United States, though the quota was set at 105. It would take until August 1946 before Chinese spouses of American military personnel were given the same rights as White spouses to enter the United States as nonquota immigrants. A year later racial restrictions on other Asian spouses were lifted, and they too were permitted to join their husbands.[46]

Black veterans who had married or hoped to marry foreign-born White women had an equally difficult time bringing their wives and children to the United States. On March 2, 1946, Roi Ottley called attention to the tragic consequences in his article "Thousands of Tan GIs Never Will See Their English-Born Children," published in *The Pittsburgh Courier*. "Much has been said in the hub-bub of English brides joining their GI husbands in the United States, but little about the tragic story of what happened to English girls who sought to form such relationships with Negro GI's. What actually happened to many is perhaps one of the blackest pages in the American 'occupation' of the British Isles." Thousands of women and children had been left behind, with little hope of uniting with their husbands and fathers. "In Manchester alone," Ottley reported, "some six hundred babies were born to British women, who were unable to marry their Negro fathers. A Red Cross worker in Manchester told me that some one hundred foundlings had been abandoned on the doorstep of the Liberty Club."* With neither the American nor the British government willing to take any action, "those Africans and West Indian Negroes living in the country [raised] money to rent a house for these wretched little ones who had been abandoned."[47]

Many Black service men and women gave up their attempts at reunion with White spouses left behind. Among those who persevered was Tennyson Henry, a Black sergeant who had fallen in love and hoped to marry Luigiana Nidasio, whom he had met in Italy. Because Henry lived in Santa Monica, California, where interracial marriages were illegal, the couple had to travel to Washington State to be married. "Interracial marriages," *The Chicago Defender* reminded its readers, were illegal in thirty states and legal in eighteen, only one of which, Washington, was "west of the Rockies." Even in Washington, "justices or ministers may refuse to perform mixed marriages . . . if they object." Fortunately, "Henry and Miss Nidasio encountered no trouble in getting their nuptial ceremony performed."[48]

Surprisingly, perhaps, it was those who had the most to come home to who appeared to have the greatest difficulty adjusting to civilian life. Married veterans and those with young children struggled, but too often failed to put back together again the families they had left behind. Though many of the veterans and their wives would re-

---

* The Liberty Clubs were organized by the Red Cross for African American servicemen in Great Britain.

marry after their postwar divorces and many more would find ways to stay together, the effects of those first postwar years would be difficult to forget or erase. The children of these marriages suffered the most. Many would eventually find ways to reunite with their veteran fathers, but only after years had passed. The war would have a lasting effect on all of them.

Chapter 14.

THE BLACK VETERANS COME HOME

In late September 1945, Marjorie McKenzie in *The Pittsburgh Courier* described for her readers the advice that the military, the press, and the experts were offering family members as they prepared to welcome home their husbands, sons, and brothers. "The men should be provided with a quiet, relaxed atmosphere, asked no questions, and made to feel that everything and everybody were just as they had left them." Such instructions, McKenzie observed, might have made sense for White families, but not for southern Black ones who were not going to succeed in creating "a relaxed atmosphere for their boys, no matter how much they may yearn and try. Most of the men I have talked with have told me that tension gripped them in the stomach, clamped itself around their heads and rose in their throats the moment they started walking down the gang plank of the boat that had brought them back to the United States. One young officer said that when he arrived he could feel the burden of jim crow settle like a big, black bird and he hasn't been able to shake it off as yet."[1]

As the historian Jennifer Brooks has written in *Defining the Peace*, "White southerners who adamantly defended Jim Crow during the war steeled themselves for the return of black soldiers, whose uniforms alone were a testament to the threatening consequences of the war. . . . From Fort Valley, Georgia, field agent Horace Bohannon reported to the SRC [Southern Regional Council]* that some white citizens anticipated that the 'returning Negro veteran is dissatisfied with conditions and will inevitabl[y] be a troublemaker.' Others similarly predicted that 'the white southerner is going to "pick on" the returning veteran to try and steer him "back into his place."'"[2]

Southern congressmen, in anticipation of the conflicts to come, fought back attempts to pass anti-poll-tax and antilynching bills. Journalists spread alarms about the coming Black insurrection. White supremacist activists in the Mississippi Delta, where Blacks outnumbered Whites, organized "vigilance committees." The FBI director, J. Edgar Hoover, in a "Survey of Racial Conditions in the U.S. . . . concluded that the war had changed not only the material conditions but also the attitudes of 'the Negro race,' now engaged in new forms of resistance to Jim Crow. 'A new militancy or aggressiveness has been reported to be existent among the Negro population' . . . that could soon sweep across the country and permanently alter its landscape."[3]

The preemptive attack against the Black veterans began on the buses and trains they boarded to bring them home from the separation centers. William Heath, who visited relatives in Jackson after being discharged, "caught the bus to go home, and it was just two or three whites on the front and the back was just full of blacks—couldn't sit down or anything. And I wasn't thinking about I was a soldier and I guess I wasn't thinking but I just took the cloth that said 'colored' and 'white' took it and moved it up two seats further. I looked back and there was some older people on there and I moved it

---

* The SRC, the successor organization to the Commission on Interracial Cooperation, was founded in 1944 to promote racial equality and economic development in the South.

up where they could sit down. And when I got ready to get off the bus . . . the driver reminded me that I'd better not ever do that again. . . . He reminded me that I was back home."[4]

Sergeant Isaac Woodard had served in New Guinea, been under enemy fire, promoted, and awarded a number of medals, including a Purple Heart. He was discharged from Camp Gordon in Georgia on February 12, 1946. Wearing his uniform and medals, he boarded a Greyhound bus for his home in Winnsboro, South Carolina. When he asked the bus driver to stop so he could use a restroom (there were none on the bus), he was told, "God damn it, go back and sit down. I ain't got time to wait," to which Woodard replied, "God damn it, talk to me like I am talking to you. I am a man just like you." The bus driver said nothing, but farther down the road stopped the bus and told Woodard, "Get up, some one outside wants to see you." It was the police chief, Lynwood Shull, who asked Woodard if he had been discharged. "I says 'yes,' just like that. So he said, 'don't say "Yes" to me, say "yes, sir."' . . . He started beating me." Woodard tried to wrest the billy club from him, but a second officer pointed his gun and told him to drop the billy. Shull continued to batter him with the billy, at one point "driving it into my eyeballs." Woodard did not get home that day, or the day after. He spent the night in the jail, woke up blind, was taken to court, fined $50, then moved to the VA hospital thirty miles away, where he was told that there was nothing that could be done to restore his sight. Two months later, his sisters arrived at the hospital to take him to the Bronx, where his parents now lived.[5]

Southern Whites were committed to maintaining segregation on public transportation—and punishing Black veterans who disobeyed Jim Crow restrictions. But of even greater concern was their fear that the returning Black veterans would attempt to register to vote and pressure others to follow their lead. In Georgia, Eugene Talmadge, a candidate in the July 1946 gubernatorial primary, warned that "wise Negroes will stay away from the white folks' ballot boxes on July 17. . . . We are the true friends of the Negroes, always have been and always will be as long as they stay in the definite place we have provided for them."[6]

In Mississippi, Senator Theodore Bilbo was even more direct—and violent—in his attempt to suppress the Black vote. "The white people of Mississippi are sleeping on a volcano," Bilbo warned, "and it is left up to you red-blooded men to do something about it. The white men of this State have a right to resort to any means at their command to stop it. . . . I call on every red-blooded white man to use *any means* to keep the niggers away from the polls. If you don't understand what that means you are just plain dumb."[7]

Elected and appointed state and local officials, courts, and police departments, separately and together, retaliated against Black veterans who dared challenge Jim Crow. In Birmingham, where the police force was led by Commissioner of Public Safety Eugene "Bull" Connor, five Black veterans[*] were, according to the historian John Egerton, murdered by policemen in the first six weeks of 1946.[8] In Atlanta, the local Communist newspaper, the *Daily World*, reported that the police were "beating up discharged and disabled Negro Veterans at the slightest provocation and practicing a general 'get-them-in-line' with post-war attitude. A number of veterans have been arrested on vagrancy and loitering charges because they happened not to be at work when stopped by police for questioning."[9]

In Columbia, Tennessee, a small town forty-three miles south of Nashville, in late February 1946, nineteen-year-old James Stephenson, recently discharged from the navy, accompanied his mother, Gladys, to the radio repair shop, which, she claimed, had taken her money but failed to fix her radio. Billy Fleming, a White army veteran

---

[*] Because Connor controlled the flow of information from inside the city government, we cannot, according to Egerton, be sure of the exact number of Black veterans murdered.

who was apprenticing in the radio shop under the GI Bill, claimed that James had looked at him "in a threatening manner" and punched him in the back of the head. Stephenson returned the punch, and the two veterans, one Black, one White, tumbled through a small window. James and his mother were arrested, pleaded guilty, and paid a $50 fine, but instead of being released, they were charged with attempted murder and removed to the county jail. As word of the confrontation spread through the town, young White men "gathered in the town square, drunk, armed, angry. Many, though not all, were in their late teens and early twenties. World War II veterans," according to the historian Gail O'Brien, "comprised the most volatile element in the crowd."[10]

The Stephensons were not released until 5:00 that evening. James was hidden in the "Bottoms," the Black district of town, to protect him from the lynching the White mob was already talking about. Black veterans armed themselves, set up lookout posts, and drove Stephenson away to safety. When four local policemen were shot as they marched into the "Bottoms" to locate and arrest him, the governor ordered the Tennessee Highway Patrol into Columbia. Sixty to seventy-five patrolmen arrived, followed by a crowd of armed Whites, veterans among them. Homes and businesses in the Black district were ransacked, cash registers looted, property destroyed, weapons seized, and hundreds arrested. Three days later, after calm had returned, two of the Black men who had been arrested were shot and killed after one of them grabbed a gun seized in the raid and stored in the jail office where they were being interrogated.

A federal grand jury was empaneled, but the all-White jurors refused to bring charges against any law enforcement officials. Twenty-five Blacks were subsequently tried for murder in state court. In the end, only one served a sentence, which was, in itself, rather remarkable. "Perhaps the most significant message to come out of the Columbia incident," Egerton concludes in *Speak Now Against the Day*, "was this: Besieged black citizens had stood up and fought back, and lived to tell about it."[11]

For months to come, the Columbia "race riot," as it was commonly referred to, made headlines in the African American press. The events—and the press coverage—frightened Whites throughout the South. The result was not an end to the violence against Black veterans and citizens, but an acceleration. "The months of July and August [1946] witnessed the heaviest lynching outbreak in recent years," *Race Relations* reported in its August–September issue. "During this period there were six confirmed reports of lynchings and at least three unconfirmed allegations of lynching." The victims included Maceo Snipes, a veteran who after becoming the first Black to register to vote in Taylor County, Georgia, was shot to death on his home porch, and the veteran John Jones of Minden, Louisiana, who had been marked as "uppity" and a "smart nigger" for, among other things, bringing home "a foreign pistol, a German Luger." Jones was arrested for reportedly entering a White woman's yard with his seventeen-year-old nephew. They were released when the woman refused to press charges. On their way home, they were waylaid by a group of White men who tortured the veteran to death with blowtorch and meat cleaver.[12]

The most egregious of the lynchings took place at Moore's Ford in Walton County, Georgia. Roger Malcolm, a Black sharecropper, charged with stabbing a White farmer, was on his way home from the jail where he had posted a bond. With him were his pregnant wife, Dorothy, the veteran George Dorsey and his wife, Mae, and the White landowner for whom Malcolm worked. Their car was stopped by a mob of thirty armed but unmasked Whites who tied the men to a tree. When Dorothy Malcolm recognized several men in the mob and asked them to let her husband and George Dorsey go, she, Mrs. Dorsey, and their husbands were shot and killed. Malcolm was castrated. One of the mob leaders later explained that George Dorsey had to be killed because he had been a "good nigger" before the war, but afterward, like other Black veterans, "thought he was as good as any white people." The murders were widely and graphically reported in the national press through the late summer of 1946. President Truman demanded a full investigation. The FBI director, J. Edgar Hoover, assigned twenty agents to the case who interviewed almost three thousand people and compiled more than ten thousand pages of reports. The FBI then sought the indictments of ten suspects. Only one was indicted—"for lying to an FBI agent."[13]

Black veterans in the South were fully aware that the resurgence of lynchings and violence in 1946 was a direct response to White fears that, having served in the military, they would no longer be willing to accept the Jim Crow regime they had lived under before the war. Clemon Jones recalled of his return to Jackson, Mississippi, that "if you'd meet one [White person] on the streets, or two of them on the streets, they'd look at you like you was an alligator or something, afraid or something, they was going to bite."[14]

And what do you do with a dangerous alligator? You shoot it. According to a Baltimore *Afro-American* editorial on August 31, 1946, "Reporters covering the reign of terror which has held a large part of Dixie in its grip for several weeks have pointed out that most of the South's venom is directed against men who have served in the armed forces of the U.S. . . . The blood which some of them spilled on the battle field was not enough to guarantee the fundamental liberties of which they heard so much. Events of the past few weeks demonstrate conclusively that without Federal intervention, the lives of those who dwell in the South are not safe. . . . Local law enforcement officials have not only shown themselves powerless, but in some instances those supposed guardians of law and order have been in the vanguard of the mobbists."[15]

That White southerners did all they could to reenforce segregation and keep Black veterans from voting came as no surprise to politicians, journalists, and public opinion outside the South. What was shocking and frightening, at least for John Gunther, who published *Inside U.S.A.* in May 1947, was the unanticipated and startling increase in violence and lynching. "I had heard words like 'discrimination' and 'prejudice' all my life, but I had no concrete knowledge, no fingertip realization, of what lies behind them. I knew that 'segregation' was a problem; I had no conception at all of the grim enormousness of the problem." He was sickened by the racist violence, an "effect," he believed, of the war. "Almost every victim of lynching since the war has been a veteran." Lynching was a crime, one seldom prosecuted and never punished, but it was much more than that. "The significance of lynching is often not the crime itself, horrible as that may be, but the terrorizing and demoralizing effect of the *threat* of lynching on a community."[16]

In the fall of 1946, Walter White of the NAACP, responding to the surge in lynchings, invited representatives of forty civil rights, religious, and labor organizations to join a new coalition, the National Emergency Committee Against Mob Violence. On September 19, White and members of the committee met with President Truman and urged him to publicly support antilynching legislation and "rouse the American people by radio, press and other media to oppose actively every form of mob violence." Truman listened sympathetically, then dismissed their proposals. "Everyone," he told them, according to David Niles, his administrative assistant who was present at the meeting, "seems to believe the president by himself can do anything he wishes to on such matters as this. But the president is helpless unless he is backed by public opinion." Niles intervened and suggested that a "blue-ribbon committee" be established "to make recommendations for federal action.... Walter White warmed to the idea and pledged to work with the president's staff to put together a first-rate committee."[17]

On September 23, 1946, four days after White's group had visited the White House, a second delegation, this one of members of the American Crusade to End Lynching, led by Paul Robeson, met with the president and presented him with an open letter, signed by the nation's most respected civil rights, religious, and education leaders and entertainment celebrities, including Henry Sloane Coffin, president of the Union Theological Seminary, W. E. B. Du Bois, Albert Einstein, John Garfield, Oscar Hammerstein II, Yip Harburg, Lena Horne, Gene Kelly, Alan Ladd, Canada Lee, Joe E. Lewis, Burgess Meredith, Gregory Peck, Edward G. Robinson, Artie Shaw, Frank Sinatra, and Orson Welles. "A wave of lynchings and mob violence is sweeping across America," the letter declared. "Though its roots are in the South, it marks the whole nation with the scourge of lawlessness, violence, and race hate.... The total number of recorded lynchings during the last six months exceeds the number for the entire period of the war. At least 41 have been reported since V-J Day—in Georgia, Louisiana, Florida, South Carolina, and Mississippi. The number has mounted monthly. In almost every instance, the victim was a veteran, recently returned from service in a war to win freedom from fear. The lynchings are intended to strike fear into the hearts of Negro servicemen who have come back to their homes determined to vote and take an equal part in the birth of a democratic South."[18]

In the evening after their visit to the White House, the Robeson group held a mass meeting at the Lincoln Memorial to mark the eighty-fourth anniversary of Lincoln's Emancipation Proclamation with songs and speeches, punctuated by eyewitness accounts of lynchings. Similar antilynching rallies were held across the country; newspapers published editorials, urging the president to act. In New York City, Mayor William O'Dwyer designated September 23, the day of the Robeson group's visit to the White House and mass meeting on the Mall, as "End Lynching Day."[19]

Truman did not respond to requests that he issue a public condemnation of lynching. Instead, on December 5, 1946, after the midterm elections, he announced the organization of the President's Committee on Civil Rights, which his aide, David Niles, had recommended. The committee's report was released a year later. It decried the "devastating consequences of lynchings," which, it emphasized, "go far beyond what is shown by counting the victims. When a person is lynched and lynchers go unpunished, thousands wonder where the evil will appear again and what mischance may produce another victim.... Lynching is the ultimate threat by which his inferior status is driven home to the Negro. As a terrorist device it reinforces all the other disabilities placed upon him. The threat of lynching always hangs over the head of the southern Negro." Because federal laws did nothing to prevent lynchings or punish the perpetrators, the committee called on Congress to enact an antilynching law.[20]

On February 2, 1948, Truman requested that Congress adopt the program outlined in his Civil Rights report, including a federal antilynching bill. Eugene "Goober" Cox of Georgia responded by shouting from the House floor that the president's program "sounds like the platform of the Communist party. The Harlem district of New York still is wielding more influence with the Administration than the entire white South." Senator John Eastland of Mississippi declared that "Truman's message to Congress was proof that the government was controlled by 'mongrel minorities' out to 'Harlemize' the nation. Texas senator Tom Connally called it a lynching of the Constitution." Southern Democrats began discussions on seceding from the Democratic Party.[21]

An antilynching bill was passed by the House Committee on the Judiciary in June 1948, but never brought to the floor. The Senate Committee on the Judiciary watered down the House bill, but not enough to garner any southern support. In July 1948, the Senate adjourned without taking a vote. It would be another three-quarters of a century before the Senate approved the Emmett Till Antilynching Act, which President Joseph Biden signed into law on March 29, 2022.[22]

The violence, the lynchings, and the failure of the federal government to protect them did not deter southern Black veterans from organizing and participating in voter registration campaigns. In Georgia, between 135,000 and 150,000 Black voters were registered in 1946 alone. "Black voters helped to defeat entrenched political machines in Savannah and Augusta and to elect a new mayor in Macon in 1947. . . . Other southern states made significant, if less striking, progress." Still, as Jennifer Brooks concludes, these successes "hardly tell the whole story. Ultimately, the voter registration drives of the postwar 1940s failed to evolve into ongoing grassroots movements. . . . The potential for progressive racial change that seemed so promising within the first couple of years after the war quickly dissipated."[23]

The backlash against the Black veterans who attempted to organize voter registration drives or register themselves was near universal and often violent. Those who remained in the South understood only too well the penalties that would be paid for registering to vote—for them and their families. Some were willing to take the risk, but for most the first priority was not fighting a losing battle against Jim Crow but completing their schooling, getting good jobs, making money to support their families, and establishing themselves in leadership positions in their communities. "What most black ex-servicemen wanted," Horace Bohannon, a veteran and field agent for the Southern Regional Council, recalled in an interview with Jennifer Brooks, "was a decent job. They wanted to work. They wanted to make it."[24]

Having served their country and picked up new skills in doing so, they sought jobs better than the ones they had held—or were pointed toward—before the war. "The returning Negro veteran," Vincent Malveaux of the American Council on Race Relations reported after a fact-finding tour of twenty-one cities, was "more concerned with his

DEMOCRACY: *government by the people collectively by elected representatives. (Webster's)*

opportunity in the fields of new employment rather than with his rights to old employment under the Selective Training and Service Act of 1940. The old job so very often was that of the mop and broom type. In many instances his army experience has given him deeper ambitions and a keener awareness of his possibilities of development."[25]

Henry Murphy, who returned from Europe to Hattiesburg, Mississippi, in 1946, told the historian Neil McMillen that he did not attempt to register to vote until a decade later. "In '46 I was trying to get a job. I wasn't thinking too much about that. I was trying to get situated.... I had some children. I was trying to find a place for them to stay.... I didn't have all of the necessities that we needed.... And I could not take care of political situations when I needed the necessity of a place to stay and my family, you know, this and that and the other, food and so forth."[26]

While the majority of veterans, like Murphy, stayed away, a small but significant number attempted to register. On July 2, 1946, Medgar Evers's birthday, he and his brother Charles, also a veteran, and four friends "walked to the polls. . . . Not a Negro was on the streets, and when we got to the courthouse, the clerk said he wanted to talk with us. When we got into his office, some 15 or 20 armed white men surged in behind us, men I had grown up with, played with. We split up and went home. Around town, Negroes said we had been whipped, beaten up and run out of town. Well, in a way we were whipped, I guess, but I made up my mind then that it would not be like that again—at least not for me."[27]

"This incident," his wife, Myrlie, recalled in her autobiography, *For Us, the Living*, might have "helped Medgar decide to return to school" instead of continuing his campaign for Black voter registration. With the GI Bill paying his tuition and a living allowance, he got his high school diploma at Alcorn A&M's laboratory high school, then enrolled in the college, majoring in business administration. After graduation, Evers did not return to his hometown of Decatur, Mississippi, but took a job with the Magnolia Mutual Insurance Company, which had been founded by Dr. T. R. M. Howard and other Negro businessmen, and moved to Mound Bayou, a tiny, all-Black town in the Delta. In 1952, six years after his discharge, he joined Dr. Howard, local businessmen, and a group of veterans who would become active leaders of the emerging civil rights campaign, including Aaron Henry and Amzie Moore, in the Regional Council of Negro Leadership, a new civil rights and economic development organization in the Delta. Together, they organized a boycott of gas stations that refused to allow Black customers to use their restrooms. In late November 1954, Evers applied to and was rejected by the University of Mississippi Law School. Soon afterward, he left the insurance company to become NAACP field secretary in Mississippi, a position he would hold until his assassination in June 1963.[28]

Amzie Moore, who would become a key organizer in SNCC (Student Nonviolent Coordinating Committee) voter registration campaigns in Mississippi in the early 1960s, had served in Burma, India, and China before returning to Cleveland, Mississippi, in 1946 and taking up his old job as a janitor at the post office. Moore, who claimed in an oral history that he had "lost his fear of whites" in the army and was already a member of the NAACP, decided, nonetheless, to focus his attention, as Evers had, on establishing himself in business. "I had in mind one time to get rich. I thought this was the answer," he told Howell Raines in the mid-1970s. "I built a brick house, and I built a service station, and I had a store. . . . I was buying lots and trying to get ahead, and suddenly one day somebody came to see me and asked me if I would go out east of Mound Bayou. They wanted me to look at something, and I went out there, and I went in the house. . . . There was a woman there with about fourteen kids, naked from the waist down. . . . They were burning cotton stalks . . . to keep warm. Not a single bed in the house. . . . Just looking at that I think really changed my whole outlook on life. I kinda figured it was a sin to think in terms of trying to get rich in view of what I'd seen." Moore, who had not previously been "involved in civil rights activity," joined the Regional Council of Negro Leadership in 1951 and was named president of the Cleveland NAACP branch in 1955.[29]

Aaron Henry, another Mississippi veteran and future movement leader, registered to vote when he returned to Clarksdale and was, in July 1946, the first Negro in Coahoma County to vote in a primary election. To support himself and his family, he planned to use his GI Bill benefits to train as a pharmacist. Since there was no pharmacy school open to African Americans in Mississippi, he enrolled at Xavier University, a small Black Catholic college in New Orleans, and got a degree in pharmacology. He passed his qualifying exams in Mississippi, married, and opened a pharmacy in Clarksdale in 1950. Like Evers and Moore, Henry joined the Regional Council of Negro

Leadership in 1951 and, in 1953, was instrumental in organizing an NAACP chapter in Clarksdale. He would be catapulted into full-time activism, like his veteran colleagues in Mississippi, only in the mid-1950s.[30]

Hosea Williams, the future civil rights leader who would work alongside Martin Luther King Jr., was discharged from the army on October 30, 1946. On traveling by bus home to Georgia, still in his uniform, he had filled an empty cup with water from the wrong fountain. "And those white men beat me until I was unconscious. They thought I was dead . . . and called the undertaker to come and pick me up. . . . But my heart was beating, and they carried me to a hospital in Thomasville, Georgia . . . a veteran hospital, and I laid there eight weeks, crying. Hating and wishing that I had fought on the side of Hitler." Williams recovered, returned to high school, got his diploma, then undergraduate and advanced degrees in chemistry under the GI Bill, and a well-paying job at the Savannah office of the U.S. Department of Agriculture's Chemical Division. "I thought you could escape Black America by being educated and professional and being rich, and you just cain't do it." After almost twenty years as an "upper middle class Negro," with a new Cadillac every year and annual vacations in Bermuda, "it finally began to come to me, you're the same thing that the house n****s was in slavery. They're using you, Hosea, to keep your own people down. And brother, I began to take note and to rebel."[31]

These and other future civil rights leaders had learned overseas that segregation was not ordained by some superior being, but was a man-made and enforced social system, designed to sustain White supremacy in the South. It was inevitable that this system fall, but how and when, they did not know. What they did know was that conditions in the South in 1946 were not conducive to successfully challenging Jim Crow. The White community and its elected leaders were prepared to use every means, including violence, to keep Blacks from voting; their neighbors were not yet ready to join them in a sustained campaign against White supremacy; the federal government was not going to protect them or punish those who used violence to block challenges to Jim Crow; and they lacked sufficient White allies, including veterans' groups, to support their campaigns.

Throughout the South, Black veterans were denied the right to vote or run for elected office. The opposite was the case for their White counterparts, who were vigorously courted as voters and candidates by political leaders of both parties.

Sixteen million men and women had been mobilized for war, more than 90 percent of them White. Should they vote as a bloc, they could, in the 1946 midterms, the 1948 presidential election, and for a long time thereafter, play a decisive role in local, state, and national politics. In the halls of Congress, the White House, state and city capitals across the country, and wherever the political class gathered, the question that kept everyone awake at night was how the veterans were going to vote.

Chapter 15.

THE WHITE VETERANS' VOTE

"The most interesting political development in 1946," the veteran journalist and political commentator Raymond Moley* observed in February, "will be the way in which veterans participate in politics and cast their votes. Politicians are already quaking in their boots about it. Experienced campaigners are free to confess that they don't know what veterans will do." Moley's only prediction, shared by party leaders on both sides of the aisle, was that returning veterans would most likely vote for other veterans. The party that nominated the most veterans was going to have the advantage moving forward. Early proof of the efficacy of such a strategy, Moley pointed out, was the political ascendance of Harold Stassen, who, at age thirty-six, had resigned as Minnesota governor to enlist in the navy. Discharged in November 1945, he was by early 1946 a front-runner for the Republican nomination for president in 1948.[1]

Dozens of elected officials had, like Stassen, resigned to enlist in

---

* Moley, once a supporter and adviser to FDR, had turned against him and become one of the New Deal's most consistent and virulent critics.

the armed services, some so that on their return from war they could campaign as veterans, not stay-at-home politicians. Joseph McCarthy, who was, as a circuit court judge in Wisconsin, exempt from the draft, enhanced his reputation as a fearless man's man by enlisting in the marines in 1942. Big Jim Folsom of Alabama, who had been defeated when he ran for Congress in 1936 and 1938 and for governor in 1942, recognized early in the war that a military tour, preferably in combat, would enhance his future status as a candidate. His problem was that he was six feet, eight inches tall and, for that reason alone, was rejected when he tried to enlist in the army. He volunteered instead for the merchant marines. Carl Zeidler, the mayor of Milwaukee, resigned to join the navy. Strom Thurmond, at thirty-nine too old to be drafted, left his position as judge on the Eleventh Judicial Circuit in South Carolina to enlist. The Chicago alderman and future Illinois senator Paul Douglas joined the marines the day after he lost a primary election for the Senate in 1942. He was fifty, far beyond the age at which he might be drafted. William O'Dwyer, aged fifty-one, took a leave of absence from his position as Kings County (Brooklyn) district attorney—and a $15,000 pay cut—to accept a commission as major in the army.[2]

Twenty-seven members of Congress also resigned their seats or took leaves of absence to serve in the armed forces. Washington congressman and future senator Warren Magnuson served on an aircraft carrier in the Pacific. Henry Cabot Lodge Jr. while still a senator served as an Army Reserve officer until July 1942, when President Roosevelt ordered congressmen in the military to either return to Washington or leave the armed forces. After winning re-election in November 1942, Lodge resigned his Senate seat and returned to active duty.[3]

The politicians who served in the war were almost uniformly successful in running for office again when they returned. The future

Illinois governor William G. Stratton, elected to Congress in 1940 and state treasurer in 1942, enlisted in the navy in 1944 and on his return home was elected to an at-large congressional seat. Warren Magnuson from Washington, Henry Cabot Lodge Jr. from Massachusetts, Joseph McCarthy from Wisconsin, Paul Douglas from Illinois, and Lyndon Johnson from Texas won Senate seats; Strom Thurmond was elected governor of South Carolina; William O'Dwyer, New York City mayor in 1945. Carl Zeidler never made it back to Milwaukee—his ship was sunk by a German U-boat near Cape Town, South Africa, on his first and only voyage as a naval officer—but his brother won election as mayor in 1948 and was re-elected in 1952 and 1956.

The prewar officeholders were but a portion of the veterans who ran for office in 1946 and by far the most successful. They were joined on primary and general election ballots by a host of political neophytes who on returning home decided to run for office. "It is a natural for the returning veteran to think of a term or two in the lawmaking body as a means of getting set for his life work back home," Raymond Brooks reported for the *Austin American-Statesman* in January 1946.[4]

Jacob Javits, who had served as an officer with the army's Chemical Warfare Service, ran for Congress in 1946. "The time was right. The war was over and many returning veterans were getting ready to run for office. A new era was beginning and I wanted to be part of it." He introduced himself to the voters in a letter to the editor of the *New York Herald Tribune* in February. "Many veterans in all walks of life are coming back imbued with a sense of responsibility for what goes on in the world. . . . Twelve million strong, young men and women veterans constitute an enormous voting strength. . . . The Republican party should be especially ready for the veterans' participation."[5]

The Republicans jumped to an early lead in the veteran candidate sweepstakes. In Cook County, Illinois, Republicans had a twelve-to-one edge in veterans nominated for office. In California, the Republican Party outpaced the Democrats in locating veteran candidates. Richard Milhous Nixon of Whittier, California, recently discharged from the navy, was invited by local Republican leaders to run against the five-term incumbent congressman and New Deal advocate Jerry Voorhis. Accepting the invitation, Nixon noted that Voorhis's "lack of a military record won't help him, particularly since most of the boys will be home and voting." Nixon never let voters forget that he had spent the last four years in the navy. He avoided mention of the fact that he had been an officer and campaigned "as just another civilian who had fought for his country." To reach as many veterans as possible, he joined the VFW and American Legion and established three different veterans' groups in his congressional district.[6]

On the other side of the continent, John Fitzgerald Kennedy, like Nixon, with no prior political experience, "introduced himself to voters as a combat veteran returning to help lead the country for which he had fought." He referred often to his older brother, Joseph Kennedy Jr., who had died in a flight over Germany on August 12, 1944, and established a VFW post named for him. Just days before the primary election his campaign used his father's money to mail voters reprints of John Hersey's article about his own heroism in the Pacific.[7]

In Wisconsin, Judge Joe McCarthy, now "Tail Gunner" Joe, never dropped an opportunity to talk about his war service while accusing his primary opponent, Robert La Follette Jr., of sitting "out the war" while "he and millions of other guys kept you from talking Japanese."[8]

In Grand Rapids, Michigan, Gerald Ford, running for Congress in 1948, called attention to his military service when he "rented a

Navy surplus Quonset hut for his headquarters, painted it red, white, and blue, and set it up on space he leased in the parking lot of . . . a popular downtown department store."[9]

Though they proudly pointed out their military service, the veteran candidates did not campaign on issues that would benefit veterans as a bloc, in part, perhaps, because they did not want to call attention to the generous rewards the government already offered them. To ask for more GI benefits might alienate the majority of voters who were not receiving any. "If veterans, considering their number and influence, ever get off to a flying start as a pressure group after bonuses and special privileges," Jacob Javits warned, "it will be bad for the country."[10]

To avoid alienating the majority of voters who were not veterans, they put their uniforms in the closet and toured their districts in blue suits, when they could afford them. Orval Faubus, running for county judge in Arkansas, with only a few civilian outfits to his name, campaigned in his "army garments. One day a friend approached and said to me in intense, subdued tones, 'For God's sake! Get out of those army clothes! It's costing you votes every day.'" Richard Nixon was more fortunate. "Pat had given Dick's outdated suits away during the war, and he couldn't keep campaigning in uniform. Roy Day [one of his backers] prevailed upon a Pomona haberdasher, who dug out a suit from the store's basement. Nixon wore it for months."[11]

The veterans, in particular those running against incumbents or party regulars, made much of their youth and energy. Kennedy's campaign slogan, "The New Generation Offers a Leader," could have been used—and, in one way or another, was—by almost every other veteran candidate. Nixon campaign billboards declared it was TIME FOR A CHANGE.[12]

Strom Thurmond in South Carolina and Big Jim Folsom in Alabama who had held office before the war campaigned nonetheless as new-generation, antiestablishment reformers. They opposed poll taxes, supported economic development programs and paved roads, and favored increased expenditures for education, including for African Americans. They were, they proudly proclaimed, not backed, funded, or supported in any way by the political bosses who ruled the Democratic Party. If and when elected, they would be beholden to the people and no one else. It was taken for granted—and they didn't have to spend much time proclaiming it—that they would also do whatever was necessary to protect White supremacy and Jim Crow. Folsom stumped the state with the Strawberry Pickers, his "hillbilly band," a suds bucket to collect donations (and call attention to the fact that no big-pocketed bosses were contributing to his campaign), and "a corn-shuck mop which he promised to use in Montgomery to scrub out the capital and wash away 'the political ring that is strangling Alabama.'" Thurmond compared his opponent and the bosses backing him to the "'gangs' of 'scheming, conniving, selfish men' who had gained power in Germany and Italy. 'I was willing to risk my life to stamp out such gangs in Europe.... I intend to devote my future to wiping out the stench and stain [that have] smeared the government of South Carolina.'"[13]

In Georgia, "good government veterans, as they often labeled themselves, organized voter registration drives, rallied popular support behind moderate candidates, ... blasted local incumbents as impediments to change," and won 20 percent of the seats in the General Assembly in 1946. What they did not do, if only because it would have destroyed any chance of victory, was challenge White supremacy and Black voter suppression.[14]

The southern veterans' campaign against the party bosses reached its crescendo in the 1946 primary in Athens, Tennessee, which attracted national attention when it turned violent. The incumbent sheriff and his deputies, backed by the party bosses, recognizing they were about to be outvoted, removed three ballot boxes and carried them off to the jailhouse. The veterans armed themselves and deployed outside the jailhouse, demanding the return of the ballot boxes. Shots were fired and the deputies, outnumbered and outgunned, surrendered. The stolen ballot boxes were retrieved, and the county court declared the members of the GI slate duly elected.[15]

The journalists who reported on the event were divided on the outcome. The veterans had prevailed against the bosses, but only because they were armed and had employed violence to prevent them from stealing the election. Here was another frightening instance of the dangers posed by the return of young men who had been armed and taught to fight by the military. The "shooting veterans," *Time* magazine observed, "had spectacularly rid themselves of one type of tyranny. But thoughtful citizens knew they had set an ominous precedent." Harold Hinton of *The New York Times* had much the same reaction. "In the eyes of the veterans who won the pitched battle here on election night, Aug. 1, the incident was nothing less than the uprising of the people to regain their liberties from tyrannical and unlawfully acting officials. To the outsider with a more objective point of view, it appears as a dangerous, desperate expedient which was lucky to come off with no deaths and only two dozen known wounded." Hinton predicted that the bosses, in Tennessee and elsewhere, had learned their lessons, would loosen their grip on the ballot boxes, reduce graft and abuse, and, in doing so, give "the veterans nothing concrete to shoot at either politically or militarily."[16]

In the end, the veterans' vote turned out to be little more than "a chimera." The prognosticators were wrong. Veteran voters were not automatically drawn to veteran candidates. On the contrary, the ex-GIs were, as Harold Hinton concluded, "in matters of general political scope . . . as divided in their ballots as any other group of American citizens of comparable size."[17]

As the 1946 primary season drew to a close, it had become clear that there would be no political revolution or, indeed, any noteworthy changes wrought by the return of the veterans. As *The New York Times* reported on August 12, thirty veterans had won their primary races, but thirty-four others had been "defeated in contests for ten Senate and eighteen House nominations, and in six Governorship candidacies."[18]

The New York Times, in its post-primary election editorial, called attention to the failed prophecies "about the veteran [and] his behavior at the ballot box. . . . Long before the end of the war the soothsayers were preparing us for what the boys would do to this sadly imperfect country of ours when they came back from the war and took charge of things. . . . The forecasters were sure that the American status quo was in for some rough handling from the returned GIs and predicted far-flung changes would be decidedly in a leftward direction. Actually the nation-wide swing in the primary elections this fading summer has been away from the left."[19]

The week before Election Day, Sam Stavisky reported in *The Washington Post* that though "the veteran vote—estimated anywhere from eight million upward—holds statistically-wonderful possibilities," there was no indication that it was going to have any major effect on election results. "The fact is that the former GIs don't vote as a bloc. . . . Nor is there any indication that the veterans, as a group, are more liberal in their political thinking than the rest of the country." The election results confirmed Stavisky's analysis. In Arkansas, usually a reliably Democratic state, the future governor, Orval Faubus, lost his campaign for county judge, as did five of the six veterans running as Democrats for county offices. Nationwide, the Republicans gained fifty-five seats in the House, twelve in the Senate, and control over both houses for the first time since 1929.[20]

The veterans did not vote as a bloc, because, by the summer and fall of 1946, they did not regard themselves as members of a bloc. Nor, despite the rhetoric of candidates like Kennedy and Nixon, were they committed to banding together to lead the nation in new directions. They had put away their uniforms and were trying to put the war behind them and forge new identities as civilians. Explaining his and the defeat of the other Democratic veteran candidates, Orville Faubus concluded that by November 1946, "the urgency of the war was gone. The high appreciation that once was felt for the men who left home to defend the country, had faded away."[21]

Veteran status was a double-edged sword. Those who were successful as candidates were those whom the public already knew—and had previously voted for, like Joe McCarthy and the dozens of other officeholders who had enlisted in the armed forces—or those with substantial fortunes like Kennedy, those who ran for office in safe districts, and those with other credentials, like Javits and Nixon, who had law degrees. Otherwise, as Faubus noted, "the veterans were at a disadvantage . . . in the battle of civilian life, in politics, business and otherwise. . . . Many were worn and weary, others shell shocked and wounded. Oftimes they were broke."[22] To get elected, they had to convince voters that they were fit, hearty, and psychologically sound, that they were not among those who had been damaged by the war. This was not an easy task to accomplish.

Expectations that the veterans' vote would push the nation leftward, or toward the extreme right, were misplaced, a symptom of the fears and anxieties with which they were greeted on their return from war. As Samuel Stouffer concluded, based on surveys he conducted for the research branch of the army, the returning soldier tended to think of the postwar world "in terms of his own job and his chances to compete either for security or advancement. . . . The soldier did not come home to reform America—there was little trace of any such attitude in responses at any period of the war." This was true of White and Black veterans alike, though for different reasons. Whites did not, by and large, envision the need for any radical social changes. Blacks did, but recognized the impossibility of overturning Jim Crow on their own.

Part 3
Readjusting to Civilian Life

"Haw! You shoulda seen where I spent my nights last winter."

Chapter 16.

"HOME, SWEET HOME IS A NIGHTMARE CRISIS"

For many if not most of the veterans, homecoming was a bittersweet experience, marked by elation tempered by fear of what was to come. "Concern about future jobs led the list in personal anxieties," Samuel Stouffer of the Research Branch of the War Department concluded, based on "various surveys in the closing year of the war.... In the background of the thinking of many was the probability of a postwar depression, which had been widely predicted." A June 1945 study disclosed that 56 percent of GIs "anticipated a widespread depression, 15% were undecided."[1]

The veterans' fears were fed by the economic projections of government officials. On May 10, two days after V-E Day, Fred Vinson, Truman's director of war mobilization and reconversion, predicted that 1.5 million civilian workers were going to be laid off in the next six months, another 3 million in the following six. In mid-August, the public's anxieties were heightened by John Snyder, Vinson's successor, who warned that "the jobless legions were destined to grow. [He] predicted there would be 3,000,000 unemployed war workers by November and possibly 8,000,000 by spring."[2]

The large number of layoffs came as no surprise, certainly not to the authors of the GI Bill, who, anticipating them, had included specific provisions "to ease the strain during demobilization" and keep the veterans occupied and off unemployment lines. Title IV provided job counseling and placement services and $20-a-week readjustment allowances for unemployed veterans (equivalent to $355 in 2024 dollars)* for up to fifty-two weeks. While the general public, the press, and the veterans and their families referred to this money as "unemployment pay," Major Thomas M. Nial in his August 1945 "Veterans' Postwar Notebook" columns for *The Atlanta Constitution* pointed out that the GI Bill had labeled them "readjustment allowances." His advice to the veterans was that they should have no compunctions about collecting their $20-a-week checks until they had found jobs that they liked and "with a chance of being permanent."[3]

Similar advice was offered by the country music songwriters and performers Bill Carlisle and Lonnie Glosson in "Rockin' Chair Money," which Carlisle recorded in November 1946, Red Foley and Johnny Tyler and their respective groups covered in March 1947, and Hank Williams Jr. in 1960. The term had been used by New Deal critics to deride unemployment insurance, but Carlisle and Glosson claimed instead that the veterans collecting their $20 checks had earned every penny the government was giving them:

> Now I got rockin' chair money
> But I got it the hard, hard way
> I fought in every battle
> From the start to the VJ day.[4]

The readjustment allowance provisions of the GI Bill served several functions: They rewarded the veterans for their service, soothed

---

* Estimate based on changes in Consumer Price Index, www.measuringworth.com/calculators/uscompare/relativevalue.php.

the anger of those who returned angry because they had sacrificed and so many others had not, and pumped dollars into the pockets of the servicemen and, from there, into a reviving consumer economy. John Snyder, director of the Office of War Mobilization and Reconversion, had predicted that unemployment numbers might well reach eight million by the spring of 1946. He was off by more than five million. In his April 1, 1946, "Report to the President, the Senate, and the House of Representatives," he offered as a major reason for this huge forecasting error "the temporary withdrawal of some 2 million veterans, who were resting, reestablishing homes, or attending to personal affairs before looking for jobs, the vast majority of them while supporting themselves on their readjustment allowance checks."[5]

To receive their $20 a week, the veterans had to pay a visit to their local United States Employment Service (USES) offices, which certified those for whom no "suitable" job was available as unemployed and eligible for readjustment allowance checks. Veterans not ready to return to work, so long as they were White and male, had little trouble getting approved. "You don't have to take any job at all," a New York City veteran told the journalist and historian Henry Pringle. "It's easy. You apply for every job the USES refers you to, of course. But you have a few beers on the way and then blow your breath in the boss's face. Or maybe you talk a little red. He don't want you naturally."[6]

Thomas Varns of Springfield, Illinois, had served as a medic with Patton's Third Army. In high school, he had learned to operate an engine lathe. On his return to Springfield, he tried to get a job in a machine shop, but because the pay was only $28 a week and he could collect $20 a week in readjustment allowance checks, he "laid around and just went and got into trouble.... I stayed up half the night and did things I shouldn't do."[7]

Joseph Argenzio of Bay Ridge, Brooklyn, had no such luck. After two weeks at home drawing government checks because he was unemployed, "my father said to me one morning, 'Joseph, we don't have any bums in this family. Go get a job.'

"I said, 'I've been away three years.'

"'Go-get-a-job!'"[8]

Readjustment allowance checks enabled the returning veterans to buy a bit of time before looking for work or enrolling in school or college, but they offered them no assistance whatsoever in solving their most immediate and pressing problem: finding a decent, affordable home for themselves and their families. The housing shortage that had marked the Depression had intensified during the war years. In 1925, builders had begun construction on 937,000 units; in 1935, on 221,000; in 1944, on 142,000. There were far too few affordable and available houses to buy or rent for the returning veterans, particularly those with wives and children.[9]

Married veterans moved in with their parents or in-laws. In the small midwestern city studied by Robert Havighurst and his team of researchers, almost every married vet was living with relatives. "Their ultimate aim, of course, was to establish a new home, but in trying to accomplish this they were faced not only with the shortage of housing but with inflated prices in real estate, lumber, home furnishings, and anything else a permanent household requires."[10]

Jack Gutman, who had served as a navy medic, returned to his parents' house in New York City before meeting a young woman and getting married. He and his wife moved in with her family until they found a home of their own to rent. "Apartments were hard to get at that time. Our first apartment was shared with a woman who rented us the back part of the apartment she owned. We had to share the kitchen. The only problem was that she was an alcoholic, and many times we had to pick her up, and put her to bed. Not a way to start married life."[11]

The housing shortage, already in crisis mode, intensified as more and more GIs were discharged. Congressman Wright Patman, Democrat of Texas, sounded the alarm on the floor of the House in mid-October 1945. "Every boat from Europe and the far Pacific brings thousands of our servicemen back to us. They are pouring home at every port.... That is not some problem to confront us in the hazy future. It is here, now, demanding action." It was essential that government do something to alleviate the housing shortage, not only because the veterans deserved this assistance, but because if nothing were done, there was no telling how they might respond. "Our housing problem must be solved speedily if we are to avoid the seething unrest that might provoke housing riots here."[12]

By early November, John Blandford, administrator of the National Housing Agency, predicted that an additional two million families would be forced "to 'double up' on housing accommodations by the end of 1946."[13] The shortage was most acute on the West Coast, where veterans looking for housing competed with war workers who had decided to stay put rather than return to their prewar communities. Richard and Pat Nixon, on returning to Whittier, California, where he was running for Congress, lived with his parents until their first child, Tricia, was born. They were able to find a place to rent on Walnut Street, but quickly discovered, as John Farrell writes in his Nixon biography, "the reason for the vacancy: there were hundreds of minks, kept in cages . . . on the lot next door, that squealed and stank. 'They're kind of noisy, aren't they?' Nixon asked his landlord, after several sleepless nights. . . . 'The odor is something terrible,'" Pat told a friend, but the family was stuck because they couldn't find anywhere else to live.[14]

The Nixons were more fortunate than most. "For the past week, I have been pounding the pavements of Los Angeles looking, looking for a place (other than my $4-a-day hotel) where my wife, 2-year-old child and self might lay our weary heads," the army air corps veteran Lucien C. Haas wrote to the editor of the *Los Angeles Times* in late October 1945. "It didn't surprise me to find that there was a housing shortage. I expected that. But it did surprise me to find that no one is doing a thing about it. . . . Those people who with tongues in cheek are leaving this to chance are soon going to be confronted by an angry minority of veterans. How can the poor man spending his whole day looking for a home find the time to hunt for a job?"[15]

"Let's Get Housing—NOW!" demanded Frank George, a navy veteran, in another letter to the editor that came close to predicting mayhem should immediate action not be taken. "Something must be done about the housing situation in Southern California—and done quick, not within 'a year or so,' nor six months, nor three months, but NOW! . . . With more veterans returning, the situation will get more critical. Something will have to break—and we hope it won't be heads! Make no mistake—we don't want sympathetic understanding: we demand action!"[16]

Threats like this were empty. They were expressive of the veterans' anger, not their intentions. There would be no violent demonstrations and no organized protest movement, in part because the major veterans' organizations did not regard the housing shortage as a primary postwar problem or one easily solved by Congress. In fact, the Legion used its political power in Congress to oppose programs for public housing that benefited civilians as well as veterans but, from their vantage point, smacked of socialism. The American Veterans Committee, which had been formed in 1943 as a progressive alternative to the American Legion, the VFW, and other established organizations, focused its attention on housing, but its influence in Washington was limited.

For the majority who were not members of the American Veterans Committee, the only outlets for their distress were complaints to their local newspapers and elected officials, whom they flooded with written protests.

In an attempt to extricate the Truman administration from blame for the crisis, John Blandford contacted the mayors of cities with more than twenty-five thousand residents with the request that they organize emergency housing committees "to establish or expand veterans' housing services." Fiorello La Guardia, mayor of New York City and president of the U.S. Conference of Mayors, seized the occasion to blast Washington for abdicating responsibility. Blandford's letter, La Guardia charged, "conveys the impression that the cities are not doing all they can. For your information, they are. The Federal Government is not doing all that it should. Congress has not yet acted.... We ask for bricks and stones and plumbing and you give us a mimeograph press release."[17]

On November 19, 1945, just days after the Blandford–La Guardia exchange, the nationally syndicated columnist Marquis Childs in a column headlined "Housing Shortage Menacing" reported that "the White House is being told in no uncertain terms that the problem of finding homes for veterans to live in is one that carries a dangerous charge of political dynamite."[18]

"Home, sweet home is a nightmare crisis instead of a song for America's war-shifted millions," *The New York Times* reported on December 9, 1945. "The scarcity picture, which has been intensified since V-J Day, is a hectic composite in which thousands of families are doubling up, living in substandard dwellings, even sleeping in cars, sheds, railroad stations, streets, garages, cellars, or trailers; or occasionally in a pup tent, school or filling station."[19]

The December 17 issue of *Life* magazine featured photographs of families searching for living space. "In San Francisco a family of four moved into a renovated mortuary and happily called it home. In Omaha a newspaper advertisement read, 'Big icebox 7 by 17 feet inside. Could be fixed up to live in.'"[20]

Truman, with midterm elections less than a year away, had to do something. On December 12, 1945, he announced that he was creating a new position, housing expediter, and appointing the former mayor of Louisville, Wilson Wyatt, to fill it. The housing plan Wyatt submitted to the president in February, titled the Veterans' Emergency Housing Program, called for the start-up of "construction of 2,700,000 low and moderate cost homes" within the next two years, 1.2 million in 1946, the remainder in 1947. Veterans would be given preference for the purchase of these units. To accelerate the construction of new housing, Wyatt proposed federal subsidies for the prefabricated housing industry, which, he claimed, would enable it to build 250,000 metal prefabs in 1946; another 600,000 in 1947.[21]

The Veterans' Emergency Housing Program relied on private industry to solve the housing crisis, even though, as the Republican senator Robert A. Taft of Ohio, no fan of federally supported or subsidized New Deal–style public works projects, declared in January 1946, "private initiative has not provided a sufficient supply of decent houses in the past" and could not be counted on to do so in the near future. Together with the Democratic senators Allen Ellender of Louisiana and Robert Wagner of New York, Taft proposed legislation that would establish a public housing program with federal subsidies to construct housing for low-income citizens, regardless of wartime service. Without an expansion of public housing, the three senators predicted, the current crisis would last forever.[22]

The underlying problem was that prices for new and previously built homes were higher than the veterans could afford. Frank Gervasi, writing in *Collier's* in February 1946, cited a letter from a returned GI from Mount Vernon, Ohio, who complained that he and his fellow veterans couldn't "possibly pay the outrageous prices some of our so-called good citizens are asking." In Nashville, Tennessee, home prices had climbed from 25 percent to 425 percent above prewar levels; in Joplin, Missouri, from 40 percent to 200 percent. *Col-*

lier's correspondents across the country "reported similar spiraling prices."[23]

"When our veterans were in service, they used to hear a lot about home in the magazine ads," O'Brien Boldt of the Philadelphia City Planning Commission told the NAACP Annual Convention in Cincinnati in June 1946. "Home was pictured as a shining little bungalow where the wife and kids were waiting. Home was the symbol of what our men were fighting for. Home was the symbol of promise of a better America our men would come back to. But when we came back home, we found that shining little bungalow—built in 1940 for $5,000.00—had a $10,000.00 price tag on it." The veteran and his family were forced to move "in with Mother-in-law. Friction—overcrowding—mental and physical misery—hope and energy dissipated in fruitless searching for a place of their own—that is the housing deal which America is serving up to its returned veterans."[24]

In August 1946, *The Milwaukee Sentinel* reported that a veteran and his three daughters had "stationed themselves downtown on Wisconsin Avenue and held signs pleading for housing. 'I'm Barbara—Age 2—Mommie, Daddie and us kids won't have a place to sleep next month.'"[25]

In September, the otherwise obsessively cheery *This Is America* screen magazine tied "America's skyrocketing divorce rate" to the housing shortage. Veterans forced to live with their wives and children in their in-laws' homes found it difficult to keep their marriages intact. Some got rooms of their own to escape, leaving wife and children alone, until they could find shelter for all of them together. Others just ran away from their marriages. "We could have reconciled most of these couples with a decent room or apartment or a little hope," the conciliation court judge Georgia P. Bullock declared. "But our hands are tied. . . . The veteran seems to be losing the very thing he fought for above all else—his home. The housing situation threatens to explode into a national menace unless something is done."[26]

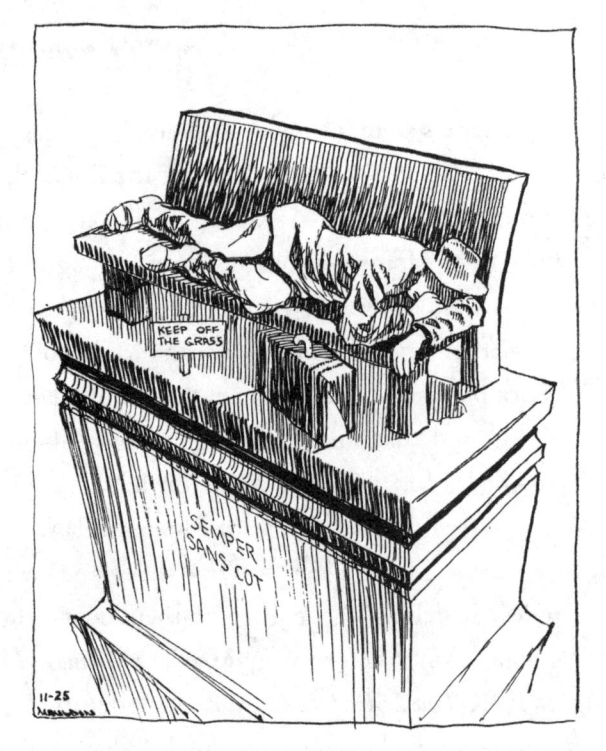

The Unknown Soldier—1946.

As the crisis worsened, federal efforts stalled. By December 1946, almost a year after Wyatt's appointment as Truman's housing czar, construction had been started on only 1 million homes, rather than the 1.2 million promised; worse yet only 600,000 had been completed. Having failed to meet his goals and unable to secure Reconstruction Finance Corporation subsidies for the prefab industry or prevent Truman from lifting price controls on building materials, Wyatt resigned. With his departure, the Veterans' Emergency Housing Program was effectively ended. The Taft-Ellender-Wagner housing bill, which might have helped reduce the shortage by funding new public housing, remained stuck in the House Committee on Banking and Currency. And the GI Bill, which was supposed to alleviate the crisis by offering mortgage guarantees to the returning veterans, was, by late 1945, proving to be an abject failure.[27]

By December 1945, only one-half of 1 percent of eligible veterans had applied for and secured GI Bill mortgage guarantees. In a rather futile attempt to expand that number, both houses of Congress, frightened by the political and social dangers posed by the expanding veterans' housing shortage, approved and Truman signed into law an amended bill that they hoped would provide more veterans with the financial boost they needed to purchase housing. The newly enhanced provisions of the amended bill doubled the loan guarantee limit for housing from $2,000 to $4,000, extended the repayment period from twenty to twenty-five years, and lengthened the time available for applying from two to ten years. These amendments, as the Veterans Administration concluded in a later "legislative history," transformed Title III from a "home loan benefit aimed at immediate readjustment aid [to] a long-range benefit open to any eligible veteran wishing to buy a home.... These changes constituted an almost complete revision of the loan guaranty program.... It was now open to all veterans who might decide to avail themselves of the benefit at any time within 10 years after the official end of the war. In terms of aiding the economy over the conversion period the objectives had also changed. It was now a long-range housing program for veterans."[28]

As generous and wide reaching as the amendments were, they did not come close to solving the veterans' housing shortage. A year after the amendments had taken effect, the percentage of eligible returned veterans who had received home loan guarantees had increased from 0.05 percent to 3.3 percent. The underlying problem remained a shortage of affordable housing, which the GI Bill, now amended, did not attend to.[29]

There were other problems as well. The veteran hoping to buy a house needed bank approval for a mortgage before he could apply to get that mortgage guaranteed. The banks, unfortunately, were discovering that the paperwork involved and the rates allowed made it less profitable for them to issue mortgages that met GI Bill requirements than to make non-guaranteed loans to those who had the collateral to back them. Veterans without that collateral were, the historian Kathleen Frydl has written, being "turned away without any recourse. 'The power of veto and discrimination is now in the hands of local lending agencies,' a frustrated realtor wrote the VA and, though he was 'for free enterprise,' he added, importantly, that 'free enterprise is failing to do the job.' Surrendering Title III to the whim of the market meant that banks had no incentive to make marginal investments."[30]

Only six of the forty-eight White male veterans in the University of Chicago study *The American Veteran Back Home* had been able to secure GI loans; another eight had attempted to do so but given up. Clarence Ardent had "tried my damndest to get a loan so I could buy a house.... Those S.O.B.'s down at the bank want you to sweat blood before they'll do anything. Well, I sweated blood and everything else for three months and didn't get anything at all."[31]

While low- and middle-income married White male veterans had a difficult time using their GI benefits to purchase homes, their difficulties were minor compared with those encountered by single veterans, those in same-sex relationships, and Blacks and women.

Federal Housing Administration (FHA) underwriting guidelines, which the banks and the VA relied on for guidance in assessing the creditworthiness of the applicant, gave precedence to the "mortgager who is married and has a family [because he] evidences more stability [and] has responsibilities holding him to his obligations." These same guidelines actively discouraged the award of housing loans to "mortgagers [like those in same-sex relationships] who are unrelated [but] have a partnership arrangement under which they jointly own a property which is used as their home.... The probabilities of dissatisfaction, disagreement, and other contingencies which might arise between members of the partnership are strong and may seriously affect the desire for continuing ownership on the part of any one of the principals." As the historian Clayton Howard notes, veterans in same-sex couples were also less likely to be approved for loans and loan guarantees wherever "queer sex acts" and sex-related offenses like "lewd vagrancy" were criminalized.[32]

Single woman veterans who applied for loans were denied them because local bank officers assumed they would eventually get married, leave their jobs, and stop making payments. Married women were rejected because their incomes were considered "merely supplemental to their husbands' and were likely to be temporary as well." In some states, woman veterans were barred from getting GI loans by laws that "forbid the lending of money to married women without the consent and responsibility of their husbands." As Nancy McInerny reported in *The New York Times*, former WACs and WAVEs had abandoned efforts to secure mortgages guaranteed by the GI Bill. "No women veterans' applications for GI house loans have been received in this [the New York] region."[33]

Black veterans had the most difficult time securing the bank loans they required to apply for GI Bill mortgage guarantees. In June 1946, E. A. Crawford, a veteran from Corpus Christi, Texas, contacted the local NAACP for assistance. "Since my release from the service, January 15, 1946, I have made several attempts to take advantage of the provisions made for veterans of World War II according to the GI Bill of Rights. So far all my attempts have been in vain. . . . Leading financial backers of the GI Bill in Corpus Christi have so divided locations of residential sections and placed restrictions on certain areas that as it is, under the present set-up, *NO NEGRO VETERAN* is eligible for a loan." The *Corpus Christi Times*, Crawford reported, had "stated that 'more than 500 GI home loans [have been] approved since Jan. 1st.' To the best of my knowledge not one single Negro was included in that number."[34]

William Richard Miles of Maryland contacted the NAACP with the same request for assistance in getting a mortgage. "I am an honorable discharge veteran. . . . I tried to borrow money on the GI bill of rights but no one around here would loan me any. . . . We colored veterans down here on the Eastern Shore cannot get any loan." His letter was duly acknowledged, but there was little the NAACP could do to help him. He was directed to "write a letter to the Veterans' Administration, Washington 25, DC and state your proposition to them." Though there was barely one chance in a thousand that the VA would take up the case, the NAACP had no other options to offer.[35]

The discrimination against Black veterans seeking housing loans was not confined to the South. In Cleveland, according to the *Call and Post*, the banks had reached a secret, unwritten agreement to deny mortgages to Blacks trying to buy houses in White neighborhoods. "The bank discrimination has stripped hundreds of Negro veterans of the opportunity to buy homes under the GI Bill of Rights. . . . The policy has channeled interested Negro home buyers into Negro communities where, because of the terrific shortage of houses, the prices have soared to high heaven."[36]

In the New York–northeastern New Jersey metropolitan area in 1950, as the historian Lizabeth Cohen discovered, only one-tenth of 1 percent of VA mortgages were held by non-White veterans. The cumulative nationwide effect of bankers' reluctance to grant mortgages and discriminatory FHA guidelines was that, according to the sociologist Chinyere O. Agbai, the home loan guaranty provisions of the GI Bill "resulted in 0.6 percent of Black men becoming homeowners" by 1960, compared to "9 percent of White men."[37]

With federal programs doing little or nothing to solve the overall housing shortage, prices out of reach, and GI Bill mortgage benefits of little minimal use to the vast majority of veterans, state and city governments stepped up their efforts to find housing for the returning veterans. City housing authorities selected and prepared sites for the unused military structures, including "surplus panelized frame houses and quonset huts," which Washington made available, free of charge. In New York City, the parks commissioner, Robert Moses, selected sites for veterans' housing on Clason Point in the Bronx, Canarsie Beach and Ulmer Park in Brooklyn, and Rego Park in Queens, ignoring the complaints of local officials and residents that the sites were either slated for the construction of new schools or uninhabitable for any creatures other than rats.[38]

In Milwaukee, "plans to house veterans included proposals to convert unused storefronts, vacant schools, and under-used public buildings, including the former North Milwaukee City Hall." The Milwaukee County Parks Commission "secured approximately 900 trailers and oversaw the construction of 765 prefabricated houses" accommodating a total of five thousand people.[39]

One of the by-products of these efforts was the racial violence that ensued when, as occurred on several occasions in Chicago, public housing authorities attempted to move a handful of Black veterans and their families into projects where Whites lived or hoped to live. Crowds of Whites violently resisted, rioted, and blocked the Blacks from moving in. To forestall future incidents and rioting, the Chicago City Council mandated that the Chicago Housing Authority secure its approval before assigning construction sites for public housing. The result was that the public housing built by the Chicago Housing Authority would be occupied almost exclusively by White veterans.[40]

In the end, city and state efforts failed to do much to solve the housing shortage. With the demise of the Veterans' Emergency Housing Program and private industry's reluctance to build low-income dwellings, it became more imperative than ever that the Taft-Ellender-Wagner bill be approved in Congress and federal subsidies be made available to municipalities to build low-cost public housing units. Two of the veterans elected in 1946, the Republican-Liberal Jacob Javits of New York and John F. Kennedy, Democrat of Massachusetts, took the lead in securing passage of the bill in the House. "We had a natural affinity in respect to anything that affected housing," Javits recalled in an oral history, "because there was a shortage of housing and the veterans were feeling the brunt of this, especially the newly-married veterans. So we consulted together about housing.... That was probably the first thing either of us did that got us any public attention."[41]

Jack Kennedy, his sister Eunice confessed, "wasn't totally engrossed in what he was doing" in Congress, with the striking exception of his steady and sometimes striking advocacy of public housing for veterans. "Veterans need homes," the freshman congressman from Massachusetts declared forcefully at a housing conference in Chicago on March 10, 1947, "and they need them quickly.... I don't believe that they will sit quietly by and 'take it' if Congress ignores the plain facts of a critical situation and yields to the do-nothing policy of pressure groups who admit their inability to cope with that situation with their present tools." At a housing rally at Faneuil Hall in Boston in May 1947, Kennedy attacked the American Legion for its opposition to the Taft-Ellender-Wagner bill. "'You know, the American Legion hasn't done a damn thing for the veterans since World War I, if ever!... How many here need homes?' Every hand went up whether they needed a home or not, and you could hear the crowd from the outside after they had quieted the crowd on the inside and he got a tremendous hand."[42]

The Legion did not take kindly to being criticized. Kennedy was asked to apologize, but instead doubled down, declaring that "the American Legion is the major stumbling block in the path of unified veterans' housing action in Massachusetts.... The national leadership of the American Legion has sold out the younger veterans by its action on housing."[43]

As the House prepared to adjourn in July, without Taft-Ellender-Wagner having been brought to the floor for a vote, Kennedy, in a rare first-term speech, blasted Republicans for their failure to take "any action to meet the most pressing problem with which this country is now confronted—the severe ever-growing shortage of housing which faces our veterans and others of moderate income. . . . There were 160,000 veterans of World War II in the Boston area in July of 1946. Forty-two percent of the veterans who were married among this group were living in rented rooms or doubled up. Their need is drastic. . . . I was sent to this Congress . . . to help solve the most pressing problem facing this country—the housing crisis. I am going to have to go back to my district on Saturday, a district that probably sent more boys per family into this last war than any in the country, and when they ask me if I was able to get them any homes, I will have to answer, 'Not a one—not a single one.'"[44]

Congressmen Javits and Kennedy were not the only veterans elected in 1946 who focused their attention on housing. For Senator Joseph McCarthy as well housing was the perfect issue to make a name for himself but on the other side of the issue, as an advocate for private industry and an opponent of public housing. Though a junior member of the Senate Banking and Currency Committee, McCarthy introduced a bill creating a Joint Committee on Housing and maneuvered to have himself appointed as vice-chairman. He was, he informed the American Legion's committee on housing, "not wedded to the T-E-W [Taft-Ellender-Wagner] bill." After a visit with members of the Legion to a veterans' housing project in Rego Park, Queens, he held a press conference, "denounced what he described as 'garbage-dump' veterans' housing" as "breeding grounds for communism [and] announced that he was dropping all other committee work from now until Jan. 1 to devote himself exclusively to the housing problem."[45]

He would spend the next four months on a marathon, highly publicized tour of the country, as vice-chairman of the Joint Committee on Housing, holding public hearings in more than thirty cities and taking testimony from 1,286 witnesses. Everywhere the committee went it was presented with detailed and graphic descriptions of an acute housing crisis that was daily growing worse. In Pittsburgh, "thirty three percent of all married World War II [vets were] doubling up with relatives or friends or living in rented rooms, trailers, or tourist cabins." In St. Louis, the Veterans Service Center had been able to find homes for only 5,000 of the 19,310 veterans who contacted it. In Miami, the housing shortage was so severe that the city government was finding it difficult to recruit civil servants, especially firemen and policemen. In Dallas County, between ten and fifteen thousand veterans with families remained without decent housing.[46]

McCarthy did not deny the severity of the shortage, but argued that the solution lay not in public housing but with the private housing industry. "Private enterprise must be our chief reliance." At the conclusion of the hearings, he drafted his own housing bill as an alternative to Taft-Ellender-Wagner. "The principal departure," *The New York Times* reported, "was the complete omission by Senator McCarthy of any provision for public housing." McCarthy's bill was voted down and Taft-Ellender-Wagner approved by the Senate, only to be blocked again by the House Banking and Currency Committee.[47]

To pressure House members to bring the bill out of committee and onto the floor, Kennedy and Javits, together with a coalition of veterans' groups, convened a conference and rally in Washington for February 29, 1948. Sponsors included the VFW, represented by Kennedy; the Jewish War Veterans, which Javits represented; the American Veterans Committee, with Franklin D. Roosevelt Jr., a veteran who would be elected to Congress in 1949; the Catholic War Veterans, with Robert Wagner Jr.; and the Disabled American Veterans, with Audie Murphy. The day after the rally, according to *The Washington Post*, thirteen hundred veterans "stormed Capitol Hill, . . . buttonholed Congressmen in their offices and in legislative halls, questioned Senators and Representatives at a public meeting and passed resolutions." The veterans failed to get the bill to the House floor, but succeeded in forcing the American Legion to change its position and endorse Taft-Ellender-Wagner.[48]

The Republican leadership, alarmed by the American Legion's support for Taft-Ellender-Wagner and worried that by opposing it they would forfeit veterans' votes in the upcoming 1948 elections, was compelled now to counter Democratic claims that they cared not a whit for homeless veterans. At 3:30 on the morning of June 19, 1948, just before adjournment, and, not coincidentally, two days before the Republican presidential nominating convention in Philadelphia, the Republican congressman Jesse Wolcott of Michigan, a World War I veteran, fervent opponent of public housing, and the ranking member of the Banking and Currency Committee that had bottled up the Taft-Ellender-Wagner bill, introduced legislation to establish a "secondary market" for GI mortgages, which, in theory, would incentivize local banks to issue more loans. The Democrats assailed this last-minute maneuver as a blatant attempt at face-saving, which it was. The first-term congressman Richard Nixon, who had until then avoided taking sides for or against Taft-Ellender-Wagner, endorsed the "secondary market" bill as "primarily in the interest of veterans." It passed, but, as predicted, did little to alleviate the veterans' housing shortage.[49]

Truman, blasting "Do-Nothing" Republicans for ignoring the needs of the veterans, called a special August session to force them to vote Taft-Ellender-Wagner up or down. This time around, Taft and the advocates for public housing on both sides of the aisle, knowing they did not have the votes, capitulated early. Instead of reintroducing the bill he had sponsored, which had passed the Senate on three separate occasions, Taft switched his vote to Senator McCarthy's substitute bill, which provided no funds for public housing but included lucrative loan guarantees for private builders and developers.

Truman's surprise election victory in November 1948 emboldened him to try one more time to resuscitate and pass some version of Taft-Ellender-Wagner. This time, he succeeded. The Housing Act of 1949, signed into law in July, was a long time coming, but not worth the wait. The bill approved loans and grants for 810,000 low-rent public housing units to be built over the next six years, not nearly enough to house the hundreds of thousands of low-income veterans in need. It was a start in the right direction, or would have been had President Truman, now worried about the war in Korea and its effect on inflation and shortages of materials, not cut the program back to 30,000 public housing units per year, just over 20 percent of the 810,000 authorized by the new law.[50]

The Republicans and the housing and real estate industries had won the battle and the war. With the federal government abandoning any meaningful attempt to subsidize public housing, private industry was in control and for the moment uninterested in constructing houses the nation's low- and middle-income veterans could afford.

Chapter 17.

GET A JOB?

There were as many paths back into civilian life as there were discharged veterans, but the final step for almost all of them was a good, well-paying job. The returning veteran, as Robert Havighurst and his associates from the University of Chicago observed, was "no longer a serviceman, but neither was he a civilian in the fullest sense. To be completely a civilian . . . required, as the veteran himself clearly understood, that he become an active participant in the civilian economy." President Truman agreed. In his twenty-one-point reconversion message to Congress on September 6, 1945, he declared that "placing demobilized veterans and displaced war workers in new peacetime jobs is the major human problem of our country's reconversion to a peacetime economy. It is imperative that this work be done swiftly and efficiently."[1]

Among the first veterans to return to work were those who took advantage of Section 8 of the Selective Training and Service Act of 1940, which guaranteed them their old jobs back if they showed up and asked for them within forty (later extended to ninety) days of discharge. Fred Hochschild of Milwaukee had been drafted in 1942 and discharged in early 1946. "When I got back to Milwaukee, I went to my mother's house and went back to work [at Western Electric] several days after that. They were glad to have me." Roy Duff had worked at Cook's Grocery in Whitefish, Montana, before the war "and, hell, I wasn't home two days until they had hold of me.... That damned store grabbed me and made me go back to work."[2]

Most but not all employers welcomed the veterans back to their old jobs. One veteran WAVE who had worked for Michigan Bell before the war had been warned that "her job would not be waiting for her when she returned." And it wasn't. She had been a supervisor when she enlisted. "When she returned, she was put back as a low-level operator—although Bell was forced to continue paying her supervisory wages. She didn't fight the assignment.... 'We didn't challenge it like we would today,' she said. 'You just accepted it that you were treated like a second-class citizen.'"[3]

African American veterans, in particular, had a difficult, sometimes impossible, time getting their old jobs back. "Some employers," a speaker at the 1946 NAACP convention noted, "have developed crafty methods of getting around the provision of the Selective Service Act on the matter of reemployment." They insisted that because the job the veteran had held before the war had been upgraded, it was now "too elevated ... and he is denied reinstatement on the grounds that the job he formerly held no longer exists." There were instances as well where the returning veteran was rehired, then dismissed, when his boss discovered that the once "docile and subservient" employee had become "much more aggressive about his rights and his citizenship than he was before his induction."[4]

Job prospects for the veterans, those seeking new work as well as those returning to their old jobs, were constrained by the unprecedented wave of strikes and factory closings that occurred after V-J

Day and the expiration of the no-strike, no-lockout pledges that the unions and management had agreed to abide by until the war was won. Unionized workers had done comparatively well during the war, but management and stockholders had done even better, with bloated executive salaries and record government-guaranteed profits. The war now over, overtime cut, and inflation rising, the unions demanded immediate wage increases of 30 percent; management refused; strike votes were called, and one after another, factories were closed as workers walked off the job and onto the picket line.

Seven million workers went out on strike in the eighteen months that followed the end of the war. The UAW "shut down eighty General Motors plants in fifty cities, with 175,000 workers on strike for 113 days. The Steelworkers were out for only twenty-five days, but there were 750,000 of them.... Some 400,000 United Mine Workers of America struck twice.... Other strikers included lumber workers in the Northwest; oil workers in the Southwest; retail clerks in Oakland; utility workers, transit workers, and truck drivers all over; teachers, other local government workers, and even the first airline pilots strike."[5]

In October 1945, *The Christian Science Monitor* warned that the nationwide strikes, if not resolved quickly, were going to aggravate the dangers posed by the demobilization of servicemen who were now looking for work, but were not going to find it in industries locked down by strikers. "If veterans of World War II remain for long months without prospect of employment, some will become easy grist for exploiters and demagogues . . . who hope to use the veterans to whip up class and group turmoil and ride to power with the backing of embittered men."[6]

Anticipating, wrongly it turned out, that the returning veterans would willingly serve as strikebreakers, Congressman John Rankin of Mississippi introduced legislation to exempt them from closed-shop laws and regulations so that they might "work without having to pay tribute [union dues] to anyone. That would do more to break these strikes," he insisted, than anything else Congress could do. Rankin's assumption that ex-servicemen would volunteer for strikebreaker duty, Charles Hurd, chief reporter on veterans' affairs for *The New York Times*, observed, was far-fetched. "Mr. Rankin, despite his long experience, does not, or will not, recognize that some veterans are union men and some do not like unions." Many would support the strikes quietly; others would join the picket lines. Very, very few would volunteer to be strikebreakers.[7]

Joe Tauchin Jr. had worked as a drill press operator at the Gisholt Machine Company in Madison after graduating from high school in 1941. In 1942 he was drafted and sent to the Pacific. On his return home, he went back to Gisholt to get his old job, "and the guy that I went back and talked to, he said, 'Well,' he said, 'I don't know if you want to come back or not. We're going to have a strike in two or three days.' So, I says, 'I gotta get to work.' So I worked there three days, and they went on strike. And I says, 'Well, I can't afford this.' So I went across the street to the Anderson Milking Machine Company, and I worked over there for a buck an hour, 'til they settled the strike, and then I come back."[8]

Steve Hutchinson had gone to work just out of high school as a semiskilled operator in a U.S. Steel finishing mill in Pittsburgh. He returned to the job after the war. "When the union officers began talking strike I got nervous, I admit.... But what the hell—we read in the papers about what the big corporations were making, and you could tell that U.S. Steel sure wasn't hurting.... The way I had it, I'd rather risk losing pay for a few months ... when I was young, than take an ass-kicking the rest of my life."[9]

The veterans stood by the unions, in part, because the unions had stood by them on their return from war. Union locals set up apprenticeship programs; assisted the veterans in securing proper security and pay; and helped them get medical and hospital care, find housing, and apply for disability pensions. The Greater New York CIO Council was particularly proud of its "record of accomplishment in serving, guiding and fighting for CIO veterans. . . . In late '45 and early '46 more than 100,000 veterans," it claimed, had "returned to jobs in CIO shops."[10]

In the South, the CIO, convinced that White veterans could be a critical element in the Southern Organizing Committee's campaign, waived initiation fees and developed programs "to reintegrate veteran members back into the workforce, to solicit their support of organizing campaigns, and to dispel the impact anti-union propaganda might have had." World War II veterans, according to historian Jennifer Brooks, "not only joined new textile unions, but actively supported and often led local organizing drives and strikes." Those recently returned "quickly emerged as leaders within many locals."[11]

The striking unions proudly publicized both the assistance they had given the returning veterans and the support they received in return. "One of the worst insults ever directed against America's fighting men," *The CIO News* declared on January 7, 1946, "was the assumption made by some anti-union employers that veterans might be used to break strikes and undermine labor conditions. Every such attempt, however, has failed miserably to date and America's veterans as might have been expected, have proved to be the most loyal and active of unionists. . . . After all, men who have fought and licked the world's most powerful dictatorships are least of all likely to tremble before domestic industrial dictators, or to allow themselves to be pushed around as pawns in a campaign to undermine American wage and living standards."[12]

Veterans who went out on strike paid a price for doing so. Congressman Rankin, with the full support if not encouragement of the American Legion, had inserted in the GI Bill a provision that barred veterans who were not working "because of a labor dispute" from receiving readjustment allowance checks. The VFW and the striking unions protested, the American Legion did nothing, and General Omar Bradley, who had been appointed to head up the Veterans Administration on August 15, 1945, refused to intervene. The result was that thousands of veterans, thirteen thousand in the GM strikes alone, though unemployed, could not receive their $20-a-week checks.[13]

In Newark, New Jersey, the local navy commander harassed striking veterans at the Westinghouse plant by directing shore patrol "to question persons wearing Navy uniforms or distinctive parts thereof and appearing in picket lines." Three navy veterans were pulled off the picket line, one of them, an African American, was arrested for picketing while wearing "a white Navy hat, bell-bottomed blue trousers and a Navy-issue sweater under a leather jacket." He spent three hours in the local jail and was released when the FBI, called in to investigate, "said it did not want him held for unlawfully wearing parts of his uniform."[14]

Despite the impediments put in their way, veterans marched with fellow union members, wearing their uniform jackets and caps, waving American flags, and holding signs that proclaimed WE FOUGHT FOR YOU OVER THERE, FIGHT FOR US *HERE!*; VETS WHO DID THE FIGHTING ARE ALSO STRIKING; WE SERVED ON THE FRONT LINE, NOW ON THE PICKET LINE; TOKYO, ROME, BERLIN, NOW E. PITTSBURGH.[15]

By March 1946, the CIO strikes that had shut down GE, GM, U.S. Steel, and other manufacturing giants had been settled. By the summer, the national strike wave was over. The postwar clash between labor and management, as the historian Joshua Freeman has written, ended in a draw. The workers did not achieve everything they had demanded, but those in the large industrial unions won wage hikes of 15 percent or greater. Workers in a number of smaller unionized and some nonunion firms got comparable wage hikes.[16]

The congressmen who wrote the employment provisions of the GI Bill, and the VA and USES agents charged with implementing them, were aware that the veterans were going to need help finding and holding on to jobs. Too many had no idea what they wanted to do, what they were capable of doing, and how they might transfer the skills they had acquired in the military to civilian jobs. They were, it appeared, in limbo, never quite satisfied with the current job, always on the search for a position better than the one they had landed in. "Voluntary shifting between jobs," the President's Commission on Veterans' Pensions reported in its 1956 study, had been "much more frequent among newly returned veterans than among most other groups of workers." A *Monthly Labor Review* study of veterans working in manufacturing found that they were less likely than nonveterans to be fired, but much more likely to quit their jobs. "Higher veteran quit rates reflect in part the problems and conflicts peculiar to this group of employees. It would be unrealistic to expect masses of men to make the transition from warfare to factory routines without some degree of shifting from job to job."[17]

Sam Stavisky of *The Washington Post* suggested in early December 1945 that the root of the veterans' disquiet was that they had set their "sights too high both on amount of pay and kind of job." They had matured, grown, acquired new confidence and skills in service, but little of that seemed to matter now that they were civilians again. "Experience in the armed forces—chiefly aimed at killing and defeating the enemy—generally have [sic] little value in peaceful, civilian life." In D.C., Stavisky found that the vast majority of available jobs were low paying and in the "hard work trades and service industries . . . which the veterans frankly don't want. . . . The better-paying, more-pleasant jobs in the commercial and professional fields demand skills and experiences which the GI just doesn't have."[18]

The first stop for those looking for work was their local USES office and the veterans' counselors stationed there. "Some men turn up there in uniform," Richard Kelley, a returned veteran, reported in *The Boston Globe* in January 1946. "Others tell by the newness of their clothes that they have just recently been discharged. Most men who are in the third or fourth stages of return to civilian life, wear combat jackets, khaki shirts and denim pants. Almost all carry the morning paper and, while waiting . . . , turn to the want ads. . . . The veteran will tell you, 'Stop telling us we can take it, that we are the best, the finest, the bravest, and that times might be bad. Of course we can take it! But make it so we don't have to take more. Make it so we find work.'"[19]

Jack Boyd, who oversaw job placement services for veterans in a small midwestern city, told researchers that those who sought his help were "good steady men, I think. And so far, we haven't had much trouble finding them jobs. Of course, the trouble is they come out of the army full of ideas of jobs that pay a dollar-twenty-five or a dollar-fifty an hour. And all we can give them here in Midwest are jobs that pay maybe sixty-five cents or seventy-five cents an hour. I start right in by laying the cards on the table and telling them I wish I could get them a good-paying job but I can't."[20]

Ralph Martin, writing for *The New Republic*, visited an office in Los Angeles filled with veterans who, unable to find decent-paying work in their hometowns, had migrated west, some with their families. A short, bald man who had been a rug salesman in Detroit, then a radar specialist in the navy, had been warned by the doctor that he could no longer handle rugs, but had to "do something else." He had looked for a job in Detroit but, finding none, "came to Los Angeles. . . . 'Do

"Sorry. We can use only men who learned something useful in the service."

you know the only job offer I've got so far?'" he asked Martin. "'Night janitor at thirty-four a week.... You know what? I may even take it. What can you do when you've got three kids?'"[21]

By late February 1946, with 10.5 million veterans returned to civilian life, the unemployment problem had, according to Charles Hurd of *The New York Times,* reached a "critical stage," with a million vets idle and 1.5 million more who would soon be on the job market. The job counselors at the seventeen hundred USES offices across the country were, the veterans complained, offering them only "the lowest paid and the most undesirable jobs in industry." Part of the problem was that large employers were, for one reason or another, not listing "their better jobs with the USES."[22]

Black veterans in the South who sought counseling and assistance from the USES staffers were routinely ignored or insulted by agents who were, with few exceptions, White and beholden to the unwritten and unassailable conventions that dictated that African Americans were fit only for underpaid, unskilled jobs as porters, dishwashers, farm help, janitors' assistants, and the like. Had there been more Black counselors, the situation might have improved, but few were hired and fewer placed in positions where they might be of assistance to veteran job seekers.

Between 1944 and 1946, as the historian David Onkst has written, the USES employed only a handful of Black counselors whom they routinely regarded and treated as second-class employees servicing second-class veterans. In Atlanta, an African American "interviewer" in the "colored" section of the USES Veterans Service Center resigned on December 10, 1945, because she had been ordered to take over the janitor's work in his absence. "This type of work is not in the scope of a trained worker. . . . I spent four years in college, two years in graduate work, leading to a Master's degree, preparing to become a professional social worker. . . . I am sorry I can no longer endure the physical and mental strain of working under these circumstances."[23]

White USES counselors and employers throughout the nation, but especially in the Jim Crow South, refused to acknowledge the fact that the Black veterans had acquired employable skills while in the armed forces. As Ambrose Caliver of the U.S. Office of Education reported at a December 1944 conference, Black servicemen had been trained as "linemen, draftsmen, cable splicers, truck drivers, clerks, clerk-typists, auto mechanics, carpenters, toolroom keepers, radio operators, smoke generator operators, welders, and instructors." They had, according to the army historian Ulysses Lee, acquired "a wider variety of technical experience than most of them would have gained in a greater number of years of civilian life. Men who had had little chance to work as interstate truckers, as heavy construction workers, and as telephone repairmen were now carrying tons of matériel in heavy trucks and trailers over strange roads, operating bulldozers and cranes in exotic ports, and stringing wire and setting up communications systems."[24]

Those who had "gone into the Army largely without mechanical skills," Lieutenant Colonel Campbell Johnson, General Lewis B. Hershey's executive assistant at the Selective Service System, observed, "are coming out with them and there is no doubt but that many of these veterans will choose to follow the lines of their new-found skills rather than their old agricultural or unskilled occupation." Asked in the spring of 1943 whether they believed their army training would help them get better jobs than they had held before the war, 61 percent of Blacks answered in the affirmative, compared with only 39 percent of Whites.[25]

The Black veterans who expected that their newly acquired skills would lead to better jobs would be sorely disappointed. No matter what their work assignments during the war, they were, on returning to the South, offered only low-skilled, low-paid farmwork and menial jobs. In Arkansas, Charles Bolté and Louis Harris, the future pollster, found that "95 per cent of the placements made by the USES for Negroes were for service and unskilled jobs." In Mississippi, according to David Onkst, White veterans got 86 percent of the professional, skilled, and semiskilled placements made by USES counselors in October 1946; Blacks, 92 percent of the unskilled and service-oriented jobs.[26]

William Hayes of Birmingham, Alabama, had served with the signal corps for almost three years, building telephone lines through North Africa and Italy. When he asked the counselor at the Birmingham USES office to find similar work for him, he was told that no such positions were available. Hayes discovered on his own that several White signal corps veterans were now working for the Birmingham

Power Company. "They were getting the jobs while he was being put on unemployment compensation."[27]

Even in those cases where the counselors recommended Black veterans for positions commensurate with their skill levels, employers refused to hire them for jobs traditionally reserved for Whites. In Greensboro, North Carolina, Ulysses Watkins, a wounded veteran who prior to the war had worked in a "local office machine sales and service store," was recommended by a VA counselor for job training and employment as an office machine serviceman for Remington Rand. After expressing interest in Watkins, Remington Rand discovered that he was a Negro and rejected his application because "it was not the policy of the organization to employ Negroes in that capacity. . . . Local customs prevented the use of a Negro for the position because of the circumstances under which repair work is usually done outside the local office."[28]

The designation of certain jobs as Whites only was not confined to the South. In Cleveland, William T. Caldwell, a Black army veteran, was refused "a referral to openings as punch press operators on the grounds that the job designated 'white only.'" Such racial discrimination in employment was legal in every state, north and south, with the exception of New York, which in 1945 had passed the nation's first and only Law Against Discrimination.[29]

Black veterans were too often faced with an impossible choice. They could either accept the menial jobs offered or reject them, in which case they risked losing their $20 weekly readjustment allowance checks. The Southern Regional Council field agent Marcus Gunter reported from Tennessee that when veterans turned down the jobs they were offered, "in the majority of cases . . . digging ditches," they were denied their checks. John Berry of Brookhaven, Mississippi, refused jobs sweeping leaves "and this kind of thing," and was removed from the eligible lists—and never did "get any of the fifty-two week payments, nor did I get any employment."[30]

Black veterans were not the only ones discriminated against by VA and USES job counselors. In Los Angeles, the "small, round man" who worked in the USES office told the journalist Ralph Martin that he was unable to find jobs for "the colored boys. . . . Same with the Mexicans and the Filipino and Japanese boys." Martin approached "a broad-shouldered Mexican American, an engineer-gunner on a B-17 who had spent most of the war in a PW camp in Nuremberg. He was an experienced bookkeeper, he said. Had all kinds of references. Almost a year without a job. 'How do you think a grown man like me feels to have his wife support him?'" Also waiting was a "tall girl, Joy Windsor Kennedy, [who] was mad because nobody would hire women truck drivers."[31]

"Finding jobs, the right jobs, is the worst problem," Nancy McInerny of *The New York Times* reported in "The Woman Vet Has Her Headaches, Too" on June 30, 1946. The WACs and WAVEs she interviewed all wanted to work. "They want satisfying jobs with opportunities to use their abilities. They want jobs leading somewhere. . . . In the services most of the women did clerical jobs," but there were others "who served as aviation machinist's mates, hospital corpsmen, draftsmen, parachute riggers, truck drivers." When, however, they tried to "obtain employment commensurate with the skills and experience they had acquired during the war," they were discouraged or dismissed. Less than half of the former WACs surveyed in 1946 had found jobs that made use of their wartime job experiences. "I'm willing to step aside for a man who is married and has family responsibilities, but I don't understand why single men veterans should have a priority over me. I did the same jobs as they in the Army," one former WAC told McInerny.[32]

Lorraine Allord, who had enlisted in the marines when her husband joined the navy, had served stateside as an air traffic controller at Cherry Point in North Carolina. After discharge, Lorraine tried to get a job at Truax Field, a military facility just outside Madison, Wisconsin. "I had a civilian air traffic control license and was told flat out, they didn't hire women." Hundreds of women who had flown for the WASPs (Women's Airforce Service Pilots) tried to find work as pilots after the war, but were similarly turned away.[33]

The VA and USES focused their attention on the veterans who had gone off to war as boys and returned as young men. So did the newspapers, magazines, and advice literature. Much less notice was paid to the 42.6 percent who were between twenty-six and thirty-seven and the 7.5 percent who were thirty-eight or older when they returned from service. Having been away for three or four years, they had fallen behind colleagues who had stayed home and learned new skills and feared they were too old to catch up. They were concerned, as well, about health problems that might affect their work.[34]

Among the older veterans who had the toughest time returning to their jobs were those who had been at the top of highly competitive professions. Too old to be drafted, Frank Capra had enlisted in early 1942 at the peak of his career, six months after the release of *Meet John Doe*. He was discharged in June 1945. Forty-eight years old, he was unsure about the future. "It's frightening to go back to Hollywood after four years . . . wondering whether you've gone rusty or lost touch," he confided to the *New York Times* reporter Thomas M. Pryor in November. Believing "that after the war moviegoers were yearning to retreat into nostalgia and fantasy," Capra's first postwar film, which he produced and directed, was *It's a Wonderful Life*. He recruited army air force veteran Jimmy Stewart to play the role of a good-natured, well-meaning, middle-aged banker who was not a war veteran and hero but a gaunt, graying, anxious father and husband. Capra had badly misjudged the moviegoers' need for escape. The war was too recent, the wounds and pain too raw to be ignored.

Capra's Christmas fantasy, which would become a classic in later years, did not come close to breaking even at the box office.[35]

William Wyler, who had made films for the army air force, was sent home in April 1945, when, after filming from a B-25 over Rome, his "hearing just went." Deaf in one ear with some hearing loss in the other, a disability that would last for the rest of his life, he was transported to an army hospital at Mitchel Field on Long Island. Lillian Hellman, who visited him there, recalled that she had "never seen anybody in such a state of horror in my life." Wyler feared he would never be able to direct again. In September, he "frankly admitted" to reporter Thomas Pryor "that he was 'scared' about his future." He said at the time, "I wish that I could go back quietly and make a small picture just to get the feel of things." Unfortunately, that was not possible because he owed Samuel Goldwyn one more picture on a contract he had signed before the war. Goldwyn wanted him to make a film about Dwight D. Eisenhower, but Wyler preferred to make one about "the ordinary GI—not a general." That film was *The Best Years of Our Lives*, and it was, according to Wyler, "the best film he has yet made," because he knew the characters in the story he was telling. "I've come home twice myself from the war and I know just how these fellows would feel and act. One character is very much like myself in the sense he comes back to a nice family, a good job, and a little money. This fellow has lived with the same woman for twenty years, yet he feels a bit strange and out of place at first. No man can walk right into the house after two or three years and pick up his life as before."[36]

Those who returned to professions that privileged youthful good looks and vigor were especially fearful that they might not be able to resume the careers they had left behind. Jimmy Stewart was thirty-two when he enlisted in the army air corps. He returned home after almost four and a half years, two of them in combat, thinner and grayer, and feeling much, much older. Like other veterans, he took time off before returning to work, moved in with his friend Henry Fonda, recently returned from navy service, and lived in the Fonda kids' playhouse. The two veterans spent the first months after discharge building and flying kites and gas-powered model airplanes.

Stewart delayed returning to work, in part because he didn't quite know how he would fit into a Hollywood that had survived the war by casting new actors, including Gregory Peck, Dana Andrews, Van Johnson, John Wayne, and Cornel Wilde, in the roles that would have been Stewart's had he stayed stateside. Part of the problem, as Henry Fonda later remarked, was that "the fellas who'd been big stars before the war came back looking like hell. That happened to Clark Gable. He looked ten years older. Jim had also aged quite a bit." Stewart agreed. "I'm just not a young fella anymore. I guess I'd only be suitable for playing grandfather to Mickey Rooney." Louis B. Mayer tried to capitalize on Stewart's war record by inviting him to star in "The James Stewart Story." Stewart turned down the offer. He had no desire to play the hero in a war movie.[37]

The lifespan of a Hollywood leading man was limited, though a good actor could, as Stewart did, age into other types of roles. It was much more difficult for the professional athletes who could not grow old gracefully and retain their skills. More than 90 percent of all baseball players active in 1941 served in the military. Most spent the war coaching and playing in exhibition games; there were no fatalities, a few were wounded, but, like other older veterans, they all lost years, paychecks, and skills that could not be recovered. On their return from service, pitchers appeared in and won fewer games and struck out fewer batters; position players hit fewer home runs, drove in fewer runs, and had lower batting averages.[38]

While Joe DiMaggio would enjoy a stellar career before and after the war, he lost almost three years during his prime and was never again as productive a batter as he had been before the war. He returned home in September, underweight, sat out the rest of the 1945 season, and, according to Richard Ben Cramer, his biographer, "went in the tank, and the Yankees with him," for the first time in his major-league career batting under .300. In his seven prewar seasons, he had, every year, accumulated more than a hundred RBIs, with a slugging percentage over .600. In the six years after his return, he drove in more than a hundred runs only twice, and his slugging percentage never reached .600.[39]

The war years took an even greater toll on Hank Greenberg, who was almost four years older than DiMaggio. From 1933 to 1940, Greenberg had never hit below .300. In 1940, his last full season before entering the military, he batted .340, had a slugging percentage of .670, hit 41 home runs, and drove in 150 runs. He was twenty-nine years old, the age when hitters approach their prime, and the highest-paid player in the game. He would not return to baseball until late in the 1945 season and had a good year in 1946. But he was thirty-five years old now, and his skills had diminished, especially in the field. He was traded to Pittsburgh from Detroit for the 1947 season and retired soon afterward.[40]

The exception to the rule might have been Ted Williams, who returned after missing three full seasons of baseball to win the Most Valuable Player award in 1946. Called back to service during the Korean War, he would lose another two seasons. Even with these interruptions, he remained one of baseball's top performers, and might, had it not been for those lost years, have surpassed Babe Ruth's home run record.[41]

For those who had aged out of their former jobs or preferred not to return to them; those who discovered, to their disgust, that they could not convert their wartime skills into peacetime employment;

and those who were dissatisfied with what was available to them in an economy still in the process of converting from war to peace, the GI Bill provided two stopgap measures to reward them for their service and keep them off the unemployment rolls. There were $20 weekly readjustment allowances for the unemployed, but only 52 of them and they expired two years after discharge or the end of the war. And there were educational and job-training benefits with living allowance checks that were far more generous and longer lasting. By June 30, 1955, 7.8 million veterans had received educational or job-training assistance paid for by the federal government, 2.2 million of them in institutions of higher education.[42]

Chapter 18.

THE VETERANS AT COLLEGE

The GI Bill, as originally written, offered veterans a two-year window to make use of its education and training benefits. These benefits included a year of tuition-free schooling for all veterans and three more years for those whose education had been interrupted by the war.

No one could predict how many veterans were going to take advantage of these benefits to get a college degree, but the consensus was that the number would be manageable. In March 1945, Earl J. McGrath, later U.S. Commissioner of Education, estimated that "in no academic year will more than 150,000 veterans be full-time students in colleges and universities. . . . Colleges and universities may expect an enrollment increase of from 10 to 15 percent from veterans." The younger veterans would stay away because, having lost much of their youth in the military, they needed to get on with their lives instead of detouring into school for four years; the older veterans, with jobs to return to and families to care for, would, except for those close to graduation, be just as reluctant to spend their first years as civilians in school.[1]

In August 1945, Stanley Frank, writing in *The Saturday Evening Post*, confirmed the prevailing wisdom that only a minority of veterans would make use of the GI Bill's offer of free tuition. The soldiers he interviewed at two large military hospitals, Percy Jones at Battle Creek, Michigan, and Thomas M. England at Atlantic City, planned to get a job, not go to school, when they were discharged. "I want to get a piece of that hundred and fifty bucks a week war workers are making," a twenty-three-year-old sergeant who had lost his left arm in the war told Frank. "I've got to get it while it lasts. I can't waste six months going to school." Another soldier told Frank that he was just "too old to go back to school"; a third that "pushing a pencil isn't for me." The GI Bill, Frank concluded, "is a splendid bill, a wonderful bill, with only one conspicuous drawback. The guys aren't buying it. They say 'education' means 'books,' any way you slice it, and that's for somebody else." Frank's predictions proved only too accurate. By the end of 1945, only 88,000 of the 8.3 million veterans who had returned to civilian life had taken advantage of the GI Bill's education and training benefits.[2]

The safety net that Congress had hoped would catch the vets before they fell into unemployment was not doing its job. To entice more veterans to enter training programs or school, and in so doing stay off the unemployment rolls, Congress amended the bill in December 1945. All veterans, regardless of age or whether their schooling had been disrupted, were made eligible for four full years of benefits. Living allowances for single veterans were increased from $50 to $65 a month and from $75 to $90 for those with dependents. The time frame for enrolling in school or training programs was extended from two to four years and the period for completing one's schooling or training from seven to nine years after the termination of the war. Tuition and allowance payments were made available to veterans taking correspondence courses.[3]

As with the amendments to Title III, the housing provisions, the December 1945 amendments to Title II, "Education of Veterans," were transformative. "The original act," the VA declared in an August 1950 report to Congress, had been "designed to provide Federal Government aid to returning World War II veterans in making a satisfactory readjustment to civilian life after separation from active service. It was not intended to be a relief act. It was not intended to be a bonus act. It was not intended to be a subsidy to education or training institutions." The December 1945 amendments changed all that. "Under the law, as amended, practically every person who served during World War II is eligible for education or training benefits," regardless of age, aptitude, or whether their schooling had been disrupted by the war.[4]

Never before and never again would an American government bestow so freely on so many, and with so few strings attached, a gift like Title II of the Servicemen's Readjustment Act: free tuition, books, and fees to attend college, vocational school, or a job-training program of your choice and a living allowance while you were enrolled.

The number of returning servicemen who took advantage of the amended and enhanced GI Bill to go to college was far greater than anyone had anticipated.

"We set our sights pretty high," Jack Short of Poughkeepsie told Studs Terkel. "I come from a working-class family. All my relatives worked in factories. They didn't own any business. They worked with their hands. High school was about as far as they went. . . . I thought to myself, this isn't what I want out of life. I want to have a good job, a respectable life. Fellas I had gone in the service with, five or six, we all had the same feeling. We all went back to school. . . . We just didn't want to go back and work in a factory in the hometown. The GI Bill was a blessing."[5]

Despite delays in getting admitted, the difficulties in finding living quarters, the shortages of labs, classrooms, equipment, and faculty, and the necessity of finding and taking on part-time jobs to supplement their GI Bill living allowances, veterans attended college in record numbers in the fall of 1946 and 1947, more than a million in each year, accounting for "nearly half the total enrollment" and 70 percent of male enrollments.[6]

By early August 1946, a year after Stanley Frank had written "The G.I.'s Reject Education," *The Saturday Evening Post* declared that the problem facing the colleges now was not too few but too many veterans. "The college dilemma is that of the man who inherited a herd of elephants: where to put them.... Boom town has come to the campus, and boom town is there to stay.... Because of the Government subsidy to servicemen, the opportunity is here; men who could never come to college under ordinary circumstances are enrolling or knocking at the doors."[7]

The nation's colleges and universities, which, almost without exception, had suffered wartime slumps in matriculants and a near-precipitous fall in revenues, admitted as many veterans with government tuition checks as they could fit into their classrooms. In a spring 1946 article titled "S.R.O.," *Time* magazine described the chaos that arrived with the onrush of veteran students at the beginning of the spring 1946 term. "Pitt was so crowded that classes had to be held on a day & night shift.... Texas Christian University set up geology labs in a gymnasium. Wisconsin quartered 1,877 veterans in a power plant 35 miles from the campus, 1,660 more at an Army airfield. Columbia established a 'trailer campus,' charging veterans for parking space but not for rent. At Rhode Island State, 28 Quonsets on Vet Row were jammed, eleven students to a hut. The president of Ohio's Marietta College took in boarders. Some hardy students at U.C.L.A. slept in all-night movies and parked cars. Everywhere student families played house in gyms, attics and cellars (40% of the ex-G.I.s were married).... Rutgers wrestled with a freshman class larger than the three upper classes combined. Enrollment at Michigan (13,714) was the biggest in its 109-year history."[8]

Congress responded by authorizing the transfer, renovation, and transportation of abandoned military installations and surplus equipment, including Quonset huts, barracks, mess tents, and prefabricated buildings. With assistance from federal and state governments—and stretching their own resources—colleges built trailer parks and tent cities and took over hotels and apartment buildings. Rensselaer Polytechnic Institute in Troy, New York, "leased four surplus LSTs (Landing Ship Tanks) and moored them on the Hudson River, where 600 veterans turned them into floating dormitories." Notre Dame converted former prisoner of war barracks into veteran housing units. Rutgers University, which had only formally become New Jersey's state university in 1945, expanded so rapidly that it had to house veterans in abandoned army barracks at Fort Kilmer and a converted prefabricated steel factory, once destined for the Soviet Union.[9]

To accommodate the onrush of veteran applicants, public universities hired new faculty members and built new campuses. California's public colleges and universities estimated that they were going to have to add at least 5,820 instructors to teach the 120,000 veterans they anticipated would matriculate in 1946. Ohio State enlisted faculty wives to teach. Other colleges hired high school teachers to fill in or asked beginning graduate students to postpone their coursework to take on full-time teaching positions. At the University of Wisconsin, the number of associate and full professors increased by 41 percent, graduate assistants and instructors by 110 percent, between the 1939–40 and the 1947–48 school years.[10]

In Illinois, "a military training center on the city's Navy Pier [was converted] into a two-year college called the Chicago Undergraduate

Center," with four thousand students, three-quarters of them veterans. It would later be relocated and expanded into the University of Illinois Chicago campus. In New York, the demand of veterans for admission, combined with an antidiscrimination campaign by the NAACP and Jewish and mainstream Protestant organizations, led to the establishment of what would become the State University of New York.[11]

Congress had, in drafting Title II of the GI Bill, given the veterans carte blanche to decide where they wanted to go to college. So long as they were accepted and remained enrolled, the federal government would cover the costs of tuition, fees, and books, up to $500 a year, and provide living allowances. Because $500 a year was enough to pay for tuition at the nation's most prestigious schools, including Harvard, which charged $400, *Time* magazine, pointedly and only partly in jest, asked the veterans, "Why go to Podunk College when the government will send you to Yale?"[12]

Michael Gold had, before the war, hoped to earn enough money to take night classes at Brooklyn Polytechnic. Under the GI Bill, he was able to attend Cornell University for free, then after two years transfer to Columbia University's School of General Studies, "the university's attempt to accommodate the surge of veterans into college."[13]

Henry Kissinger had studied accounting at City College before the war. With the GI Bill, he was able to pay the same tuition, $0, to attend any private university that accepted him. In April 1947, he applied to "leading Eastern universities" and was turned down at Columbia, Cornell, NYU, the University of Pennsylvania, and Princeton, but accepted at Harvard. He spent his first few weeks living in a makeshift barracks in a converted gym, then was moved to the least comfortable and prestigious dorm, which housed other Jewish students. At the start of his fourth semester, Kissinger married. Because his wife had a steady job, he did not have to take on part-time jobs to supplement his living allowance and was able to focus full-time on his coursework, in which he excelled.[14]

George Esser, a native of Virginia, had earned a degree in chemistry at the Virginia Military Institute but decided while in the service that he didn't want to pursue a career in that field. "All during the war I was thinking what I was going to do, and I ran into a man who said, 'Why not go to law school?'" He visited Harvard for an interview in February 1946 and, among other things, was asked what he had done during the war. He was there more than two hours before he was told that he would be admitted. "The G.I. Bill . . . pretty much covered all of the expenses. . . . There were lots of people in law school at that time who were from all over the country who would not have normally gone to Harvard Law School."[15]

To make room for veterans like Kissinger and Esser, Harvard increased its undergraduate enrollment from thirty-five hundred to fifty-four hundred and total enrollments including graduate and professional schools from eight thousand to twelve thousand. In one of its many feel-good postwar features, *Life* magazine praised the veterans at Harvard for their dedication, high standards, and good work, and cited President James Conant, who saluted them "as a heartening sign that the democratic process of 'social mobility' is . . . piercing the class barriers which, even in America, have tended to keep a college education the prerogative of the few."*[16]

The GI Bill was indeed democratizing higher education, though nowhere near as dramatically as Conant boasted. The veterans in the Harvard class of 1947 came from families with an average income of $7,400; the average income for all American families in 1947 was $2,620.[17]

Wherever they happened to land, the veterans found ways to nav-

---

* President Conant had eighteen months earlier criticized the GI Bill for awarding educational benefits to all veterans instead of those with demonstrated exceptional abilities.

igate the GI Bill requirements to secure maximum benefits. Because the bill paid tuition and living expenses to attend graduate and professional schools, savvy veterans figured out that if they began their college education in state schools where they could afford the tuition on their own, they could use their GI benefits to enroll in higher-priced, prestigious graduate and professional schools. After two years at the University of Chicago, Fredric Steinhauser transferred to Mankato State in Minnesota for his junior and senior years, then returned to the University of Chicago and used his last two years of GI benefits to get a master's degree.[18]

The newspapers and magazines that had recently focused their attention on GIs in foxholes followed them onto the college campuses. In the early spring of 1947, *Life* magazine sent Margaret Bourke-White, the first accredited female war correspondent allowed into combat zones, to the University of Iowa to photograph veterans wheeling baby carriages, holding squirming infants while studying, hanging out laundry to dry. One-third were married and most, married or not, worked to supplement the $65 to $90 living allowance checks they received every month. "They work in junk yards, soda fountains, laboratories, grocery stores. They drive trucks and taxis. Five have jobs as assistant policemen. Eighty percent of the office buildings in Iowa City are cleaned, swept and serviced by student veterans." And yet, despite it all, two-thirds of the 48 percent of veterans who would not have been able to attend college "without GI Bill Aid" were earning "above-average grades."[19]

Half a continent away, in Berkeley, California, Robert Meyerhof supported himself, his wife, and his mother, who lived with them, by taking on "two or three jobs always. I worked in the bookstore on the campus. I worked at football games taking tickets and whatever jobs

I could get. I did gardening on the side. . . . And then one time I got a marvelous job at the racetrack." All this in addition to the eight hours a week "dishwashing or babysitting" for the professor who, in exchange, gave Meyerhof and his family a room in his house.[20]

Despite the obstacles in their paths, the veterans did as well as, if not better than, their younger, nonveteran classmates. At Brooklyn College, according to President Harry Gideonse, "veterans as a group maintained a slight but consistent superiority in academic performance over comparable nonveterans." Studies comparing veteran with nonveteran grades at the University of Southern California, the University of Wisconsin, Ohio State, the University of Michigan, UCLA, and Iowa recorded the same results.[21]

As astonishing as the grades they attained were the choices they made in their courses of study. Twenty-eight percent of the veterans enrolled in the fall of 1947 were taking general education courses in social studies and the humanities, far higher than had been anticipated. At the more "selective" public and private colleges and universities, the percentage of liberal arts majors was even greater. At the University of Wisconsin, 38 percent of veterans in the class of 1949 were liberal arts majors. Large numbers had enrolled in college for the sole purpose of getting better jobs when they graduated, but many were there because they needed a hiatus of sorts between the military and the civilian worlds, time to decide what came next.[22]

Joseph Heller of Coney Island, who would write one of the most important and widely read World War II novels, *Catch-22*, enrolled in college because it allowed him "to delay, to buy time. I didn't want—I felt myself much too young—to have to decide right away what I was going to do for the rest of my life. . . . Going to college was easier and more appealing than going to work and certainly, then, more respected. And what work could I have found that would not have been a blow to the spirit after my jubilant homecoming from the war?" Because he had, while in the army, enjoyed a few brief stays in "lower California," he enrolled at the University of Southern California, then, after a year, transferred to NYU, got his BA in two years, followed by an MA at Columbia, all paid for by the GI Bill.[23]

The GI Bill made it possible for large numbers of lower-income high school graduates to attend college, but it offered no financial assistance to the 59 percent of White and 83 percent of Black veterans without high school degrees. "In most U.S. cities," *Time* magazine reported in September 1945, "battle veterans of Europe and the Pacific who need a few more credits to enter college must return to regular teen-age classrooms." Several cities, including Houston, Baltimore, Washington, Detroit, and Philadelphia, set up special programs to provide veterans with other routes toward their diplomas, including separate classrooms or schools, some, as in Philadelphia, where they were allowed to smoke in class.[24]

John Berry of Brookhaven, Mississippi, had been drafted out of high school at age eighteen. On his return home, unemployed and, it appeared, unemployable, he went back to his old high school to talk to the principal. "They had some type of program at that time where you could take some courses during the summer and so forth and also you could take a test, and if you passed that test you could go on to college." Berry took the test, passed it, and was admitted to Alcorn A&M, the first Black land grant college in the nation. Berry's mother had wanted him to go to college and had saved some money, but not nearly enough. Without the GI Bill he would never have been able to attend and graduate. One of his classmates was Medgar Evers, another veteran attending Alcorn on the GI Bill.[25]

Roscoe Simmons Pickett's first stop after being discharged was the Mississippi high school he had attended before being inducted. Because the principal agreed to give him credit for "some study" he had done in the navy, he was able to get his diploma in four months and apply to college.[26]

Berry, Evers, and Pickett were the exceptions to the rule. Most Black veterans had neither the time nor the resources nor the assistance of local educators necessary to help them get their high school degrees and go on to college. The substantial gap in high school graduation rates for White and Black males, especially in the South, was one reason why a smaller percentage of Blacks were able to use their GI benefits to attend college. But it was not the only or the most important impediment placed in their path.

The GI Bill was designed, written, and passed into law with the active support of southern congressmen who were not going to permit it to interfere with the racial status quo by granting the same level of benefits to Black veterans as Whites. Title II, as the Loyola University law professor Juan Perea has noted, was "carefully race-neutral on its face, making no distinctions between qualified veterans because of their race. The Bill was also carefully designed to require federal benefits to be administered locally and so to conform to local prejudices." Paragraph 8 of Part VIII explicitly forbade every "department, agency, or officer of the United States [from exercising] any supervision or control, whatever, over any State education agency, or State apprenticeship agency, or any educational or training institution." Here was an open invitation to the seventeen states from Florida to Delaware that required the segregation of educational institutions to bar the admission of African American veterans.[27]

Black veterans who sought to attend colleges and universities in the South were restricted to the historically Black colleges and universities, which, unfortunately, lacked the capacity to accommodate the majority of those who applied. "An estimated 20,000 black veterans were turned away from the Negro colleges, and a survey of 21 of the southern black colleges indicated that 55 percent of all veteran applicants were turned away for lack of space, compared to about 28 percent for all colleges and universities."[28]

The Black veterans, as the historian Sarah Ayako Barksdale has written, fought back with lawsuits against the colleges and universities that refused to admit them. With the assistance of the NAACP and Southern Regional Council attorneys, they were able to open some doors that had been closed. The University of Arkansas Law School admitted two Black veterans in 1948, though it did not provide them with campus housing. Johns Hopkins, the University of Maryland, and William and Mary graduate schools opened their doors to Black veterans between 1948 and 1950.[29]

Despite the difficulties they encountered, significant numbers of Black veterans were able to get their degrees. Bryson C. Armstead Sr. of Haddonfield, New Jersey, entered the navy right out of high school. He hadn't considered going to college until a neighbor across the street and his wife who had gone to St. Augustine's College, a historically Black college in Raleigh, North Carolina, suggested he apply there. "My parents had no money [but] at that time, the G.I. Bill, they paid everything. The G.I. [Bill] in those days was better than a job. I can make out better going to school than I'd be working at RCA. Yes, because they paid for everything, everything, and then gave me spending change.... I went to St. Aug. for three years, finished. Then they paid for my graduate work at Glassboro [State College in New Jersey]. Hadn't put out a cent. Hadn't put out one cent. Then they paid for me over at Temple. I had thirty-two hours above my Master's over at Temple and the G.I. [Bill] paid it. The best thing I have ever done in my life, the best thing." With his degree from Glassboro, Armstead was able to leap into the middle classes as an elementary school teacher.[30]

Millie Dunn Veasey, a WAC veteran born and raised in Raleigh, enrolled in St. Augustine's in 1948, then after a year withdrew because her husband asked her to. She returned in 1950 and graduated in 1953, her tuition paid by the GI Bill. She was one of only two woman veterans at St. Augustine's.[31]

Dempsey Travis had been shot in the leg at the Shenango Personnel Replacement Depot in Pennsylvania by White soldiers who feared that African Americans shut out of the base post exchange and the movie theater were going to riot. After recovering from his wound, he was transferred to the Aberdeen Proving Ground in Maryland, where he spent the war as a clerk and eventually graduated to running the post exchange. His commanding officer suggested he go to officer candidate school. "But I'd had enough. I said, 'Let me out as early as you can, so I can at least go to school under the GI Bill.' I took entrance exams at Roosevelt, at DePaul, at Northwestern. I got three letters back saying pretty much the same thing: Look, you dumb son of a bitch, don't ever try to get into college, 'cause you just ain't got what it takes. Try usin' your arms, try usin' your back. They never said, Try usin' your head." Travis went to work in the stockyards, like his father. An old teacher whom he met on the street suggested he go to Englewood Evening Junior College in Chicago, which he did, and then transferred to "Roosevelt and finished two years in one. That's the story of me and the GI Bill. It paid my tuition and that made the difference. If anything positive came out of the war, that was it."[32]

While the GI Bill made it possible for many Black veterans to get their college degrees, the percentage that did so was considerably lower than that of White veterans. A 1973 report by the Princeton University Educational Testing Service found that while "more than 28 percent of whites in the 1923–1928 birth cohorts enrolled in collegiate level training, ... less than 12 percent of returning black veterans chose this option." Those Black veterans who were best positioned to take advantage of the bill's educational benefits were, according to economists Sarah Turner and John Bound, those who were "most likely to have access to colleges and universities outside the South." For those who were "limited to the South in their collegiate choices, the G.I. Bill exacerbated rather than narrowed the economic and educational differences between blacks and whites."[33]

The GI Bill had similar effects on gender inequities in higher education. Through the 1930s, males had outnumbered females in higher education by about three to two. The war changed all that. As men were pulled out of the classroom to enter the military, colleges and universities adjusted to the shortage of students—and tuition—by admitting more women and offering them opportunities previously denied because they were women. For the first time in its history, Harvard College allowed Radcliffe students to attend some upper-division classes and opened the undergraduate library to them, but only on Saturday afternoons. In colleges across the country, women were permitted if not encouraged to enroll in what had been considered "male only" science and math undergraduate majors. The number of science bachelor's degrees awarded to women increased by nearly one-third. "Greater numbers of women enrolled in engineering programs.... The war also provided a boost for women with career aspirations in medicine."[34]

When the men returned from war, the opportunities for women in higher education declined precipitously. The colleges and universities that had welcomed women during the war turned them away in favor of veterans with their tuition, fees, and books guaranteed by the federal government. Male enrollments spiked from 300,000, or 30 percent of total enrollments in the 1943–44 school year, to more than 1.8 million, or 70 percent in 1947–48.[35]

Benjamin Fine of *The New York Times*, perhaps the most acute observer of higher education trends and the only one, it appeared, interested in female students, reported as early as January 6, 1946, on "the growing difficulty of women students to get into college. During the war many colleges upset their existing ratio between men and women by admitting large numbers of women students. Now the colleges are frequently putting the women last in their category of those who are to be admitted." Swarthmore announced that "no additional women are to be admitted in March"; the University of Illinois was admitting "few out-of-State women"; Syracuse University had sharply curtailed its enrollment of women; North Carolina had turned away several hundred; Cornell University, "where women had been in the majority during the war, had cut back their proportion to 20 percent."[36]

In August 1946, Milton MacKaye reported for *The Saturday Evening Post* that public colleges and universities were conserving dormitory space for veterans by denying admission to "out-of-state women. . . . Speaking off the record, and regretfully, a number of educators predict such a tightening of the situation that many American girls presently of college age will never be allowed to matriculate."[37]

St. Cloud State Teachers College, part of the Minnesota state system, had had no housing for men before the war. That all changed with the return of the veterans. To expand the number of male veterans enrolled, the school converted a nursery school into a men's rooming house and Carol Hall, "an expansion dormitory for girls, freshman girls," into a men's dormitory.[38]

The women's colleges could not pick up the slack, because they lacked dormitory space. The federal government had been generous in supplying institutions that enrolled veterans with Quonset huts, army barracks, and prefabricated buildings of every variety, but no such assistance was available for the women's colleges. To take advantage of GI tuition payments and government largesse, several women's colleges turned coeducational. In New York, Adelphi opened its doors to men, Finch Junior College welcomed male veterans to its summer session, and Sarah Lawrence and Hunter College considered going coed.[39]

Even woman veterans eligible for GI Bill education benefits had problems making use of them. Had the colleges provided day-care facilities or had Congress extended the nine-year limit for completing a degree, woman vets might have been able to use their GI benefits to attend school and get degrees. But without these changes, they had to choose either marriage and children or school; most chose the former.

Dorothy Dempsey had grown up in Pelham Bay in the Bronx, attended business school after graduating from a Catholic high school, and got a job at the local Oscar Mayer meatpacking plant. When the war came, she joined the coast guard. After the war, taking advantage of the GI Bill, she applied for and was accepted into an early childhood program at NYU. After a year she withdrew to get married. She wanted to go back to school—and did briefly, at Rutgers—but she had three children to raise and that came first. By the time she was able to return to school, her GI Bill benefits had run out. It would take her a full thirteen years to get her degree.[40]

On May 21, 1946, *The New York Times Forum*, a radio program, considered the question "Should women stay away from college to give veterans a chance?" Dr. Charles Harold Gray, the president of Bard College, declared that the decline in female admissions threatened "to set education back a hundred years. 'It has been a long struggle,' Dr. Gray declared, 'for women to get into professional schools—into medicine, engineering and architecture. If they are not admitted during the next few years, there will very likely be a throwback. Granting the emergency, to make a distinction between students on the basis of sex is to revert back to the ideas of the Victorian age and is not defensible even in an emergency.'"[41]

Despite the warnings, no steps were taken by the colleges and universities or federal or state governments to reverse the growing gender disparities. "As male veterans stormed the colleges and universities with their G.I. Bill benefits," the historian Suzanne Mettler has written, "women's enrollment rates declined precipitously to 24 percent of graduates in 1950, nearly the same level as in 1910. Not until 1970 did the proportion of women among college graduates return to its prewar levels." The same dynamics were at play in professional and graduate schools. "The proportion of women among those attaining master's or second professional degrees declined from 38 percent in 1940 to 29 percent in 1950, and did not return to the former level until 1970." There was a similar decline in the percentage of women who earned doctorates and advanced professional degrees. As the historian Susan Hartmann has written, "The brief promise of greater educational equity which surfaced amidst the imperatives of war vanished as another imperative, the need to compensate those who had defended the nation, increased the distance between women's and men's opportunities."[42]

The federal government's infusion of billions of GI Bill dollars into higher education transformed the nation's colleges and universities. The success of working- and lower-middle-class students in schools that had once spurned them, but now needed their guaranteed tuition payments to offset wartime enrollment shortfalls, dramatically altered the public's and the institutions' conviction that higher education should be restricted to those from affluent families and the few who had demonstrated extraordinary intellectual prowess in secondary schools.[43]

Week after week, the daily press, opinion journals, glossy magazines, and newsreels highlighted the ways in which veteran college students did not fit the norm. They were older and less affluent, had come from public high schools or arrived without diplomas, refused to wear beanies or play childish games, were married with children, and worked menial jobs to support themselves. And they were serious, studious, mature students who were more interested in their classroom work than extracurricular activities. It had become clear that they—and others like them—belonged right where they were: in the colleges and universities that had once looked down on them.

Large numbers of lower-middle-class Catholic and Jewish veterans who, before the war, would have been excluded because they didn't have the money to attend or were victims of quota systems were, with GI Bill support, able to attend college. In New York State, Jewish organizations, including the Jewish War Veterans, worried that long-standing traditions of discrimination would limit the number of veterans admitted to private colleges, pressed for a bill that would bar institutions of higher education that received tax dollars from discriminating against Blacks and Jews and lobbied Governor Dewey for the establishment of a state university. They succeeded in getting both the antidiscrimination bill and a state university. Pressure in other states, including New Jersey, Massachusetts, and Pennsylvania, resulted in similar antidiscrimination legislation and an increase in the admission of Jewish students.[44]

The democratization of higher education that the GI Bill made possible was a double-edged sword. Extending educational benefits to veterans only, a population that was 98 percent male and well over 90 percent White, had the effect of leaving behind those population groups underrepresented in the military. The number of White males who had not been college-bound prior to the arrival of the GI Bill but were now able to acquire a degree and the tangible lifetime benefits of better-paying positions increased dramatically. This was not the case for as large a proportion of women and Black men.

The veterans attending college became the face of the GI Bill. Former soldiers, sailors, airmen, and marines wheeling baby carriages on campus were infinitely more photogenic than apprentices in coveralls training to become auto mechanics. Still, for all the publicity they received—almost all of it positive—the veterans enrolled in institutions of higher education constituted only 28.2 percent of the nearly eight million service men and women who had by June 30, 1955, received education and training benefits under the GI Bill. The number who used their benefits to enroll in vocational education and job-training programs was far greater: 45 percent, or 3.5 million veterans, in nondegree vocational programs; 27 percent, or 2.1 million, in on-job and on-farm training programs.[45]

Some of these noncollege schools and programs imparted employable skills, but many others, too many, were little more than money-making scams that benefited the schools' founders rather than the students. The newspapers and magazines that had praised the college-bound veterans and the schools that accepted them had little but disdain, much of it richly deserved, for the numerous for-profit schools and job-training programs created to take advantage of the billions of dollars authorized for veterans' schooling by the GI Bill. What went largely unnoticed were those vocational programs that were passing on skills to veterans who had returned from war and were contemplating careers in the arts.

Chapter 19.

VOCATIONAL SCHOOLS AND JOB-TRAINING PROGRAMS

The GI Bill, as Congressman Thomas Abernethy of Mississippi triumphantly declared on the floor of Congress, was a "States' right bill." As a trusted and admiring colleague of John Rankin and a member of the Committee on World War Veterans' Legislation, which wrote and reported out the bill to the full House, Abernethy knew what he was talking about. Under the bill he presented to the House in May 1944, the federal government allocated the monies to be spent on veterans' schooling and job-training programs, but local and state authorities would decide how, for what, and where they would be spent. "As long as I am a Member of Congress," Abernethy promised, "I shall never support any bill that permits the Government to encroach in the slightest upon State Control of Education."[1]

In their crusade to throw money at veterans and their communities with no federal oversight, the solons of D.C. seeded the growth of a monstrous boondoggle. The prohibition against federal control opened the door to hustlers and schemers who saw a way to make quick money by starting up vocational schools or job-training programs, enrolling veterans, and collecting the tuition paid for by the federal government. "More than 5,600 of the 8,800 approved schools below college level which operate for profit have been established since the date of the enactment of the Servicemen's Readjustment Act," the VA reported to Congress in 1950. "Since most of these schools have few students other than veterans, practically all of their financial support comes from the Federal Government. They are really operated on public funds but privately conducted for profit by private interests." The education and training of veterans at government expense had turned into a "billion dollar business. . . . People with no previous experience or interest in the field of education, whose prime interest is a quick and excessive return on invested capital, have discovered the lucrative business of training veterans. These individuals have established schools—sometimes chains of schools—in which the training of veterans is a necessary incidental to the profits to be gained." The businessmen/school founders paid themselves huge salaries and profited additionally from sweetheart rental agreements and dummy corporations that provided the students with supplies and then sold the goods they produced. Agents on commission were hired to recruit veterans; large sums were spent on advertising.[2]

It was almost as if the bill had been written, then amended, to line the pockets of the new breed of education grifters. Congressman William R. Poage of Texas had predicted as much when he rose on the floor of the House of Representatives to support an amendment that restricted tuition payments to "existing" institutions, not those founded after the passage of the GI Bill. "There is not a man or woman on this floor who does not know . . . that there is going to be a racket established all over this country of so-called institutions of learning that are simply going to spring up here, there, and yonder to get the kids' money. . . . Do not tell me that such schools will not spring up, because you and I know that they will." Congressman Poage's warnings went unheeded.[3]

Thousands of schools appeared out of nowhere. In its 1950 report to Congress, the VA included thirty-seven pages of ads from schools that catered to returning veterans. There was the American School of Upholstering in Baltimore; the National Meat & Food Institute in Miami; the Lee Auto Body School and the Hazleton Woodworking Institute in Hazleton, Pennsylvania; the Independence Trade School for "White Veterans" in Ponchatoula, Louisiana; the Upholstery Trades School in Philadelphia. "Colored veterans" were invited, in ads published in the Black press, to enroll in the Vocational Institute of Texas in San Antonio, which offered classes in cooking and baking, auto mechanics, shoe repair, woodworking, tailoring, and radio repair; the Mel Walker School for tailoring in Chicago; the Bolivar County Trades School in Shelby, Mississippi; the Temple Vocational School in Temple, Texas. *The Afro-American* published hundreds of advertisement for hundreds of vocational schools in Baltimore, including the Painting and Paperhanging Division of the Maryland Vocational School; the National Institute of Music Inc.; the Buildings Trades School Inc.; the Tailoring Institute; and the American Training School of Clothing and Designing.[4]

Henry J. Walker, general supervisor of the National Education Council of Associated Master Barbers and Beauticians of America, the barbers' equivalent, he claimed, of the American Medical Association, testified before a congressional subcommittee about his visit to a state-approved barber school in Pittsburgh. Though the entire city had only seventy licensed barbers, the school enrolled 153 students "with 22 barber chairs and only three teachers." Of the 87 students who graduated, "only 16 of those boys . . . have gotten jobs in barber shops. The rest of them are driving cabs or something of that kind, yet the Veterans' Administration under the law has to pay that tuition to those schools for inferior training."[5]

Albert Q. Maisel, writing for *Collier's* magazine, had a field day describing vocational school scams. Vets were going to school, their tuition and living allowances paid by the federal government, to become chicken sexers, bartenders, ballroom dancing instructors, photographers, radio and television mechanics, barbers, and commercial pilots, though there was no labor shortage in any of these fields. The Johnny Johnson Dancing Studios of Chicago, approved by the State of Illinois "to give a one-year course of teacher-training instruction for ballroom dancing," enrolled two hundred students. "If all the students of this school were actually planning to pursue the profession of dancing instruction, this single institution could turn out enough teachers in a year to man every dancing school in the entire city of Chicago."[6]

Maisel portrayed the GIs enrolled in these schools as victims of fraudsters and profiteers. Some might have been, but the majority knew what they were doing. They enrolled not because they were hoodwinked by clever advertisements or recruiting agents on commission but because they too profited from the fraud. Living allowances had in February 1948 increased from $65 to $75 a month for unmarried vets, $105 for married, and $120 ($1,520 in 2023 dollars*) for those with two or more dependents. For veterans who had used up their unemployment compensation allowances, these checks proved a godsend.[7]

Investigators for the President's Commission on Veterans' Pensions found that the states with the highest unemployment rates and the lowest wages enrolled the greatest percentage of veterans in vocational programs. "The available data suggest that, particularly in the

---

* Estimate based on changes in Consumer Price Index, www.measuringworth.com/calculators/uscompare/relativevalue.php.

South, many veterans may have taken below college training in preference to taking jobs or used such benefits as a disguised form of unemployment benefits." The percentage of Black veterans who used their GI Bill educational benefits to enroll in vocational schools was almost double that of Whites, most likely because the living allowances they collected paid more than the menial jobs that were available.[8]

Henry Kirksey, a Black veteran who needed a job to support himself and his family while he was at Jackson State College, "started teaching at a white-operated Magnolia Trade School for black troops, black veterans." When he was approached by two Black businessmen who wanted to start their own vocational school, he "made one thing very clear, I said, 'Look, I've been down at Magnolia Trade School. The thing that bothers me the most is that I'm in class with a lot of veterans who go to sleep all the time.'" He agreed to teach at the school, but only if he were allowed to dismiss students who slept through class. He later admitted that he had been "stupid for doing that . . . because those guys worked all day real hard and this was a way for them to make extra money, to get that veteran's benefit. And I was just too stupid—I was so committed to the fact that if they were in there, being paid to learn, that they were supposed to learn."[9]

In Palmer's Crossing in Hattiesburg, Mississippi, two White men established the Southland Development Foundation, which offered Black veterans classes in auto mechanics and radio technology. Veterans with an eighth-grade education could enroll in radio, those without in auto mechanics. William J. Heath, a Black veteran who at the time was attending college on the GI Bill, taught adult education courses there from 5:00 to 10:00 p.m. The vocational school was a scam, but profitable for the owners who collected the tuition, Heath who got a decent salary, and the veterans who got living allowances for showing up. "A lot of them didn't get any training. They were getting the subsidy . . . and that's all they were interested in. . . . You'd have grown men sitting there who could hardly write their names and you couldn't get their attention enough or know whether to blame them or blame me." None of it really mattered because there were no jobs in the skilled trades available for Black veterans. The best they could hope for was employment as "a grease monkey.... Now, he might have fixed a transmission and whatnot but was paid as a grease monkey."[10]

Eugene Russell Sr. of Scott County, Mississippi, on his return from the Pacific, had no intention of going back to school to get a high school diploma. "What do a twenty-three-year-old man look like, done got married, going back to the seventh grade or sixth grade?" He enrolled instead in a local vocational school, which he hoped might teach him skills that would enable him to get a decent paying job. "It was just a rip-off. We was getting sixty dollars a month [living allowance]. You'd stay there five hours every day. If it's mechanic, painting, anything, they're going to take you out where there's an old tractor, ain't run in twenty years. And set you around there and just talk about it.... You ain't learned nothing. What is to learn? The tractor ain't going to run. They ain't going to teach you how to make it run. It's just a sham."[11]

"Southern congressmen, in the passing of the [GI] bill," the Reverend W. A. Bonder of Tougaloo, Mississippi, declared in a letter to the U.S. Congress, had "dropped a wrench in the wheel" by giving untrammeled authority to "State Committees appointed by Southern governors" to decide whether or not to grant "schools permission to teach veterans, under the GI Bill.... These State Committees, as a rule, start off with a determination that Negro soldiers shall not be trained under this bill, and they never let up. In fact, it's practically impossible now for a school to get a permit from these committees to operate a school to teach Negro GI's ... any of the standard trades, like carpentry, brick masonry, plumbing, interior decoration or any of the journeyman trades.... But if a school wants to teach Negro veterans such non-essentials like 'beauty culture,' radio mechanics (when the average good radio doesn't have to be repaired once in five years), or wants to teach 'furniture finishing,' whatever that is, or patching old shoes, or something in which certain people are not interested, they may get by; but never will they pass, if they want to teach worthwhile skills." The Black-owned Carver Trades School in Jackson, Mississippi, had been closed down after two months, when the state education department refused to certify it. "Many feel that about the only way Negroes can operate a private veteran's school in certain southern states is to give a white man about half interest in the school, and get this white man to 'front' for them."[12]

The end result was that decent vocational schools, which taught real skills and admitted Black veterans, were in very short supply. When, in December 1946, I. W. Paxton of Palatka, Florida, wrote to Jesse Dedmon Jr., the secretary of veterans affairs at the NAACP, "concerning what assistance they could give me in entering a school in radio under the G.I. Bill of Rights," Dedmon referred him to the Hilltop Radio Electronics Institute in Washington, D.C., eight hundred miles away. There was apparently no other school "you will be able to attend."[13]

In the final analysis, it didn't much matter. In the Jim Crow South no amount of vocational training was going to lead to a job that had always been restricted to White men. The director of the Brunswick Vocational School in southern Georgia explained to Horace Bohannon of the Southern Regional Council that "as a Christian . . . it really hurt him to see a Negro veteran enter his office because he had so little to offer them. He said he had wanted to establish a vocational school with bricklaying, carpentry, and plastering as the courses offered. He disfavored offering some of modern skills because he said 'there is no need training a man for a job he can't do around here.'"[14]

After his return from the Philippines, Ulysses Lee Gooch, "juggling things around as to . . . what am I going to do with my life?"

found ads in the local Memphis papers for all sorts of training programs. "There was GI training on how to cook, how to do anything, everything . . . anywhere between becoming a medical doctor to being a truck driver." One of the ads was for a flight-training school, and "that appealed to me. So I walked in thinking that I'm going to start learning to fly airplanes. . . . And they informed me, indirectly, . . . this is a white folks school." Hooked now on the idea of becoming a pilot, Gooch enrolled in a flight-training school for Black veterans in Nashville and completed his training, only to discover that no commercial companies were hiring Black pilots.[15]

Robert Coronado Villalobos had the same sort of experience. After using his GI education benefits to study accounting, he found that "there was nothing available for a Mexican American. So I delivered Coke on a truck, just to have a job. There wasn't much choice." He eventually applied for a job with the post office and got one as a custodian, then a mail carrier. He never did get to use the accounting skills he had acquired.[16]

Vocational school grift was the largest but by no means the most egregious scam authorized and paid for by the GI Bill. That honor went to the fraudulent job-training programs. State agencies, according to the historian Kathleen Frydl, lacking "guideposts or standards" to evaluate training programs, often "opted to approve all of the applications received." Store owners who wanted to add clerks or salesmen applied for and received approval to run on-the-job training programs, then hired veterans and used their living allowances to supplement their salaries. "Insofar as employers used the GI Bill as a form of bonus pay, and employees agreed, both were defrauding the government by undermining the purpose of the law."[17]

The worst scams, according to Maisel, were the flight-training schools that offered far less instruction than was needed to qualify as a commercial pilot. Of the 339,300 veterans who entered flight-training vocational courses by November 1947 at a cost to the government of nearly $200 million, 204,000 dropped out in the early stages and only 16,300, or fewer than 5 percent, completed the advanced courses necessary to qualify as commercial pilots. Even those who did qualify found it near impossible to get jobs in a field already overcrowded with military pilots who were soaking up every available commercial job.[18]

Local governments joined in the fleecing of the feds. "Rookie policemen and firemen," Henry Pringle reported in "Are We Making a Bum out of G.I. Joe?" in the *Ladies' Home Journal*, were being hired because the living allowances they received for job training enabled cities and towns to "cut their salaries proportionately. Officials in Montgomery County, Maryland, publicly boasted that four G.I.s had been employed in the engineer's office. They would get $60 each from the county and $90 monthly from Washington. Thus the county would save $360 monthly."[19]

While there appeared to be an abundance of job-training programs for White veterans, some of them legitimate, far fewer admitted Blacks. In Savannah, Georgia, "the local State Veterans Service Officer" told SRC field reporter Horace Bohannon "that few or no white shops admitted Negro workers. . . . He also said that in cases where Negroes were in white shops, they were only being exploited. He cited an example of a veteran in a furniture shop, supposedly taking upholstering. However, a visit to the shop proved that the boy was unloading and uncrating furniture."[20]

"Negro veterans complain that they are only considered for such training as porter, truck driver helper, or barber," Vincent Malveaux declared at a June 1946 NAACP conference. The head of the USES office in Houston, Texas, told Malveaux "that the white people in the community seemingly felt that as a matter of customs Negroes should not be taught any skills. Most white counselors are of the opinion that

Negroes will not find future employment in skilled and new fields so they immediately discourage these veterans about pursuing such courses."[21]

Black businessmen in the South, like their White counterparts, were cashing in on job-training scams. Adrian L. Oliver, a graduate student at Atlanta University, interviewed twenty-one veterans who had enrolled in job-training programs in Black-owned shops. Most were getting no training but had been put to work at menial tasks. "Interestingly, Oliver observed that even though the veterans felt abused, they were still hesitant to leave their programs because they 'believed that the compensation received from "on-the-job" training far exceeds any salary that they could receive from jobs that were open to them.'"[22]

The for-profit vocational schools and job-training programs established for the primary purpose of enriching local businessmen were numerous and notorious. But there were legitimate programs as well whose objective was not to make money for their founders but to train veterans for trades and industries.

James Anderson served with the marines in the Pacific. His first priority after his discharge was figuring out "how am I going to make a living. I really didn't want to farm so I went out and looked around. I did get training as a mechanic . . . under the GI Bill of Rights. They paid the fellow that I was working for, they paid him some amount, and I was paid to go to the Rice Lake Vocational School [in northwest Wisconsin] and learn how to weld, and that was taken care of by the GI Bill." With training as an auto mechanic and a welder, Anderson was able to support himself. He would later go to work for the post office.[23]

David Fuentes, who lived in the Los Angeles area, used the GI Bill to go "to tailoring school. I ended up in the garment business.

That's what I did all my life for 44 years. I made mink coats. Before that I used to make high fashion dresses for movie stars. . . . I made good money. I had a good life." John López, also of Los Angeles, enrolled in a carpenter's apprenticeship program. "The GI Bill paid for it, tools . . . whatever I needed." López acquired a journeyman certification and later joined the union. He "was unstinting in his praise of the GI Bill: 'I wouldn't have what I have now if it wasn't for the help from the military.'"[24]

Vocational programs administered by public high schools and not-for-profit state-funded institutions provided more meaningful job training than the for-profit ones. Unfortunately, they were universally oversubscribed and too often designed and operated as dumping grounds for students who had been detoured away from academic programs. The equipment in the shops and labs was substandard and outdated, the instruction less than adequate. Congress could have helped out by providing funds for public high schools to develop programs for veterans. Spokesmen for the CIO Veterans Committee and the director of veterans' activities for the United Electrical, Radio, and Machine Workers of America urged Congress to appropriate funds as part of the amended GI Bill so that public high schools might remain open at night to offer adult education programs and high school accredited courses to returning veterans. Their suggestions were not taken up.[25]

A few states, recognizing that public high schools were not prepared to accommodate the veterans, established their own special vocational programs. Sherby Woods, who suffered a serious facial wound in Italy, returned home to northern Minnesota in 1945. "I couldn't have gone back to a factory job because I was beat up too much. . . . I just wanted to find a job and have some comfort. I was, uh, I was pretty shaky." His county in Minnesota had set up a program for veterans who wanted to learn "heavy equipment maintenance." On graduating from the program, he got a job with the county that he would hold for the next thirty-eight years.[26]

In the southern states, the only schools that provided Black vets with instruction in the trades were those organized and run by African American educators. In Monroe, North Carolina, "Black veterans . . . took advantage of the school set-up for them at the Winchester Avenue School and dozens of farming and non-farming veterans enrolled in the various courses. . . . They could take general education and other vocational courses. . . . Most of the veterans worked during the day and attended the veterans' school at night." The GI Bill living allowance they received "was added family income."[27]

In Crowley, Louisiana, the wife of the Black high school principal told Wesley Brazier of the SRC that a large number of veterans were returning to "the high school trying to complete their work and then they plan to go and learn a technical trade." German Levy of Brookhaven, Mississippi, asked by an interviewer whether he had taken advantage of the GI Bill, answered with pride that he had "used all forty-eight months of it," received his high school diploma—"during that time they didn't care how old a Black person was"—then gone to tailoring school.[28]

In Memphis, Marcus Gunter, an SRC field agent, visited "two high schools teaching veterans vocational subjects from three in the afternoon to nine in the evening. The equipment is very good, the instructors competent, but there are men who will be waiting for 18 months before they can enter the school, due to the lack of space and instructors."[29]

Though the fraudulent schools got the most attention from the press and congressional oversight committees, there were scattered across the nation vocational programs founded by well-meaning citizens, businessmen, and educators who saw in the GI Bill an opportunity to train veterans for trades and industries that were experiencing postwar labor shortages. In New Haven, Connecticut, restaurant owners, short of cooks, chefs, bakers, and other essential staff, founded the New Haven Restaurant Institute in May 1946 to retrain ships' cooks and mess sergeants to work in restaurants. The institute was housed in a "defunct restaurant in the packing house district" until Mrs. James Rowland Angell, the wife of the former Yale president, arranged for it to move to a five-acre site across from the Yale Divinity School. By its third year of operation, the school enrolled 114 men, all but 5 of whom were veterans. In 1951, it changed its name to the Culinary Institute of America. Twenty-one years later, it relocated to Hyde Park, New York. It is today recognized as one of the premier schools of culinary education in the world, the "think tank of the food industry," with master's, bachelor's, and associate's degrees, certificate programs, courses for professionals, conferences, and consulting services, on several campuses across the country.[30]

In Elkhart, Indiana, the C. G. Conn Band and Orchestra Instrument Manufacturing Company, like the New Haven restaurateurs, facing a shortage of skilled labor, founded what it proudly declared was the first and only full-time musical instrument repair school. "A number of the students now enrolled formally," a local newspaper article reported, "were musicians with some of the nation's big-name dance bands" who on returning from the military had been unable to find steady work. Instead of "drifting about the country on one-night hops," they used their GI Bill benefits to learn a new trade. Within a year of operation, the school claimed it had graduated forty-seven veterans, every one of them employed in instrument repair work, many in "repair shops of their own."[31]

Among the programs that offered the veterans, White and Black, real opportunities to enhance their skills were those housed in the hundreds of reputable, long-established art, theater, music, and dance schools that had fallen on hard times during the war but were rescued by the GI Bill. By November 1947, almost 7 percent of the veterans enrolled in school below the college level were attending programs "related to art, music, and entertainment."[32]

There is no evidence that either John Rankin, chair of the House committee that reported out the GI Bill, or Bennett Champ Clark, his counterpart in the Senate, or the elected officials who voted for it did so because they wanted to provide ballet dancers, jazz musicians, actors, and painters with support, training, and, in many cases, instruction by Europeans in exile who introduced them to new styles, techniques, genres, and approaches that would, in the end, contribute to a postwar renaissance in the American arts.

The critic Ben Davis, noting that "art-historical convention speaks of 'postwar American art' as a distinct epoch," attributes much of the "broad ferment in art" to the "unusually broad-minded generosity of the GI Bill's Title II, which funded school for veterans at the institution of their choice (if they could get in).... For a number of people who would never otherwise have considered higher education, let alone studying art, the assist was decisive." Among the World War II veterans who studied painting under the GI Bill were Robert Rauschenberg, Roy Lichtenstein, Ellsworth Kelly, Romare Bearden, Donald Judd, Cy Twombly, Noah Purifoy, John Hultberg, Jon Schueler, and Ernest Briggs.[33]

The GI Bill, according to the art historian Richard Cándida Smith, was "one of the most important pieces of legislation ever affecting the arts." It enabled aspiring painters and visual artists to study their craft at government expense while collecting living allowance checks. Some enrolled in art schools because that had always been their dream, others because the GI Bill gave them the chance to experiment, to find out if they had what it took to become an artist.[34]

In Atlanta, the High Museum of Art, founded in 1926, enrolled ninety-five veterans in the fall of 1947. "Many of them have never studied art before," the school director reported, "although they knew they had talent. Now the GI Bill of Rights is giving them an opportunity to develop latent talents."[35]

The future abstract expressionist painter Jon Schueler, after teaching literature at San Francisco State, enrolled at the California School of Fine Arts with "a lot of guys who were in a similar situation to myself, who had not necessarily thought of becoming painters before. I had wanted to be a writer but got involved with painting and the GI Bill made it possible to make that kind of dramatic shift which would have been much more difficult under other circumstances."[36]

Noah Purifoy, a visual artist, sculptor, cofounder of the Watts Towers Arts Center, and central figure in the postwar West Coast art scene, earned an undergraduate degree at Alabama State Teachers College in Montgomery before the war. "When I got out of the service, I went to Atlanta U., where I . . . got my degree in social work, and I worked at it for two or three, or three or four years, in Cleveland and Los Angeles." Finding social work unfulfilling, he applied to the Chouinard Art Institute in Los Angeles "just out of the clear blue" and was accepted "without portfolio or anything." Before enrolling, he "had to overcome his misgiving that art was too frivolous an endeavor for a black person. He decided that since it was government money, he could afford to experiment. He would spend a trial year in art school. If his teachers felt he had promise, he would continue, otherwise not. The whole prospect was a frightening gamble."[37]

Milton Ernest Rauschenberg, who would later change his name to Robert, had, as a child, loved to draw, but never considered making art his career. On his discharge from the navy, he spent a year doing menial jobs in Los Angeles, then studied painting at the Kansas City Art Institute, the Académie Julian in Paris, Black Mountain College in North Carolina, and the Art Students League in New York City, his living expenses and tuition covered by the GI Bill.[38]

The art schools the veterans enrolled in had barely survived the war and would have had to close their doors had they not been rescued by the GI Bill. The Art Students League, founded in New York City in 1875, lost half its students and half its revenue in the first two years of the war, but with veterans comprising two-thirds of the postwar student body, their tuition paid by the GI Bill, it was able to triple the number of instructors.[39]

In California, between 1946 and 1952, veterans accounted for "never less than 70 percent of students" and "frequently well over 80 percent" in the top art schools. The California School of Fine Arts in San Francisco, founded in 1874, which had during the war lost so much of its tuition revenue that the director had to quit because "there was no money to pay his salary," bounced back in the fall of 1945 as the first class of veterans enrolled. "By the following spring term, the change in the school's fortunes was stunning. Enrollment leaped to 1,017 full- and part-time students, 350 percent greater than the previous year." In Los Angeles, the Chouinard Art Institute, established in 1921,* came close to closing during the war, but survived into the postwar period from tuition received from veterans.[40]

The GI Bill would have the same positive impact on music schools across the country and on the thousands of young musicians who, with few exceptions, found it near impossible to find work after the war. By 1946, the most successful of the big bands, including those led by Benny Goodman, Harry James, and Tommy Dorsey, had lost their venues and disbanded, because nightclubs could not afford to pay the 30 percent cabaret tax, later reduced to a slightly less ruinous 20 percent, that had been slapped on them in 1944. Unable to find steady gigs, veterans discovered that they could make ends meet and enhance their skills by enrolling in classically oriented programs in

---

* It would in 1961 merge with the L.A. Conservatory of Music and become CalArts.

newborn or resurrected music schools and collecting the living allowance checks authorized by Title II of the GI Bill.[41]

John Coltrane, on turning eighteen in September 1944, enlisted in the navy and was assigned to Manana, Oahu, Hawaii, where he played with the Melody Masters. Discharged in August 1946, he returned to Philadelphia and enrolled at the Granoff School of Music. The school's founder and director, Isidore Granoff, a Russian émigré violinist, "offered a traditional classical training," but, after the war, admitted a large number of veterans who played jazz and hired instructors who could teach jazz. One of them, Dennis Sandole, a guitarist and big band arranger, introduced Coltrane to "advanced harmonic techniques" and helped him with his compositions. Coltrane also studied the saxophone at Granoff, rehearsed with colleagues, and gave recitals. The living allowance checks he collected while enrolled supplemented his meager income as a freelancer.[42]

Dave Brubeck, who had earned an undergraduate degree before the war, enrolled after his discharge as a graduate student at Mills College in Oakland, a women's college that had decided to admit male veterans with GI Bill benefits. At Mills, he studied under Darius Milhaud, "one of the few great accepted classical composers that absolutely liked and accepted jazz." Milhaud "guided the 26 year old's studies in counterpoint, theory, polyrhythms, and polytonality," lessons that he would incorporate into the music he composed and played in the decades to come. While at Mills, Brubeck fronted an octet, with Paul Desmond and Cal Tjader, veterans who were attending nearby San Francisco State College under the GI Bill.[43]

"The G.I. Bill," Brubeck told the author Marc Myers, "allowed me to become exposed to one of the great classical composers of our time.... For most of the musicians I knew, the G.I. Bill gave us a chance to study. We were pulled away from worrying about how to make a living. I was in the service for four years, from 1942 to 1946, and was out of touch with the jazz world when I returned. Under the

G.I. Bill, you were able to study with the best teachers right across the country. The sound of jazz changed as musicians became more educated" by European classical artists exiled from their homes and now teaching at American schools.[44]

At Juilliard, the number of veterans who enrolled in the summer program "jumped from 21 in 1945 to 650 in 1946, pushing the total enrollment from 1,380 to 2,134." Latin jazz drummer, arranger, and bandleader Tito Puente was one of them. He had enlisted in the navy shortly after Pearl Harbor and spent more than three years on the aircraft carrier USS *Santee*, where he was encouraged first by the chaplain onboard, then by the top officers, to put together a band to entertain the crew on its long voyages to and from North Africa, then back and forth across the Pacific. He learned about the GI Bill when he was discharged. "We could go to school; we could buy a house; we could have our old jobs back." Unable on his return home to find a steady position as a Latin big band drummer, he auditioned for and was accepted at Juilliard on the GI Bill to study "composition, orchestration, and arranging, and naturally transcribing and copying." He stayed there for a few years, collected his living allowance checks, worked part-time, and then left to develop "my style and all that by actually performing and playing."[45]

Veterans who, like Puente, had played in army and navy bands during the war but could not find paying jobs in peacetime enrolled in music programs at the University of North Texas in Denton; Schillinger House, the future Berklee School of Music in Boston; and several schools in Los Angeles, including Jefferson High School, the Los Angeles Conservatory, Los Angeles City College, and the Westlake College of Music, where they studied with European classical musicians and composers who had fled Germany and eastern Europe during the war. As a result of "the cross-fertilization" of classical music and jazz fueled by the GI Bill, "jazz," according to the composer, conductor, horn player, and author Gunther Schuller, "steadily became much more intricate and developed." The changes in the music composed and performed were unmistakable. Because of the GI Bill, the returning veterans were able to expand their musical vocabularies, learn theory, classical harmony, and counterpoint, and position themselves to supplement their incomes by doing studio work, composing, arranging, teaching, and crossing over into pop and commercial music (and later rock and roll) for film and radio.[46]

Very much like the nation's art and music schools, theater programs that had come close to collapsing during the war rebounded in the immediate postwar period by enrolling as many veterans as they could. Aspiring actors, Black and White, many from working-class backgrounds, opted to take a flier on a career in the arts rather than accept the low-paying, sometimes menial jobs available to them. At best, they would learn enough to make a living and get noticed; at worst, they would have taken a few years off, as payback for their service, before entering the labor market on the ground floor.

In New York City, recently discharged vets, including a sizable number who would later make it to Broadway and Hollywood, attended the non-degree Dramatic Workshop at the New School, which had been founded in 1940 by the German theater director Erwin Piscator. On returning home from Guam, the navy veteran Bernie Schwartz, the future Tony Curtis, moved into his parents' apartment on Stebbins Avenue in the Bronx. Instead of looking for work suitable for a Jewish street kid who had "barely learn[ed] to read and write in high school" and knew no arithmetic, Schwartz finished school at Seward Park High School on Grand Street in Manhattan and tried to break into show business. He got nowhere, and when he discovered that the GI Bill would pay for acting lessons, he applied to the Dramatic Workshop, "auditioned, got up and acted [his] guts out." Only later did he learn that no one was paying attention. "You couldn't be turned down." The school, which had barely survived the war, needed the veterans' tuition payments to stay afloat; the veterans needed the living allowances. "A lot of GIs who went to that school," Curtis recalled in a memoir, "were just scammers. They went through the motions so they could draw their GI Bill stipend of $60 bucks a month without having to get a job. Others came so they could learn a little diction or have some fun up on stage." Curtis was different. He was going to school to learn how to act.[47]

Walter Matthau was one of his classmates. On being discharged from the army air force in Sacramento in October 1945, he moved to Reno, worked as a loader for Railway Express, and gambled to his heart's content. On the advice of a girlfriend who worried that he was on the way to becoming a "depraved gambler," Matthau returned to New York City, moved in with his mother on the Lower East Side, and enrolled in the Dramatic Workshop. "I could not have afforded to go to drama school without the GI Bill. Not in a million years.... There were nice people at the school, and every month there was a check from the government. It was simple."[48]

Harry Belafonte, who had dropped out of high school after one semester and joined the navy in 1944 at age seventeen, also found his way to the Dramatic Workshop. On his discharge in December 1945, he moved in with his mother, his stepfather, and their three children on Amsterdam Avenue in Harlem and found work as an assistant janitor. "I mopped halls, stoked furnaces, and made small repairs. Almost immediately, I sank into a funk much deeper than I had ever known.... As far as I could tell, janitorial work was what I'd be doing for the rest of my life, and I knew I could never settle for that." He had no notion of becoming an actor or performer and had never been to the theater when a tenant, as a tip for hanging her venetian blinds, gave him a ticket to the American Negro Theater (ANT). Enthralled by what he had seen, he wanted now to be part of the theater, "not as an actor but just ... a helper of some kind." He volunteered as a stagehand and was later asked to read for a part, which he got. While at the ANT, he heard about "the most exciting theater workshop in New York," the Dramatic Workshop. "Everybody at the ANT was talking about it. Best of all, the G.I. Bill would cover my tuition." Despite the objections of his fiancée and mother, who were "horrified I'd blown my G.I. Bill money on drama school," Belafonte enrolled.[49]

Other veterans including Jason Robards, Charles Durning, and the future comedian Don Rickles attended the older, prestigious American Academy of Dramatic Arts in New York City. And still more enrolled in the new program organized by the nonprofit American Theatre Wing, which, after surveying the wishes and needs of five hundred returned veterans, shifted resources and talents from its stage-door canteens to creating "a trade-art-business school of a new type." The new school was launched and, with appropriate theatrical flair, publicized in a July 8, 1946, press release. "Happy School Days are here again for approximately four hundred veterans of the entertainment world enrolled in the American Theatre Wing's unique 'university' organized on an industry-wide basis to give highly advanced technical and professional courses under the GI Bill of Rights. . . . This 'strictly non-academic' school opens . . . with a schedule of hours that would set regular school authorities to hair-tearing."[50]

Courses, paid for through the GI Bill, were offered in acting, tap dancing, ballet, modern dance, fencing, makeup, publicity, playwriting, stage design, and radio, which was taught in broadcast studios provided by the networks and local stations. The major focus was on the theater—and on veterans who had been union members. "'This crowd,' a Wing spokesman pointed out, 'didn't run away with the carnival, you know. They're pretty well educated, but they want to be taught styles in acting Shakespeare. They don't need a lot of gymnasium, but somebody's got to teach them how to take a stage fall without killing themselves.'" Agnes de Mille headed up the dance department; Jerome Robbins taught modern dance; Lincoln Kirstein directed the ballet program. Other well-known professionals offered classes in their specialties. Within a year, 1,650 "veterans of the entertainment industry" were enrolled in the program. The original twenty-three courses expanded to fifty (not counting the individual vocal lessons and special coaching arranged through the program).[51]

Anthony Dominick Benedetto was one of veterans who enrolled. Benedetto had been drafted in late 1944 and sent to the front lines in Germany as a replacement rifleman. "I saw things no human being should ever have to see. I know I'm speaking for others as well when I say that life can never be the same once you've been through combat. I don't care what anybody says: no human being should have to go to war, especially an eighteen-year-old boy." After V-E Day, far short of the points needed for demobilization, the GI who would become Tony Bennett was "assigned to Special Services, the division of the military that had the task of entertaining the occupying troops." Discharged in August 1946, he moved back to his parents' home in Astoria, Queens. "Everything was different than it had been before.... All I knew was that I wanted to get my life started again as soon as possible." He was "determined to do whatever I had to do to become a professional singer." He auditioned, sat in with every band that invited him, knocked "on the door of every booking agent, club and promoter in town," and took whatever part-time jobs he could find, including singing waiter jobs. Like so many other vets, he was saved by the GI Bill. Though he had never graduated from high school, he was admitted to the American Theatre Wing's Professional School, his tuition paid for, with a living allowance that far exceeded what he had been able to earn at his odd jobs. He took acting classes and voice lessons with "amazing teachers.... I've since applied the techniques I learned there to my singing."[52]

Veterans who lived outside New York City and Los Angeles were able to locate acting schools closer to home. Ernest Borgnine, a navy veteran from a blue-collar family in New Haven, returned to his parents' house at war's end. "I went out looking for work." Unable to find a factory job—and not sure he even wanted one—Borgnine came home after a day of job hunting "and I guess I looked despondent. My mother asked me what was the matter. I said, 'Mom, for two cents I'd go back and join the navy again. At least I'd get a pension at the end of my twenty years.' I wasn't sure whether she'd approve or disapprove. All I know is I didn't expect what she actually said to me. 'Son,' she said, 'have you ever thought of becoming an actor. . . . You always like to make a damn fool of yourself, making people laugh. Why don't you give it a try.'" The next day, Borgnine hitchhiked to Yale to see if he could get into the Drama School on the GI Bill. He was told that he could be admitted, but only after he completed two years of undergraduate classes. "Asking around at other schools—those with a little less ivy—I finally found out about the Randall School up in Hartford, Connecticut. . . . They were glad to see me. They didn't care what credentials I had." He stayed in school, tuition paid for by the GI Bill, and collected his living allowance checks long enough to get rave reviews in a student production, after which he took the train to Virginia, where he found work moving scenery in a repertory theater.[53]

In the June 1945 issue of *Dance Magazine*, the publisher, Rudolf Orthwine, reprinted a letter from Master Sergeant Joseph E. Kowatch, who asked if the magazine could furnish him and other veterans interested in dance—"most of them would like to study ballet!"—with information on schools that would accept them and their GI Bill benefits. The publisher answered in an editorial that Kowatch's "suggestion makes action on our part imperative. We must all be instrumental in assisting the returned soldier to find himself in a peaceful occupation to his liking, where he may be happy and able to earn a livelihood." *Dance*, he pledged, would serve "as a clearing house for gathering all obtainable information" about schools and benefits and make this information available to the servicemen and the "proper authorities."[54]

Robert Barnett, who would join the New York City Ballet in 1949 and in 1962 become artistic director of the Atlanta Ballet, attended his first ballet performance while he was in the service. "I was living in San Pedro in a barracks, and I'd just been in Los Angeles on liberty for that day. I walked by the theater and decided I was going to go in. It was a revelation." Stationed in Japan after the war, Barnett danced in a pseudo-ballet show for American servicemen, then, after his discharge, informed his parents he was going to "Los Angeles and see if I can find a place to study. I questioned my mother's aunt because she taught at Pasadena Community College." She suggested that he inquire at the school's theater department, which he had trouble finding. A girl at the college theater box office directed him instead to a dance school in West Los Angeles where a friend of hers studied. "I got on a bus, transferred and went down La Brea Avenue, and finally found the school. It was over a movie theater. There was a blond lady at the desk. She said they had classes for older students. In fact they had a program under the GI Bill. The teacher turned out to be Bronislava Nijinska," the exiled dancer, choreographer, teacher, and sister of the legendary Vaslav Nijinsky. "They signed me up, got all the papers. I took twelve classes a week: Tap, ballet, and character class. We had music theory. We had French classes. It was like a little academy."[55]

Twenty-nine veterans were listed on the January 1947 register, forty-one on the final 1948 class roster for Bronislava Nijinska's Hollywood Ballet School in Los Angeles. Here was yet another example of the serendipitous journeys that brought together through the GI Bill American veterans recently returned from war and European artists in exile.[56]

Everywhere but in the southern states, White and Black veterans could and did study tap, ballet, and modern dance under the GI Bill at a variety of schools, including the prestigious San Francisco Ballet School and the Katherine Dunham School of Dance and Theatre on West Forty-Third Street in New York. Paid advertisements in *Dance* featured dozens of schools that accepted students under the GI Bill. Veterans in New York City could receive free tuition and living allowances at the School of Dance Arts, Ballet, Tap, and Spanish and Mabel Horsey's Studio, which offered classes in "Tap, Toe, Ballet, Acrobatic dance, as well as Drama, Music, Sight Reading, and Piano."[57]

Veteran enrollments in dance schools, studios, and academies ballooned as state education departments across the country authorized "social dancing" courses as eligible for GI Bill benefits, even though it was quite apparent that few, if any, of the veterans were going to make a living as ballroom dancing instructors. The Arthur Murray Studios were a prime recipient of GI Bill funding. "By 1946, Murray operated seventy-two dance studios across the United States and generated $20 million per year in revenue," much of it from veterans.[58]

There was another, lesser-known feature of the GI Bill that was especially beneficial to aspiring Black and White chefs, writers, painters, musicians, and dancers. To provide schooling for veterans who remained overseas as part of the occupation army, improve relations with foreign countries, and "spread American business influence," veterans were permitted to use their GI Bill tuition payments and living allowances to study abroad.[59]

Hundreds, some of whom had fallen in love with European cities, Paris in particular, returned courtesy of the GI Bill, some to go to school, others to register, collect their living allowances, and enjoy the sights, sounds, and cultural institutions. The former marine and future humorist Art Buchwald "discovered that, for a small price, the woman who took attendance at his language school, the Alliance

Française, would mark him present each day. A friend told him that if all the veterans who were enrolled there actually showed up for class, 'they would need a soccer stadium to accommodate them.'"[60]

Ellsworth Kelly, who had served with the 603rd Camouflage Engineers, had been in Paris briefly during the war and wanted to return "and the G.I. Bill allowed that. . . . But as soon as I got there, I realized I wasn't French, you know, and I wasn't European. . . . And I stopped painting for a short while and went to museums and traveled on my bicycle all over France."[61]

Norman Mailer used his advance money from *The Naked and the Dead* to travel to Paris, where he and his first wife, Bea, who had served in the WAVEs, with hundreds of other veterans enrolled in the Cours de Civilisation Française, a private language institute. Their tuition was fully paid, and the two of them received a total of $180 a month from the GI Bill. Other veterans in Paris studied music, art, and cooking. "Robert Owens, an African American from Berkeley, California, persisted through four years of piano training at the tough Ecole Normale de Musique. . . . So many veterans attended the classes at the Cordon Bleu cooking school that it set up a separate course for Americans."[62]

Other veterans had come to Paris, *Life* magazine explained in a feature story, "for all manner of reasons, some just to have a good time; a few because their particular neuroses failed to fit a Stateside moral code; many among the Negroes to climb over the walls surrounding them at home."[63]

For Black veterans locked out of higher education, Paris on the GI Bill was both godsend and necessity. *The Afro-American* reported in April 1947 on "eight members of the American minority population" studying under the GI Bill at the University of Paris; another at the Sorbonne; two more at L'École Normale, and one taking classes in dress design at L'École de la Chambre Syndicale de la Couture Parisienne. Herbert Gentry had been stationed in a Parisian suburb at war's end. "I just fell in love with that city. And when I was discharged, I decided I wanted to go back to school in Paris." He studied French at the Alliance Française, painting and drawing at L'Académie de la Grande Chaumière, and political science at L'École des Hautes Études, all on the GI Bill.[64]

Romare Bearden, who before the war had his first gallery show in Washington, D.C., then another in New York, still "felt that I really didn't know enough about painting, that I hadn't really gone to art school enough." In 1950, at age thirty-nine, he "still had the GI Bill of Rights which I hadn't used. And I decided to go to Paris." He enrolled in a course of philosophy taught by Gaston Bachelard at the Sorbonne, pocketed his GI Bill living allowance, and spent his time wandering the city and meeting poets and artists. "I didn't paint at all. I thought that I would like to but I was so absorbed in seeing and walking in Paris from one end of the city to the other that I could never get around to doing any painting."[65]

Paris was the major attraction for veterans who chose to use their GI Bill benefits to travel and live outside the States, but it was not the only one. Veterans studied in Sweden, Ecuador, Australia, Mexico, and elsewhere. *Life* magazine focused its attention on those in Mexico in "GI Paradise," a January 1948 photo essay. A beguiling shot of a reclining female nude being sketched on a rooftop may have helped boost veterans' enrollment in Mexico to a thousand by the summer of 1948.[66]

The GI Bill provided incalculable assistance to the millions of returning veterans who took advantage of its generous educational benefits, collected living allowances while doing so, and enhanced their self-esteem, skills, and marketability. Its impact on postwar America was not, however, limited to the benefits it bestowed on individual veterans. As the President's Commission on Veterans' Pensions declared in its 1956 report, the bill had been designed not only to reward the men and women who had fought and won the war but to "ease the strain during demobilization" on an economy in transition from war to peace and forestall "a postwar unemployment crisis."[67]

And that is precisely what it did by bestowing nearly $4 billion in tuition payments on colleges, universities, vocational schools, and job-training programs across the country and an additional $10 billion on veterans for living allowances. The White House Office of Management and Budget figures for government spending on "veterans education benefits" from 1946 through 1952 put the total at more than $17.3 billion. These cash infusions into the cities, towns, and communities with schools certified to receive GI Bill tuition payments and into the pockets, household budgets, and bank accounts of the 7.8 million veterans who participated went a long way toward stabilizing the postwar economy. This federal government pump priming was not accidental, but an intentional and a critical element in the design, drafting, and implementation of the 1944 bill and subsequent amendments to it.[68]

Chapter 20.

AFTER FIVE YEARS

Despite the rather dire prognostications of politicians, the press, the public, and the veterans, a booming wartime economy, with fits and starts, but no real backward sliding, was converted to a vibrant peacetime one. The fears of a return to depression and massive unemployment vanished as rapidly as they had appeared. So too the unsettling images of hordes of unemployed veterans provoking civil unrest and political chaos, as had happened in Germany, in Italy, and, to a much lesser extent, in the United States after World War I.

The economy had not righted itself by itself. The GI Bill had played an outsized role in the relatively smooth reconversion from war to peace. The two million veterans whom John Snyder, director of the Office of War Mobilization and Reconversion, identified as "resting" before looking for work were able to do so because they were collecting $20-a-week readjustment allowance checks. These checks benefited not only the returning servicemen but the overall economy by transferring $1 billion of federal funds in 1946 and $1.4 billion in 1947 to the veterans and their families to spend as they saw fit. As the President's Commission on Veterans' Pensions concluded in its 1956 report, this "outpouring of purchasing power in readjustment benefits during the first postwar years played a part in the Nation's speedy economic adjustment. Payments to veterans helped to offset the drop in factory payrolls, and to maintain the high demand for goods and services." They fed consumer demand, which, in turn, led to increased production of consumer goods and new jobs producing and selling them.[1]

Title II of the GI Bill, "Education of Veterans," provided the veterans with a second, more lucrative and rewarding alternative to employment: free tuition, fees and expenses up to $500 a school year, and living allowances for up to four years to attend college, university, or vocational school. Some 7.8 million veterans profited from the GI Bill education programs, but so too did the overall economy, as the federal government poured $14.5 billion into Title II benefits: $10 billion in living allowances, $4 billion in tuition fees, and $500 million for supplies, equipment, and other fees. The direct and beneficial effects of this spending on the overall economy and social stability cannot be underestimated.[2]

As Samuel Stouffer concluded in the second volume of *The American Soldier*, published in 1949, "The combination of liberal benefits under the GI bill and a continuation of employment at a high level in the postwar period provided an almost ideal situation for the reabsorption into civilian life of the millions of men who laid down their arms at the end of the war."[3]

Five years after V-J Day, the economy was booming; consumer goods were available again; homicides, manslaughters, robberies, burglaries, and auto theft, which had reached new heights in the immediate postwar period, had tailed off. The predictions that marriages that had stayed intact through the war would not survive the first years of peace proved largely true, but the impact of the marriage apocalypse was much less significant than the experts had warned.

The national divorce rate reached new heights in the first three postwar years, more than double that of the Depression era. But so had the marriage rate. The birth rate had also risen far more than had been expected, with 3.8 million births in 1947, an almost 60 percent increase from ten years earlier.[4]

The singular failure of the GI Bill's readjustment assistance—and the one that might have been felt most acutely by large numbers of veterans—was the Title III mortgage guaranty program, which had done little, if anything, to solve the housing crisis. In July 1949, *Collier's* magazine, surveying the plight of the hundreds of thousands of inadequately housed or unhoused veterans and their families, published "Our Shameful Record in Veterans' Housing" by Frank D. Morris. The article was unsparing in its condemnation of Washington for not doing more for the veterans and of the public for not demanding that more be done. "Mr. G.I. Veteran, in case you've forgotten, is the fellow to whom we promised a decent American home; a place where he could settle down to citizenship and family life. Does he, after four years of peace, now have that home or even a reasonable facsimile thereof?" The magazine's answer was a resounding no. There were, *Collier's* declared, based on its survey of thirty American cities, "approximately 1,500,000 ex-servicemen who live under appalling conditions." The base problem was that there were not enough affordable housing units available for purchase or in construction.[5]

The GI Bill had, since its passage into law in June 1944, done precious little to relieve the housing shortage. By December 1949, only 10.6 percent of World War II veterans had made use of GI Bill mortgage guarantees to purchase homes.[6] Housing and VA officials blamed the bankers for not issuing mortgages and the builders for not constructing sufficient family-size affordable homes. The bankers and the builders, in turn, accused the government and the VA for not doing more to remove the restrictions and regulations that made the GI Bill provisions less than attractive to lenders and recipients alike. Despite the recriminations on all sides, the underlying problem, which Senator Taft had identified in August 1945 and had not been solved, was that "private initiative" was not supplying "sufficient . . . decent houses" at affordable prices. Congress attempted, belatedly, to stimulate the housing market by passing Public Law 475 in 1950, which increased the percentage of the purchase price guaranteed by the federal government from 50 percent to 60 percent, the maximum loan guaranteed from $4,000 to $7,500, and the repayment period from twenty-five to thirty years.[7]

It would take until the early 1950s before a solution was found to the veterans' housing shortage. Between 1950 and 1955, the number of veterans who used GI Bill mortgage guarantees to buy new homes increased by an astounding 250 percent. Though the 1950 housing bill (Public Law 475), which liberalized the requirements for loan guarantees, played a role in this increase, it was not a major one. Of far greater significance were two other factors. Five years after the end of the war, the younger veterans who had possessed little or no liquid assets when they returned from service were, now older and better educated or with several years on the job, able to carry the monthly payments on a guaranteed GI mortgage. Of even greater importance was the fact that private builders, five years after V-E Day, were finally beginning to construct homes the veterans could afford—and enough of them to make a significant dent in the postwar housing shortage.[8]

Wilson Wyatt, Truman's housing expediter, had in 1946 tried to jump-start the construction of affordable housing by subsidizing the prefabricated home industry. The attempt failed miserably. William Levitt, whose family was in the construction business on Long Island, found a better, cheaper, and more efficient way to mass-produce affordable houses. Instead of manufacturing prefabs on an assembly line in a factory, separately preparing building sites, and trucking them to their final destinations, Levitt built his houses on-site, thousands at a time, dramatically lowering the costs of land, building materials, labor, marketing, and sales. "The construction process itself was divided into twenty-seven distinct steps—beginning with laying the foundation and ending with a clean sweep of the new home. Crews were trained to do one job—one day the white-paint men, then the red-paint men, then the tile layers. Every possible part, and especially the most difficult ones, were preassembled in central shops."[9]

To cut costs even further, the Levitts subverted union rules that protected workers and their wages. "Long Island's building trades 'Czar,'" Big Bill DeKoning, who was "arrested and convicted on ninety-two counts of extortion, coercion and conspiracy" in 1953, looked the other way as the contractors and subcontractors who worked at Levittown, in return for kickbacks, violated the rules DeKoning, as a union official, was supposed to enforce.[10]

Levitt's cost-saving building techniques were a necessary but not the only source of his success. As important was his ingenious deployment of GI and FHA loan guarantees. At almost every step of the process, from building to sales, Levitt, while honored as "the apostle of private enterprise," fed off and profited from government money. He secured advance FHA "commitments" to insure 90 percent of the mortgages on the houses he intended to build and then, with these "commitments" in hand, sought and was granted "production advances" from local banks. This, as Eric Larrabee wrote in *Harper's Magazine* in September 1948, "made it possible" for him "to bring together the capital without which a many-thousand-house development could not be undertaken." Having built his houses with federal loan guarantees, Levitt then sold them to veterans who used their GI Bill benefits to secure mortgages, backed by the federal government.[11]

Federal munificence paid off not only for Levitt and the developers who followed his lead but for the veterans as well. The two-bedroom Cape Cod–style houses with radiant heating, name-brand appliances, landscaped grounds, and nearby schools, shopping centers, and a swimming pool were both affordable and irresistible to veterans who had hitherto been priced out of the single-family home market.

"We'd been staying with our folks in the Bronx," the wife of the veteran Al Ludwig recalled, "because no one could find a place after the war; there were no developments. Levittown was like a godsend." Asked about her neighbors, all of whom were White, most of them in households headed by a male veteran, Mrs. Ludwig replied that "we all got along because we all started with a clean slate, we were all in the same situation. It was a great experience."[12]

Through the 1950s, the Levitt organization expanded its operations from Long Island to Bucks County, Pennsylvania, where it put up sixteen thousand houses, and then on to Willingboro, New Jersey. Other builders deployed similar mass production and financing practices to put up huge developments, occupied by large numbers of veterans and their families, in the suburbs of almost every large metropolitan area, including Boston, Portland, Los Angeles, Phoenix, Houston, Denver, Memphis, San Antonio, Cleveland, Washington, Chicago, Baltimore, and San Francisco.[13]

To a great extent as a result of the efforts of suburban developers like the Levitts, single-family housing starts reached "1,692,000 in 1950, an all-time high." As the number of new-built affordable houses increased, so did the number of veterans ready and able to purchase them with federal loan guarantees. Between December 1949 and December 1955, the percentage of veterans who made use of GI Bill guaranteed mortgages rose from 10.6 percent to 26.7 percent. By October 1955, there were "more than 10.7 million veteran homeowners, of whom all but a small proportion were veterans of World War II." By December 1955, 4.1 million veterans had purchased homes with GI

Bill mortgage guarantees and millions more with FHA loans or conventional loans.[14]

With so many veterans now in the market for single-family homes, the VA felt obliged to issue a warning "To the HOME-BUYING Veteran" in a June 1950 letter, warning them that the loans they were taking out would have to be repaid, that they should be careful not to "overobligate" themselves to spending more than they could afford, that they should bear in mind the future cost of taxes, insurance, "repairs, heat, light, water and other utilities," that they had only until July 25, 1957, to use their guaranty entitlements, and that the VA did not "warrant that the home you buy is a good one.... Remember that the purchase of a home will probably be the biggest investment in your family's lifetime. DO NOT TREAT IT LIGHTLY."[15]

As had been the case with every other provision of the GI Bill, Title III, though race neutral in theory, was, in execution, far from it. It did not provide veterans with mortgages or funds for down payments or financial assistance in securing mortgages. What it did was guarantee mortgages if and when the veterans were able to secure them. It was of no use at all to veterans who, because they were not White, male, and married, were denied mortgages by their local banks.

Black veterans were further discriminated against by the builders, developers, real estate agents, and homeowners who refused to sell to them because they were Black. Because neither the courts, nor Congress, nor any state, save Pennsylvania, and any city, save San Francisco, had passed antidiscrimination housing legislation, Black veterans had no recourse when developers like Levitt turned them away because, they claimed, integrated developments were bad for business.

Eugene Burnett, like so many other veterans, had read the ads about the new Levittown houses and drove out from East Harlem to see for himself. "I found the salesman," he later told journalist Paula Span, "and said 'I like your house and I'm considering buying one. Could you give me the application?' . . . He said, 'It's not me. But the owners of this development have not yet decided to sell to Negroes.' I was shocked out of my shoes."[16]

The Levitts' refusal to sell their houses to Black veterans and civilians meant that, as the NAACP's executive secretary, Walter White, declared on a visit to Long Island in 1951, there was now "almost as much quiet segregation on Long Island as there is open segregation in Georgia." The Levitts made no attempt to disguise the fact that their suburban villages were as segregated as any in the South. While he was not personally prejudiced, William Levitt explained to a reporter, his potential buyers were, and as a businessman he had to cater to them. "As a Jew, I have no room in my mind or heart for racial prejudice. But, by various means, I have come to know that if we sell one house to a Negro family, then ninety to ninety-five per cent of our white customers will not buy into the community. That is their attitude, not ours. We did not create it, and cannot cure it. As a company, our position is simply this: we can solve a housing problem, or we can try to solve a racial problem. But we cannot combine the two."[17]

Labor unions, Jewish organizations, the NAACP, and veterans' groups protested against the Levitts' refusal to sell to Black veterans. In November 1948, Thurgood Marshall of the NAACP requested that the FHA "cease issuing mortgages for the financing of Levittown until the signing of racial restrictive covenants is removed as a condition of occupancy." Such covenants, he reminded the commissioner, Franklin Richards, had been declared unenforceable by the Supreme Court. Commissioner Richards replied that the court decision notwithstanding, the FHA had no "authority to refuse to insure mortgages for private projects practicing race discrimination."[18]

Even had the Levitts been fully willing to integrate their developments, they would have been blocked from doing so by the FHA, which not only refused to oppose housing segregation but actively enforced it. In determining the value of a property, the FHA assessed "the degree of compatibility of the inhabitants of the neighborhood. The presence of incompatible groups in a neighborhood tends to lessen or destroy owner-occupancy appeal." Loan guarantees would be approved for houses in segregated neighborhoods but not in integrated communities.[19]

As the National Park Service concluded in its March 2021 study, *Racial Discrimination in Housing*, "The contributions and consequences of FHA and VA policies in the residential segregation of postwar American cities and suburbs turned out to be sweeping and enduring.... In a 1950 survey of metropolitan New York, nonwhite families... received only 0.1 percent of VA mortgages through the GI Bill.... In metropolitan Los Angeles, FHA or VA loans covered 46.6 percent of all owner-occupied homes by 1960, with racially segregated developments the rule and 97 percent of new housing closed to African Americans. In the San Francisco Bay area, the FHA and VA together subsidized 60 percent of the homes constructed in the 1950s, with 98.5 percent barred from purchase by nonwhites."[20]

Just thirty-five miles from the first Levittown on Long Island, another huge development was built in the late 1940s to alleviate the postwar housing shortage and provide decent, affordable homes for returning veterans, so long as they were White. Frederick Ecker, chairman of the board of the Metropolitan Life Insurance Company, whose housing projects were nearly as large as William Levitt's, offered the same rationale for barring African Americans. In an affidavit in a lawsuit challenging the decision to bar Blacks from leasing apartments in Stuyvesant Town, Ecker declared, as had Levitt, that "the implication that I, personally... entertain any prejudice against colored people is ridiculous and false." The decision to prohibit Blacks from occupying apartments in his complexes was purely a business decision. "It is the legal duty of the management of Stuyvesant to adopt such policies as . . . will best protect the safety of this investment. In fulfilling this duty, it had been decided that Negroes should not, at this time, be accepted as tenants."[21]

Robert Moses, with the approval of Mayor La Guardia, both of them fearful that the postwar urban housing shortage combined with the growth of slum areas would discourage veterans from resettling in the city, encouraged Ecker and Metropolitan Life to build a walled-in town within the city for middle-class veterans and other New Yorkers. Stuyvesant Town would be erected between Fourteenth and Twentieth Streets in the Gas House District, an area of modest tenements that housed eleven thousand low-income New Yorkers. Robert Moses and Mayor La Guardia referred to the district as a slum and its replacement by Stuyvesant Town as a "slum-clearance" project. Questioned as to why the Stuyvesant Town plans included no public school, Ecker replied "that the Company desires to restrict the use of the entire area to its own tenants . . . if there were a public school in the project the City would allow some children, including Negroes, to attend from outside the area." To counter the claim that Metropolitan Life was biased against "Negroes," the company agreed to build Riverton, a second, though smaller, development in Harlem.[22]

Veterans were given first priority in leasing Stuyvesant Town apartments. In late June 1947, after the families of two White veterans were given leases and moved into apartments, three Black veterans who had also applied but were turned down sued Metropolitan Life Insurance for violating their constitutional rights. Joseph R. Dorsey had held the rank of captain in the army, had a master's degree, and was employed as a supervisor of casework for the probation department. He lived with his mother and aunt on West 108th Street. Calvin B. Harper, a disabled veteran with a good job and good salary who lived in the Bronx and commuted three hours a day to work, applied for an apartment because he needed to live closer to his job. Monroe D. Dowling, who had been discharged at the rank of captain, had undergraduate and graduate degrees from Harvard, and lived with his wife and child in a one-bedroom apartment in the Bronx. "I have tried many times to get better living quarters closer to my place of work but have been unsuccessful. I am informed and believe that I would qualify for an apartment except for the intention of the Stuyvesant Town corporation not to permit Negroes to occupy apartments in that project."[23]

The three Black veterans were represented by Charles Abrams of the American Civil Liberties Union and attorneys from the American Jewish Congress and the NAACP. The Metropolitan Life Insurance lawyers did not deny that Stuyvesant Town barred Black veterans and other African Americans but insisted that, as a private entity, it could choose whomever it wanted to live in its buildings. The company won its suit in the New York Supreme Court in December 1948; the decision was affirmed by the Appellate Division in July 1949; a year later the U.S. Supreme Court, after eight months of deliberations, refused to hear the case.[24]

Charles Abrams, writing in *Commentary*, declared that in sanctioning the right of the Metropolitan Life Insurance Company to discriminate against African Americans in New York City, the courts had provided developers in other cities and states carte blanche to do the same. "The entrepreneur may be single-minded in his quest for profit," but government, Abrams argued, should be "bound to the principle of non-discrimination and the equal protection of the laws." Instead, New York City and State and the courts had become complicit, if not active partners, in extending Jim Crow northward.[25]

In August 1949, Hardine Hendrix, a war veteran, and his wife and son were invited by a Stuyvesant Town tenant to occupy his apartment for the summer. In mid-September a second tenant, a professor at City

College who had been fired for political reasons, extended the Black family's residence by inviting them to stay in his apartment, rent free. Metropolitan Life retaliated by sending eviction notices to both tenants and more than a dozen others who had supported the integration of Stuyvesant Town. In the end, a compromise of sorts was reached. The tenants who had allowed the Hendrix family to live in their apartments were forced out, but in 1952, after a three-year fight and the mediation efforts of the city council president, Metropolitan Life dropped eviction proceedings against nineteen tenants and granted the Black veteran Hardine Hendrix a lease.[26]

It would take five to ten years from the end of the war before a substantial number of veterans were able to use their GI Bill benefits to purchase new housing built by private developers with federal mortgage loans and guarantees. With few exceptions, these new developments were racially segregated. By 1953, there were no Blacks among the 70,000 residents of Long Island's Levittown. By 1960, there were 57. Stuyvesant Town admitted its first Black tenants in 1952 and by 1960 had a total of 47 among its 22,405 residents.[27]

This discrimination would have far-reaching consequences for the veterans, their families, and the nation at large.

Part 4

Legacies

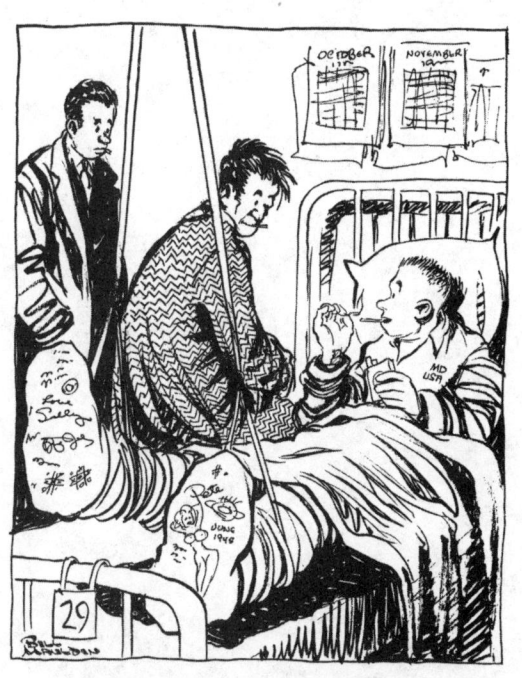

"How's things outside, boys? Am I still a war hero or a drain on th' taxpayer?"

Chapter 21.

THE VETERANS' WELFARE STATE

Congress, dominated during the war by a coalition of Republicans and southern Democrats, had thwarted all attempts to maintain or extend New Deal welfare programs, but had instead, as the sociologists Edwin Amenta and Theda Skocpol have written, constructed "what the New Deal reformers had hoped to avoid: a special welfare state for a substantial sector of the population deemed especially deserving. The social reformism of the New Deal had been channeled into expanded public provision for veterans."[1]

This post–World War II veterans' welfare state was constructed piece by piece from 1940 through 1950.

The Selective Training and Service Act of 1940 guaranteed only World War II veterans, not those who had left their jobs to work in the war industries, their former positions back when the war was over. By March 1947, almost 900,000 veterans had taken advantage of this provision of the act.[2]

Public Law 10, signed on March 17, 1943, provided them with "medical and hospital treatment, domiciliary care, and burial benefits ... regardless of whether the disability suffered was service incurred."[3]

The Disabled Veterans' Rehabilitation Act, also signed into law in March 1943, authorized medical assistance and vocational rehabilitation for veterans. By 1955, some 220,000 veterans had received these benefits at a total cost of $1.6 billion.[4]

The Veterans' Preference Act of 1944 gave disabled veterans who were applying for federal jobs 10 extra points on their civil service test scores, 5 for those not disabled. It also exempted veterans from age, height, and weight requirements and offered them credit for military service in meeting the experience requirements for positions. Ten years after the law had been enacted, the percentage of veterans employed in the federal civil service had jumped from 420,439, or 15 percent of the total, to 1,066,534, or 50 percent.[5]

The GI Bill of June 1944 provided generous short-term financial assistance, including readjustment allowances for the unemployed, education and training benefits, and loan guarantees to purchase a home, farm, or business. The bill also directed the VA to build new hospitals for veterans and appropriated $500 million for this purpose.

The December 1945 amendments extended the bill's already generous educational benefits to those whose schooling had not been disrupted by war and its mortgage guarantees to those who had never dreamed of owning their own single-family homes.

The War Brides Act of December 28, 1945, offered veterans, and veterans only, the opportunity to bring their "White" war brides into the country, without regard to immigration quotas and at government expense. Subsequent amendments provided veterans' fiancées and fiancés entry into the country and removed the racial restrictions on the entry of Asian war brides.

Public Law 293, signed by President Truman on January 3, 1946, established the Department of Medicine and Surgery within the Veterans Administration. The law provided exemptions for VA medical staff from civil service rules, and spearheaded the modernization and expansion of medical and hospital care for the returning veterans. The number of physicians in the VA hospitals rose from 2,300 on June 30, 1945, to 4,000 a year later. "By 1950, the VA administered 136 hospitals, which had a total of 577,715 admissions that fiscal year. Another twenty-six hospitals were under construction that year, slated to provide 20,000 additional beds."[6]

National Housing Acts passed into law in 1948, 1949, and 1950 "revised GI Bill loan provisions," as Congress, according to historian Kathleen Frydl, "infused billions of dollars into the housing program."[7]

These were the building blocks for the construction of the veterans' welfare state. They required the expenditure of billions of dollars now available with the cessation of hostilities abroad. Between 1945 and 1948, as spending for "national defense" fell by 900 percent from $83 billion to $9 billion, spending on veterans' benefits ballooned from $110 million in 1945 to $2.5 billion in fiscal 1946, $6.3 billion in 1947, and $8.8 billion in 1950. According to the political scientist Michael Brown in *Race, Money, and the American Welfare State*, by 1950 "veteran's payments made up 21 percent of federal outlays and 65 percent of transfer payments." By December 31, 1955, $24.5 billion had been spent on World War II veterans, nearly double the $13.3 billion Congress had appropriated for the Marshall Plan. An additional $34 billion was made available to guarantee loans to veterans for houses, businesses, and farms. Billions more funded medical care, hospitalization, and pensions for the disabled. By 1970, the total costs of World War II veterans' benefits approached $90 billion.[8]

Fortune magazine, surveying the American welfare state in February 1952, reported that two-thirds of the federal "welfare" bill of approximately $10 billion went for veterans' benefits. While it considered these benefits "excessive," *Fortune* did not recommend that they be cut. Its concern was that the Truman administration's Fair Deal would extend to the rest of the population the benefits granted to World War II veterans: enhanced unemployment compensation, housing assistance, funding for education, and a national health program that would provide "hospitals for everybody" and "doctors for everybody." The editors of *Fortune* need not have worried.[9]

The president and the politicians, on both sides of the aisle, the newspapers, magazines, radio, and newsreels had repeatedly emphasized that the war would be won by citizens, war workers, and volunteers on the home front as well as by those in uniform. This inclusive rhetoric notwithstanding, those who contributed to the war effort in capacities other than as members of the armed forces would not receive the benefits reserved for veterans. The exclusion of civilians from the postwar welfare state was not a foregone conclusion. President Roosevelt, according to his domestic adviser Samuel Rosenman, envisioned his proposal for "federal financial aid for educating GI's . . . as a kind of entering wedge" to pry loose federal funding to "states that could not provide decent educational facilities out of their own resources." General Bradley, having pushed an extensive and expensive veterans' health-care reorganization plan through Congress, believed that it might serve as a model for a national health-care program.[10]

These hoped-for extensions of benefits from veterans to civilians would not come to pass. While Congress in the postwar decades allocated billions of dollars for medical care, hospital treatment, and domiciliary care for veterans, $154 million in 1947 alone on the construction of new VA hospitals and domiciliary facilities, it balked at establishing complementary programs for nonveterans. The end result was, as Paul Starr has written of health care, that a "large group of working-class, predominantly white males was able to receive government-financed health services, which when advocated for other Americans were denounced as likely to undermine self-reliance."[11]

This was the case as well for unemployment compensation, job training and counseling, rehabilitation assistance for the disabled, tuition and living allowances to attend colleges, universities, and vocational schools, and loan guarantees in purchasing a home. These benefits, authorized and funded between 1940 and 1950 for veterans, were denied the 100 million nonveteran adults alive in 1945. They were denied as well to the almost quarter million men who had risked their lives in the merchant marines;* the more than a thousand women who served as WASPs (Women's Airforce Service Pilots);† and the thousands of Red Cross volunteers, including the Donut Dollies,‡ who accompanied the troops into every theater of war, served them food, danced with them, cared for and comforted the wounded in field hospitals, general hospitals, and hospital ships, and drove and staffed the clubmobiles, cinemobiles, trailer kitchens, and trucks that transported hundreds of tons of supplies and equipment.[12]

By the early 1960s, the postwar portraits of discontented, angry, restless, violent, sometimes criminal veterans returning from war had given way to those of smiling family men with college degrees and good jobs, living with their wives and children in suburban single-family homes with a television in the den, a kitchen full of appliances, and a shiny new car in the garage.

The benefits offered the World War II veterans had, in fact, so

---

* In 1988, after a court decision in their favor, the merchant marines who had served in the war were made eligible for VA benefits.

† In 1977, the WASPs were retroactively reclassified as military personnel eligible for VA benefits.

‡ In 2012 the Red Cross volunteers' contribution to the war effort was officially recognized in a Senate resolution, sponsored by Senator Susan Collins of Maine. No financial assistance or veterans' benefits of any sort were offered those still living or the families of the deceased.

successfully accomplished their purpose and facilitated the reinsertion of millions of veterans into the economic, social, and cultural life of the nation that some outside the Beltway, most notably Martin Luther King Jr., suggested that it might now be time for the federal government to extend them to all Americans.

In the summer of 1963, Dr. King, in speeches in Harlem, Baltimore, and elsewhere, proposed a bill of rights for the disadvantaged, modeled on the GI Bill. "During World War II," he wrote in *Why We Can't Wait*, published in June 1964, "our fighting men were deprived of certain advantages and opportunities. To make up for this, they were given a package of veterans rights, significantly called a 'Bill of Rights.' . . . In this way, the nation was compensating the veteran for his time lost, in school or in his career or in business. Such compensatory treatment was approved by the majority of Americans. . . . I am proposing, therefore, that, just as we granted a GI Bill of Rights to war veterans, America launch a broad-based and gigantic Bill of Rights for the Disadvantaged, our veterans of the long siege of denial. Such a bill could adapt almost every concession given the returning soldier without imposing an undue burden on our economy. . . . While Negroes form the vast majority of America's disadvantaged, there are millions of white poor who would also benefit from such a bill."[13]

In July 1964, King presented his plan to the Republican Party platform committee; in August, to the Democrats. Neither party endorsed it. The price tag was too large—$15 billion—there was little support for raising taxes or slashing military spending to fund it, and the proposal was aimed at providing financial support for two of the constituencies Congress believed it could ignore: poor Blacks and Whites.

King did not give up. In July 1965, in a series of speeches, thirty-five in Chicago, another eight in Cleveland, he again took up his call for a GI Bill–style program for the disadvantaged. In October 1967, testifying before the Kerner Commission (National Advisory Commission on Civil Disorders), he argued that "a broad-based and gigantic bill of rights for the disadvantaged," patterned on the GI Bill, "will do more than the most massive development of troops to quell riots and still hatred." What was required, he wrote in a *New York Times* opinion piece the following month, was nothing less than a "revolution in values" and the redirection of "the billions of dollars now directed toward destruction and military containment" toward a bill of rights that would provide for all citizens what the GI Bill had offered the World War II veterans.[14]

In December 1967, King and the Southern Christian Leadership Conference launched the Poor People's Campaign to mobilize a massive nonviolent campaign to compel the government to "address the issues afflicting America's poor and weak" and fund a bill of rights for the disadvantaged. In April 1968, he was assassinated. The campaign to extend the benefits of the GI Bill that had profited White males and their families to poor and Black Americans who most needed them died with him.[15]

A little more than a quarter century after Dr. King's death, President Bill Clinton, celebrating the GI Bill's fiftieth anniversary, declared that it had given the World War II veterans "a ticket to the American dream. . . . And look what they did. . . . Out of the World War II class, 450,000 became engineers; 360,000 became schoolteachers; 240,000 became accountants. . . . One hundred and eighty thousand became doctors and nurses; 150,000 became scientists, paving our way to the next century."* The outpouring of praise for the 1944 bill and its amendments in providing opportunities for the World War II veterans was well deserved. But President Clinton was only

---

* The figures are impressive, though questionable. These figures were probably compiled by the Veterans Administration, but we have no idea how or when.

half right when he declared that the GI Bill "arguably was the greatest investment in our people in American history." That investment was not "in our people," writ large, but in the 11.8 million veterans who received one or more GI Bill benefits.[16]

Had the demographics of the uniformed armed forces been congruent with the general population, the GI Bill and the organization of the veterans' welfare state might have had a vastly different impact on the construction and expansion of the American middle class. But this was not the case. Through the first postwar decade, as Michael Brown has written, the incomes of the World War II veterans, who were 98 percent male and more than 90 percent White, "rose relative to those of nonveterans. Income advantages were reinforced by differences in possession of assets. Most veterans had more liquid assets than nonveterans. . . . Veterans of all ages made substantial gains in home ownership compared to nonveterans. . . . Veterans were disproportionately concentrated in high-paying occupations; compared to nonveterans, they were substantially more likely to be professionals, managers, or skilled workers."[17]

The bestowing of benefits on the veterans, but not on other citizens, had the effect of widening the gender and racial inequalities in education, assets, income, and opportunities that had begun to narrow during the war years.

The GI Bill reinforced what the historian Lizabeth Cohen has referred to as the "male-directed family economy" that predated the war, but had become somewhat less dominant during it. Male adults who had served in the military were disproportionately afforded "access to career training, property ownership, capital, and credit"; their "control over family finances" was legitimized and strengthened; "their wives' claim to full economic and social citizenship" weakened. They were able to secure loan guarantees that enabled them to purchase houses, farms, and businesses, further cementing their role as the family's primary and dominant breadwinner.[18]

"I ain't got a chance, Joe. I had too many blood transfusions overseas."

The construction of a veterans' welfare state had an even greater effect on sustaining and extending racial inequities. While large numbers of White male veterans were able to ascend into an enlarged American middle class because the GI Bill provided them with college and professional degrees, job training, and mortgage guarantees, this was true for a much smaller percentage of Black veterans.

Most significant in exacerbating the racial inequities in the decades following the war was the differential in homeownership between White and Black veterans. Between 1950 and 1960, as the number of GI loans doubled, White homeownership increased by 7 percent, Black, by half that, 3.5 percent.[19]

"Home ownership," according to the sociologists Melvin L. Oliver and Thomas M. Shapiro, "represents not only an integral part of the American Dream but also the largest component in most Americans' wealth portfolios.... Families with modest to average amounts of wealth hold most of that wealth in their home. As home prices appreciate, as they have through the postwar years, that wealth grows and can be passed on from generation to generation." Black veterans who were barred from buying homes in the new suburban developments were locked "out of the greatest mass-based opportunity for wealth accumulation in American history."[20]

In the Whites-only Levittown development on Long Island, as in the other subdivisions constructed in the late 1940s and the 1950s, the veteran's first house served as a stepping-stone to upward mobility for the entire family. As the "starter" home appreciated in value, so did the family's assets. Some of the increase was due to inflation, some to improvements and additions that were only possible because the carrying costs of the GI Bill guaranteed mortgages were low. Whatever the reasons, it was White veterans, not Black, who, having purchased a house with the help of the GI Bill, were able to trade up to more expensive houses and pass on to future generations their appreciated capital and credit.[21]

The sociologist Chinyere O. Agbai, in her study of VA and FHA housing loan guaranty programs, found that while White veterans were 13 percent more likely than nonveterans to own homes in the newly built subdivisions in the suburbs, there was no measurable increase in ownership for Black veterans compared with nonveterans. Black veterans barred from buying decent, affordable homes in good neighborhoods in the suburbs with or without VA mortgages had no choice but to purchase homes in poorer suburban communities or urban areas that appreciated in value far less than the single-family houses in the new developments purchased by White veterans.[22]

On November 5, 2021, seventy-six years and three months after V-J Day, congressmen Seth Moulton of Massachusetts and James Clyburn of South Carolina introduced a bill in the House of Representatives* to correct the "pattern of discrimination against racial minorities, especially African Americans," in the administration and allocation of GI Bill educational and housing guaranty benefits. Moulton and Clyburn proposed that access to the VA Loan Guaranty Program and post-9/11 education assistance benefits be extended to the "surviving spouse and certain direct descendants of Black veterans who had served on active duty during World War II." The bill had forty-seven sponsors, all Democrats, and was referred to the Committee on Veterans' Affairs, where it died. It was reintroduced in 2023 and 2025. According to govtrack.us, an independent entity that monitors congressional legislation, the 2025 bill had a "2% chance of being enacted."[23]

---

* The full name of the 2021 and 2023 bills was the Sgt. Isaac Woodard, Jr. and Sgt. Joseph H. Maddox GI Bill Restoration Act.

Chapter 22.

AFTERMATHS

"In 1982," Studs Terkel writes in the introduction to *"The Good War,"* "a woman of thirty, doing just fine in Washington, D.C., let me know how things are in her precincts. 'I can't relate to World War Two. It's in schoolbook texts, that's all. Battles that were won, battles that were lost. Or costume dramas you see on TV. It's just a story in the past. It's so distant, so abstract. I don't get myself up in a bunch about it.' It appears that the disremembrance of World War Two is as disturbingly profound as the forgettery of the Great Depression."[1]

Terkel published his oral history of the "disremembered" war in 1984 and won the Pulitzer Prize for general nonfiction in 1985. Ten years later, the former sergeant Andy Rooney published the first edition of *My War*. Terkel had attempted to counter the "disremembering" of the war by collecting oral histories of those who had lived through it. Rooney, on the contrary, claimed that he was writing to expunge his memories. "For three of my four years in the Army, I saw the fighting from close up. I can't forget much of what I saw and I want to write it down.... Once you've put something down on paper, you can dismiss it from your mind. Having told it, I'll be able to forget it."[2]

Terkel circumscribed his title, *"The Good War,"* with quotation marks "not as a matter of caprice or editorial comment, but simply because the adjective 'good' mated to the noun 'war' is so incongruous." Andy Rooney, interviewed by Tom Brokaw for his book *The Greatest Generation*, "challenged [the] premise that his was the greatest generation any society could hope to produce."[3]

Terkel's and Rooney's dismissal of the notion that America's war was a "good" one fought by its "greatest generation" would, in the years following the publication of their books, be consigned to the dustbin of history, replaced by the elaborate and endless celebrations of what the West Point professor and author Elizabeth Samet has called the "World War II myth" and the historian John Bodnar "the mythical images of a powerful nation and righteous citizen-soldiers."[4]

Beginning in the mid-1980s and with greater emphasis in the next two decades, GI Joe was, according to Samet, reconfigured as "an archetype of stoic humanity rather than a readily identifiable individual.... World War II veterans gradually became objects of veneration who no longer needed the reality, the complexity, the ambivalence—in short, the humanity—that [Ernie] Pyle and others bestowed on them during the war."[5]

A nation hungry for heroes after the Vietnam debacle and primed to celebrate victory after the fall of the Soviet Union was in no mood to heed the quotation marks that Studs Terkel had added to *"The Good War"* or question, with Andy Rooney, the characterization of those who had fought it as "the greatest generation." World War II had ended in a resounding victory. The injuries, wounds, illnesses, insecurities, fears, and nightmares visited upon those who had fought it could be safely buried as the past; their difficulties readjusting to civilian life minimized, if not forgotten, in a narrative that focused on the triumphalist moment when America and its people embarked on a moral crusade backed by military might to crush Nazism and Fascism, eradicate evil, reinforce democracy and capitalism at home, and extend their blessings to the rest of the world.⁶

This campaign of historical re-remembrance, reconstruction, and mythmaking was exemplified and enhanced on the fortieth anniversary of D-Day, when, standing atop the cliff that the GIs had ascended in June 1944, President Ronald Reagan saluted the veterans who had "stood and fought against tyranny in a giant undertaking unparalleled in human history." Reagan's widely publicized and expertly orchestrated visit to Normandy, according to historian David Greenberg, writing in *Slate*, "kicked off the D-Day mania," which would be amplified with subsequent visits by Presidents Clinton in 1994, George W. Bush in 2002 and 2004, Barack Obama in 2009 and 2014, Donald Trump in 2019, and Joe Biden in 2024."⁷

The surviving veterans of World War II honored at Normandy and elsewhere over the last half century deserve the praise bestowed on them. Still, we do them a disservice by reducing them to stick-figure avatars of progress, confining the effects of their war service to a character-building, maturing experience that prepared them for postwar roles as nation builders, and overlooking the difficulties they encountered on returning from war.

In the introduction to *Bringing Mulligan Home: The Other Side of the Good War*, Dale Maharidge explains that he needed to write about the homecoming of his father and the marines who fought alongside him in the Pacific, "because World War II followed a lot of men back to the United States. Ignored in many 'good war' narratives is . . . what really happened overseas—and most important, what occurred after the men came home. Many families lived with the returnee's

---

* Jimmy Carter was the first to visit Normandy during a seven-nation tour of Europe, but he did so in January 1978, not on the anniversary of D-Day, and his brief, unheralded stopover did not have the impact of future D-Day anniversary celebrations.

demons and physical afflictions. A lot of us grew up dealing with collateral damage from that war—our fathers."[8]

In part because of medical advances that saved lives on the battlefield, the number of World War II veterans who returned home wounded was larger than anyone had expected. Of the 16 million who went to war, 670,846 service men and women, 565,861 in the army alone, returned with physical wounds; hundreds of thousands more with wounds to mind and body that were not as visible but would affect them for the rest of their lives.[9]

After the PT boat he had commanded in the Pacific was sunk, the navy lieutenant John Fitzgerald Kennedy swam for miles with an injured sailor in tow, causing irreparable damage to an already damaged back and frail and injured body. Tests at military hospitals revealed that he had developed an ulcer and malaria and was dangerously emaciated. He was ordered back to the States for a thirty-day furlough in mid-December 1943. In June 1944, he was operated on in an attempt to alleviate or cure his back problems. The operation was not successful. On January 18, 1945, the navy's Retirement Board found that he was "incapacitated for active service in the Naval Reserve by reason of colitis, chronic; that this incapacity for naval service is permanent, and is the result of an incident of the service." After his retirement from the navy, his physical condition, already compromised before he entered the service, deteriorated further. He would spend the rest of his shortened life in pain and reliant on painkillers.[10]

The future Republican senator Robert Dole of Kansas was wounded in Italy in April 1945 and would spend the next three and a quarter years in American hospitals. At Percy Jones Army Hospital in Battle Creek, Michigan, he met the future senator Daniel Inouye, who had been wounded in Italy a week after he had. "We were both learning how to do everything from smoking a cigarette to opening a letter with one hand." Dole had lost the use of his right arm; Inouye's had been amputated.[11]

Joshua J. Nasaw served as a medical officer in Eritrea. While dismantling and evacuating a military hospital for which there was no further use—and doing so under extreme time pressure—he had a heart attack, was transported to Jerusalem, repatriated to Rhoads General Hospital in Utica, New York, and then Tilton General Hospital at Fort Dix, New Jersey, where he was discharged with a full disability rating. He had his second heart attack at age sixty-one, this one fatal, rated by the VA as service connected.[12]

The number of service men and women who, wounded, injured, and ill, applied for disability pensions after discharge was greater than had been anticipated. "Based on past experience," General Omar Bradley recalled in his autobiography, "the VA had estimated that about 10 percent of all World War II veterans would apply for pensions. We were astonished to find that the actual figure came to about 25 percent. . . . We had geared up for about 60,000 applications a month. They came in at the rate of about 400,000 a month. By February 1, 1946, we had received over 2 million pension claims from World War II veterans." By June 30, 1947, almost half a million veterans with neuropsychiatric disabilities had been awarded pensions at a cost of nearly $20 million monthly.[13]

Among the veterans whose lives were most grievously affected by their service were those who returned to civilian life with drinking problems. There is a wealth of evidence from VA studies, memoirs, oral histories, interviews, and the reminiscences of family members that the incidence of alcoholism among the veterans was staggering—and for many, long-lasting and deadly. Because neither the VA nor the general public initially considered alcoholism a service-connected disability, these veterans received neither disability pensions nor directed, effective treatment in VA facilities.

Frank O'Hara, art critic and poet, developed his "legendary" drinking problem in basic training and then in sonar school in Key West. "At Key West," he wrote to his parents, "there is Duval Street. . . . There are bars up and down and you drink rum or vodka, sometimes brandy-and-vodka, but the scotch is watered." O'Hara reassured his father and alcoholic mother that they need not "worry" about his drinking, because "I don't like cheap liquor and anything else is out of my wage bracket, so I am in the same position as the repulsive spinster who prided herself on her virginity." But the fact was that he was becoming a heavy drinker. Twenty years after his return, he would die of injuries, the most serious to his liver, sustained when he was hit by a taxi, late at night, on Fire Island. The anesthetist who had treated him told his friend and former lover, Joseph LeSueur, that he would "very likely have survived . . . if his liver hadn't been in such terrible shape. In other words he had drunk so much that he couldn't withstand the horrible thing that happened to him that night. In a sense he died of alcoholism." O'Hara was forty years old.[14]

Alcoholism contributed to the debility or death of countless veterans like O'Hara. A 1979 study that compared the death rates of World War II servicemen hospitalized for chronic alcoholism in 1944 and 1945 with a control group of nonveteran nonalcoholics found that thirty years after the war "mortality was significantly higher" for the alcoholic veterans, who were more likely to die from cirrhosis, accidents, suicides, homicides, tuberculosis, pneumonia, upper respiratory tract infections, and a variety of other causes. Studies of World War II veterans in VA hospitals between 1970 and 1980 found that between 23 percent and 28 percent were "defined alcoholics or problem drinkers."[15]

Even greater perhaps than the damage done by alcoholism were the long-term effects of nicotine addiction, which the military had nurtured, unknowingly perhaps, by supplying service men and women with abundant quantities of free and low-cost cigarettes. Addicted to tobacco, the veterans and civilians who had taken up smoking during the war found it difficult, if not impossible, to give it up in peacetime. By 1987, 24 percent of World War II veterans, with a mean age of 66.2 years, were smokers. Five years later, 14.4 percent of the surviving veterans, their mean age over 71, were still smoking.[16]

The results, for those who continued to smoke, were disastrous. The Veterans Administration's Office of General Counsel recognized as much in 1993 when it issued the opinion "that an injury or disease resulting from tobacco use in the line of duty in active military, naval, or air service could serve as the basis for a service-connected claim for compensation." In a study comparing World War II and Korean veterans with nonveterans, researchers found that mortality rates for veterans, twenty-five to fifty years after discharge, were significantly higher and that "military service caused approximately 2 million *additional* premature deaths . . . between the ages of 40 and 75." The researchers concluded that because "military service increased the smoking rate . . . by 30 percentage points," veterans were more susceptible to heart disease and lung cancer. "Military induced smoking explains 65 to 79 percent of excess veteran deaths due to heart disease and 35 to 58% of excess deaths due to lung cancer." A study comparing mortality rates of World War II veterans who smoked with their twins who did not found death rates twenty-four years after discharge more than twice as high for the veterans who smoked.[17]

Large numbers of veterans were able to live for decades with the deleterious aftereffects of military service in the belief, nurtured by the military medical establishment, that time would cure their ills. That was, regrettably, not the case for the hundreds of thousands who had been treated or should have been treated for psychiatric disabilities incurred during their service.

More than half of the patients in VA hospitals in 1965 were receiving care for psychiatric problems. For those who did not require hospitalization, the VA opened outpatient clinics. Veterans seeking help for psychological problems made "more than 180,000 visits to day treatment centers. Over 69,000 patients were on the mental hygiene clinic rolls at the end of the year." Another 14,000 psychiatric patients were being treated in community care programs and 7,200 "in halfway houses, and special arrangements other than their own homes."[18]

And yet, despite the best of intentions, the treatments the VA offered provided minimal relief. A twenty-year follow-up study of patients in the Oakland VA mental hygiene clinic found "reason to believe that the symptoms following from sufficiently severe traumatic stress may persist over very long intervals, if indeed they ever disappear." More ominously, perhaps, "the passage of time, even after two decades, has not sufficed to free [the veterans] of their symptoms. Indeed, there is a distinct possibility that changes incident to age are exacerbating their problems and reducing their power to cope with the stresses of civilian life."[19]

The essential problem might have been, as Professor Hans Pols of the University of Sydney suggested, that "psychiatric disability commencing after the war was believed to be related to factors which predated the war. Consequently, military psychiatrists devoted relatively little attention to post-war psychiatric syndromes."[20]

The patients who sought help invariably came away from their treatment with no noticeable improvement, but no aggravation of their symptoms. This was not the case with the small but significant number with psychoses or severe depression who were lobotomized.

Lobotomy, as the medical historian Jack Pressman reminds us, "did not cure any patients of a specific disease," nor was it intended to. "More accurately, it transformed them into persons whose characteristics, physiological as well as psychological, were quite different than they had been before the operation. . . . Recipients 'paid a price' in unfortunate side effects. Psychosurgery was a form of human salvage, not rescue."[21]

When, in 1969, Hanna M. Moser, the associate chief of staff at the VA hospital in Lyons, New Jersey, did a follow-up study on 147 patients who had had lobotomies, she found that a number of them had been "disabled by undesirable side effects. Seizures occurred in almost half. Intellectual loss was severe in 25 percent. . . . Fewer than 10 percent . . . were able to be discharged." Eighty-four percent, on the other hand, had become "better" hospital patients, and the number who had exhibited "frequent assaultive behavior" had declined from 81 percent preoperative to 51 percent postoperative.[22]

Much of what we know about the long-term effects of lobotomy on World War II veterans comes from "The Lobotomy Files," a three-part series by the *Wall Street Journal* reporter Michael Phillips, published in December 2013.* Phillips, at the outset of his research, was able to locate only one living lobotomized veteran, Roman Tritz, a former bomber pilot. Tritz, on returning from England in 1945, had been given a "clean bill of health" by army doctors and discharged. He found work and appeared to be doing well, according to his sister, until the late 1940s, when his behavior turned "alarming" and his parents had him committed to the VA hospital in Tomah, Wisconsin, where he underwent twenty-eight rounds of electroshock therapy, several rounds of "insulin-induced temporary comas," and sixty-six treatments of high-pressure water sprays of alternating hot and cold water to stimulate his nerves. When these treatments failed, he was given a lobotomy and, in 1957, discharged from the VA hospital after 2,272 days.

---

* A fourth follow-up article was published on January 24, 2015.

Tritz was far from cured. His "symptoms ebbed and flowed over the decades that followed. He grew separated from family and wary of friends, persecuted by thoughts of government conspiracies and the magnets he believes were placed in his head. For more than 30 years," Phillips wrote, "he has eaten alone, twice a day, at the King Street Kitchen, a La Crosse restaurant. . . . He won't use a phone. So out-of-town relatives visit when they can and check on him by calling the restaurant to make sure he is showing up for meals. . . . He says there are several Roman Tritzes, but he isn't one of them. He believes he was born in England and spirited away to America by the FBI." His delusions are multiple: He worked for the Secret Service (he didn't), the FBI broke up his two marriages (he was never married), he met Osama bin Laden, he served in Vietnam (none of this true).[23]

After his three-part series appeared, Phillips was contacted by the family of Dorothy Dieffenwierth, who had enlisted as a navy nurse in 1943 and worked in military hospitals in the Northwest, caring for "men wounded in the Pacific." She had suffered a nervous breakdown at a naval hospital near Seattle, was released from active duty in 1946, and eventually committed to a VA hospital in Tuscaloosa, Alabama. Like Tritz, she was treated with electroconvulsive shock therapy and, when that didn't work, given a lobotomy. Dieffenwierth was released from the hospital in 1951, married in 1955, and had three sons. She was beautiful and charming, had a lovely voice, and was a caring mother, according to her son. But she was also "childlike and volatile. . . . The boys never knew if she was going to blow up in public. She once doused Bob [her husband] with a glass of water during a spat at a restaurant . . . and occasionally threatened to kill him." She chased one of her son's friends out of the house "while brandishing a butter knife. Dorothy sometimes seemed to believe she was an aristocrat with a maid named Hephzibah—a figure in the Bible—whom she would ask to fetch tea and perform other chores." She was distant, unemotional. When her youngest son committed suicide, "her displays of grief appeared veneer-thin, 'not something coming out of the very, very, very deepest part of her heart.'" Her memory was mostly gone, but when interviewed by Phillips, she recalled Tuscaloosa. "'They put me under and doctors gave me an operation.' She can't recall why, and the missing thought frustrates her. Her face screws up as she tries to grasp it. 'Dear, dear, dear, dear,' she says."[24]

The vast majority of veterans who lived with war-connected psychological distress did not seek help from VA doctors. They suffered quietly, learned to tough it out on their own, to detour around their symptoms, some with the help of alcohol, others by diving obsessively into work. They did not talk about their wartime experience, avoided triggers like war films, went to work every day, and had nightmares nearly every night. They told themselves over and over again that they would be okay as long as they managed to behave okay. "The stigma of mental illness, and seeing a mental health professional," according to the psychotherapist Ron Langer, who practiced at the Denver Veterans Affairs Medical Center, was "quite strong, and the use of alcohol to deal with emotional pain was widely accepted. They were also conditioned not to complain about their hardships, so many combat veterans may have suffered in silence after the return from the war."[25]

The lack of understanding of what had happened to them combined with the absence of effective treatment modalities left many feeling "isolated and crazy," according to Paula Schnurr, executive director of the National Center for PTSD. "They thought it was just them. And they didn't talk about it." Absent knowledge of a source or cause of their discomfort, they could not escape the suspicion that there was something lacking or deficient in their psychological makeup that rendered them susceptible to these disorders. Inebriated or sober, they stumbled along at home, at work, and everywhere else, beset by what others regarded as personality "quirks" or "flaws": nightmares, insomnia, restlessness, irritability, sudden recourses to near-violent anger, abrupt "startle reflexes" when a car backfired or some loud noise disturbed them.[26]

Veterans have silently endured postwar psychological disorders in every campaign, every army, every war. The roots of their distress have been known by many names: "wind contusions" during the Napoleonic Wars (the "wind" came from a projectile that came close but did not wound the soldier); "soldier's heart" in the American Civil War; "disordered action of the heart," or DAH, in the Boer War; "shell shock" during and immediately after World War I; traumatic war neurosis and combat fatigue during World War II.[27]

In 1952, the American Psychiatric Association (APA) in the first edition of the *Diagnostic and Statistical Manual of Mental Disorders*, or *DSM*, introduced a new category: "gross stress reaction to describe a temporary condition suffered by emotionally stable soldiers who had been exposed to 'exceptional physical or mental stress.'" As Nadia Abu El-Haj writes in *Combat Trauma*, "The key term here was *temporary*." In 1968, after it had been rather conclusively determined that whatever the cause of the veterans' condition it was not a temporary one, the APA in "*DSM-II* eliminated gross stress reaction as a diagnosis, in favor of the far less specific and seemingly benign category, Adjustment Reaction to Adult Life. Among possible causes of this disorder was 'fear of combat'—which was understood to be a transient rather than chronic condition, whose appearance coincided in time with the stressful experience, rather than presenting with a delayed onset." There was still no recognition that the traumatic events experienced during the war could have a delayed and extended "post-traumatic" impact on the veteran's psychological health.[28]

Relying on *DSM-II*, "mental health professionals across the country assessed disturbed Vietnam veterans using a diagnostic nomenclature that contained no specific entries for war-related trauma," the sociologist Wilbur Scott of the University of Oklahoma and the U.S. Air Force Academy has written. "VA physicians typically did not collect military histories as part of the diagnostic work-up. Many thought that Vietnam veterans who were agitated by their war experiences, or who talked repeatedly about them, suffered from a neurosis or psychosis whose origin and dynamics lay outside the realm of combat." They were diagnosed and treated in the same ways as the World War II veterans had been, with no understanding that their delayed traumatic reactions might be war related.[29]

For more than a decade after the publication of *DSM-II* in 1968, members of Vietnam Veterans Against the War, and the antiwar activists, social workers, and psychiatrists who worked with them, assembled evidence that the difficulties so many veterans were having were caused not by some underlying, undiscovered psychiatric disorder but by a specific traumatic event or series of events they had experienced during the war. Their symptoms—guilt, depression, difficulties in forming intimate connections, psychic numbing—were in fundamental ways similar to those of women who had been sexually abused, to concentration camp victims, and to those who had survived catastrophic events of one sort or another. A consensus was developing that war-related traumas were but one example of a broader spectrum of "catastrophic stress disorders" that might manifest themselves as acute, chronic, or delayed. In 1980, the American Psychiatric Association, in *DSM-III*, recognized "post-traumatic stress disorder" as a distinct diagnostic category.[30]

The PTSD diagnosis and the treatments developed to deal with it were at first extended only to Vietnam veterans. The prevalence and persistence of PTSD symptoms among World War II veterans went virtually unnoticed and undiagnosed. Writing in 1994 on the fiftieth anniversary celebration of D-Day, the *Newsweek* reporter David Gelman observed that "in all the solemn ceremonials . . . scarcely anyone has noted the continued, debilitating presence of PTSD among surviving veterans of World War II. . . . It comes as a shock to find that there are an estimated 210,000 survivors of that earlier conflict who continue to suffer full-blown symptoms of traumatic stress. In their 70s and 80s now, these old soldiers have borne the crushing emotional weight of their experiences for half a century. . . . 'It's amazing,'" Brian Engdahl of the Veterans Administration Medical Center in Minneapolis told Gelman, "'to encounter so many veterans who've lived 40, 50 years with stress symptoms yet didn't see a strong connection with their combat experience.'"[31]

As memories of the war, submerged for years, resurfaced and could no longer be ignored, many elderly, retired veterans, having "lost the daily structure that sheltered them for years," sought help at VA hospitals and clinics. "They don't always come voluntarily," Gelman reported. "Their wives, who may have been taking the brunt of their erratic behavior, are often the ones to seek help for them." One veteran's wife whose husband had recurrent nightmares and had been hospitalized after he had gone on a rampage at a hamburger joint had lived with his "obsession" for decades before she "brought him to a psychiatrist, who diagnosed PTSD. 'I don't know why it took so long for us to figure out what was wrong,' she says. 'I guess we all had to soldier on; it was part of that period.'"[32]

"These are men who held jobs, raised families, and thought that they had put the war behind them," a 1992 study found. "Careful examination, however, revealed that the war was not entirely behind them. . . . They worked hard, in some cases extremely long hours, apparently to deal with chronic anxiety. . . . It is as if the constant activity of work and family and the avoidance of war reminders were successful in preventing the more disabling aspects of PTSD."[33]

"Most of the World War II men that I worked with came to me in their 70s or 80s, after retirement or the death of a spouse," Dr. Joan

Cook, professor of psychiatry at Yale and a VA researcher on PTSD, told the journalist Tim Madigan. "Their symptoms seemed to be increasing, and those events seemed to act as a floodgate."[34]

Melvin Dahlberg, who had fought in Italy and Germany and was wounded at the Battle of the Bulge, did not seek help until he watched *Band of Brothers*, the 2001 HBO series. He was seventy-nine years old. "It all brought me back to combat. I darned near lost it. I can't explain it, but it was just horrible. I broke down." Dahlberg sought help at a VA hospital. "They gave me 100% disability." For the next decade and more, he took part in a group meeting, until one after another of his fellow aged veterans died and the group was disbanded.[35]

Hollace "Red" Ditterline, a decorated infantryman in the European theater who served with Audie Murphy, treated his PTSD symptoms with alcohol for most of his adult life. His oldest son, Dennis, who was a self-proclaimed "psychology nut—Oh God, I read all the books"—did his best to persuade him to visit a VA outpatient clinic. "I said, 'Damn, Dad. They got psychologists down there. They got psychiatrists down there. They got people down there who can help you with your problem that *you* won't admit you have.'" It wasn't until "Red was nearly seventy that he took his son's advice." A few years later, in an interview for the Audie Murphy Research Foundation, Red mentioned that he "heard that Murph had PTSD too. I never stopped and thought that Murph might have it. But I think every one of us who was in that company had it. I still got it. When we got home, people didn't understand about post-traumatic stress disorder. A lot of the guys would go to the tavern and try drinking their blues away. People would tease 'em. Somebody'd toss a firecracker and they'd fall off the stool and crawl around in the spit on the floor. Some people thought that was real funny. My doctor says there's no cure for it. When I go to bed at night I don't know if I'm gonna sleep in the bed or sleep on the floor. I kicked the wall and broke two toes here a while back. And my knuckles are black and blue where I beat the walls. I don't say this to brag, 'cause I wish I didn't have it. Anyhow, a lot of guys have it a lot worse than me. I go to the VA Outpatient Center and I can just about tell looking into the guys' eyes if they have post-traumatic stress disorder. . . . Talking about it is what helps it. You got to get it off your chest. You got to talk about it."[36]

Jack Gutman, a former navy medical corpsman, after returning home, marrying, and making money working with his father, "was still having terrible flashbacks about the war," but kept quiet about it. "We had never heard of Post-Traumatic Stress Disorder, and I never sought treatment until years later." Instead, he buried his memories as best he could. "I would not talk about my war years, nor seek treatment for it. . . . I covered up the pain . . . originally with alcohol, but also by using humor. Plus, I kept busy with other personal and family projects as well as working hard on my various jobs." Gutman had been "going to the Veterans' Administration for some other medical and dental assistance, and I finally told them about my flashbacks from the war. The doctor said I had Post Traumatic Stress Disorder (PTSD)" and recommended therapy. Only after two years of therapy was Gutman able to "talk about what I experienced in the war, the fears, and other memories, without falling apart or having to resort to the bottle."[37]

During his third-year psychiatry rotation at a VA hospital, Stewart Alan Stancil interviewed "an 86 year old veteran of the second world war, who had voluntarily visited the emergency department. . . . I asked what had brought him to the hospital. . . . He replied that he had felt depressed and suicidal for about 65 years and became tearful as he began his story. . . . Like millions of other veterans of the second world war, he returned home to the role of husband and employee, but he never escaped from the nightmares and guilt that plagued him. He explained that after the war it was more acceptable to drink away 'the shakes and blues' rather than to seek psychological help. . . . He had chosen not to speak of his experience in the second world war . . . before speaking to me."[38]

Again and again, the veterans who had suffered silently or delayed seeking help at VA hospitals, clinics, and emergency rooms until they were in their seventies and eighties, when asked why they had waited so long, explained that they were hesitant to say anything that might worry their wives and children. It was easier to live quietly with their wounds or to make believe they weren't there than to put a name to them and announce them to the world.

The World War II veterans most likely to have been afflicted by long-lasting, persistent PTSD symptoms were the 116,000 POWs who survived captivity and returned to civilian life. A 1989 study found that fully half of them met the "DSM-criteria for PTSD in the year following repatriation." Twenty-nine percent "continued to meet the criteria . . . forty years later." Wherever they were held captive, the POWs suffered from boredom, beatings, physical ailments from which they would never fully recover, from cold in Europe, oppressive heat in the Pacific, thirst and dehydration, and debilitating hunger from a diet that was monotonous and lacking in nutrition. Poor diet led to poor health, weight loss, and, after liberation, food-hoarding habits similar to those of concentration camp survivors. The physical injuries were, for the most part, curable. Broken limbs could be set, weight put on, vitamin deficiencies remedied, and bodies treated for malaria, tuberculosis, typhus, and dysentery. It was much more difficult to cure minds, to erase the flashbacks, to ease the consciences of those who survived.[39]

Ray "Hap" Halloran, a B-29 navigator who was shot down and imprisoned by the Japanese in a cage in downtown Tokyo and lost close to a hundred pounds in captivity, was stricken by PTSD long before the disorder was given a name. Halloran spent ten months in a military hospital after returning home. "There were no psychiatrists involved who tried to find out what happened to us. The nurses and doctors were gentle and helpful and that sort of thing, but they didn't know what was going on inside our minds, the thoughts all day long, the nightmares at night. When I went home . . . I had a great mother and father, and four brothers, but I didn't fit in anymore. My whole life changed and I did not want to discuss with them the things that had happened to me. . . . I went back to the hospital, where I was more comfortable, with the other prisoners of war. Even though we did not talk about those things, we had some common understanding." Halloran eventually left the hospital, found work, and was visibly successful. Still, "for 39 years, I had pretty severe nightmares, pretty disruptive to the family. . . . I would wake up screaming, and I was waving my hands, trying to hold off the gun butts. I'd try to hide. I'd get under the bed. . . . Or I'd run outside. I'd be screaming, trying to find something to hold onto."[40]

Norman Bussel, who had been shot down and taken prisoner on April 29, 1944, spent a year in German POW camps, where he endured unremitting cold, boredom, and a nearly deadly shortage of food. Within weeks of his return to the States and discharge from the army hospital in Memphis, near his home, Bussel "began to have difficulty breathing in close quarters or in a crowd. I felt as if I was smothering, and I could not draw a complete breath. Panic would set in and I believed I might pass out." He could not ride on a bus or sit in a movie theater or eat in a restaurant if there were others there. "Unexpected noises threw me into a frenzy." When a taxi driver slammed his trunk lid with a bang, "I came completely unglued. My first reaction was to dive for cover." The only release, the only relief, came from alcohol, but it was temporary.

Bussel took over his father's grocery business, bought a house using the GI Bill, and tried to make a go of his marriage, but he never stopped drinking, would fly into sudden rages, had little time for his children. In 1984, forty years after he was taken prisoner by the Germans, he attended a meeting of American Ex-Prisoners of War and discovered that his "phobias were not peculiar to me alone. The others suffered the exact same symptoms. It was a great relief to know that I was not unique. That I was not afflicted with some progressive insanity that would one day destroy my mind." This knowledge did not cure his symptoms or alleviate his pain. "I know that my private war with PTSD will never come to an end. I have my own 'demilitarized zone' and I must remain constantly on the alert for a surprise attack. . . . Some symptoms of PTSD may never completely disappear."[41]

Michael Gold, one of the veterans Thomas Childers wrote about in *Soldier from the War Returning*, had been taken prisoner by the Germans in January 1944 and remained in captivity until May 1945. He survived his homecoming—though with difficulty—and learned to cope with the nightmares that came almost every night. Gold was a model veteran in almost every way, used the GI Bill to get his undergraduate degree, went off to medical school, received a prestigious residency at Mount Sinai in New York City, and had a successful private practice in New Jersey. "No one would have described Michael Gold as a tormented man, and although he had always had something of a temper, no one would have thought of him as an angry man. . . . And yet he was subject to sudden eruptions of explosive anger, outbursts that his family first witnessed when he returned from the war. They seemed so out of character, so incomprehensible, coming without warning and ending just as abruptly, triggered by apparently trivial things."

Friends and family were surprised when Gold divorced his wife and moved into a furnished apartment. He was voted out of his group practice in 1984 because he had become too difficult, too erratic, too angry to get along with. He remarried in 1986 and moved to Vermont. "The nightmares persisted, and so did the periodic outbursts of temper." In 1995, fifty years after his return to the United States, Michael broke down again, this time at an air show. On his return home, he "made inquiries with the American Legion, received advice about benefits [available to POWs], and then made an appointment at the VA hospital." At the hospital, he filled out forms and was given a physical. At the end of his visit, the doctor "studied him for a moment, a quizzical expression on his face. 'Dr. Gold,' he said, 'you have nightmares, symptoms of depression, and sudden outbursts of rage that, as best you remember, go all the way back to the Second World War. Fifty years.... These are classic symptoms of PTSD, Dr. Gold.'"

Gold joined a PTSD group and in the years that followed engaged in group therapy sessions with other veterans who suffered as he did. "It has been a long, turbulent struggle," Thomas Childers concludes of Gold's battle to put the war behind him, "waged with much pain, denial, and disruption over the course of decades. The truth is that for Michael, as for tens of thousands of others, the war will never be completely over. Its echoes linger in the crevices of his soul; it is a part of him. But more than sixty years after coming home, Michael Gold has found peace with himself and with his family, and, at long last, even with his war."[42]

Veterans with PTSD and brain injuries live their lives in two dimensions, the past involuntarily floating into the present. Like Billy Pilgrim, Kurt Vonnegut's POW stand-in at the bombing of Dresden, the veterans are "unstuck in time," traveling back to the war, mostly at night, in dreams, nightmares, flashbacks, what the PTSD literature calls "intrusive recollections."[43]

The veterans fought against the trauma, pushing it back, finding ways to live their lives and move forward. They did their best to forget. They married, had children, got college degrees, bought homes, pursued careers. But the war they brought home remained with them.

Norman Gordon, who as a medic in Europe had seen "pain and

death all the time," told his stepdaughter that "when he came home . . . he had to go to bed for several years with a bottle of whiskey in order to get to sleep." But over time he found the strength to fall asleep without that bottle.[44]

Eugene Sledge, the author of two classic books on his war experience, *With the Old Breed* and *China Marine*, "was haunted by vivid, terrifying nightmares" for twenty years after his return from war. "Science was my salvation!" He conquered "the curse of combat nightmares" by concentrating on his studies and his professional work as a professor of biology. But the war never left him. "In later years, some memory of the war has flashed through my mind nearly every day. Old buddies tell me it has been the same with them. . . . Needless to say, I read as little about World War II and watch as little film as possible." Sledge regarded himself not as a victim but as a survivor. Until the day he died, he mourned his slain comrades and refused to romanticize the war he had fought. "Over fifty years later I look back on the war as though it were some giant killing machine into which we were thrown to endure fear to the brink of insanity—some fell over the brink—and physical fatigue to near collapse. Those who survived unhurt will never forget—and cannot forget—the many friends lost in their prime and the many articles of civilization ruthlessly destroyed."[45]

John Wenzel was a fighter pilot in northern Italy and Austria in early 1945. In April, his plane was struck and badly damaged by a German shell, and he was slightly wounded. He returned home in late 1945, graduated from Swarthmore, moved to New York City, where he "drank a lot, and he kept to himself." He would much later, in an interview with the *New York Times* reporter Michael Wilson, call this "the dark times." Like other veterans, he eventually pulled himself together, married, started a family, "stayed busy, and the war faded into the background. And, for more than seven decades, that was where the war stayed." When he was in his late nineties and living in a senior apartment in Brooklyn Heights, a decade after his wife had died, the nightmares arrived. "He dreamed of falling from the sky. He awoke feeling helpless and afraid." His daughters arranged for him to meet on Zoom with a counselor. After seventy years, he began to tell stories about his war experience and allowed his daughters to bring him his medals, long hidden away. Shortly before his hundredth birthday, "his vision and hearing diminished, he spoke with effort about staying quiet for so long. 'There was no place to talk about it, and no way to express myself,' he said. He glanced toward the medals. 'For many years, these were tucked away. We didn't have much reason to pull them out.' . . . He hoped stories like his would keep the war from being forgotten. 'I'm afraid people are going to take it lightly—it shouldn't be taken lightly,' he said. 'They've got their own wars, and World War II is getting to be smaller and smaller.'"[46]

Acknowledgments

This book, like other works of scholarship, has been a group endeavor. At every step of the way, I have been able to call on friends, family, colleagues, former graduate students, archivists, and librarians for assistance.

I am grateful to Dr. Karen Binder-Brynes, George Chauncey, Dr. Anna Fels, Lynn Garafola, Ron E. Gregg, John McManus, and Steve Shepard for answering my queries and filling in some blanks.

Peter-Christian Aigner, Stephen Brier, Matt Broggie, Joshua Freeman, Dewar Macleod, Daniel Nasaw, Edward Rotundo, and Dinitia Smith read every chapter of the final draft and offered incisive commentary, corrections, and editorial advice.

Amy Reeve was a superb fact-checker.

Veronica Hylton and Kate Reeve helped me prepare my endnotes and bibliography.

Much of my research was done during the extended period in which libraries and research centers were closed because of the COVID crisis. My deepest gratitude goes to the librarians, curators, and archivists who, nonetheless, went out of their way to respond to my questions and supply me with the information and the documents I needed. Among them were Debra Brookhart, curator/archivist, American Legion National Headquarters; Jessica Clark, assistant curator, Historical Manuscripts, Special Collections, McCain Library and Archives, University of Southern Mississippi; Sarah D'Antonio Gard, senior archivist and head of collections, Robert and Elizabeth Dole Archives and Special Collections, Robert J. Dole Institute of Politics; Lauren Gray, head of reference, Kansas Historical Society State Archives; Anneliese Jakle, archivist, Montana Historical Society Library and Archives; Chris McDougal, former director of archives and library, National Museum of the Pacific War; Maggie Rivas-Rodriguez, founder and director, Voces Oral History Center, University of Texas at Austin; Nicole Semenchuk, archives and digital collections specialist, the Culinary Institute of America; Clancy Smith, former records management specialist, University Archives, Special Collections, University of Southern Mississippi; Luke Sprague, oral historian, Wisconsin Veterans Museum, Wisconsin Department of Veterans Affairs; Charice Thompson, manuscript librarian, Moorland-Spingarn Research Center, Howard University; Sara Wilson, administrative specialist, University of North Texas Oral History project; Cameron Wood, oral history coordinator, Ohio History Connection; and closer to home, Steven Klein and the Interlibrary Loan staff at the CUNY Graduate Center; William Kelly and Brent Reidy, past and present Andrew W. Mellon Directors of the Research Libraries of the New York Public Library; and Ian Fowler, curator of maps, History and Government Information, New York Public Library.

In this, as in my previous books, I have had the good fortune to be represented by Andrew Wylie and edited by Ann Godoff. Andrew was, as always, my first and most encouraging reader. Ann read and reread every word in numerous drafts and offered invaluable assistance. My thanks, as well, to Katie Cacouris at The Wylie Agency, to Casey Denis, Victoria Laboz, Sharon Gonzalez, Sarah Hutson, and Jessie Stratton at Penguin Press, and to Aileen Boyle.

Dinitia Smith has with incredible patience, goodwill, and her incomparable editorial skills made this a better book from first words to last. I am grateful to my son Daniel, another superb editor,

ACKNOWLEDGMENTS

for reading the final manuscript. I thank him, my son Peter, my daughter-in-law, Layla Moughari, and my brother, Jonathan Nasaw, for their support.

Finally, I wish to express my gratitude to the veterans who recounted their experiences in memoirs, letters, and oral histories and to the men and women who took the time to share with me their stories of growing up with fathers who brought the war home with them.

Abbreviations

Newspapers

AA: *Afro-American* (Baltimore)
AA-S: *Austin American-Statesman*
AC: *Atlanta Constitution*
ADW: *Atlanta Daily World*
BG: *Boston Globe*
BS: *Baltimore Sun*
CC&P: *Cleveland Call and Post*
CD: *Chicago Defender*
CDT: *Chicago Daily Tribune*
CSM: *Christian Science Monitor*
HC: *Hartford Courant*
HCRIM: *Harvard Crimson*
LAS: *Los Angeles Sentinel*
LAT: *Los Angeles Times*
Nday: *Newsday*
NJ&G: *New Journal and Guide* (Norfolk, Va.)
NYAN: *New York Amsterdam News*
NYHT: *New York Herald Tribune*
NYT: *New York Times*
PC: *Pittsburgh Courier*
PP: *Pittsburgh Press*
PT: *Philadelphia Tribune*
RCJN: *Rockland County Journal News*
USA: *USA Today*
WP: *Washington Post*

Periodicals

ALM: American Legion Magazine
AM: American Mercury
BHG: Better Homes & Gardens
CR: Congressional Record
GH: Good Housekeeping
HCP: Hospital & Community Psychiatry
HQ: Hollywood Quarterly
HR: Hollywood Reporter
JAH: Journal of American History
LCP: Law and Contemporary Problems
LHJ: Ladies' Home Journal
MLR: Monthly Labor Review
NH: Naval History
NR: New Republic
NW: Newsweek
NYer: New Yorker
NYRB: New York Review of Books
POQ: Public Opinion Quarterly
PQ: Psychiatric Quarterly
SEP: Saturday Evening Post
TLS: Times Literary Supplement
WD: Woman's Day

Archives and Archival Repositories

APP: American Presidency Project, UC Santa Barbara, Santa Barbara, Calif.
ASWW2: American Soldier in World War Two, Virginia Tech, Blacksburg, Va.
CIA: Culinary Institute of America Archives, Hyde Park, N.Y.
DDEPL: Dwight David Eisenhower Presidential Library, Abilene, Kans.
Dole: Dole Institute of Politics, Lawrence, Kans.
FDRPL: Franklin Delano Roosevelt Presidential Library and Museum, Hyde Park, N.Y.
FOX: Fox Movietone News: The War Years, Digital Collections, University of South Carolina Libraries, Columba, S.C.
HSTPL: Harry S. Truman Presidential Library and Museum, Independence, Mo.
JFKPL: John F. Kennedy Presidential Library and Museum, Boston, Mass.
Marshall: George C. Marshall Papers, George C. Marshall Foundation, Lexington, Va.
MC: Miller Center of Public Affairs, Presidential Speeches Collection, University of Virginia, Charlottesville, Va.
Mills: Saul Mills Papers, Special Collections, New York University, New York, N.Y.
MSRC: Moorland-Spingarn Research Centers, Howard University, Washington, D.C.

NAACP: Papers of the NAACP, History Vault, ProQuest
NLM: National Library of Medicine, Bethesda, Md.
NVMM: National Veterans War Memorial & Museum, Columbus, Ohio
NWW2M: National World War Two Museum, New Orleans, La.
RRPL: Ronald Reagan Presidential Library and Museum, Simi Valley, Calif.
SRC: Southern Regional Council Papers, on microfilm, New York Public Library
Stimson: H. L. Stimson Papers, Manuscripts and Archives Department, Yale University Library, New Haven, Conn.

Oral History Collections

AAA: Archives of American Art, Smithsonian Institution, Washington, D.C.
ALPL: Oral History Program, Veterans Remember, Abraham Lincoln Presidential Library, Springfield, Ill.
AMDA: American Masters Digital Archive, Interviews, PBS
BOHP: Brubeck Oral History Project, University of the Pacific Library, Stockton, Calif.
CCSU: Veterans History Project, Central Connecticut State University, New Britain, Conn.
GLBT: GLBT Historical Society, Primary Source Set: Lesbians in the Military, San Francisco, Calif.
GPP: Georgia Political Papers and Oral History Program, University of West Georgia, Special Collections, Carrollton, Ga.
KU: World War II: The African American Experience, KU Libraries, Digital Collections, University of Kansas, Lawrence, Kans.
LdG: Lawrence de Graaf Center for Oral & Public History, World War II Collections, 10th Mountain Division, California State University, Fullerton, Calif.
MAVC: Mexican American Veterans Collection, Center for Oral and Public History, California State University, Fullerton, Calif.
MDL: Minnesota Digital Library, World War II Veterans Collection, St. Cloud State University, Milaca, Minn.
MOHP: Mississippi Oral History Project, Center for Oral History & Cultural Heritage, Special Collections, University of Southern Mississippi, Hattiesburg, Miss.
MWBOHP: Montana War Brides Oral History Project, Montana Historical Society, Helena, Mont.
NWW2M: National World War Two Museum, New Orleans, La.
OHP-UCLA: Oral History Project, UCLA, Los Angeles, Calif.
ROHA: Rutgers Oral History Archives, Military History, New Brunswick, N.J.
SOHPC: "Documenting the American South," Southern Oral History Program Collection, University Library, University of North Carolina at Chapel Hill, Chapel Hill, N.C.
TL: "Texas Liberators of World War II Concentration Camps Oral History Project," Baylor University Institute for Oral History, Waco, Tex.

ABBREVIATIONS

UTK: WWII Oral Histories, Digital Collections, University of Tennessee, Knoxville, Tenn.

VHP: Veterans History Project, Library of Congress, Washington, D.C.

VMI: VMI Archives Digital Collections, Adams Center, Virginia Military Institute, Lexington, Va.

VOHC: Voces Oral History Center, Moody College of Communication, University of Texas at Austin, Austin, Tex.

VOHP: Veteran's Oral History Project, Center for the Study of War and Society, Department of History, University of Tennessee, Knoxville, Tenn.

WVHP: Women's Veterans Historical Project, University of North Carolina, Greensboro, N.C.

WVMOHC: Wisconsin Veterans Museum Oral History Collection, World War II oral histories, Wisconsin Veterans Museum, Madison, Wis.

Notes

Introduction

1. Mauldin, *Up Front*, 8, 12–13.
2. Mauldin, *Up Front*, 12–13; U.S. Census Bureau, *Historical Statistics . . . to 1970*, Part 2, 1140; "Research Starters: U.S. Military by the Numbers," NWW2M; Tuttle, *"Daddy's Gone to War,"* 31.
3. Selective Service System, *Selective Service as the Tide of War Turns*, 199, 192.
4. Menninger, *Psychiatry in a Troubled World*, 132.
5. U.S. Department of Health, Education, and Welfare, *100 Years of Marriage and Divorce Statistics*, table 1, 22, stacks.cdc.gov/view/cdc/12831/; Mintz and Kellogg, *Domestic Revolutions*, 171.
6. Tuskegee University Archives Repository, http://archive.tuskegee.edu/repository/digital-collection/lynching-information/lynchings-stats-year-dates-causes.

Chapter 1: The Return of the Wounded

1. Manchester, *Goodbye, Darkness*, 175.
2. Chambers and Anderson, *Oxford Companion to American Military History*, 304; Leckie, *Helmet for My Pillow*, 78–79.
3. Cummings, interview, Sept. 2010, Theodore R. Cummings Collection, CCSU (AFC/2001/001/78232), Video recording (MV01), Sept.–Oct. 2010, transcript, VHP.
4. Manchester, *Goodbye, Darkness*, 175–82.
5. Leckie, *Helmet for My Pillow*, 96.
6. "How We Licked the Japs," *CDT*, Sept. 11, 1942, 12; "1942 United Newsreel Report on Guadalcanal," C-SPAN video 00:08:33; see, for example, Sept. 1, 1942, www.c-span.org/video/?458711-1/1942-united-newsreel-report-guadalcanal.
7. Weinberg, *World at Arms*, 344.
8. U.S. Army, Surgeon General's Office, *Neuropsychiatry in World War II*, 2:460.
9. Theodore Lidz, "Psychiatric Casualties from Guadalcanal," 194.

10. E. Rogers Smith, "Neuroses Resulting from Combat," 94. See also Albert Rosner, "Neuropsychiatric Casualties from Guadalcanal."
11. Leon Frank Jenkins Collection (AFC/2001/001/9162200), VHP.
12. U.S. Army, Surgeon General's Office, *Neuropsychiatry in World War II*, 2:8.
13. Lidz, "Psychiatric Casualties from Guadalcanal," 201.
14. E. Rogers Smith, "Neuroses Resulting from Combat," 96.
15. Office of War Information, "Report on Recovery of American Wounded," news release no. OWI-1830, May 19, 1943; "OWI Traces Great War Hospital Route," *WP*, May 20, 1943, 6.
16. Waldemar Kaempffert, "Our Medical Army Does a Vast Job," *NYT*, June 13, 1943, SM3.
17. Elizabeth Henney, "Gen. Hines; They'll Be Coming Back This Time," *WP*, Feb. 20, 1944, S2.
18. Fox Movietone News, Feb. 1, 1944, FOX.
19. U.S. War Department, *Helpful Hints to Those Who Have Lost Limbs*, 12–13; Video Recording no. 956, *Meet McGonegal*, 1944, Records of the Office of the Chief Signal Officer, Documentary Films Online version, National Archives and Records Collection.
20. Childers, *Soldier from the War Returning*, 60–65, 147–69, 247–54.
21. Ernie Pyle, "War in Italy Tough on Our Troops; Weather, Terrain Both Against Us," *AC*, Dec. 14, 1943; Pyle, *Ernie's War*, 172–73.
22. "The Psychiatric Toll of Warfare," *Fortune*, Dec. 1943, 141.
23. U.S. War Department, *You're on Your Way Home*, iii, 8; "Vacationists Warned Invasion May Cancel Train and Bus Space," *BG*, June 11, 1944, D18.
24. Bowker, *Out of Uniform*, 91.
25. U.S. Department of Agriculture, Bureau of Agricultural Economics, *Veterans' Readjustment to Civilian Life*, 5.
26. Mary Hornaday, "As the Wounded Come Back Home," *CSM*, Jan. 19, 1944, 20.
27. "U.S. Hospital Ship Acadia Back from Italy with 776 Casualties," *NYHT*, Jan. 10, 1944, 1A; "Army Hospital Ship Lands . . . ," *CDT*, Jan. 10, 1944; "The U.S.S. Acadia Hospital Ship Brings War Wounded Home WWII Newsreel Archival Footage"; Fox Movietone News, Jan. 14, 1944, FOX.
28. "U.S. Hospital Ship Acadia Back from Italy with 776 Casualties . . . ," *NYHT*, Jan. 10, 1944, 1A.
29. Colonel Thomas B. Protzman, *Journal*, entries for Dec. 22, 25, 26, 31, 1943; Jan. 1, 3, 1944; Dec. 25, 1943, www.med-dept.com/veterans-testimonies/timeline-usahs-acadia-lt-colonel-thomas-b-protzman/.
30. Mack Morris, "Hospital Ship," in Kluger, *Yank, the Army Weekly*, 155.
31. Ralph McGill, "Where Headlines Come Home," *AC*, Oct. 5, 1944, 8.
32. Jones, *WWII*, 128.
33. Garland, *Unknown Soldiers*, 197.
34. DePastino, *Bill Mauldin*, 145–46; Mauldin, *Up Front*, 36–37.
35. Palmer, Wiley, and Keast, *Procurement and Training of Ground Combat Troops*,

28; Selective Service System, *Dependency Deferment*, table 4, 77; Mapheus Smith, "Populational Characteristics of American Servicemen in World War II," 249.
36. George C. Marshall, "Editorial Note on Army Personnel Shortages, Feb.–April 1944, #4-420," in *Aggressive and Determined Leadership*, 285–86; Palmer, Wiley, and Keast, *Procurement and Training of Ground Combat Troops*, 39.
37. Franklin E. Kameny Collection (AFC/2001/001/5208), Video recording (MV01), Oct. 2003, VHP.
38. Shields, *And So It Goes*, 48–51.
39. Ferguson, *Idealist*, 114–22.

Chapter 2: War Stories

1. Fussell, *Wartime*, 145.
2. Hackett, in Harris, Mitchell, and Schechter, *Homefront*, 195.
3. Kim Guise, "Mail Call: V-Mail," Dec. 7, 2019, NWW2M; "World War II: Victory Mail (V-Mail)," Veteran Voices Military Research, veteran-voices.com/victory-mail/; Linderman, *World Within War*, 303.
4. Sweeney, *Secrets of Victory*, 31–32.
5. Steinbeck, *Once There Was a War*, vii–ix, xi; Boomhower, *Dispatches from the Pacific*, 16.
6. Boomhower, *Richard Tregaskis*, 113–15.
7. Richard Tregaskis, "Georgian 'Stalwart' in Solomon Battle," *AC*, Sept. 5, 1942, 5; Richard Tregaskis, "'I Trampled Him to Death,' Marine Says," *WP*, Oct. 11, 1942, 14; Richard Tregaskis, "Break a Communique into Individuals," *A-AS*, Oct. 8, 1942, 9.
8. Boomhower, *Richard Tregaskis*, 146–50; John Chamberlain, "Books of the Times," *NYT*, Jan. 21, 1943, 19.
9. Hersey, *Into the Valley*, xi; John Hersey, "The Battle of the River," *Life*, Nov. 23, 1942, 114–15.
10. Herbert L. Matthews, "Road of Mud, Fatigue—and Glory," *NYT*, Dec. 26, 1943, SM6.
11. Pew Research Center, "Newspapers Fact Sheet," June 29, 2021, www.pewresearch.org/journalism/fact-sheet/newspapers/; population figures derived from *Vital Statistics of the United States, 1945, Part 1* (Washington, D.C.: GPO, 1947), table 8, 15; *Magazine Circulation and Rate Trends, 1937–1955* (New York: Association of National Advertisers, 1956), 12–13, 31.
12. Lewis Gannett, "Books," in Goodman, *While You Were Gone*, 451; Steinbeck, *Once There Was a War*, 2.
13. Boomhower, *Richard Tregaskis*, 146–50; John Chamberlain, "Books of the Times," *NYT*, Jan. 21, 1943, 19.
14. Horten, *Radio Goes to War*, 2; Emma Belle Petcher, in "Communication: News & Censorship," *The War*, directed by Ken Burns and Lynn Novick, 2007, PBS.
15. Fairchild, *They Called It the War Effort*, 87–88.

16. Horten, *Radio Goes to War*, 2.
17. Norman Corwin, "The Radio," in Goodman, *While You Were Gone*, 379–81; Blum, *V Was for Victory*, 36.
18. George A. Willey, "The Soap Operas and the War," in Lichty and Topping, *American Broadcasting*, 369–80; James Lantz, "Superman on Radio," Superman Homepage, www.supermanhomepage.com/radio.php.
19. Biesen, *Blackout*, 73.
20. Doherty, *Projections of War*, 231.
21. Doherty, *Projections of War*, 21.
22. "Mellet Boss for Hollywood," *HR*, Dec. 23, 1941, 1, 9; "Co-ordinator of Films Named," *LAT*, Dec. 24, 1941, 4; Doherty, *Projections of War*, 80–81.
23. Harris, *Five Came Back*, 144–49, 152–54.
24. *The Battle of Midway*, film produced by the U.S. Navy, distributed by 20th Century Fox, 1942, www.youtube.com/watch?v=7OBw0r28qC0.
25. Harris, *Five Came Back*, 158, 173; James Agee, "The New Pictures," *Time*, Sept. 28, 1942.
26. Koppes and Black, *Hollywood Goes to War*, vii; Dorothy B. Jones, "The Hollywood War Film: 1942–1944," *HQ* 1, no. 1 (Oct. 1945): 2, 11.
27. Bosley Crowther, "'Bataan,'" *NYT*, June 4, 1943, 17.
28. Hersey, *Into the Valley*, v; Doherty, *Projections of War*, 174.
29. Jones, *WWII*, 150–51.
30. Roeder, *Censored War*, 10–11.
31. Leo Cullinane, "Public to Get More Realistic Picture of War," *NYHT*, Sept. 5, 1943, 13; "Lifts Picture Ban on War's Realism," *NYT*, Sept. 5, 1943, 12.
32. *Life*, Sept. 20, 1943, 33–34.
33. Fox Movietone News, Oct. 1, 1943, FOX.
34. Petcher, in "Communication: News & Censorship," *The War*, PBS.
35. Sherrod, *Tarawa*, 152–83.
36. Robert Sherrod, "'Those Bloody Films,'" *NH* 7, no. 4 (Nov./Dec. 1993): 20; Peter Neushul and James D. Neushul, "With the Marines at Tarawa," U.S. Naval Institute, *Proceedings* 125, no. 4 (April 1999).
37. "New Films," *BG*, March 3, 1944, 22.
38. U.S. Marine Corps Films, *With the Marines at Tarawa*, 1944, www.youtube.com/watch?v=JolhiCbU_u8.
39. Dower, *War Without Mercy*, 8; Hersey, *Into the Valley*, 46–47; Sherrod, *Tarawa*, 149.
40. Dower, *War Without Mercy*, 79–85.

Chapter 3: Bad Habits

1. McManus, *Island Infernos*, 125–27.
2. Manning, *When Books Went to War*, 103–5.
3. Manning, *When Books Went to War*, app. B, 202–32.

4. Kennett, *G.I.*, 94; Pyle, *Brave Men*, 368; Bius, *Smoke 'Em if You Got 'Em*, 64.
5. "Army Slang in WWII," ASWW2; Bius, *Smoke 'Em if You Got 'Em*, 63, 72, 79.
6. Fussell, *Wartime*.
7. Leckie, *Helmet for My Pillow*, 118.
8. Dole, *One Soldier's Story*, 166–67.
9. Fussell, *Wartime*, 103.
10. Adams, *Best War Ever*, 69–70.
11. Grinker and Spiegel, *Men Under Stress,* 131; Medical Department, United States Army, *Preventive Medicine in World War II*, Vol. III, 247, 254.
12. Jones, *WWII*, 130.
13. Schrijvers, *Crash of Ruin*, 168.
14. Moede, 1995, OH626, WVMOHC.
15. Eckstam, 1994, OH00031, WVMOHC.
16. Bach, OH00040, 1994, WVMOHC.
17. Hirsh, *Problem Drinker*, 97.
18. Gray, *Warriors*, 61–62.
19. Roberts, *What Soldiers Do*, 162–73; "They're Both Destroyers," black and white, 1 photomechanical print (poster): 24 x 21 cm, Images from the History of Medicine, NLM.
20. Leder, *Thanks for the Memories*, xii.
21. Brandt, *No Magic Bullet*, 164.
22. U.S. Army, Surgeon General's Office, *Preventive Medicine in World War II*, 5:191.
23. U.S. Army, Surgeon General's Office, *Preventive Medicine in World War II*, 5:213; "S233: Venereal Disease," Question 23, ASWW2.
24. Burns, *Gallery*, 108, 109.
25. Sevareid, *Not So Wild a Dream*, 422. See also Anderson, "Accidental Tourists," 27, 31, 41–43.
26. U.S. Army, Surgeon General's Office, *Preventive Medicine in World War II*, 5:326.
27. Lanciotti, *Timid Marine*, 132, 134–36.
28. Eckstam, OH0031, 1994, 30, WVMOHC.
29. "German Girls," *Life*, July 23, 1945, 35, 36, 38.
30. "Nazi Girls' Rape Racket Fails to Fool U.S. Army," *CDT*, May 16, 1945, 3.
31. "Army Crimes," editorial, *CDT*, Nov. 18, 1945, 22.
32. Roberts, *What Soldiers Do*, 195–97, 210–11, 219–20; Robert J. Lilly, "U.S. Military Justice in the European Theater of Operations . . .," table 10, para. 35.
33. Ollie Stewart, "Present Reverberations of Army Bias Called Ominous," *AA*, March 17, 1945, 15.
34. Zeiger, *Entangling Alliances*, 73–74, 98, 105, 166–67; Shukert and Scibetta, *War Brides of World War II*, 20.
35. Houtz, interview, OH 2030, MWBOHP.
36. U.S. War Department, *War Department Technical Manual, TM 12-2305*, 2.

37. Menninger, *Psychiatry in a Troubled World*, 227; Bérubé, *Coming Out Under Fire*, 3.
38. Franklin E. Kameny Collection (AFC/2001/001/5208), Video recording (MV01), Oct. 2003, VHP.
39. Carpenter and Yeatts, *Stars Without Garters!*, 20.
40. Miller, *On Being Different*, 19–20.
41. Delmont, *Half American*; Hall, oral history, in Vacha, *Quiet Fire*, 159.
42. Humphrey, *My Country, My Right to Serve*, 32–34.
43. Meyer, *Creating GI Jane*, 158–59.
44. Adelman, *Long Time Passing*, 167; Meyer, *Creating GI Jane*, 177–78, n104, 249–50; Pat Bond, interview by Allan Bérubé, May 1981, www.glbthistory.org/primary-source-set-lesbians-in-the-military.

Chapter 4: Segregation in the Military

1. Guglielmo, *Divisions*, 3–4.
2. U.S. Army Center of Military History, "Asian-Pacific Americans in the U.S. Army: 100th Infantry Battalion in World War II," www.army.mil/asianpacificamericans/; "Going for Broke: The 442nd Regimental Combat Team," Sept. 24, 2020, NWW2M; Guglielmo, *Divisions*, 84–85.
3. Guglielmo, *Divisions*, 17–18; MacGregor, *Integration of the Armed Forces*, 7.
4. MacGregor, *Integration of the Armed Forces*, 18; "Negroes to Get Fair Treatment," *LAT*, Oct. 10, 1940, 5.
5. Lee, *Employment of Negro Troops*, 140–41.
6. White, *Man Called White*, 194; Guglielmo, *Divisions*, 24–25, 38.
7. John Hope Franklin, "Their War and Mine," 576–78.
8. George Q. Flynn, "Selective Service and American Blacks During World War II," 20; Lee, *Employment of Negro Troops*, 423.
9. U.S. Congress, Senate, Committee on Military Affairs, *Married Men Exemption* (drafting of fathers), 402.
10. MacGregor, *Integration of the Armed Forces*, 33.
11. Lee, *Employment of Negro Troops*, 423, 591–93; MacGregor, *Integration of the Armed Forces*, 72–74; James, *Double V*, 194–95.
12. Delmont, *Half American*, xiv–xv.
13. Harris, *Five Came Back*, 134; Koppes and Black, *Hollywood Goes to War*, 258–59.
14. Doherty, *Projections of War*, 213.
15. Stouffer et al., *Adjustment During Army Life*, 511.
16. Guglielmo, *Divisions*, 216.
17. Brooke, *Bridging the Divide*, 22.
18. Clemon Jones, oral history, Sept. 21, 1994, 13–14, MOHP.
19. Ward, *Defending White Democracy*, 44; "Bankhead's Plan Rejected by U.S. Army," *AA*, Aug. 22, 1942, 2.

20. "Armed Forces," *RR* 3, no. 1, 2 (Aug.–Sept. 1945): 9.
21. Robinson and Duckett, *I Never Had It Made*, 30–35; Jules Tygiel, "The Court-Martial of Jackie Robinson," in *Extra Bases*, 16–23.
22. Burnham, *By Hands Now Known*, 108–9.
23. Black, oral history, Aug. 11, 2009, ALPL.
24. Hervieux, *Forgotten*, 157; Ollie Stewart, "More Colored People . . . ," *AA*, Nov. 14, 1942, 1; "Tan Yanks Best Liked in London," *AA*, May 6, 1944, 1; Guglielmo, *Divisions*, 323–28.
25. Ward, *Defending White Democracy*, 46, 49.
26. Bird, *Chairman*, 187–89; McGregor, *Integration of the Armed Forces*, 43.
27. Delmont, *Half American*, 185, 228–35. For a brilliant, novelistic, but nonetheless largely accurate portrait of the 92nd Infantry Division, see McBride, *Miracle at St. Anna*.
28. Byron Greenwald, "Absent from the Front," 118–19; MacGregor, *Integration of the Armed Forces*, 51–55.
29. McGregor, *Integration of the Armed Forces*, 53.
30. Langston Hughes, "Here to Yonder: Simple and the GIs," *CD*, Feb. 9, 1946, 14.
31. David Brion Davis, "World War II and Memory."
32. Parker, *Fighting for Democracy*.
33. Williams, *Medgar Evers*, 29.
34. Langston Hughes, "Invasion!!!!," June 17, 1944, in *Langston Hughes and the "Chicago Defender,"* 130–32.

Chapter 5: The Last Bloody Year in Europe

1. "American Invaders Mass in England," *Life*, May 15, 1944, 21.
2. Harris, *Five Came Back*, 310–11, 317.
3. Franklin D. Roosevelt, "Prayer on D-Day," text of radio speech, June 6, 1944, FDRPL.
4. Raymond Daniell, "Landing Puts End to 4-Year Hiatus," *NYT*, June 7, 1944, 1; "Allies Hold 100-Mi Front," *LAT*, June 7, 1944, 1.
5. Ernie Pyle, "Roving Reporter," *PP*, June 17, 1944, 11.
6. Ernie Pyle, "The European Campaign Clarified," in *Ernie's War*, 286–87.
7. Doubler, *Busting the Bocage*; Blumenson, *Breakout and Pursuit*, 185; U.S. Army, *Army Battle Casualties and Nonbattle Deaths in World War II: Final Report*, 92.
8. Slawenski, *J. D. Salinger: A Life*, 103–7.
9. Salinger, *Dream Catcher*, loc. 1172, Atria Books ebook.
10. "Public Opinion Polls Part II: The War," *POQ* 8, no. 3 (Autumn 1944): 44.
11. Sparrow, *History of Personnel Demobilization in the United States Army*, 103, app. 4, 302–3; "Army to Give Priority to Fathers, Overseas Veterans in Demobilizing . . . ," *NYT*, Sept. 6, 1944, 14.

12. Robert C. Albright, "'Exhausted' New Deal Fears Peace, Dewey Says," *WP*, Sept. 8, 1944, 1; John Rogers, "Administration Fears Peace, Dewey Says in Opening Address," *BG*, Sept. 8, 1944, 1.
13. "President, Aides Reply to Dewey," *NYT*, Sept. 9, 1944, 16; "Stimson Denies Plans to Delay Troop Return," *NYHT*, Oct. 6, 1944, 7A.
14. Bradley and Blair, *General's Life*, 349.
15. Eisenhower, *Crusade in Europe*, 329; Kennedy, *The Library of Congress World War II Companion*, 595.
16. Joseph C. Harsch, "Little Hope Now Held for End of War in Europe This Year," *CSM*, Sept. 27, 1944, 1–2.
17. Rebecca Jo Plant, "Preventing the Inevitable: John Appel and the Problem of Psychiatric Casualties in the US Army During World War II," in Biess and Gross, *Science and Emotions After 1945*, 225–26; George C. Marshall, "Memorandum for General Clark, September 22, 1944, #4-521," Marshall; Stimson Diaries, Oct. 11, 1944, 48:134–35, Stimson.
18. John W. Appel and Gilbert W. Beebe, "Preventive Psychiatry," 1470–71.
19. Ruppenthal, *Logistical Support of the Armies*, vol. 2, table 10, 317; Bradley and Blair, *General's Life*, 354–55.
20. Greenfield, Palmer, and Wiley, *Organization of Ground Combat Troops*, 237–44; "Research Starters: US Military by the Numbers," NWW2M; Ferguson, *Idealist*, 138.
21. "Battle of the Bulge: The Greatest American Battle of the War," blog post, Dec. 16, 2020, NVMM.
22. Derived from "Total battle casualties" figures for "European Theater, all branches—officers and enlisted," in U.S. Army, *Army Battle Casualties and Nonbattle Deaths in World War II: Final Report*, 32.

Chapter 6: War Wives, Girlfriends, and Mothers

1. Hackett, in Harris, Mitchell, and Schechter, *Homefront*, 195.
2. Hendrickson, *Fighting the Night*, 11.
3. Hahne, in Terkel, *"Good War,"* 118–19.
4. Rita Sanchez, "The Five Sanchez Brothers in World War II," in Rivas-Rodriguez, *Mexican Americans & World War II*, 20.
5. Leonard Eskin, "Sources of Wartime Labor Supply in the United States," table 4, 275; Nell Giles, "What About the Women?," *LHJ* 61, no. 6 (June 1944): 23, 157, 159.
6. Hartmann, *Home Front and Beyond*, 82; Gilbert, *Cycle of Outrage*, 24–41. On "wayward girls," see Brooks, *Gotham's War Within a War*, 99–103.
7. Hartmann, *Home Front and Beyond*, 84.
8. "Paris Is Free Again!," *Life*, Sept. 11, 1944, 28, 38.
9. Carruthers, *Good Occupation*, 111.

10. "Speaking of Pictures . . . Marines Find Pin-Ups and Glamour on Guam," *Life*, June 18, 1945; Carruthers, *Good Occupation*, 140–41.
11. Overton, *Marriage in War and Peace*, 37.
12. Havighurst et al., *American Veteran Back Home*, 39–40.
13. Hackett, in Harris, Mitchell, and Schechter, *Homefront*, 197.
14. Groves, *Conserving Marriage and the Family*, 29–30.
15. Margaret Mead, "What's the Matter with the Family?" *Harper's*, April 1, 1945, 393–98.
16. Sgt. Ed Cunningham, "Jilted GIs in India Organize First Brush-Off Club," Jan. 23, 1943, in *Yank* editors, *Best from "Yank,"* 35.
17. Carruthers, *Dear John*, 3; Milton Bracker, "What to Write the Soldier Overseas," *NYT*, Oct. 3, 1943, SM14.
18. Pfau, *Miss Yourlovin*, chap. 1, paras. 20, 24, ACLS Humanities E-Book; "Some Wives Hurt Soldiers' Morale," *NYT*, Jan. 8, 1945, 20.
19. Litoff and Smith, *Since You Went Away*, 56–59, 63.
20. "Friends of the Wounded," *Life*, May 15, 1944, 28.
21. "General Kirk's Speech at Times Conference," *NYT*, Oct. 13, 1944, 14.
22. *I'll Be Seeing You*, Scripts.com, www.scripts.com/script/i'll_be_seeing_you_10542#google_vignette.
23. Franklin Reck, "Will He Be Changed?," *BHG*, Dec. 1944, 15.

Chapter 7: Washington Prepares for the Veterans' Return

1. Ross, *Preparing for Ulysses*, 25; Franklin D. Roosevelt, Address to the American Legion Convention, Chicago, Oct. 2, 1933, APP.
2. Frydl, *GI Bill*, 80, 87; Jennings, *Out of the Horrors of War*, 40–41.
3. U.S. Congress, House, Committee on World War Veterans' Legislation, *Hearings . . . to Provide for Rehabilitation of Disabled Veterans*, Oct. 2, 1942, 18.
4. President's Commission on Veterans' Pensions, *Readjustment Benefits, Part A*, 2; Childers, *Soldier from the War Returning*, 62, 227–28.
5. Dole to Registrar, Washburn University, March 2, 1949, Memorabilia Collection, me18, 13553, Dole; Dole, *One Soldier's Story*, 233, 251, 254, 259–61.
6. Robert F. Jefferson, "'Enabled Courage.'"
7. J. O. Dedmon Jr., "Memorandum on Conference . . . on Mr. Joseph H. Maddox of Boston, Mass.," Sept. 29, 1945, Part 09, Group II, Series G, folder 001540-008-0332, NAACP; Joseph H. Maddox, "Veterans' Administration Cheats Wounded Veterans," *AA*, Oct. 28, 1944, 7.
8. National Resources Planning Board, *National Resources Development Report for 1943*, ii, 3, 80.
9. Katznelson, *Fear Itself*, 379; "Washington Notes," *NR*, Aug. 2, 1943, 139.
10. FDR, "Fireside Chat 25: On the Fall of Mussolini," July 28, 1943, MC; Ross, *Preparing for Ulysses*, 92–93.

11. Burtin, *Nation of Veterans*, 60.
12. "Charges Neglect of War Wounded," *NYT*, Dec. 15, 1943, 13.
13. FDR, "Message to Congress on the Education of War Veterans," Oct. 27, 1943, APP; Ross, *Preparing for Ulysses*, 100.
14. FDR, "State of the Union Message to Congress," Jan. 11, 1944, FDRPL; Ross, *Preparing for Ulysses*, 99.
15. John E. Rankin, April 20, 1944, 78th Cong., 2nd sess., *CR* 90, pt. 3, 3591–92; Rankin to E. A. Hiller, April 25, 1944, cited in Ross, *Preparing for Ulysses*, 108.
16. "Atherton Assails Rankin for Delay," *NYT*, April 22, 1944, 14.
17. "Blames Rankin's Negro Hatred for Bill Delay," *CD*, May 6, 1944, 11.
18. Charley Cherokee, "National Grapevine," *CD*, May 27, 1944, 13.
19. "Roosevelt on Rights Bill," *NYT*, June 23, 1944, 32.
20. Olson, *The G.I. Bill, the Veterans, and the Colleges*, 23–24.
21. Frydl, *GI Bill*, 2.
22. Dave Camelon, "I Saw the GI Bill Written," 47.
23. Sherry, *In the Shadow of War*, 111.
24. Katznelson, *Fear Itself*, 182; Thomas Abernethy, May 12, 1944, 78th Cong., 2nd sess., *CR* 90, pt. 4, 4434.

Chapter 8: Victory in Europe

1. Fussell, *Doing Battle*, 153–54.
2. Ralph Martin, "The War Was Over," *Yank*, May 1945, 4.
3. Sledge, *With the Old Breed*, 243.
4. Alsen, *J. D. Salinger and the Nazis*, 91–93.
5. "The Fall of Germany," *Yank*, June 1, 1945, 18–19.
6. Eleanor Roosevelt, "My Day," May 9, 1945, in *My Day*, 103.
7. Joseph Hearst, "3,100,000 Yanks Back in '45," *CDT*, May 10, 1945, 1.
8. "Demobilization Announced," *NYT*, May 11, 1945, A4; "Army Announces System . . . ," *BG*, May 11, 1945, 1.
9. "Redeployment," *Yank*, June 1, 1945, 20.
10. Mauldin, *Back Home*, 4.
11. Fussell, *Doing Battle*, 161–62.
12. Bridgforth, oral history, NWW2M.
13. Barrett McGurn, "That Pacific War," *Yank*, Aug. 10, 1945, 3–4; Evan Wylie, "Ordeal at Okinawa," *Yank*, June 29, 1945, 2–4; Bill Davidson, "Ex-GIs in College," *Yank*, June 29, 1945, 6–8; "Paree," *Yank*, July 6, 1945, 8–9; Georg N. Meyers, "What's Cooking," *Yank*, July 6, 1945, 11.
14. "Redeployment Moves: Homeward Bound," *NYT*, May 20, 1945, E2.
15. Childers, *Soldier from the War Returning*, 110.
16. PFC Kurt Vonnegut Jr. to Kurt Vonnegut Sr. and family, May 29, 1945, in Vonnegut, *Letters*, 9; Vonnegut, *Love, Kurt*, 129.

17. Terkel, *"Good War,"* 370–71; Justin Wm. Moyer, "Black WWII Soldiers Asked a White Woman for Doughnuts. They Were Shot," *WP*, Jan. 15, 2023.
18. "Army Denies Holding Negroes," *NYT*, May 21, 1945, 21; Harry McAlpin, "First 75 Negro GI's Win Release . . . ," *CD*, May 26, 1945, 1; "Why Not Send German Prisoners," *PC*, May 26, 1945, 6.
19. Charles H. Loeb, "GI's in Pacific Await Discharge," *AA*, June 30, 1945, 9.
20. Black, oral history, Aug. 11, 2009, ALPL.
21. "GIs Protest Delay in Redeployment to States," *CD*, Sept. 22, 1945, 1.
22. "White Face Passport to Come Home," *CD*, Dec. 15, 1945, 1.
23. Childers, *Soldier from the War Returning*, 110–11; "Camp Lucky Strike: RAMP Camp No. 1," June 26, 2020, NWW2M.
24. Dana Adams Schmidt, "Somervell Views Camps in France," *NYT*, July 30, 1945, 10.
25. Roberts, *What Soldiers Do*, 1, 179, 183. On bombing of Le Havre, see Ed Vulliamy and Pascal Vannier, "D-Day's Forgotten Victims Speak Out," *NYRB*, June 20, 2024, 57–58.
26. Dana Adams Schmidt, "Americans Leave Dislike in France," *NYT*, Nov. 11, 1945, 5.
27. Mel Most, "Paris Blames Petty Crimes on Americans," *AC*, Dec. 9, 1945, 2.
28. Childers, *Soldier from the War Returning*, 113, 114.
29. Ollie Stewart, "Nazi Tactics Against Tan GI's in Paris," *AA*, June 16, 1945, 5.
30. Ziemke, *U.S. Army in the Occupation of Germany*, 98, 161.
31. Percy Knauth, "Fraternization," *Life*, July 2, 1945, 26.
32. Carruthers, *Good Occupation*, 123.
33. "Army Bars Relaxing Its Discharge Rules . . . ," *NYT*, June 1, 1945, 3.
34. Barrett McGurn, "The Jap War," *Yank*, June 3, 1945; Meier, *Morgenthau*, 451.
35. Bartelt, OH00116, 1997, 10, WVMOHC.
36. Leslie R. Groves, *The Atomic Bombings of Hiroshima and Nagasaki*, chaps. 8–10, Avalon Project, Lillian Goldman Law Library, Yale Law School, avalon.law.yale.edu/subject_menus/mpmenu.asp.
37. "Statement by the President Announcing the Use of the A-Bomb at Hiroshima," Aug. 6, 1945, Public Papers, HSTPL.
38. Boyer, *By the Bomb's Early Light*, 3–4; "The Haunted Wood," *WP*, Aug. 7, 1945, 6.
39. "The Atomic Bomb," *NYHT*, Aug. 7, 1945, 22.
40. Hanson Baldwin, "The Atomic Weapon," *NYT*, Aug. 7, 1945, 10.
41. John Bartlow Martin, "Anything Bothering You, Soldier?," *Harper's*, Nov. 1, 1945, 456.
42. "Atomic Bomb Is Loosed . . . ," *NYHT*, Aug. 9, 1945, 1A; Mac R. Johnson, "Atomic Dust . . . ," *NYHT*, Aug. 10, 1945, 1A; "Second Bomb More Potent," *BG*, Aug. 12, 1945, 3; Groves, *Atomic Bombings of Hiroshima and Nagasaki*.
43. Columbia Broadcasting System, *From Pearl Harbor into Tokyo*, 247–48, 253, 274, 279.

44. Eleanor Roosevelt, "My Day," Aug. 15, 1945, *PP*, 22.
45. Sherwin, *World Destroyed*, 5.
46. "The Quarter's Polls," *POQ* 9, no. 3 (Autumn 1945): 385.
47. Bartelt, OH116, 1997, 10–11, 13, WVMOHC.
48. Heather Hilliard, "Benerito Seferino Archuleta," Nov. 3, 2002, VOHC.
49. Sledge, *With the Old Breed*, 343.
50. Bridgforth, oral history, NWW2M.
51. Wingo, *Mother Was a Gunner's Mate*, 217, 219–20.
52. "Victory Celebrations," *Life*, Aug. 27, 1945, 23; Satterfield, *Home Front*, 366; Brooke L. Blower, "V-J Day, 1945, Times Square," in Blower and Bradley, *Familiar Made Strange*, 85; Hiltner, *Taking Leave, Taking Liberties*, 2.
53. Seymour R. Linscott, "Boston Becomes . . . ," *BG*, Aug. 15, 1945, 1, 3.
54. "Boston Keeps Up Victory Whoopee," *BG*, Aug. 16, 1945, 1.
55. *LAT*, Aug. 15, 1945; *Life*, Aug. 27, 1945, 26.
56. Farrell, *Richard Nixon*, 7.
57. Alexander Feinberg, "All City 'Lets Go,'" *NYT*, Aug. 15, 1945, 1.
58. Eisenstaedt, *Eisenstaedt on Eisenstaedt*, 74; Mendonsa, interview, Sept. 3, 2005, George Mendonsa Collection (AFC/2001/001/42868), VOHP.
59. Brooke L. Blower, "V-J Day, 1945, Times Square," 79–80.
60. Eliza Berman, "More from the Scene of That Famous V-J Day Kiss in Times Square," *Life*, Aug. 14, 1945, www.life.com/history/v-j-day-kiss-times-square/; Hariman and Lucaites, "Times Square Kiss."
61. Brooke L. Blower, "WWII's Most Iconic Kiss Wasn't Romantic—It Was Terrifying . . . ," *WP*, Feb. 22, 2019.

Chapter 9: A "Slow Demobilization"

1. "V-J to Bring . . . ," *LAT*, Aug. 11, 1945, 7; "Army of 3,000,000 Believed Plan," *NYT*, Aug. 12, 1945, 5.
2. Senator Albert "Happy" Chandler, Sept. 14, 1945, 79th Cong., 1st sess., *CR* 91, pt. 7, 8588.
3. Congressman Clare Hoffman, Sept. 13, 1945, 79th Cong., 1st sess., *CR* 9, pt. 7, 8577.
4. Thomas L. Stokes, "Demobilization: A Political Issue?," *AC*, Sept. 23, 1945, 5D.
5. Freeman, *American Empire*, 51.
6. "Army of 3,000,000 Believed Plan," *NYT*, Aug. 12, 1945, 5; Joseph A. Loftus, "Says Army Speeds Discharge Rate," *NYT*, Sept. 13, 1945, 4; "Slash of 28 Billion in Funds . . . ," *NYT*, Sept. 26, 1945, 1; "Patterson Hints More Army Cuts," *NYT*, Sept. 28, 1945, 2.
7. Bert Marvin Sharp, "'Bring the Boys Home,'" 4; "Demand 'Daddies' Back," *NYT*, Nov. 10, 1945, 20; "Send Congress 10,000 Pleas . . . ," *CDT*, Dec. 15, 1945, 10; "'Bring Back Daddy Club' Wives . . . ," *BS*, Dec. 19, 1945, 28; "Urge Services to Free Fathers," *NYHT*, Dec. 11, 1945, 25A.

8. Zeiger, *Entangling Alliances*, 116; "British Brides," *Life*, Nov. 18, 1945, 45, 48.
9. American Legion, "Our WWII Story: Here Come the War Brides," July 21, 2021, www.legion.org/honor/253045/our-wwii-story-here-come-war-brides; Senator Richard Russell, Dec. 19, 1945, 79th Cong., 1st sess., *CR*, vol. 91, pt. 9, 12342; Wolgin and Bloemraad, "'Our Gratitude to Our Soldiers,'" 37.
10. *CIO News*, Nov. 12, 1945, 6; Nov. 19, 1945, 5; Nov. 26, 1945, 2.
11. Outtakes from television series episode 15: "I Want My Daddy Back," in *Decision: The Conflicts of Harry S. Truman*, filmed, 1961–63, broadcast 1964, audio recording, Screen Gems Collection, Motion Picture MP2002-93, HSTL, www.trumanlibrary.gov/movingimage-records/mp2002-93.
12. Kleemann, OH 247, 1999, 15–16, WVMOHC; Linderman, *World Within War*, 185.
13. Lincoln Kirstein, "Rank," in Shapiro, *Poets of World War II*, 52.
14. "S234: Attitudes Towards Army Life," Nov. 1945, pt. 2, EM Form B: Questions 16, 29, ASWW2.
15. Leinbaugh and Campbell, *Men of Company K*, 283.
16. Faubus, *In This Faraway Land*, 654–55.
17. Robert Edson Lee, *To the War*, 162–63.
18. Ferguson, *Idealist*, 172, 190–91; Slawenski, *J. D. Salinger*, 143.
19. Lindesay Parrott, "Pacific Veterans Press for Return," *NYT*, Dec. 5, 1945, 6; Robert Trumbull, "GI's in Pacific Aim Fire at Congress," *NYT*, Dec. 11, 1945, 4.
20. "Home by Christmas?," *Time*, Dec. 17, 1945, 23.
21. "4,000 Manila Yanks Demonstrate When Ship Is Canceled," *CDT*, Dec. 26, 1945, 1; Preis, *Labor's Giant Step*, 273–74.
22. "Demobilization Slowed to Maintain Occupation," *CSM*, Jan. 5, 1946, 1; Sidney Shalett, "War Department to Slow Return of Overseas Troops . . . ," *NYT*, Jan. 5, 1946, 1.
23. "Disgruntled G.I.'s in Manila . . . ," *CSM*, Jan. 7, 1946, 13. See also R. Alton Lee, "The Army 'Mutiny' of 1946," *JAH* 53, no. 3 (Dec. 1966): 555–71.
24. "'Near Mutiny' Is Broken Up," *BS*, Jan. 9, 1946, 1.
25. "GIs Yell Taunts at General of European Area," *CDT*, Jan. 10, 1946, 11; Marshall Andrews, "3 Appointed to Question Eisenhower," *WP*, Jan. 11, 1946, 1.
26. "Sweating It Out . . . in Europe," *Yank*, Dec. 28, 1945, 8–9.
27. "Protesting GIs Win Eleanor's Promise of Aid," *CDT*, Jan. 12, 1946, 5.
28. "The President's News Conference," Jan. 8, 1946, APP; Dewey L. Fleming, "Truman Backs Army and Navy on Releases," *BS*, Jan. 9, 1946, 1.
29. U.S. Congress, Senate, Committee on Military Affairs, *Demobilization of the Armed Forces*, pt. 3, 340, 350, 351.
30. Dwight D. Eisenhower, "Address over Columbia and Associated Broadcast Networks," Jan. 18, 1946, Pre-presidential Speeches, 49–51, DDEPL.
31. Marshall Andrews, "Shrill Task Force Intercepts Ike on Way to Testify in House . . . ," *WP*, Jan. 23, 1946, 1.
32. "Army of 3,000,000 Believed Plan," *NYT*, Aug. 12, 1945, 5. For timeline of re-

ductions in manpower estimates, see Sparrow, *History of Personnel Demobilization in the United States Army*, 351–53.
33. Sparrow, *History of Personnel Demobilization*, 280–83; Mrs. A. H. Nickless to Eisenhower, Dec. 19, 1945; Eisenhower to Nickless, Dec. 31, 1945, in Sparrow, *History of Personnel Demobilization*, 251.

Chapter 10: Repatriated and Discharged

1. Ginsberg et al., *Lost Divisions*, table 10, 60; "'Home Alive by '45': Operation Magic Carpet," Oct. 2, 2020, NWW2M.
2. "S234: Attitudes Towards Army Life," Nov. 1945, pt. 2, EM Form B: Question 6.1; EM Form A: Questions 26.1, 58, 61, 75, 82, 87. ASWW2.
3. National Opinion Research Center, *Opinion News*, Feb. 18, 1947.
4. Transportation Corps, U.S. Army Service Forces, European Theater of Operations, "You're Staging for the States," 1945, NWW2M.
5. "3,221 Soldiers Dock Intent on Civilian Future," *NYHT*, Aug. 16, 1945, 8.
6. Argenzio, interview by Cory Bachman, Oct. 30, 2006, VMI.
7. Gambone, *Greatest Generation Comes Home*, 21; Sparrow, *History of Personnel Demobilization in the United States Army*, 216–17.
8. Louis Falstein, "You're on Your Own," *NR*, Oct. 8, 1945, 465.
9. Merle Miller, "Separation," *Yank*, Dec. 28, 1945, 16.
10. Milton Lehman, "The Last Big Sweat—and Out!," *SEP*, Nov. 3, 1945, 12.
11. Miller, "Separation," 16.
12. Falstein, "You're on Your Own," 465.
13. Miller, "Separation," 17.
14. Lehman, "Last Big Sweat," 68.
15. Sparrow, *History of Personnel Demobilization in the United States Army*, 217–18.
16. Falstein, "You're on Your Own," 466.
17. Lehman, "Last Big Sweat," 69.
18. Walter Bernstein, "A Reporter At Large: OUT," *NYer*, Sept. 1, 1945, 49.
19. McEnaney, *Postwar*, 100–103.
20. Wardlow, *Transportation Corps*, 347–48.
21. "Home-Going Veterans Fill Union Station," *LAT*, Dec. 15, 1945, 1; "GI's Stranded on West Coast," *BS*, Dec. 19, 1945, 7; L. H. Robbins, "What's Going On in the GI's Mind," *NYT*, April 7, 1946, 102.
22. Stouffer et al., *Adjustment During Army Life*, 431.
23. Hewitt, OH 00592, 1995, 20, WVMOHC.
24. Clinton E. Riddle, "World War II Oral History, Part V," March 19, 2002, 80–81, UTK.
25. Karen Matthews, "Dennis Baca," Nov. 2, 2002, VOHC.
26. "The Boom," *Fortune*, June 1946, 99.

27. Harold L. Elfenbein, "So You Want to Be a Civilian," *ALM*, June 1945, 12–13.
28. Heath, oral history, Sept. 8, 1994, 27, MOHP; Ray, OH00604, 1995, 18, WVMOHC.
29. "Hunt for Clothes," *Life*, July 30, 1940, 80.
30. Agnes E. Meyer, "Veterans' Pot Boils," *WP*, May 3, 1946, 7.
31. Carsel, *Wartime Apparel Price Control*, 148.
32. "A Good White Shirt," *NW*, Jan. 28, 1946, 56.
33. Baker, interview by Herman J. Trojanowski, Feb. 19, 1999, 16, WVHP.
34. Flink, *Automobile Age*, 275–76.
35. William Moore, "Used Car Prices Bring Protest from Veterans," *CDT*, Aug. 9, 1945, 10.
36. Mauldin, *Back Home*, 133–35, 138–40.
37. Alexander Nemerov, "Coming Home in 1945," *American Art* 18, no. 2 (Summer 2004): 62–63, https://doi.org/10.1086/424790.
38. Brooke, *Bridging the Divide*, 41–43.
39. Gooch, *City Poet*, 77, 91.
40. Davis and Dee, *With Ossie and Ruby*, 144.
41. Nancy McInerny, "The Woman Vet Has Her Headaches, Too," *NYT*, June 30, 1946, SM18, 38.
42. "S144: Post-war Plans of Negro Soldiers," Aug. 1944, Questions 63, 66.1, ASWW2; Farley and Allen, *Color Line and the Quality of Life in America*, table 5.1, 113; Modell, Goulden, and Magnusson, "World War II in the Lives of Black Americans," 839.
43. Kirksey, oral history, March 4, 1994, 81, MOHP; Sewell and Dwight, *Mississippi Black History Makers*, 77–80.
44. Conner, oral history, Dec. 2, 1993, 25, MOHP.
45. Brooke, *Bridging the Divide*, 41–43.
46. Bérubé, *Coming Out Under Fire*, 246–47.
47. Adair and Adair, *Word Is Out*, 55–57; Adelman, *Long Time Passing*, 164–71.
48. Jennifer Dominque Jones, "'To Stand upon My Constitutional Rights,'" 127; Witsell to Dedmon, Jan. 8, 1946, Papers of the NAACP, Part 09, Series C, folder 001540-007-0636, NAACP; John H. Young III, "Blue Discharges Under Fire," *PC*, Oct. 20, 1945, 5; "Blue Discharge," *PC*, Nov. 24, 1945, 6.
49. Jesse Dedmon Jr., "Monthly Report of Activities of the Secretary, Veterans Affairs for January 1946, Discrimination in the Armed Forces," Feb. 4, 1946, Part 17, folder 001451-005-0001, NAACP.
50. Canaday, *Straight State*, 141; U.S. Army, Surgeon General's Office, *Neuropsychiatry in World War II*, 2:637 and 1:237, 486–87.
51. Senator Bennett Clark, March 24, 1944, 78th Cong., 2nd sess., *CR* 90, pt. 3, 3076–77.
52. Young III, "Blue Discharges Under Fire," 10; Frank T. Hines, "Veterans Administration Instruction No. 2," April 11, 1945, in Cory, *Homosexual in America*, 44, app. A, Document 3, 278; Canaday, *Straight State*, 151.

53. Canaday, *Straight State*, 154; U.S. Congress, House, Committee on Military Affairs, *Investigations of the National War Effort*, 7.
54. Bérubé, *Coming Out Under Fire*, 230–31.
55. Humphrey, *My Country, My Right to Serve*, 34–35.
56. "Name Withheld," *Yank*, Nov. 16, 1948, 18.
57. Canaday, *Straight State*, 156–58; Bérubé, *Coming Out Under Fire*, 239–41.
58. "Samuel Cassius Discharge Case Review," Papers of the NAACP, Part 09: Discrimination in the U.S. Armed Forces, Series B: Armed Forces' Legal Files, 1940–1950, Group II, Series G, Veterans Affairs Discharge Reviews, folder 001540-005-0198, NAACP.
59. "Memorandum to Mr. White from Mr. Dedmon," June 20, 1946, Papers of the NAACP, Part 09: Discrimination in the U.S. Armed Forces, Series B: Armed Forces' Legal Files, 1940–1950, Group II, Series G, Veterans Affairs Discharge Reviews, folder 001537-008-0790, NAACP.

Chapter 11: Wounded Minds

1. U.S. Army Medical Department, *Medical Statistics*, table 25, 43.
2. Alsen, *J. D. Salinger and the Nazis*, 89; Salinger to Hemingway, July 27, 1946, Ernest Hemingway Personal Papers, box 1C36, "Salinger, J. D.," JFKPL. The postmark on the letter is incorrect and should have read "1945."
3. *What's the Score . . . in a Case Like Mine?*, War Department Pamphlet No. 21-35 (Washington, D.C.: War Department, 1945).
4. Harris, *Five Came Back*, 385–86; Edgerton, "Revisiting the Recordings of Wars Past," 34.
5. John Huston, "Let There Be Light/The Script," 206–7, in ed. Hughes, *Film*.
6. Salinger to Hemingway, July 26, 1945.
7. Huston, "Let There Be Light/The Script," 220–22.
8. Herbert C. Archibald and Read D. Tuddenham, "Persistent Stress Reaction After Combat," 475, 480; Administrator of Veterans Affairs, *Annual Report, 1965* (Washington, D.C.: GPO, 1965), 23, 38.
9. Kaminsky, *John Huston, Maker of Magic*, 44; Ben Shephard, "Here Is Human Salvage," *TLS*, no. 4988 (1998): 30.
10. Harris, *Five Came Back*, 410–13.
11. Huston, *Open Book*, 125.
12. Kupper, *Back to Life*, 99.
13. Dunn, oral history, OH00029, 1994, WVMOHC.
14. Dumas and Keen, *Psychiatric Primer for the Veteran's Family and Friends*, 6.
15. Tim Madigan, "Their War Ended 70 Years Ago. Their Trauma Didn't," *WP*, Sept. 11, 2015.
16. Fussell, *Doing Battle*, 122, 123.
17. Mailer, *The Naked and the Dead*, 3.
18. J. D. Salinger, "The Stranger," *Collier's*, Dec. 5, 1945.

19. Terkel, *"Good War,"* 202.
20. Ciardi, *Other Skies*, 45, 67, 70, 78, 80.
21. Brukman, oral history, NWW2M.
22. Ann Godoff, Oct. 9, 2022, in author's possession.
23. Shepard, *Salinger's Soul*, 41–42.
24. Herman "Hank" Josephs, "Oral Memoirs of Herman 'Hank' Josephs," Oct. 22, 2011, TL, in Sloan, Myers, and Holland, *Tattooed on My Soul*, 184, 185.
25. Canafax, "Oral Memoirs of Wilson Canafax," Sept. 14, 2011, 11, 18, TL.
26. Dippo, "Oral Memoirs of William Dippo," Oct. 21, 2011, 34, TL.
27. Sledge, *China Marine*, 149.
28. Bradley, *Flags of Our Fathers*, 308.
29. Chipman, OH0019, 1995, WVMOHC.
30. Mathews, *Our Fathers' War*, 215–16; Simpson, "Soldier's Heart," 549–50.
31. Gutman, *One Veteran's Journey to Heal the Wounds of War*, 32; Luis Alberto Urrea, "My Mother Returned from World War II a Changed Woman," *NYT*, May 12, 2023.
32. Havighurst et al., *American Veteran Back Home*, 71–72.
33. Kupper, *Back to Life*, 99.
34. Betsy Loren Plumb, "How the War Lasts."
35. Davis and Dee, *With Ossie and Ruby*, 134, 144, 168–69.
36. Brotherton, *Company of Heroes*, 7, 46, 64, 128, 170, 202.
37. Personal communication to author.
38. Terkel, *"Good War,"* 111.
39. Brotherton, *Company of Heroes*, 130–31.
40. Brotherton, *Company of Heroes*, 170–71.
41. E. M. Jellinek and Mark Keller, "Rates of Alcoholism in the United States of America," 55; Hirsh, *Problem Drinker*, 160–61.
42. Fussell, *Doing Battle*, 183.
43. Dondero, oral history, in King, *War Stories*, 10.
44. J. D. Salinger, "A Perfect Day for Bananafish," *NYer*, Jan. 31, 1948.
45. James A. Campbell, "Mental Disorder Following Service Discharge," 379; Menninger, *Psychiatry in a Troubled World*, 380; Futterman and Pumpian-Mindlin, "Traumatic War Neuroses Five Years Later," 401; Brill and Beebe, *Follow-Up Study of War Neuroses*, 121, table 108 on 122, 132.
46. Sledge, *With the Old Breed*, 78–79.
47. Ellis, *Sharp End*, 83.
48. U.S. Army, Surgeon General's Office, *Neuropsychiatry in World War II*, 1:544–45.
49. Graham, *No Name on the Bullet*, 189–90.
50. Adams, *Best War Ever*, 122–23.
51. Maharidge, *Bringing Mulligan Home*, 125–26.
52. Maharidge, *Bringing Mulligan Home*, 145.
53. U.S. Congress, House, Committee on Veterans' Affairs, *Investigation of the Vet-*

erans' Administration with a Particular View to Determining the Efficiency of the Administration and Operation of Veterans' Administration Facilities. Hearings Before the Committee on World War Veterans' Legislation, 775–76.
54. Samuel Paster and Saul Holtzman, "Experiences with Insulin and Electroshock Treatment in an Army General Hospital," 383–84.
55. Elizabeth Ruiz Garcia, interview by Hannah McIntyre, oral history, Feb. 2, 2000, VOHC.
56. Personal communication from Dr. Anna Fels.
57. Paster and Holtzman, "Study of One Thousand Psychotic Veterans Treated with Insulin and Electric Shock," 812.
58. Pressman, *Last Resort*, 147–93; Daniel Blain, "Priorities in Psychiatric Treatment of Veterans," 93.
59. Pressman, *Last Resort*, 336–42; Elliott S. Valenstein, "The History of Lobotomy," 430; Michael M. Phillips, "The Lobotomy Files," pt. 2, *WSJ*, Dec. 13, 2013.
60. Ferguson, *Idealist*, 203.
61. John L. Bratton, "Our Men Can Take It," *LHJ*, June 1945, 13.
62. David Dempsey, "Veterans Are Not Problem Children," *AM*, Sept. 1945, 326–29.

Chapter 12: Violent Veterans

1. Norman Q. Brill and Herbert I. Kupper, "Problems of Adjustment in Return to Civilian Life," in U.S. Army, Surgeon General's Office, *Neuropsychiatry in World War II* 1:722.
2. Bolté, *New Veteran*, 140.
3. "Sheriffs Warned of Crime Peril in Postwar Era," *LAT*, March 26, 1944, 13.
4. Arch Soutar, "Home Coming Isn't Easy," *SEP*, Dec. 16, 1944, 36, 38.
5. Bowker, *Out of Uniform*, 25.
6. Mauldin, *Back Home*, 53–55.
7. Manchester, *Goodbye, Darkness*, 273.
8. Lingeman, *Noir Forties*, 116.
9. Rabinowitz, *American Pulp*, 140.
10. Shuker-Haines, "Home Is the Hunter," 65.
11. Biesen, *Blackout*, 7–8; Lloyd Shearer, "Crime Certainly Pays on the Screen," *NYT*, Aug. 5, 1945, 77.
12. *Ride the Pink Horse*, Scripts.com, www.scripts.com/script/ride_the_pink_horse_16931.
13. Spillane, *I, the Jury*, 10–12, 24.
14. Nolan, *Ross Macdonald*, 80, 85–86, 91–94; Samet, *Looking for the Good War*, 158–59.
15. Krutnik, *In a Lonely Street*, 210.
16. Williams to Margaret "Margo" Jones, in *Selected Letters of Tennessee Williams*, 2:75; Lahr, *Tennessee Williams*, 123; Kazan, *Elia Kazan*, 350.
17. *Boomerang*, Scripts.com, www.scripts.com/script/boomerang!_4493.

Chapter 13: Love and Marriage . . . and Divorce

1. U.S. Department of Health, Education, and Welfare, *100 Years of Marriage and Divorce Statistics*, table 1, 22; Mintz and Kellogg, *Domestic Revolutions*, 171.
2. Fred Rodell, "Divorce Muddle," *Life*, Sept. 3, 1945, 86.
3. "Divorce Pleas by GIs Rising Sharply Here," *WP*, Nov. 17, 1945, 3.
4. Havighurst et al., *American Veteran Back Home*, 260.
5. Eliza Pavalko and Glen Elder Jr., "World War II and Divorce," 1222, 1224.
6. Mintz and Kellogg, *Domestic Revolutions*, 173.
7. *Divorce*, directed by William Nigh (Monogram Pictures, 1945), 1:11, www.tcm.com/tcmdb/title/17094/divorce#overview.
8. "Child Study Party," *NYT*, Nov. 12, 1944, 47; "Aid Offered in Solving War Tension Problems," *LAT*, Nov. 18, 1944, A3; "Favors Program on War Marriages," *NYT*, Nov. 20, 1944, 21; "PTA Managers Ask Local Units to Aid Program for Veterans," *CDT*, Dec. 2, 1944, 13; "G.I. Marital Adjustment Is Meeting Topic," *CDT*, Dec. 3, 1944, E6.
9. Toni Taylor, "Will Your War Marriage Stick?," *Redbook*, Dec. 1944, 2; Irene Stokes Culman, "You Married Him—Now Stick with Him," *GH*, May 1945, 17.
10. Eleanor B. Stevenson, "The Soldier Takes a Wife," Feb. 10, 1947, Document 5, Subgroup II, Eleanor B. Stevenson Papers, Series 5, Writings, box 1, William and Eleanor Stevenson Papers, RG 30/219, O.C.A., Digitizing American Feminisms, Oberlin College, https://americanfeminisms.org/we-cannot-change-the-world-but-we-can-change-the-people-in-it-the-eleanor-bumstead-stevenson-papers/document-5-the-soldier-takes-a-wife/.
11. "School for Brides Opens," *NYT*, April 5, 1945, 20; Jere Daniel, "The Whys of War Divorce," *NYT*, Feb. 3, 1946, SM48; "Rabbis Advocate Family Courses," *NYT*, June 28, 1946, 19; "Bids Churches Act to Check Divorces," *NYT*, Oct. 20, 1946, 15.
12. Robert M. Yoder, "Come Down from the Tree, Ma—It's Me," *WD*, Sept. 1945, 15.
13. Mona Gardner, "Has Your Husband Come Home to the Right Woman?," *LHJ*, Dec. 1945, 41.
14. Milkman, *Gender at Work*, 112.
15. Cooper, in Harris, Mitchell, and Schechter, *Homefront*, 214–15.
16. Therese Benedek, "Marital Breakers Ahead?," *Parents*, Sept. 1945, 150.
17. Hackett, in Harris, Mitchell, and Schechter, *Homefront*, 230–31.
18. Cooper, in Harris, Mitchell, and Schechter, *Homefront*, 249.
19. Baruch and Travis, *You're Out of the Service Now*, 47; Gardner, "Has Your Husband Come Home to the Right Woman?," 72. See also Lt. Frederick Robin, "When Your Soldier Comes Home," *LHJ*, Oct. 1945, 183.
20. Childers, *Soldier from the War Returning*, 190–91, 194, 288.
21. Stolz et al., *Father Relations of War-Born Children*, 33.
22. Wilson, *Man in the Gray Flannel Suit*, 78, 83, 264–66.
23. Groves, *Conserving Marriage and the Family*, 30.

24. James Hicks, "War Wives Unsung Heroes," *NJ&G*, June 22, 1946, 4.
25. "Legless Veteran Alleges Love Theft," *BS*, Aug. 1, 1945, 1; "Erring Wives of Veterans Facing Jail," *CDT*, Aug. 2, 1945, 1; "Cartoonist Mauldin Sues for Divorce," *BG*, Oct. 23, 1945, 2.
26. Fred Stanley, "Hollywood Crystal Ball," *NYT*, May 20, 1945, X1; James I. Deutsch, "Piercing the Penelope Syndrome," 33.
27. *The Best Years of Our Lives*, Scripts.com, www.scripts.com/script/the_best _years_of_our_lives_3947.
28. *The Blue Dahlia*, Scripts.com, www.scripts.com/script.php?id=the_blue _dahlia_19810&p=3.
29. Rabinowitz, *American Pulp*, 132, 137.
30. Goulden, *Best Years*, 45.
31. Minch, OH1077, 2007, 23, WVMOHC.
32. Tuttle, *"Daddy's Gone to War,"* 217.
33. Tuttle, *"Daddy's Gone to War,"* 218.
34. Mathews, *Our Fathers' War*, 3–4.
35. Cordier, July 20, 2007, ALPL.
36. De Nike, in Harris, Mitchell, and Schechter, *The Homefront*, 231–32.
37. Stolz et al., *Father Relations of War-Born Children*, 39–40.
38. Dumas and Keen, *Psychiatric Primer for the Veteran's Family and Friends*, 22; Stolz et al., *Father Relations of War-Born Children*, 36.
39. Stolz et al., *Father Relations of War-Born Children*, 43–45.
40. Hendrickson, *Fighting the Night*, 165–66.
41. Peabody, in Harris, Mitchell, and Schechter, *Homefront*, 233.
42. Stolz et al., *Father Relations of War-Born Children*, 61–63.
43. Stolz et al., *Father Relations of War-Born Children*, 71, 179, 321–22.
44. Judd, *Between Two Worlds*, 92–93.
45. Caitlyn Norma Duff, OH2043, Sept. 8, 2002, MWBOHP.
46. Jordan, "Tracing War Bride Legislation and the Racial Construction of Asian Immigrants," 8–10.
47. Shukert and Scibetta, *War Brides of World War II*, 48; Zeiger, *Entangling Alliances*, 168–79; Roi Ottley, "Thousands of Tan GIs Never Will See Their English-Born Children," *PC*, March 2, 1946, 14.
48. "Flies from Italy to Marry Ex-GI," *CD*, Aug. 16, 1947, 5.

Chapter 14: The Black Veterans Come Home

1. Marjorie McKenzie, "Pursuit of Democracy: Returning Veterans Find Little to Cheer Them in Old Hometowns," *PC*, Sept. 29, 1945, 6.
2. Jennifer E. Brooks, *Defining the Peace*, 19–20.
3. Gage, *G-Man*, 283.
4. Heath, oral history, Sept. 8, 1994, 14, MOHP.
5. Isaac Woodard testimony, "Plaintiff's Bill of Exceptions No. 1 in the Circuit

Court of Kanawha County, West Virginia," Nov. 10, 1947, in Papers of the NAACP, Part 08, Series B, NAACP; Gergel, *Unexampled Courage*, 12–23. See also, for a similar case, Burnham, *By Hands Now Known*, 103–6.

6. Joseph L Bernd, "White Supremacy and the Disfranchisement of Blacks in Georgia, 1946," 496.
7. U.S. Congress, Senate, *Report of the Special Committee to Investigate Campaign Expenditures, 1946*, 14.
8. Egerton, *Speak Now Against the Day*, 361–62.
9. *ADW*, Nov. 27, 1945, 1.
10. O'Brien, *Color of the Law*, 9–11. In this and the paragraphs to follow, I have relied on O'Brien's detailed narrative of the "Columbia riot."
11. Egerton, *Speak Now Against the Day*, 365.
12. "Violence," *RR* 4, no. 1, 2 (Aug.–Sept. 1946), 3–5, 28.
13. Equal Justice Initiative, "Moore's Ford Bridge," in *Lynching in America*, 27; Gergel, *Unexampled Courage*, 35; Gage, *G-Man*, 312–13.
14. Clemon Jones, oral history, 18, MOHP.
15. "Don't Let Congress Forget," *AA*, Aug. 31, 1946, 4.
16. Gunther, *Inside U.S.A.*, 679, 687–88.
17. "End Mob Violence, Truman Is Urged," *NYT*, Sept. 20, 1946, 27; Gergel, *Unexampled Courage*, 72–73.
18. "American Crusade to End Lynching: A Call to the American People," reel 192, no. 80, SRC; "End Lynching Crusade Lists Activities," *ADW*, Sept. 13, 1946, 1.
19. "Anti-lynching Crusade," *WP*, Sept. 21, 1946, 6; "Mayor Designates 'End Lynching Day,'" *NYT*, Sept. 22, 1946, 54.
20. Drew Pearson, "Robeson Sounded Wrong Key," *WP*, Sept. 29, 1946, B5; "To Secure These Rights: The Report of the President's Committee on Civil Rights," 24–25, HSTPL.
21. Anthony Leviero, "Anti-lynching Law, Civil Liberties Unit Sought by Truman," *NYT*, Feb. 3, 1948, 1; "Southern Threats to Democrats Rise," *NYT*, Feb. 5, 1948, 17; Freeman, *American Empire*, 75.
22. "Anti-lynching Bill Cleared to Senate," *WP*, June 15, 1948, 9; "Republicans Hint Antilynching Bill Due for Swift Action," *AA*, July 10, 1948, A2.
23. Brooks, *Defining the Peace*, 32.
24. Brooks, *Defining the Peace*, 17.
25. Vincent Malveaux, "Problems Affecting the Negro Veteran," 37th Annual Conference of the National Association for the Advancement of Colored People, Cincinnati, Ohio, June 26, 1945, Part 01: Meetings of the Board of Directors, Records of Annual Conferences, Major Speeches, and Special Reports, folder 001412-011-0687, NAACP.
26. Murphy, oral history, 36, MOHP.
27. Medgar Evers, as told to Francis Mitchell, "What I Live in Mississippi," *Ebony*, Nov. 1958, 66, in Williams, *Medgar Evers*.
28. Evers-Williams and Peters, *For Us, the Living*, 27, 72–73, 75–97.

29. Moore, oral history, March 29, April 13, 1970, MOHP, 19; Moore, oral history, in Raines, *My Soul Is Rested*, 233–34; Payne, *I've Got the Light of Freedom*, 30–32.
30. Morrison, *Aaron Henry of Mississippi*.
31. Rice, *Hosea Williams*, 33–38, 45, 51–52; Williams, oral history, May 15, 1988, 5–12, GPP.

Chapter 15: The White Veterans' Vote

1. Raymond Moley, "Veterans' Influence in Politics," *AC*, Feb. 8, 1946, 10; Paul Mallon, "War Veterans to Have Voice in Politics," *HC*, Feb. 4, 1946, 3.
2. Tye, *Demagogue*, 50; Grafton and Permaloff, *Big Mules & Branchheads*, 56; Crespino, *Strom Thurmond's America*, 38–41; Robert Howard, "Pleas of Vets Feature Races for Assembly," *CDT*, April 7, 1946, N6; "It's Major O'Dwyer . . . ," *NYT*, April 28, 1942, 23.
3. Nichter, *The Last Brahmin*, 55–56, 58, 61.
4. Raymond Brooks, "Legislative Races Will Find Many New Contenders This Year," *AA-S*, Jan. 6, 1946, A6.
5. Javits, *Javits*, 89–90, 93–94; J. K. Javits, "Veterans and the Republican Party," *NYHT*, Feb. 24, 1946, A6.
6. George Tagge, "G.O.P. in County Has 2–1 Edge in Vet Candidates," *CDT*, Jan. 16, 1946, 31; Farrell, *Richard Nixon*, 12; Gellman, *Contender*, 42, 47.
7. Logevall, *JFK*, 420–21; Nasaw, *Patriarch*, 598.
8. Tye, *Demagogue*, 70–71.
9. Cannon, *Gerald R. Ford*, 68–69.
10. Jacob Javits, "Veterans and the Republican Party."
11. Faubus, *In This Faraway Land*, 678; Farrell, *Richard Nixon*, 18.
12. Gellman, *Contender*, 64.
13. Egerton, *Speak Now Against the Day*, 392; Crespino, *Strom Thurmond's America*, 46.
14. Brooks, *Defining the Peace*, 115, 116.
15. Theodore H. White, "The Battle of Athens, Tennessee," *Harper's*, Jan. 1947, 54–61; Byrum, *McMinn County*, 112–20; DeRose, *Fighting Bunch*.
16. "Battle of the Ballots," *Time*, Aug. 12, 1946, 20; Harold B. Hinton, "Tennessee Veterans Are Wary Now," *NYT*, Aug. 18, 1946, 82.
17. Harold Hinton, "Veterans' Direct Action a Minor Post-war Fear," *NYT*, Aug. 11, 1946, 79.
18. "30 Veterans Win in Primary Races," *NYT*, Aug. 12, 1946, 11.
19. "Topics of the Times," *NYT*, Aug. 30, 1946, 13.
20. Sam Stavisky, "Veteran's Only Sure Winner in This Heat . . . ," *WP*, Oct. 27, 1946, B1; Faubus, *In This Faraway Land*, 678.
21. Faubus, *In This Faraway Land*, 678.
22. Faubus, *In This Faraway Land*, 678–79.

Chapter 16: "Home, Sweet Home Is a Nightmare Crisis"

1. Stouffer et al., *Combat and Its Aftermath*, 598.
2. Walter H. Waggoner, "What We Face Told: People Must Still Accept Many Hardships, Says Report to President . . . ," *NYT*, May 10, 1945, 1; "Thousands More Idle . . . ," *LAT*, Aug. 19, 1945, 2.
3. President's Commission on Veterans' Pensions, *Readjustment Benefits, Part A*, 13; Thomas M. Nial, "Veterans' Postwar Notebook," *AC*, Aug. 27, 1945, 12; Aug. 29, 1945, 14.
4. "'Rocking-Chair Money': Meaning and Origin," Word Histories, https://word histories.net/2022/01/15/rocking-chair-money/; "Whoops, Another Bureau," HC, June 1, 1944, 12, PQHN; "Rockin' Chair Money," Hank Williams Lyrics, www.azlyrics.com/lyrics /hankwilliams/rockinchairmoney.html.
5. U.S. Office of War Mobilization and Reconversion, *Sixth Report to the President, the Senate, and the House of Representatives*, 2.
6. Henry F. Pringle, "Are We Making a Bum out of G.I. Joe?," *LHJ*, Sept. 1946, 212.
7. Varns, oral history, Nov. 24, 2009, ALPL.
8. President's Commission on Veterans' Pensions, *Readjustment Benefits, Part A*, 71; Argenzio, oral history transcript, Oct. 30, 2006, VMI.
9. U.S. Census Bureau, *Historical Statistics . . . to 1970*, Part 2, Series N, 156–69, 639–40.
10. Havighurst et al., *American Veteran Back Home*, 80.
11. Gutman, *One Veteran's Journey to Heal the Wounds of War*, 32.
12. Congressman Wright Patman, Oct. 16, 1945, 79th Cong., 1st sess., *CR* 91, pt. 7, 9724–25.
13. "More Doubling Up Seen in Housing Crisis," *LAT*, Nov. 11, 1945, 8.
14. Farrell, *Richard Nixon*, 20.
15. Lucien C. Haas, "Looking for a Home," *LAT*, Oct. 22, 1945, A4.
16. Frank George, "Let's Get Housing—NOW!," *LAT*, Nov. 26, 1945, A4.
17. "Mayor Lays Crisis in Housing to U.S.," *NYT*, Nov. 11, 1945, 28.
18. Marquis W. Childs, "Washington Calling," *Nday*, Nov. 19, 1945, 22.
19. "Housing Shortage at 'Crisis' Stage . . . ," *NYT*, Dec. 9, 1945, 127.
20. "The Great Housing Shortage," *Life*, Dec. 17, 1945, 27.
21. *Veterans Emergency Housing Program*, 1–2.
22. U.S. Congress, Senate, Subcommittee on Housing and Urban Redevelopment, "Postwar Economic Policy and Planning," 6, 7; Philip H. Hill, "Housing-Legislative Proposals," 177; Taft, "The Housing Problem," Jan. 17, 1946, 79th Cong., 2nd sess., *CR* 92, p. 9, app., A75–77.
23. Frank Gervasi, "No Place to Live," *Collier's*, Feb. 16, 1946, 80.
24. O'Brien Boldt, "Veterans' Housing Problems," Address to 37th Annual Conference of the National Association for the Advancement of Colored People, Cincinnati, Ohio, June 26, 1945, Part 01: Meetings of the Board of Directors, Records of Annual Conferences, Major Speeches, and Special Reports, Folder 001412-011-0687, NAACP.

25. Fure-Slocum, *Contesting the Postwar City*, 266.
26. "From Courtship to Courthouse: A THIS IS AMERICA—*This Week* Short," *LAT*, Sept. 8, 1946, 29.
27. Barton Bernstein, "Reluctance and Resistance," 61–63.
28. President's Commission on Veterans' Pensions, *Readjustment Benefits, Part A*, table 4, 49; Department of Veterans Affairs, "Legislative History of the VA Home Loan Guaranty Program," 3–4.
29. President's Commission on Veterans' Pensions, *Readjustment Benefits, Part A*, table 4, 49.
30. Frydl, *GI Bill*, 276.
31. Havighurst et al., *American Veteran Back Home*, 145–47.
32. U.S. National Housing Agency, Federal Housing Administration, *Underwriting Manual*, paras. 1636 (2), 1640 (7); Howard, "Building a 'Family-Friendly' Metropolis," 938.
33. Altschuler and Blumin, *GI Bill*, 197; Charles Hurd, "Readjustment: Elimination of 'Red Tape' in 'GI Bill' . . . ," *NYT*, March 24, 1946, 38; Nancy McInerny, "The Woman Vet Has Her Headaches, Too," *NYT*, SM40.
34. Louis Lee Woods II, "Almost 'No Negro Veteran . . . Could Get a Loan,'" 405–6; Crawford to Dr. H. Boyd Hall, June 13, 1946, Part 9, Series C, folder 001540-08-0332, NAACP.
35. Miles to Mrs. Arrington, March 12, 1946; NAACP Secretary Veterans' Affairs, April 11, 1946, Part 9, Series C, folder 001540-008-0332, NAACP.
36. "Banking Policies Keep Negroes in Ghettoes," *CC&P*, Nov. 28, 1947, 1A.
37. Cohen, *Consumers' Republic*, 171; Chinyere O. Agbai, "Wealth Begins at Home," 43.
38. Carl A. Spencer, "State and Local Housing Programs After World War II," 499; "O'Dwyer Pleased with Housing Work," *NYT*, March 1, 1946, 4.
39. Fure-Slocum, *Contesting the Postwar City*, 267, 270.
40. Hirsch, *Making the Second Ghetto*, 54–56, 74–76, 94–96; Hiroshi Takei, "Unexpected Consequence of Government Manipulation . . ."; "Chicago Race Riot Balked," *LAS*, Aug. 21, 1947, 1; Moroney, *Chicagoland Dream Houses*, 9, 157–59.
41. Javits, Oral History Interview, April 4, 1966, 3–4, JFKPL.
42. Logevall, *JFK*, 443–45; Galvin, Oral History Interview, JFK#1, May 15, 1964, 2, JFKPL; *BG*, May 12, 1947, 1; Weinstein, Oral History Interview, June 3, 1982, 9–10, JFKPL.
43. "Cong. Kennedy Asked to Apologize . . . ," *BG*, May 23, 1947, 1.
44. Congressman John Kennedy, July 24, 1947, 80th Cong., 1st sess., *CR* 93, pt. 8, 10096.
45. "Senate Group Approves . . . McCarthy Housing Investigation," *WSJ*, July 18, 1947, 3; "Defeat Forecast for Housing Bill," *NYT*, Aug. 27, 1947, 3; "Rego Park Housing Called Mad Slum," *NYT*, Aug. 28, 1947, 3; Bess Furman, "M'Carthy Pledges Housing Aid Speed," *NYT*, Sept. 3, 1947, 28.
46. Baxandall and Ewen, *Picture Windows*, 90; U.S. Congress, Joint Committee on

Housing, "Study and Investigation of Housing: Hearings Before the Joint Committee on Housing," pts. 1 and 2, 143, 692, 824, 1369, 1373, 1479; pt. 3, 3172.
47. "Report of Hon. Joseph R. McCarthy, Vice Chairman to the Joint Committee on Housing," 80th Cong., 2nd sess. (Washington, D.C.: GPO, 1948); Samuel A. Tower, "GOP Leader Offers New Housing Plan," *NYT*, Feb. 28, 1948, 23.
48. "Veterans Storm Capitol Hill," *WP*, March 2, 1948, B2.
49. 80th Cong., 2nd sess., June 19, 1948, *CR*, vol. 94, pt. 7, 9324, 9326.
50. Alexander Von Hoffman, "Study in Contradictions," 310–12.

Chapter 17: Get a Job?

1. Havighurst et al., *American Veteran Back Home*, 91; Harry S. Truman, "Special Message to the Congress . . . ," Sept. 6, 1945, Public Papers, HSTPL.
2. Hochschild, OH00590, 1994, 12, WVMOH; Norma Duff, OH2043, Sept. 8, 2002, MWBOHP.
3. Susan Perry, "Female Veterans," 23.
4. Malveaux,"Problems Affecting the Negro Veteran," 37th Annual Conference of the National Association for the Advancement of Colored People, Cincinnati, Ohio, June 26, 1945, Part 01: Meetings of the Board of Directors, Records of Annual Conferences, Major Speeches, and Special Reports, Folder 001412-011-0687, NAACP.
5. Jack Metzgar, "1945–1946 Strike Wave," 216.
6. "Strike Idleness Held Threat to Veterans," *CSM*, Oct. 22, 1945, 3.
7. John Rankin, Nov. 7, 1945, 79th Cong., 1st sess., *CR* 91, pt. 8, 10473; Charles Hurd, "The Veteran," *NYT*, Oct. 7, 1945, 35.
8. Tauchin, OH00519, 1997, WVMOHC.
9. Goulden, *Best Years*, 108–9.
10. "Highlights of Council Services to Veterans," CIO Veterans Activities, 1946–1947, WAG.075, box 2, folder 7, Mills.
11. Brooks, *Defining the Peace*, 81, 83, 85.
12. "Veterans Carry On," *CIO News*, Jan. 7, 1946, 2, WAG.075, box 2, folder 7, Mills.
13. "Compensation Denied Veterans in Strike," *LAT*, Jan. 17, 1946, 4; "5,000 Steel Workers Join in Demand for Higher Pay," *AA*, Feb. 2, 1946, 8.
14. "Navy to Pick Up Strike Pickets in Its Uniform," *NYHT*, Jan. 21, 1946, 8; "Fifth of Jersey Strikers on Picket Lines Colored," *AA*, Feb. 2, 1946, 8.
15. Assorted Images, United Mine Workers of America Strike of 1946, www.google.com/search?q=united%20mine%20workers%20of%20america%20strike%20of%201946&tbm=isch&rlz=1C1CHBF_enUS889US891&hl=en&sa=X&ved=0CJwBEKzcAigAahgKEwj4muT8qvP_AhUAAAAAHQAAAAAQhQE&biw=1140&bih=914#imgrc=X1iNqITtUkgFVM.
16. Metzgar, "1945–1946 Strike Wave," 221–22; Freeman, *American Empire*, 42.

17. President's Commission on Veterans' Pensions, *Readjustment Benefits, Part B*, 273; "Veterans Return to the Nation's Factories," *MLR* 63, no. 6 (Dec. 1946), 928–29.
18. Sam Stavisky, "Discharged GI Finds Soft Job Not Open for Unskilled Hands," *WP*, Dec. 3, 1945, 1.
19. Richard M. Kelley, "Anybody Want to Hire a Machine Gun Operator?," *BG*, Jan. 13, 1946, D7.
20. Havighurst et al., *American Veteran Back Home*, 112.
21. Martin, *Best Is None Too Good*, 69–70.
22. Charles Hurd, "Readjustment," *NYT*, Feb. 23, 1946, 38.
23. David Onkst, "'First a Negro . . . Incidentally a Veteran,'" 520; Lena D. Sayles to Major John Bell, Dec. 10, 1945, reel 189, 31, 1944–1948, Series VII, Veterans Services Project, SRC.
24. Caliver, *Postwar Education of Negroes*, 11; Ulysses Lee, *Employment of Negro Troops*, 593.
25. Campbell Carrington Johnson, "Veterans and the Community," Dec. 17, 1944, 9–10, Campbell Carrington Johnson Papers, folder 61, box 57-3, MSRC; Stouffer et al., *Adjustment During Army Life*, 537.
26. Bolté and Harris, *Our Negro Veterans*, 11; Onkst, "'First a Negro . . . Incidentally a Veteran,'" 521.
27. Malveaux, "Problems Affecting the Negro Veteran," 37th Annual Conference of the National Association for the Advancement of Colored People, Cincinnati, Ohio, June 26, 1945, Part 01: Meetings of the Board of Directors, Records of Annual Conferences, Major Speeches, and Special Reports, Folder 001412-011-0687, NAACP.
28. "Vet Denied Job as Machine Serviceman," *NJ&G*, April 27, 1946, 1.
29. "Vet Charges USES Refuses Skilled Jobs," *CC&P*, Aug. 17, 1946, 5A.
30. Gunter to George S. Mitchell, April 2, 1946, reel 188, 6, SRC; Berry, oral history, Nov. 16, 1993, 10, 21–22, 46, MOHP.
31. Martin, *Best Is None Too Good*, 71.
32. Hartmann, *Home Front and Beyond*, 44; Nancy McInerny, "The Woman Vet Has Her Headaches, Too," SM38–40.
33. Allord, OH00014, 1995, WVMOHC; Sarah Parry Myers, *Earning Their Wings*, 307–8.
34. Mapheus Smith, "Population Characteristics of American Servicemen in World War II," 247.
35. Thomas M. Pryor, "Mr. Capra Comes to Town," *NYT*, Nov. 18, 1945, 49; Harris, *Five Came Back*, 421, 423.
36. Herman, *Talent for Trouble*, 275, 278–80; Thomas M. Pryor, "William Wyler and His Screen Philosophy," *NYT*, Nov. 17, 1946, 77; personal communication with Catherine Wyler, Dec. 12, 2023.
37. Matzen, *Mission*, 308–9.
38. Bullock, *Playing for Their Nation*, 126–27, 131–32, 140.
39. Cramer, *Joe DiMaggio*, 212–20.

40. Mark Kurlansky, "Henry B. Interrupted," in *Hank Greenberg*, 95–123; "Hank Greenberg," Baseball Reference, www.baseball-reference.com/players/g/greenha01.shtml.
41. Bullock, *Playing for Their Nation*, 128–29.
42. President's Commission on Veterans' Pensions, *Readjustment Benefits, Part B*, 22.

Chapter 18: The Veterans at College

1. Earl J. McGrath, "The Education of the Veteran," 85.
2. Stanley Frank, "The G.I.'s Reject Education," *SEP*, Aug. 18, 1945, 20, President's Commission on Veterans' Pensions, *Readjustment Benefits, Part B*, 26.
3. President's Commission on Veterans' Pensions, *Readjustment Benefits, Part B*, 12–15; *Part A*, table 4, 49 (on total number of returned veterans by December, 1945).
4. U.S. Congress, House, Committee on Veterans' Affairs, *Report on Education and Training*, 7.
5. Terkel, *"Good War,"* 144–45.
6. President's Commission on Veterans' Pensions, *Readjustment Benefits, Part B*, 26.
7. Milton MacKaye, "Crisis at the Colleges," *SEP*, Aug. 3, 1946, 9.
8. "S.R.O.," *Time*, March 18, 1946, 75–76.
9. "3,527 FPHA Homes Transferred to 'VETS,'" *NYT*, Nov. 18, 1945, 32; Frydl, *GI Bill*, 313; Altschuler and Blumin, *GI Bill*, 88; Clemens, *Rutgers Since 1945*, 5.
10. MacKaye, "Crisis at the Colleges," 39; "S.R.O.," *Time*, 75–76; Olson, *The G.I. Bill, the Veterans, and the Colleges*, 88.
11. Shermer, *Indentured Students*, 103; Fabricant and Brier, *Austerity Blues*, 51–54.
12. "S.R.O.," *Time*, 75–76.
13. Childers, *Soldier from the War Returning*, 27, 123, 230.
14. Ferguson, *Idealist*, 190, 222, 225–26.
15. Esser, oral history, June–Aug. 1990, Interview L-0035, SOHPC.
16. Altschuler and Blumin, *GI Bill*, 77; Charles J. V. Murphy, "GIs at Harvard," *Life*, June 17, 1946, 17, 22.
17. Karabel, *Chosen*, 183–84.
18. Steinhauser, interview by Linda Cameron, April 23, 2009, Minnesota's Greatest Generation, Minnesota Historical Society.
19. "Veterans at College," *Life*, April 21, 1947, 105–13.
20. Meyerhof, oral history, Oct. 28, 2006, 17–18, LdG.
21. Harry Gideonse, "Educational Achievement of Veterans at Brooklyn College," 467; Bradford Morse, "The Veteran and His Education," 18.
22. President's Commission on Veterans' Pensions, *Readjustment Benefits, Part B*, 27; Van Ells, *To Hear Only Thunder Again*, 151.
23. Heller, *Now and Then*, 193–94, 204.
24. Wiley, *Training of Negro Troops*, 7; "High School G.I.s," *Time*, Sept. 3, 1945, 88–91.

25. Berry, oral history, Nov. 16, 1993, 10, 22, 46, MOHP.
26. Pickett, oral history, Nov. 5, 1993, 28–29, 32, MOHP.
27. Juan F. Perea, "Doctrines of Delusion . . . ," 591; U.S. Congress, House, Committee on Veterans' Affairs, *Servicemen's Readjustment Act of 1944*, Title II, Chapter IV, Part VIII, para. 8, 10–11.
28. Keith Olson, *G.I. Bill*, cited in Turner and Bound, "Closing the Gap or Widening the Divide," 153.
29. Sarah Ayako Barksdale, "Prelude to a Revolution," 206, 215–17.
30. Armstead, oral history, March 7, 2013, ROHA.
31. Veasey, oral history, June 25, 2000, WVHP.
32. Terkel, *"Good War,"* 151–52, 156–58.
33. U.S. House of Representatives, 93rd Cong., 1st sess., House Committee Print no. 1, *Report of Educational Testing Service, Princeton University, on Educational Assistance Programs for Veterans* (Washington, D.C.: GPO, 1973), cited in Turner and Bound, "Closing the Gap or Widening the Divide," 149, n7, 172.
34. Karabel, *Chosen*, 180; Hartmann, *Home Front and Beyond*, 104.
35. Federal Security Agency, Office of Education, *Biennial Survey of Education in the United States, 1942–44*, chap. 4, 11; Federal Security Agency, Office of Education, *Biennial Survey 1946–48*, chap. 4, 11–12.
36. Benjamin Fine, "Facilities in Colleges Taxed by Returning War Veterans," *NYT*, Jan. 6, 1946, 32; Hartmann, *Home Front and Beyond*, 106.
37. MacKaye, "Crisis at the Colleges," 39.
38. Eugene Perkins and Lorraine Perkins, interview by Calvin Gower, April 2, 1982, MDL.
39. "Classes for Men at Finch College," *NYT*, April 17, 1946, 29.
40. Dempsey, oral history, March 1, 2010, ROHA.
41. "Forum Topic Announced," *NYT*, May 21, 1946, 21; Helen M. Hosp, "Student Pressures in Higher Education," 232.
42. Mettler, *Soldiers to Citizens*, 155; Hartmann, *Home Front and Beyond*, 116.
43. Altschuler and Blumin, *GI Bill*, 111.
44. Dinnerstein, *Antisemitism in America*, 158–60; Saveth, "Education," 91.
45. President's Commission on Veterans' Pensions, *Readjustment Benefits, Part B*, 22.

Chapter Nineteen: Vocational Schools and Job-Training Programs

1. Congressman Abernethy, May 12, 1944, 78th Cong., 2nd sess., *CR* 90, pt. 4, 4435.
2. U.S. Congress, House, Committee on Veterans' Affairs, *Report on Education and Training Under the Servicemen's Readjustment Act, from the Administrator of Veterans Affairs*, 9, 66, 70–74.
3. Congressman Poage, speaking on S. 1767, on May 17, 1944, 78th Cong., 2nd sess., *CR* 90, pt. 4, 4620.
4. U.S. Congress, House, Committee on Veterans' Affairs, *Report on Education*

and Training, app. E, "Typical Examples of Misleading Advertising Relating to Veterans' Training," 162–99.
5. U.S. Congress, House, Committee on Veterans' Affairs. *Hearings Before the Subcommittee on Education, Training and Rehabilitation,* Part 2, Jan. 30, 1948, 152–54.
6. Albert Q. Maisel, "What's Wrong with Veterans' Schools?," *Collier's*, May 1, 1948, 54.
7. President's Commission on Veterans' Pensions, *Readjustment Benefits, Part B*, 46.
8. President's Commission on Veterans' Pensions, *Readjustment Benefits, Part B*, 32.
9. Kirksey, oral history, March 4, 1994, 82, 97, MOHP.
10. Heath, oral history, Sept. 8, 1994, 43–46, MOHP.
11. Russell, oral history, March 3, 1994, 39–41, MOHP.
12. Bonder to U.S. Congress, Papers of the NAACP, Jan. 13, 1948, Part 09: Discrimination in the U.S. Armed Forces, Series A: General Office Files on Armed Forces Affairs, 1918–1955, folder 001535-006-0790, NAACP.
13. Paxton to Dedmon, Dec. 3, 1946; Dedmon to Paxton, Jan. 9, 1947, Part 9, Series C, folder 001540-08-0474, NAACP.
14. Bohannon to Mitchell, March 18, 1946, reel 188, 4, 1944–1948, Series VII, Veterans Services Project, SRC.
15. Gooch, oral history, June 21, 2011, KU.
16. Villalobos, oral history, OH#3808, Oct. 12, 2006, MAVC.
17. Frydl, *GI Bill*, 195.
18. Maisel, "What's Wrong with Veterans' Schools?"
19. Henry F. Pringle, "Are We Making a Bum Out of G.I. Joe?," *LHJ*, Sept. 1946, 48.
20. David Onkst, "'First a Negro . . . Incidentally a Veteran,'" 527; Bohannon to Mitchell, Feb. 22, 1946, reel 188, no. 4, SRC.
21. Malveaux, "Problems Affecting the Negro Veteran," 37th Annual Conference of the National Association for the Advancement of Colored People, Cincinnati, Ohio, June 26, 1945, Part 01: Meetings of the Board of Directors, Records of Annual Conferences, Major Speeches, and Special Reports, Folder 001412-011-0687, NAACP.
22. Onkst, "'First a Negro . . . Incidentally a Veteran,'" 525–26.
23. Anderson, oral history, 2004, WVMOHC.
24. Fuentes, oral history, OH#3078, June 21, 2005, MAVP; Steven Rosales, "Fighting the Peace at Home," 604.
25. U.S. Congress, Senate, Committee on Finance, *Amendments to the Servicemen's Readjustment Act of 1944*, Oct. 8–12, 1945, 121, 318, 323.
26. Woods, oral history, Feb. 18, 1990, MDL.
27. Marcellus Chandler Barksdale, "The Indigenous Civil Rights Movement and Cultural Change in North Carolina," 47–48.
28. Brazier to George S. Mitchell, June 21, 1946, reel 188, no. 5, SRC; Levy, oral history, Dec. 21, 1993, MOHP.
29. Gunter to George S. Mitchell, April 2, 1946, reel 188, 6, SRC.

30. Culinary Institute of America, "CIA History," www.ciachef.edu/our-story/; "Lady Lawyer Kitchen-Wise," *RCJN*, Sept. 19, 1949, 3; Nancy MacLennan, "115 Taking Courses in Culinary Arts," *NYT*, Feb. 21, 1949, 14; Marie Blizard, "They Know What's Cooking," *HC*, July 3, 1949, SM5; Second Graduating Class photo (Mislabeled as first graduating class), CIA, www.ciachef.edu/our-story/.
31. June Geserick, "Veterans Sweeten Music," *CDT*, Oct. 6, 1946, B4.
32. President's Commission on Veterans' Pensions, *Readjustment Benefits, Part B*, 32.
33. Ben Davis, "The GI Bill Made Art," *Jacobin*, Aug. 27, 2019.
34. Smith, *Utopia and Dissent*, 79.
35. Catherine Barnwell, "95 GIs Forget Rifles for Creative Study," *AC*, Sept. 15, 1947, 12.
36. McChesney, *Period of Exploration, San Francisco, 1945–1950*.
37. "Noah Purifoy," digital archive, Hammer Museum at UCLA; Purifoy, interview, Sept. 8, 1990, 16–17, OHP-UCLA; Smith, *Utopia and Dissent*, 85–86.
38. Menand, *Free World*, 228, 234.
39. Stephanie Cassidy, "Staying Power," *Linea*, July 9, 2015, asllinea.org/staying-power-art-students-league/.
40. Smith, *Utopia and Dissent*, 82, 90–93; Suzanne Muchnic, "True to a Significant School," *LAT*, July 1, 2001.
41. Eric Felten, "How the Taxman Cleared the Dance Floor," *WSJ*, March 17, 2013; Marc Myers, *Why Jazz Happened*, 50.
42. Porter, *John Coltrane*, 38–39, 50–52.
43. "Dave Brubeck on His Musical Development at Mills College Under Darius Milhaud," BOHP; Doug Ramsey and Sony Music Entertainment, "Dave Brubeck, The Biography: Part 1: 1920–1948," www.davebrubeckjazz.com/Bio-/Dave-Brubeck---The-Biography/Bio-1920-1948.
44. Myers, *Why Jazz Happened*, 62.
45. Powell, *Tito Puente*, 88–91, 125; Loza, *Tito Puente and the Making of Latin Music*, 32–34.
46. Marc Myers, "Interview: Gunther Schuller (Part 2)," JazzWax, Jan. 19, 2010, www.jazzwax.com/2010/01/interview-gunther-schuller-part-2.html. On Westlake, see Michael T. Spencer, "Jazz Education at the Westlake College of Music."
47. John Willett, "Erwin Piscator," 1–6, 9, 11; Curtis and Paris, *Tony Curtis*, 61, 67–68; Curtis, *American Prince*, 81–82.
48. Edelman and Kupferberg, *Matthau*, 45–48.
49. Belafonte, *My Song*, 56–57, 65.
50. Isadora Bennett, "Training Program of the American Theatre Wing," 34; Isidore Bennett, Director of Publicity, American Theatre Wing, "Immediate Monday News," July 1, 8, 1946, American Theatre Wing Professional Training Program: clippings, NYPL for the Performing Arts.
51. Jean Meegan, "Show Business Taught Ex-GI's," *BS*, July 7, 1946, A6; "150 Former GI's Sign for Theatre Wing 'U.,'" *NYT*, July 2, 1946, 20; "American The-

ater Wing's Professional Training Program," press release, June 18, 1947, NYPL for the Performing Arts.
52. Bennett, *Good Life*, 55, 62, 68, 79–80, 84–85.
53. Wise and Rehill, *Stars in Blue*, 117–21; Borgnine, *Ernie*, 48–50, 52–53.
54. Rudolf Orthwine, "Victory in Europe Brings Soldier Rehabilitation to the Fore," 4.
55. Joel Lobenthal, "Conversation with Robert Barnett," 37.
56. Thanks to Lynn Garafola, author of *La Nijinska* (New York: Oxford University Press, 2022), for information on Bronislava Nijinska's Hollywood Ballet School class lists.
57. Advertisements from *Dance* 21, no. 1 (Jan. 1947), Jerome Robbins Dance Division, NYPL for the Performing Arts.
58. "Dancing Instruction Under G.I. Bill O.K.'d for Vets in New York," *HCRIM*, April 16, 1946; "Dancing Lessons Are Free to GI's," *NYT*, April 17, 1946, 27; "Arthur Murray Office and Studio," Los Angeles Conservancy, www.laconservancy.org/locations/arthur-murray-office-and-studio.
59. Lisa Pinley Covert, "The GI Bill Abroad," 251.
60. Levenstein, *We'll Always Have Paris*, 101.
61. "Ellsworth Kelly, Alexander Calder," Sept. 18, 1997, AMDA, www.pbs.org/wnet/americanmasters/archive/interview/ellsworth-kelly/.
62. Lennon, *Norman Mailer*, 98; Levenstein, *We'll Always Have Paris*, 101.
63. John Stanton, "The New Expatriates," *Life*, Aug. 22, 1949, 77, 78, 84.
64. Edgar A. Wiggins, "Veterans Take Advantage of GI Bill, Study in Paris," *AA*, April 26, 1947, 11; Valerie J. Mercer, "Herbert Gentry," in *Explorations in the City of Light: African-American Artists in Paris, 1945–1965*, ed. Audreen Buffalo (New York: Studio Museum in Harlem, 1996), www.herbertgentry.com/valerie-j-mercer.
65. Romare Bearden, oral history interview, June 29, 1968, AAA.
66. "GI Paradise," *Life*, Jan. 5, 1948, 56–58; Covert, "The GI Bill Abroad," 252, 257–58.
67. President's Commission on Veterans' Pensions, *Readjustment Benefits, Part A*, 13, 55.
68. President's Commission on Veterans' Pensions, *Readjustment Benefits, Part B*, 23; White House, Office of Management and Budget, table 11.3: "Outlays for Payments by Individuals by Category and Major Program," line 33, Historical Tables, www.whitehouse.gov/omb/budget/historical-tables/.

Chapter 20: After Five Years

1. U.S. Office of War Mobilization and Reconversion, *Sixth Report to the President, the Senate, and the House of Representatives*, 2; President's Commission on Veterans' Pensions, *Readjustment Benefits, Part A*, 47.
2. President's Commission on Veterans' Pensions, *Readjustment Benefits, Part B*, 23.

3. Stouffer et al., *Combat and Its Aftermath*, 639.
4. U.S. Department of Health, Education, and Welfare, *100 Years of Marriage and Divorce Statistics*, table 3, 4, p. 24; U.S. Census Bureau, *Historical Statistics . . . to 1957*, 22.
5. Frank D. Morris, "Our Shameful Record in Veterans' Housing," *Collier's*, July 23, 1949, 57.
6. President's Commission on Veterans' Pensions, *Readjustment Benefits, Part A*, table 4, 49.
7. U.S. Senate, Subcommittee on Housing and Urban Redevelopment, "Postwar Economic Policy and Planning," 6, 7; President's Commission on Veterans' Pensions, *Veterans' Loan Guaranty and Direct Loan Benefits, Part C*, 2–3.
8. President's Commission on Veterans' Pensions, *Readjustment Benefits, Part A*, table 4, 49; President's Commission on Veterans' Pensions, *Veterans' Loan Guaranty and Direct Loan Benefits, Part C*, 69–71.
9. Jackson, *Crabgrass Frontier*, 234–35.
10. Keogh, *In Levittown's Shadow*, 60–61.
11. Eric Larrabee, "The Six Thousand Houses That Levitt Built," *Harper's*, Sept. 1948, 85–87.
12. Ron Rosenbaum, "The House That Levitt Built," *Esquire*, Dec. 1983, 385–86, Esquire Magazine Archive.
13. Jackson, *Crabgrass Frontier*, 237; Michael T. Kaufman, "Tough Times for Mr. Levittown," *NYT*, Sept. 24, 1989, SM42.
14. Jackson, *Crabgrass Frontier*, 233; President's Commission on Veterans' Pensions, *Readjustment Benefits, Part A*, table 4, 49; Altschuler and Blumin, *GI Bill*, 188–89.
15. Carl R. Gray Jr., Administrator of Veterans Affairs, *To the Home-Buying Veteran*, VA Pamphlet 4-5, June 1950; "Veterans Warned on Homes," *NYT*, July 9, 1950, 19.
16. Paula Span, "Mr. Levitt's Neighborhood," *WP*, May 27, 1997, C1.
17. Dave Rosenbluth, "NAACP Head Hits LI 'Quiet Segregation,'" *Nday*, Dec. 6, 1951, 3; Craig Thompson, "Growing Pains of a Brand-New City," *SEP*, Aug. 1954, 72. For an extended discussion of segregated housing on Long Island, see Keogh, *In Levittown's Shadow*.
18. "NAACP Attacks Covenants in Vet Housing," *CC&P*, Nov. 6, 1948, 1B; "FHA Rejects Anti-bias Plea Made by NAACP," *CC&P*, Nov. 13, 1948, 1B.
19. U.S. National Housing Agency, Federal Housing Administration, *Underwriting Manual*, para. 1320; Rothstein, *Color of Law*, 73.
20. National Park Service, *Civil Rights in America: Racial Discrimination in Housing*, 32–33.
21. Simon, *Stuyvesant Town*, 32, 37, 62; Zipp, *Manhattan Projects*, 73–113.
22. Boyden Sparkes, "Can the Cities Come Back?," *SEP*, Nov. 1944, 29; Simon, *Stuyvesant Town*, 36; Abrams, *Forbidden Neighbors*, 251–56; Zipp, *Manhattan Projects*, 120–21.

23. Affidavits of Dorsey, Dowling, Harper, Supreme Court of the State of New York, June 25, 1947, in *Dorsey v. Stuyvesant Town Corp.*, in Papers of the NAACP, Part 05, folder 001521-019-0769, NAACP.
24. Simon, *Stuyvesant Town*, 51, 57–58; "Negroes Lose in Stuyvesant Town Decision," *NYHT*, Dec. 21, 1948, 3; "N.Y. High Court's Negro Tenant Ban by Housing Project," *CDT*, July 20, 1949, A9; "Stuyvesant Town Answers Protest," *NYT*, Nov. 19, 1949, 9; Charles Abrams, "Slum Clearance Boomerangs," *Nation*, July 29, 1950, 106.
25. Charles Abrams, "Stuyvesant Town's Threat to Our Liberties," *Commentary*, Nov. 1949, 426–33.
26. Gold, *When Tenants Claimed the City*, 49–54; "Stuyvesant Town Grants Negro Family Apt.," *NYAN*, Jan. 26, 1952, 3.
27. Cohen, *Consumers' Republic*, 217; Garodnick, *Saving Stuyvesant Town*, 22.

Chapter 21: The Veterans' Welfare State

1. Edwin Amenta and Theda Skocpol, "Redefining the New Deal," in Weir, Orloff, and Skocpol, *Politics and Social Policy in the United States*, 94.
2. President's Commission on Veterans' Pensions, *Readjustment Benefits, Part A*, table 1, 259.
3. U.S. Congress, House, Committee on Veterans' Affairs, *The Provision of Federal Benefits for Veterans*, 180–81.
4. President's Commission on Veterans' Pensions, *Readjustment Benefits, Part A*, 2.
5. U.S. Civil Service Commission, *History of Veteran Preference in Federal Employment*, table 1, 39.
6. U.S. Congress, House, Committee on Veterans' Affairs, 214; Bradley and Blair, *General's Life*, 458–62; Van Ells, *To Hear Only Thunder Again*, 122–23.
7. Frydl, *GI Bill*, 265.
8. White House, Office of Management and Budget, Table 3.1: "Outlays by Superfunction and Function, 1940–2029," Historical Tables, President's Budget, www.whitehouse.gov/omb/budget/historical-tables/; President's Commission on Veterans' Pensions, *Readjustment Benefits, Part A*, table 2, 44; President's Commission on Veterans' Pensions, *Veterans' Loan Guaranty and Direct Loan Benefits, Part C*, 54; U.S. Census Bureau, *Historical Statistics . . . to 1970*, 849–55, 1140; Brown, *Race, Money, and the American Welfare State*, 169.
9. "The Spreading State of Welfare," *Fortune*, Feb. 1952, 104, 154, 156, 159–60.
10. Rosenman, *Working with Roosevelt*, 395; Frydl, *GI Bill*, 165.
11. Administrator of Veterans Affairs, *Annual Report, . . . 1950* (Washington, D.C.: GPO, 1951), 239; Starr, *Social Transformation of American Medicine*, 280–83, 289.
12. Korson, *At His Side*, 274; Urrea, "My Mother Returned from World War II a Changed Woman."
13. "Negro GI Bill Urged," *PT*, July 2, 1963, 1; "Dr. King Urges," *BS*, Dec. 20, 1963, 40; King Jr., *Why We Can't Wait*, 150–52.

14. Brown, *Race, Money, and the American Welfare State*, 169; "The Quarter's Polls," *POQ* 10, no. 3 (Autumn 1946): 437. For a discussion of public and congressional pushback against the extension of veterans' benefits, see Burtin, *Nation of Veterans*, chap. 4; Eig, *King*, 456; "King in Atlanta for 3-Day Rest," *CD*, July 31, 1965, 31; "Dr. King Urges," *CDT*, Jan. 14, 1968, A14; Martin Luther King Jr., "The American Negro," *NYT*, Nov. 12, 1967, 219.
15. Eig, *King*, 533–34.
16. William J. Clinton, "Remarks Commemorating the 50th Anniversary of the GI Bill of Rights," June 22, 1994, APP.
17. Brown, *Race, Money, and the American Welfare State*, 180, 182. See also, for an opposing analysis of veteran versus nonveteran incomes, Angrist and Krueger, "Why Do World War II Veterans Earn More Than Nonveterans?"
18. Cohen, *Consumers' Republic*, 137.
19. Cohen, *Consumers' Republic*, table 2, 222.
20. Oliver and Shapiro, *Black Wealth, White Wealth*, 18, 108.
21. John T. McQuiston, "If You're Thinking of Living In: Levittown," *NYT*, Nov. 27, 1983, R9, price data from "Levittown, New York," City-Data.com, www.city-data.com/city/Levittown-New-York.html.
22. Chinyere O. Agbai, "Wealth Begins at Home," 76. On social and geographical stratification in the suburbs, see Keogh, *In Levittown's Shadow*, 79–114.
23. U.S. Congress, House, *Sgt. Isaac Woodard Jr. and Sgt. Joseph H. Maddox GI Bill Restoration Act of 2021*, H.R. 5905, 117th Cong., 1st sess., introduced in House Nov. 5, 2021; U.S. Congress, House, *Sgt. Isaac Woodard Jr. and Sgt. Joseph H. Maddox GI Bill Restoration Act of 2023*, H.R. 1255, 118th Cong., 1st sess., introduced in House Feb. 28, 2023; "Co-sponsors of H.R. 1255 (118th): Sgt. Isaac Woodard Jr. and Sgt. Joseph H. Maddox GI Bill Restoration Act of 2023"; Seth Moulton, "Moulton, Clyburn Introduce Landmark Legislation," press release, Nov. 11, 2021; "H.R. 1725: Sgt. Isaac Woodard, Jr. . . .," www.govtrack.us/congress/bills/119/hr1725.

Chapter 22: Aftermaths

1. Terkel, *"Good War,"* 3.
2. Rooney, *My War*, 5.
3. Terkel, "Note," in *"Good War"*; Brokaw, *Greatest Generation*, 293.
4. Samet, *Looking for the Good War*, 5, 16; Bodnar, *"Good War" in American Memory*, 1.
5. Samet, *Looking for the Good War*, 274–75.
6. See, for example, Brokaw, *Greatest Generation*, xxvii–xxviii; Ambrose, *Citizen Soldiers*, 472.
7. Ronald Reagan, "Remarks at a Ceremony Commemorating the 40th Anniversary of the Normandy Invasion, D-Day," June 6, 1984, RRPL; David Greenberg, "D-Day OD," *Slate*, June 4, 2004. See also David Jackson, "D-Day Has Become a Presidential Pilgrimage," *USA*, June 5, 2014.

8. Maharidge, *Bringing Mulligan Home*, xiv.
9. DeBruyne and Leland, *American War and Military Operations Casualties*, April 26, 2017, table 1, 2.
10. Logevall, *JFK*, 354–56, 368–69, 382; R. T. McIntire, Chief of Bureau, to BuPers, Jan. 18, 1945, JFK Personal Papers, Naval Retiring Board, JFKPP-011-034, 13, JFKPL.
11. Dole, *One Soldier's Story*, 214–15.
12. Joshua J. Nasaw's service and discharge records in author's possession.
13. Bradley and Blair, *General's Life*, 453–54; Menninger, *Psychiatry in a Troubled World*, 380.
14. Gooch, *City Poet*, 68, 74, 464.
15. C. Denis Robinette, Zdenek Hrubec, and Joseph F. Fraumeni Jr., "Chronic Alcoholism and Subsequent Mortality in World War II Veterans," 693, 697; Donald Stockford and Alice P. Carmody, *1980 Supplement to "Alcoholism and Problem Drinking, 1970–1975,"* 16.
16. Jeffrey E. Harris, "Cigarette Smoking Practices, Smoking-Related Diseases, and the Costs of Tobacco-Related Disability Among Currently Living U.S. Veterans . . . ," Report Commissioned by the Department of Veterans Affairs Assistant Secretary for Policy and Planning, Sept. 15, 1997, table 4, 11; table 6, 15, www.mit.edu/people/jeffrey/HarrisVARept97.pdf.
17. Harris, "Cigarette Smoking Practices," 1; Bedard and Deschênes, "Long-Term Impact of Military Service on Health," 177–78; Carmelli and Page, "Twenty-Four Year Mortality in World War II US Male Veteran Twins . . . ," 557.
18. Administrator of Veterans Affairs, *Annual Report, 1965*, 23, 38.
19. Herbert C. Archibald and Read D. Tuddenham, "Persistent Stress Reaction After Combat," 475, 480.
20. Hans Pols, "Waking Up to Shell Shock," 148–49.
21. Pressman, *Last Resort*, 10.
22. Hannah M. Moser, "Ten-Year Follow-Up of Lobotomy Patients," 381.
23. Michael M. Phillips, "The Lobotomy Files," pt. 1, *WSJ*, Dec. 12, 2013.
24. Michael M. Phillips, "A Nurse's Story: World War II Vet's Lobotomy Scarred Family She Raised," *WSJ*, Jan. 24, 2015.
25. Ron Langer, "Combat Trauma, Memory, and the World War II Veteran."
26. Schnurr quoted in Madigan, "Their War Ended 70 Years Ago. Their Trauma Didn't," *WP*, Sept. 11, 2015.
27. Matthew J. Friedman, "History of PTSD in Veterans"; Edgar Jones, "Historical Approaches to Post-combat Disorders."
28. Abu El-Haj, *Combat Trauma*, 38–39.
29. Wilbur J. Scott, "PTSD in DSM-III," 297–307.
30. American Psychiatric Association, *DSM-III*, section 309.81, 236–37.
31. David Gelman, "Reliving the Painful Past," *NW*, June 13, 1994.
32. Gelman, "Reliving the Painful Past," 22.
33. Robert Hierholzer et al., "Clinical Presentation of PTSD in World War II Combat Veterans," 819.

34. Tim Madigan, "Their War Ended 70 Years Ago. Their Trauma Didn't," *WP*, Sept. 11, 2015.
35. Dahlberg, oral history, NWW2M.
36. Mathews, *Our Fathers' War*, 241–42; "Excerpts from July 1997 Interview with Hollace 'Red' Ditterline," *Audie Murphy Research Foundation Newsletter* 2 (Spring 1997): 3.
37. Gutman, *One Veteran's Journey to Heal the Wounds of War*, 32, 88–89.
38. Stewart Alan Stancil, "After the War Is Over."
39. U.S. Department of Veterans Affairs, "American Prisoners of War (POWS) and Missing in Action (MIAs)," table 1, 4; Speed et al., "Posttraumatic Stress Disorder as a Consequence of the POW Experience."
40. Halloran, March 12, 2004, Military Oral History Collection, VMI.
41. Bussel, *My Private War*, 202–3, 260–61, 317.
42. Childers, *Soldier from the War Returning*, 256–57, 267–68, 274.
43. Vonnegut, *Slaughterhouse-Five*, 29; Matthew J. Friedman, "PTSD History and Overview."
44. Ann Godoff, Oct. 9, 2022, in author's possession.
45. Sledge, *China Marine*, xiii, 149–50, 159–60.
46. Michael Wilson, "He Bombed the Nazis. 75 Years Later, the Nightmares Began," *NYT*, April 30, 2023. John Wenzel died, on October 2, 2023, at the age of a hundred.

Bibliography

Abrams, Charles. *Forbidden Neighbors*. New York: Harper, 1955.

Abu El-Haj, Nadia. *Combat Trauma: Imaginaries of War and Citizenship in Post-9/11 America*. London: Verso, 2022.

Adair, Nancy, and Casey Adair. *Word Is Out: Stories of Some of Our Lives*. San Francisco: New Glide Publications, 1978.

Adams, Michael C. C. *The Best War Ever: America and World War II*. Baltimore: Johns Hopkins University Press, 1994.

Adelman, Marcy, ed. *Long Time Passing: Lives of Older Lesbians*. Boston: Alyson Publications, 1988.

Agbai, Chinyere O. "Wealth Begins at Home: The Housing Benefits of the 1944 GI Bill and the Making of the Racial Wealth Gap in Homeownership and Home Value." PhD diss., Brown University, 2022.

Alsen, Eberhard. *J. D. Salinger and the Nazis*. Madison: University of Wisconsin Press, 2018.

Altschuler, Glenn C., and Stuart M. Blumin. *The GI Bill: A New Deal for Veterans*. New York: Oxford University Press, 2009.

Alvah, Donna. *Unofficial Ambassadors: American Military Families Overseas and the Cold War, 1946–1965*. New York: New York University Press, 2007.

Ambrose, Stephen E. *Citizen Soldiers: The U.S. Army from the Normandy Beaches to the Bulge to the Surrender of Germany, June 7, 1944–May 7, 1945*. New York: Simon & Schuster, 1997.

American Psychiatric Association. *DSM-III: Diagnostic and Statistical Manual of Mental Disorders*. 3rd ed. Washington, D.C.: American Psychiatric Association, 1981.

Anderson, Carolyn. "Accidental Tourists: Yanks in Rome, 1944–1945." *Journal of Tourism History* 11, no. 1 (2019): 22–45.

Angrist, Joshua, and Alan B. Krueger. "Why Do World War II Veterans Earn More Than Nonveterans?" *Journal of Labor Economics* 12, no. 1 (Jan. 1994): 74–97.

Appel, John W., and Gilbert W. Beebe. "Preventive Psychiatry—an Epidemiologic Approach." *Journal of the American Medical Association* 131, no. 18 (1946): 1469–75.

Archibald, Herbert C., and Read D. Tuddenham. "Persistent Stress Reaction After Combat: A 20-Year Follow-Up." *Archives of General Psychiatry* 12, no. 5 (1965): 475–81.

Astor, Gerald. *The Greatest War: The Battle of the Bulge to Hiroshima*. New York: Warner Books, 2001.

Barksdale, Marcellus Chandler. "The Indigenous Civil Rights Movement and Cultural Change in North Carolina: Weldon, Chapel Hill, and Monroe, 1946–1965." PhD diss., Duke University, 1977.

Barksdale, Sarah Ayako. "Prelude to a Revolution: African-American World War II Veterans, Double Consciousness, and Civil Rights, 1940–1955." PhD diss., University of North Carolina at Chapel Hill, 2014.

Baruch, Dorothy Walter, and Lee Edward Travis. *You're Out of the Service Now: The Veteran's Guide to Civilian Life*. New York: D. Appleton–Century, 1946.

Baruch, B. M., and J. M. Hancock, United States. Office of War Mobilization. *Report on War and Post-war Adjustment Policy*. Washington, D.C.: GPO, 1944.

Baxandall, Rosalyn, and Elizabeth Ewen. *Picture Windows: How the Suburbs Happened*. New York: Basic Books, 2000.

Bedard, Kelly, and Olivier Deschênes. "The Long-Term Impact of Military Service on Health: Evidence from World War II and Korean War Veterans." *American Economic Review* 96 (2006): 176–94.

Beebe, Gilbert W., and Michael E. De Bakey. *Battle Casualties, Incidence, Mortality, and Logistic Considerations*. Springfield, Ill.: Charles C. Thomas, 1952.

Belafonte, Harry. *My Song: A Memoir*. With Michael Shnayerson. New York: Knopf, 2011.

Bennett, Isadora. "The Training Program of the American Theatre Wing." *Educational Theatre Journal* 7, no. 1 (March 1955).

Bennett, Tony. *The Good Life*. With Will Friedwald. New York: Pocket Books, 1998.

Bernd, Joseph L. "White Supremacy and the Disfranchisement of Blacks in Georgia, 1946." *Georgia Historical Quarterly* 66, no. 4 (1982): 492–513.

Bernstein, Barton J. "Reluctance and Resistance: Wilson Wyatt and Veterans' Housing in the Truman Administration." *Register of the Kentucky Historical Society* 65, no. 1 (1967): 47–66.

———. "The Removal of War Production Board Controls on Business, 1944–1946." *Business History Review* 39, no. 2 (Summer 1965): 243–60.

Bérubé, Allan. *Coming Out Under Fire.* 1990. Chapel Hill: University of North Carolina Press, 2010.

Biesen, Sheri Chinen. *Blackout: World War II and the Origins of Film Noir.* Baltimore: Johns Hopkins University Press, 2005.

Biess, Frank, and Daniel M. Gross, eds. *Science and Emotions After 1945: A Transatlantic Perspective.* Chicago: University of Chicago Press, 2014.

Bird, Kai. *The Chairman: John J. McCloy and the Making of the American Establishment.* New York: Simon & Schuster, 1992.

Bius, Joel R. *Smoke 'Em if You Got 'Em: The Rise and Fall of the Military Cigarette Ration.* Annapolis, Md.: Naval Institute Press, 2018.

Blain, Daniel. "Priorities in Psychiatric Treatment of Veterans." *Military Surgeon* 102, no. 2 (1948): 85–97.

Blower, Brooke Lindy, and Mark Bradley, eds. *The Familiar Made Strange: American Icons and Artifacts After the Transnational Turn.* Ithaca, N.Y.: Cornell University Press, 2015.

Blum, John Morton. *V Was for Victory: Politics and American Culture During World War II.* New York: Harcourt Brace Jovanovich, 1976.

Blumenson, Martin. *Breakout and Pursuit.* Washington, D.C.: Center of Military History, U.S. Army, 2005.

———. *Kasserine Pass.* Boston: Houghton Mifflin, 1967.

Bodnar, John E. *The "Good War" in American Memory.* Baltimore: Johns Hopkins University Press, 2010.

Bolté, Charles G. *The New Veteran.* New York: Reynal & Hitchcock, 1945.

Bolté, Charles G., and Louis Harris. *Our Negro Veterans.* New York: Public Affairs Committee, 1947.

Boomhower, Ray E. *Dispatches from the Pacific: The World War II Reporting of Robert L. Sherrod.* Bloomington: Indiana University Press, 2017.

———. *Richard Tregaskis: Reporting Under Fire from Guadalcanal to Vietnam.* Albuquerque: University of New Mexico Press, 2021.

Borgnine, Ernest. *Ernie: An Autobiography.* New York: Citadel Press, 2008.

Bowker, Benjamin C. *Out of Uniform*. New York: Norton, 1946.

Boyer, Paul S. *By the Bomb's Early Light: American Thought and Culture at the Dawn of the Atomic Age*. New York: Pantheon, 1985.

Bradley, James. *Flags of Our Fathers*. With Ron Powers. New York: Bantam Books, 2000.

Bradley, Omar, and Clay Blair. *A General's Life: An Autobiography*. New York: Simon & Schuster, 1983.

Brandt, Allan M. *No Magic Bullet*. New York: Oxford University Press, 1987.

Brill, Norman Q., and Gilbert W. Beebe. *A Follow-Up Study of War Neuroses*. Washington, D.C.: National Academies Press, 1955.

Brokaw, Tom. *An Album of Memories*. New York: Random House, 2002.

——— . *The Greatest Generation*. New York: Random House, 1998.

——— . *The Greatest Generation Speaks*. New York: Random House, 1999.

Brooke, Edward W. *Bridging the Divide: My Life*. New Brunswick, N.J.: Rutgers University Press, 2007.

Brooks, Emily M. *Gotham's War Within a War: Policing and the Birth of Law-and-Order Liberalism in World War II–Era New York City*. Chapel Hill: University of North Carolina Press, 2023.

Brooks, Jennifer E. *Defining the Peace: World War II Veterans, Race, and the Remaking of Southern Political Tradition*. Chapel Hill: University of North Carolina Press, 2004.

Brooks, Richard. *The Brick Foxhole*. New York: Harper, 1945.

Brotherton, Marcus. *A Company of Heroes: Personal Memories About the Real Band of Brothers and the Legacy They Left Us*. 2010. New York: Dutton Caliber, 2020.

Brown, Michael K. *Race, Money, and the American Welfare State*. Ithaca, N.Y.: Cornell University Press, 1999.

Bullock, Steven R. *Playing for Their Nation: Baseball and the American Military During World War II*. Lincoln: University of Nebraska Press, 2004.

Burnham, Margaret A. *By Hands Now Known: Jim Crow's Legal Executioners*. New York: Norton, 2022.

Burns, John Horne. *The Gallery*. 1947. New York: New York Review of Books, 2004.

Burtin, Olivier. *A Nation of Veterans: War, Citizenship, and the Welfare State in Modern America*. Philadelphia: University of Pennsylvania Press, 2022.

BIBLIOGRAPHY

Bussel, Norman. *My Private War: Liberated Body, Captive Mind: A World War II POW's Journey*. New York: Pegasus, 2008.

Byers, Jean. *A Study of the Negro in Military Service*. Washington, D.C.: Department of Defense, 1950.

Byrum, C. Stephen. *McMinn County*. Memphis: Memphis State University Press, 1984.

Caliver, Ambrose. *Postwar Education of Negroes: Educational Implications of Army Data and Experiences of Negro Veterans and War Workers*. Washington, D.C.: Federal Security Agency, U.S. Office of Education, 1945.

Camelon, Dave. "I Saw the GI Bill Written." *The American Legion Magazine* 47, no. 3 (Sept. 1949).

Campbell, James A. "Mental Disorder Following Service Discharge." *Psychiatric Quarterly* 20, no. 3 (1945): 375–80.

Canaday, Margot. "Building a Straight State: Sexuality and Social Citizenship Under the 1944 G.I. Bill." *Journal of American History* 90, no. 3 (2003): 935–57.

———. *The Straight State: Sexuality and Citizenship in Twentieth-Century America*. Princeton, N.J.: Princeton University Press, 2009.

Cannon, James M. *Gerald R. Ford: An Honorable Life*. Ann Arbor: University of Michigan Press, 2013.

Carmelli, Dorit, and William F. Page. "Twenty-Four Year Mortality in World War II US Male Veteran Twins Discordant for Cigarette Smoking." *International Journal of Epidemiology* 25, no. 3 (1996): 554–59.

Carmody, Alice P., Louis Mesard, and William F. Page. *Alcoholism and Problem Drinking, 1970–1975: A Statistical Analysis of VA Hospital Patients*. Washington, D.C.: Reports and Statistics, Office of the Controller, Veterans Administration, 1977.

Caro, Robert A. *Means of Ascent*. Vol. 2 of *The Years of Lyndon Johnson*. New York: Knopf, 1990.

Carpenter, C. Tyler, and Edward H. Yeatts. *Stars Without Garters! The Memoirs of Two Gay GI's in WWII*. San Francisco: Alamo Square Press, 1996.

Carruthers, Susan L. *Dear John: Love and Loyalty in Wartime America*. New York: Cambridge University Press, 2022.

———. *The Good Occupation: American Soldiers and the Hazards of Peace*. Cambridge, Mass.: Harvard University Press, 2016.

Carsel, Wilfred. *Wartime Apparel Price Control*. Washington, D.C.: Office of Temporary Controls, Office of Price Administration, 1947.

Casey, Steven. *When Soldiers Fall: How Americans Have Confronted Combat Losses from World War I to Afghanistan*. New York: Oxford University Press, 2014.

Chambers, John Whiteclay, and Fred Anderson, eds. *The Oxford Companion to American Military History*. New York: Oxford University Press, 1999.

Childers, Thomas. *Soldier from the War Returning: The Greatest Generation's Troubled Homecoming from World War II*. Boston: Houghton Mifflin Harcourt, 2009.

Ciardi, John. *Other Skies*. Boston: Little, Brown, 1947.

Clemens, Paul G. E. *Rutgers Since 1945: A History of the State University of New Jersey*. New Brunswick, N.J.: Rutgers University Press, 2015.

Coady, Christopher. *John Lewis and the Challenge of "Real" Black Music*. Ann Arbor: University of Michigan Press, 2016.

Cohen, Lizabeth. *A Consumers' Republic: The Politics of Mass Consumption in Postwar America*. New York: Vintage Books, 2004.

Collins, Julia. *My Father's War: A Memoir*. New York: Da Capo Press, 2002.

Columbia Broadcasting System. *From Pearl Harbor into Tokyo*. New York: Columbia Broadcasting System, 1945.

Cory, Donald Webster. *The Homosexual in America: A Subjective Approach*. New York: Greenberg, 1952.

Costello, John. *Virtue Under Fire: How World War II Changed Our Social and Sexual Attitudes*. Boston: Little, Brown, 1985.

Covert, Lisa Pinley. "The GI Bill Abroad: A Postwar Experiment in International Relations." *Diplomatic History* 40, no. 2 (April 2016): 244–68.

Cramer, Richard Ben. *Joe DiMaggio: The Hero's Life*. New York: Simon & Schuster, 2001.

Crespi, Leo P., and G. Schofield Shapleigh. "'The' Veteran—a Myth." *Public Opinion Quarterly* 10, no. 3 (1946): 361–72.

Crespino, Joseph. *Strom Thurmond's America*. New York: Hill and Wang, 2012.

Cuber, John F. "Family Readjustment of Veterans." *Marriage and Family Living* 7, no. 2 (1945): 28–30.

Curtis, Tony. *American Prince: A Memoir*. With Peter Golenbock. New York: Harmony Books, 2008.

Curtis, Tony, and Barry Paris. *Tony Curtis: The Autobiography*. New York: William Morrow, 1993.

Davis, David Brion. "World War II and Memory." *Journal of American History* 77, no. 2 (1990): 580–87.

Davis, Ossie, and Ruby Dee. *With Ossie and Ruby: In This Life Together.* New York: Morrow, 1998.

DeBruyne, Nese F., and Anne Leland. *American War and Military Operations Casualties: Lists and Statistics.* CRS Report for Congress. Washington, D.C.: Library of Congress, Congressional Research Service, 2015.

Dechter, Aimée R., and Glen H. Elder Jr. "World War II Mobilization in Men's Work Lives: Continuity or Disruption for the Middle Class?" *American Journal of Sociology* 110, no. 3 (2004): 761–93.

Delmont, Matthew F. *Half American: The Epic Story of African Americans Fighting World War II at Home and Abroad.* New York: Viking, 2022.

DePastino, Todd. *Bill Mauldin: A Life Up Front.* New York: Norton, 2008.

DeRose, Chris. *The Fighting Bunch: The Battle of Athens and How World War II Veterans Won the Only Successful Armed Rebellion Since the Revolution.* New York: St. Martin's Press, 2020.

Deutsch, James I. "Piercing the Penelope Syndrome: The Depiction of World War II Veterans' Wives in 1940s Hollywood Films." *Humboldt Journal of Social Relations* 16, no. 1 (1990): 31–42.

Dinnerstein, Leonard. *Antisemitism in America.* New York: Oxford University Press, 1994.

Doherty, Thomas Patrick. *Projections of War: Hollywood, American Culture, and World War II.* New York: Columbia University Press, 1993.

Dole, Robert J. *One Soldier's Story: A Memoir.* New York: HarperCollins, 2005.

Doubler, Michael D. *Busting the Bocage: American Combined Arms Operations in France, 6 June–31 July 1944.* Electronic resource. Fort Leavenworth, Kans.: U.S. Army Command and General Staff College, Combat Studies Institute, 1988.

Dower, John W. *War Without Mercy: Race and Power in the Pacific War.* New York: Pantheon Books, 1986.

Dumas, Alexander G., and Grace Graham Keen. *A Psychiatric Primer for the Veteran's Family and Friends.* Minneapolis: University of Minnesota Press, 1945.

Edelman, Rob, and Audrey Kupferberg. *Matthau: A Life.* Lanham, Md.: Taylor Trade, 2002.

Eden, Maya. "Quantifying Racial Discrimination in the 1944 G.I. Bill." *Explorations in Economic History* 90 (Oct. 2023).

Edgerton, Gary. "Revisiting the Recordings of Wars Past: Remembering the Documentary Trilogy of John Huston." *Journal of Popular Film and Television* 15, no. 1 (Spring 1987).

Egerton, John. *Speak Now Against the Day: The Generation Before the Civil Rights Movement in the South.* New York: Knopf, 1994.

Eig, Jonathan. *King: A Life.* New York: Farrar, Straus and Giroux, 2023.

Eisenhower, Dwight D. *Crusade in Europe.* Garden City, N.Y.: Doubleday, 1948.

Eisenstaedt, Alfred. *Eisenstaedt on Eisenstaedt: A Self-Portrait.* New York: Abbeville Press, 1985.

Ellis, John. *The Sharp End: The Fighting Man in World War II.* New York: Scribner, 1980.

Equal Justice Initiative. *Lynching in America: Targeting Black Veterans.* Montgomery, Ala.: Equal Justice Initiative, 2017.

Eskin, Leonard. "Sources of Wartime Labor Supply in the United States." *Monthly Labor Review* 59, no. 2 (1944): 264–78.

Evers-Williams, Myrlie, and Manning Marable, eds. *The Autobiography of Medgar Evers: A Hero's Life and Legacy Revealed Through His Writings, Letters, and Speeches.* New York: Basic Civitas Books, 2006.

Evers-Williams, Myrlie, and William Peters. *For Us, the Living.* 1967. Jackson: University Press of Mississippi, 1996.

Fabricant, Michael, and Stephen Brier. *Austerity Blues: Fighting for the Soul of Public Higher Education.* Baltimore: Johns Hopkins University Press, 2016.

Fairchild, Louis. *They Called It the War Effort: Oral Histories from World War II, Orange, Texas.* Austin, Tex.: Eakin Press, 1993.

Farley, Reynolds, and Walter R. Allen. *The Color Line and the Quality of Life in America.* New York: Russell Sage Foundation, 1987.

Farrell, John A. *Richard Nixon: The Life.* New York: Doubleday, 2017.

Faubus, Orval Eugene. *In This Faraway Land.* Conway, Ark.: River Road Press, 1971.

Federal Security Agency, Office of Education. *Biennial Survey of Education in the United States, 1942–44.* Washington, D.C.: GPO, 1949.

———. *Biennial Survey of Education in the United States, 1946–48.* Washington, D.C.: GPO, 1951.

Ferguson, Niall. *The Idealist, 1923–1968.* Vol. 1 of *Kissinger.* New York: Penguin Press, 2015.

Flink, James J. *The Automobile Age.* Cambridge, Mass.: MIT Press, 1988.

Flynn, George Q. "Selective Service and American Blacks During World War II." *Journal of Negro History* 69, no. 1 (1984): 14–25.

Franklin, John Hope. "Their War and Mine." *Journal of American History* 77, no. 2 (1990): 576–79.

Freeman, Joshua Benjamin. *American Empire: The Rise of a Global Power, the Democratic Revolution at Home, 1945–2000.* New York: Viking, 2012.

———. *Working-Class New York: Life and Labor Since World War II.* New York: New Press, 2001.

Friedman, Matthew J. "History of PTSD in Veterans: Civil War to DSM-5." In *U.S. Department of Veterans Affairs.* Washington, D.C.: GPO, 2017.

Frydl, Kathleen. *The GI Bill.* New York: Cambridge University Press, 2009.

Fure-Slocum, Eric Jon. *Contesting the Postwar City: Working-Class and Growth Politics in 1940s Milwaukee.* New York: Cambridge University Press, 2013.

Fussell, Paul. *Doing Battle: The Making of a Skeptic.* Boston: Little, Brown, 1996.

———. *Wartime: Understanding and Behavior in the Second World War.* New York: Oxford University Press, 1989.

Futterman, Samuel, and Eugene Pumpian-Mindlin. "Traumatic War Neuroses Five Years Later." *American Journal of Psychiatry* 108, no. 6 (1951): 401–8.

Gage, Beverly. *G-Man: J. Edgar Hoover and the Making of the American Century.* New York: Viking, 2022.

Gambone, Michael D. *The Greatest Generation Comes Home: The Veteran in American Society.* College Station: Texas A&M University Press, 2005.

Garland, Joseph E. *Unknown Soldiers.* Rockport, Mass.: Protean Press, 2009.

Garodnick, Daniel R. *Saving Stuyvesant Town: How One Community Defeated the Worst Real Estate Deal in History.* New York: Three Hills, 2021.

Gellman, Irwin F. *The Contender, Richard Nixon: The Congress Years, 1946–1952.* New York: Free Press, 1999.

Gerber, David A., ed. *Disabled Veterans in History.* Ann Arbor: University of Michigan Press, 2012.

Gergel, Richard. *Unexampled Courage: The Blinding of Sgt. Isaac Woodard and the Awakening of President Harry S. Truman and Judge J. Waties Waring.* New York: Farrar, Straus and Giroux, 2019.

Gerstle, Gary. *American Crucible: Race and Nation in the Twentieth Century.* Princeton, N.J.: Princeton University Press, 2017.

Gideonse, Harry. "Educational Achievement of Veterans at Brooklyn College." *Educational Record* 31, no. 4 (1950): 453–68.

Gilbert, James Burkhart. *A Cycle of Outrage: America's Reaction to the Juvenile Delinquent in the 1950s*. New York: Oxford University Press, 1986.

Ginsberg, Eli, et al. *The Lost Divisions*. New York: Columbia University Press, 1959.

Gold, Roberta. *When Tenants Claimed the City: The Struggle for Citizenship in New York Housing*. Urbana: University of Illinois Press, 2014.

Goldin, Claudia, Lawrence F. Katz, and Ilyana Kuziemko. "The Homecoming of American College Women: The Reversal of the College Gender Gap." *Journal of Economic Perspectives* 20, no. 4 (Fall 2006): 133–56.

Gooch, Brad. *City Poet: The Life and Times of Frank O'Hara*. New York: Knopf, 1993.

Goodman, Jack, ed. *While You Were Gone: A Report on Wartime Life in the United States*. New York: Simon & Schuster, 1946.

Goulden, Joseph C. *The Best Years, 1945–1950*. New York: Atheneum, 1976.

Grafton, Carl, and Anne Permaloff. *Big Mules & Branchheads: James E. Folsom and Political Power in Alabama*. Athens: University of Georgia Press, 1985.

Graham, Don. *No Name on the Bullet: A Biography of Audie Murphy*. New York: Viking, 1989.

Gray, J. Glenn. *The Warriors: Reflections on Men in Battle*. 1959. New York: Harper & Row, 1967.

Greenfield, Kent Roberts, Robert R. Palmer, and Bill I. Wiley. *The Organization of Ground Combat Troops*. 1947. Washington, D.C.: Center of Military History, U.S. Army, 1987.

Greenwald, Bryon. "Absent from the Front: What the Case of the Missing World War II Black Combat Soldier Can Teach Us About Diversity and Inclusion." *Joint Force Quarterly*, no. 111 (4th Quarter 2023): 112–23.

Grinker, Roy R., and John P. Spiegel. *Men Under Stress*. Philadelphia: Blakiston, 1945.

Groves, Ernest R. *Conserving Marriage and the Family: A Realistic Discussion of the Divorce Problem*. New York: Macmillan, 1944.

Guglielmo, Thomas A. *Divisions: A New History of Racism and Resistance in America's World War II Military*. New York: Oxford University Press, 2021.

Gunther, John. *Inside U.S.A.* 1947. New York: New Press, 1997.

Gutman, Jack. *One Veteran's Journey to Heal the Wounds of War*. Jack Gutman, 2016.

BIBLIOGRAPHY

Hariman, Robert, and John Louis Lucaites. "The Times Square Kiss: Iconic Photography and Civic Renewal in U.S. Public Culture." *Journal of American History* 94, no. 1 (2007): 122–31.

Harris, Mark. *Five Came Back: A Story of Hollywood and the Second World War*. New York: Penguin Press, 2014.

Harris, Mark Jonathan, Franklin D. Mitchell, and Steven J. Schechter, eds. *The Homefront: America During World War II*. New York: Putnam, 1984.

Hartmann, Susan M. *The Home Front and Beyond: American Women in the 1940s*. Boston: Twayne, 1982.

Havighurst, Robert James, et al. *The American Veteran Back Home: A Study of Veteran Readjustment*. New York: Longmans, Green, 1951.

Heller, Joseph. *Now and Then: A Memoir from Coney Island to Here*. New York: Scribner, 1999.

Hendrickson, Paul. *Fighting the Night: Iwo Jima, World War II, and a Flyer's Life*. New York: Knopf, 2024.

Herman, Jan. *A Talent for Trouble: The Life of Hollywood's Most Acclaimed Director, William Wyler*. New York: Da Capo Press, 1997.

Hersey, John. *Into the Valley: A Skirmish of the Marines*. 1943. New York: Schocken Books, 1989.

Hervieux, Linda. *Forgotten: The Untold Story of D-Day's Black Heroes, at Home and at War*. New York: HarperCollins, 2015.

Hierholzer, Robert, et al. "Clinical Presentation of PTSD in World War II Combat Veterans." *Hospital & Community Psychiatry* 43, no. 8 (Aug. 1992): 816–20.

Hill, Philip H. "Housing-Legislative Proposals." *Law and Contemporary Problems* 12, no. 1 (Winter 1947): 173–85.

Hiltner, Aaron. *Taking Leave, Taking Liberties: American Troops on the World War II Home Front*. Chicago: University of Chicago Press, 2020.

Hirsch, Arnold R. *Making the Second Ghetto: Race and Housing in Chicago, 1940–1960*. 1983. Chicago: University of Chicago Press, 2021.

Hirsh, Joseph. *The Problem Drinker*. New York: Duell, Sloan and Pearce, 1949.

Hobson, Laura Z. *Gentleman's Agreement*. Atlanta: Cherokee Publishing Company, 1947.

Horten, Gerd. *Radio Goes to War: The Cultural Politics of Propaganda During World War II*. Berkeley: University of California Press, 2002.

Hosp, Helen M. "Student Pressures in Higher Education." *Journal of the American Association of University Women* 39, no. 4 (1946).

Howard, Clayton. "Building a 'Family-Friendly' Metropolis: Sexuality, the State, and Postwar Housing Policy." *Journal of Urban History* 39, no. 5 (2013): 933–55.

Huebner, Andrew J. *The Warrior Image: Soldiers in American Culture from the Second World War to the Vietnam Era*. Chapel Hill: University of North Carolina Press, 2008.

Hughes, Langston. *Langston Hughes and the "Chicago Defender": Essays on Race, Politics, and Culture, 1942–62*. Edited by Christopher C. De Santis. Urbana: University of Illinois Press, 1995.

Humphrey, Mary Ann. *My Country, My Right to Serve: Experiences of Gay Men and Women in the Military, World War II to the Present*. New York: HarperCollins, 1990.

Huston, John. "Let There Be Light/The Script." In *Film*, edited by Robert Hughes. New York: Grove Press, 1962.

———. *An Open Book*. 1980. New York: Da Capo Press, 1994.

Jackson, Kenneth T. *Crabgrass Frontier: The Suburbanization of the United States*. New York: Oxford University Press, 1985.

James, Rawn. *The Double V: How Wars, Protest, and Harry Truman Desegregated America's Military*. New York: Bloomsbury Press, 2013.

Javits, Jacob K. *Javits: The Autobiography of a Public Man*. With Rafael Steinberg. Boston: Houghton Mifflin, 1981.

Jefferson, Robert F. "'Enabled Courage': Race, Disability, and Black World War II Veterans in Postwar America." *Historian* 65, no. 5 (2003): 1102–24.

Jellinek, E. M., and Mark Keller. "Rates of Alcoholism in the United States of America, 1940–1948." *Quarterly Journal of Studies on Alcohol* 13 (1952): 49–59.

Jennings, Audra. *Out of the Horrors of War: Disability Politics in World War II America*. Philadelphia: University of Pennsylvania Press, 2016.

Jones, Edgar. "Historical Approaches to Post-combat Disorders." *Philosophical Transactions of the Royal Society of London: Series B, Biological Sciences* 361, no. 1468 (2006): 533–42.

Jones, James. *WWII: A Chronicle of Soldiering*. New York: Ballantine, 1975.

Jones, Jennifer Dominique. "'To Stand upon My Constitutional Rights': The NAACP and World War II–Era Sexual Exclusion." *Journal of Civil and Human Rights* 2, no. 2 (Fall/Winter 2016): 121–50.

Jones, Patrick. "A History of the Armed Forces School of Music." PhD diss., Pennsylvania State University, 2002.

Jordan, Caitlyn. "Tracing War Bride Legislation and the Racial Construction of Asian Immigrants." *Asian American Research Journal* 1, no. 1 (2021).

Judd, Robin. *Between Two Worlds: Jewish War Brides After the Holocaust*. Chapel Hill: University of North Carolina Press, 2023.

Kaminsky, Stuart M. *John Huston, Maker of Magic*. Boston: Houghton Mifflin, 1978.

Karabel, Jerome. *The Chosen: The Hidden History of Admission and Exclusion at Harvard, Yale, and Princeton*. Boston: Houghton Mifflin, 2006.

Katznelson, Ira. *Fear Itself: The New Deal and the Origins of Our Time*. New York: Liveright, 2013.

———. *When Affirmative Action Was White*. New York: Norton, 2005.

Katznelson, Ira, and Suzanne Mettler. "On Race and Policy History: A Dialogue About the G.I. Bill." *Perspectives on Politics* 6 (Sept. 2008): 519–37.

Kazan, Elia. *Elia Kazan: A Life*. New York: Da Capo Press, 1997.

Kennedy, David M., ed. *The Library of Congress World War II Companion*. New York: Simon & Schuster, 2007.

Kennett, Lee B. *G.I.: The American Soldier in World War II*. New York: Scribner, 1987.

Keogh, Tim. *In Levittown's Shadow: Poverty in America's Wealthiest Postwar Suburb*. Chicago: University of Chicago Press, 2023.

King, Martin Luther Jr. *Why We Can't Wait*. New York: Harper & Row, 1964.

King, R. T., ed. *War Stories*. Reno: University of Nevada Oral History Program, 1995.

Klarman, Michael J. *From Jim Crow to Civil Rights: The Supreme Court and the Struggle for Racial Equality*. New York: Oxford University Press, 2004.

Klein, Maury. *A Call to Arms: Mobilizing America for World War II*. New York: Bloomsbury, 2013.

Kluger, Steve, ed. *Yank: The Army Weekly*. New York: St. Martin's Press, 1991.

Knightley, Phillip. *The First Casualty: From the Crimea to Vietnam: The War Correspondent as Hero, Propagandist, and Myth Maker*. New York: Harcourt Brace Jovanovich, 1975.

Koppes, Clayton R., and Gregory D. Black. *Hollywood Goes to War: How Politics, Profits, and Propaganda Shaped World War II Movies*. Berkeley: University of California Press, 1990.

Korson, George Gershon. *At His Side: The Story of the American Red Cross in World War II*. New York: Coward-McCann, 1945.

Kroeger, Brooke. *Undaunted: How Women Changed American Journalism*. New York: Knopf, 2023.

Kruse, Kevin M., and Stephen Tuck, eds. *Fog of War: The Second World War and the Civil Rights Movement*. New York: Oxford University Press, 2012.

Krutnik, Frank. *In a Lonely Street: Film Noir, Genre, Masculinity*. New York: Routledge, 1991.

Kupper, Herbert I. *Back to Life: The Emotional Adjustment of Our Veterans*. New York: L. B. Fischer, 1945.

Kurlansky, Mark. *Hank Greenberg: The Hero Who Didn't Want to Be One*. New Haven, Conn.: Yale University Press, 2010.

Lahr, John. *Tennessee Williams: Mad Pilgrimage of the Flesh*. New York: Norton, 2014.

Lanciotti, Joseph. *The Timid Marine: Surrender to Combat Fatigue*. New York: iUniverse, 2005.

Langer, Ron. "Combat Trauma, Memory, and the World War II Veteran." *War, Literature, and the Arts: An International Journal of the Humanities* 23, no. 1 (2011): 50–58.

LaRossa, Ralph. *Of War and Men: World War II in the Lives of Fathers and Their Families*. Chicago: University of Chicago Press, 2011.

Leckie, Robert. *Helmet for My Pillow: From Parris Island to the Pacific*. 1957. New York: Bantam, 2010.

Leder, Jane Mersky. *Thanks for the Memories: Love, Sex, and World War II*. Westport, Conn.: Praeger, 2006.

Lee, Robert Edson. *to the wa*r. New York: Knopf, 1968.

Lee, Ulysses. *The Employment of Negro Troops*. 1963. Washington, D.C.: GPO, 2001.

Leinbaugh, Harold P., and John D. Campbell. *The Men of Company K: The Autobiography of a World War II Rifle Company*. New York: Bantam Books, 1987.

Lennon, J. Michael. *Norman Mailer: A Double Life*. New York: Simon & Schuster, 2013.

Levenstein, Harvey A. *We'll Always Have Paris: American Tourists in France Since 1930*. Chicago: University of Chicago Press, 2004.

Lichtenstein, Nelson. *Labor's War at Home: The CIO in World War II*. Philadelphia: Temple University Press, 2003.

Lichty, Lawrence Wilson, and Malachi C. Topping. *American Broadcasting: A Source Book on the History of Radio and Television*. New York: Hastings House, 1975.

Lidz, Theodore. "Psychiatric Casualties from Guadalcanal." *Psychiatry* 9, no. 3 (1946): 193–213.

Lilly, J. Robert. "U.S. Military Justice in the European Theater of Operations (ETO), World War II: Judging Crimes, Targeting Populations, and Sentencing Patterns. . . ." In *Justices militaires et guerres mondiales*, edited by Jean-Marc Berlière. Louvain-La-Neuve: Presses Universitaires de Louvain, 2013.

Linderman, Gerald F. *The World Within War: America's Combat Experience in World War II*. New York: Free Press, 1997.

Lingeman, Richard R. *The Noir Forties: The American People from Victory to Cold War*. New York: Nation Books, 2012.

Lipsitz, George. *Rainbow at Midnight: Labor and Culture in the 1940s*. Urbana: University of Illinois Press, 1994.

Litoff, Judy Barrett, and David C. Smith, eds. *Since You Went Away: World War II Letters from American Women on the Home Front*. New York: Oxford University Press, 1991.

Lobenthal, Joel. "A Conversation with Robert Barnett." *Ballet Review* 41 (2013).

Logevall, Fredrik. *JFK: Coming of Age in the American Century, 1917–1956*. New York: Random House, 2020.

Loza, Steven Joseph. *Tito Puente and the Making of Latin Music*. Urbana: University of Illinois Press, 1999.

MacGregor, Morris J., Jr. *Integration of the Armed Forces, 1940–1965*. Washington, D.C.: Center of Military History, 2001.

Maharidge, Dale. *Bringing Mulligan Home: The Other Side of the Good War*. New York: PublicAffairs, 2013.

Mailer, Norman. *The Naked and the Dead*. 1948. New York: Picador, 1998.

Maloney, Thomas N. "Wage Compression and Wage Inequality Between Black and White Males in the United States, 1940–1960." *Journal of Economic History* 54, no. 2 (June 1994): 358–81.

Manchester, William. *Goodbye, Darkness: A Memoir of the Pacific War*. 1980. Boston: Back Bay Books, 2002.

Manning, Molly Guptill. *When Books Went to War: The Stories That Helped Us Win World War II*. Boston: Houghton Mifflin Harcourt, 2014.

Marble, Sanders. *Rehabilitating the Wounded: Historical Perspective on Army Policy.* Office of Medical History, Office of the Surgeon General, June 2008.

Marshall, George C. *Aggressive and Determined Leadership, June 1, 1943–December 31, 1944.* Vol. 4 of *The Papers of George Catlett Marshall.* Edited by Larry I. Bland and Sharon R. Ritenour. Baltimore: Johns Hopkins University Press, 1996.

Martin, Ralph G. *The Best Is None Too Good.* New York: Farrar, Straus, 1948.

Mathews, Tom. *Our Fathers' War: Growing Up in the Shadow of the Greatest Generation.* New York: Broadway Books, 2005.

Matzen, Robert. *Mission: Jimmy Stewart and the Fight for Europe.* Pittsburgh: GoodKnight Books, 2016.

Mauldin, Bill. *Back Home.* New York: W. Sloan Associates, 1947.

———. *Up Front.* New York: Holt, 1945.

McBride, James. *Miracle at St. Anna.* New York: Riverhead Books, 2002.

McChesney, Mary Fuller. *A Period of Exploration, San Francisco, 1945–1950.* Oakland: Oakland Museum, Art Department, 1973.

McEnaney, Laura. *Postwar: Waging Peace in Chicago.* Philadelphia: University of Pennsylvania Press, 2018.

McGrath, Earl J. "The Education of the Veteran." *Annals of the American Academy of Political and Social Science* 238 (March 1945): 77–88.

McGurn, Barrett. *"Yank, the Army Weekly": Reporting the Greatest Generation.* Golden, Colo.: Fulcrum, 2004.

McManus, John C. *The Deadly Brotherhood: The American Combat Soldier in World War II.* Novato, Calif.: Presidio, 1998.

———. *Island Infernos: The US Army's Pacific War Odyssey, 1944.* New York: Dutton Caliber, 2021.

Meier, Andrew. *Morgenthau: Power, Privilege, and the Rise of an American Dynasty.* New York: Random House, 2022.

Menand, Louis. *The Free World: Art and Thought in the Cold War.* New York: Picador, 2022.

Menninger, William Claire. *Psychiatry in a Troubled World: Yesterday's War and Today's Challenge.* New York: Macmillan, 1948.

Mettler, Suzanne. *Soldiers to Citizens: The G.I. Bill and the Making of the Greatest Generation.* New York: Oxford University Press, 2005.

Metzgar, Jack. "The 1945–1946 Strike Wave." In *The Encyclopedia of Strikes in*

American History, edited by Aaron Brenner, Benjamin Day, and Immanuel Ness. Armonk, N.Y.: M. E. Sharpe, 2009.

Meyer, Leisa D. *Creating GI Jane: Sexuality and Power in the Women's Army Corps During World War II*. New York: Columbia University Press, 1996.

Milkman, Ruth. *Gender at Work: The Dynamics of Job Segregation by Sex During World War II*. Urbana: University of Illinois Press, 1987.

Miller, Merle. *On Being Different: What It Means to Be a Homosexual*. New York: Random House, 1971.

———. *That Winter*. New York: W. Sloane, 1948.

Mintz, Steven, and Susan Kellogg. *Domestic Revolutions: A Social History of American Family Life*. New York: Free Press, 1988.

Modell, John, Marc Goulden, and Sigurdur Magnusson. "World War II in the Lives of Black Americans: Some Findings and Interpretation." *Journal of American History* 76, no. 3 (1989): 838–48.

Moore, Deborah Dash. *GI Jews: How World War II Changed a Generation*. Cambridge, Mass.: Harvard University Press, 2004.

Moroney, Siobhan. *Chicagoland Dream Houses: How a Mid-century Architecture Competition Reimagined the American Home*. Urbana: University of Illinois Press, 2024.

Morrison, Minion K. C. *Aaron Henry of Mississippi: Inside Agitator*. Fayetteville: University of Arkansas Press, 2015.

Morse, Bradford. "The Veteran and His Education." *Higher Education* 16, no. 7 (March 1960): 3-6, 16-19.

Moser, Hanna M. "A Ten-Year Follow-Up of Lobotomy Patients." *Psychiatric Services* 20, no. 12 (Dec. 1969): 381.

Murray, Paul T. "Blacks and the Draft: A History of Institutional Racism." *Journal of Black Studies* 2, no. 1 (Sept. 1971): 57–76.

Myers, Marc. *Why Jazz Happened*. Berkeley: University of California Press, 2012.

Myers, Sarah Parry. *Earning Their Wings: The WASPs of World War II and the Fight for Veteran Recognition*. Chapel Hill: University of North Carolina Press, 2023.

Nasaw, David. *The Patriarch: The Remarkable Life and Turbulent Times of Joseph P. Kennedy*. New York: Penguin Press, 2012.

National Parks Service, U.S. Department of the Interior, National Historic Landmarks Program. *Civil Rights in America: Racial Discrimination in Housing*. Washington, D.C.: National Historic Landmarks Program, National Park Service, U.S. Department of the Interior, 2021.

National Resources Planning Board, National Resources Development Report for 1943. Washington, D.C.: GPO, 1943.

Nemerov, Alexander. "Coming Home in 1945: Reading Robert Frost and Norman Rockwell." *American Art* 18, no. 2 (2004): 58–79.

Nichter, Luke A. *The Last Brahmin: Henry Cabot Lodge Jr. and the Making of the Cold War.* New Haven, Conn.: Yale University Press, 2020.

Nolan, Tom. *Ross Macdonald: A Biography.* New York: Scribner, 1999.

O'Brien, Gail Williams. *The Color of the Law: Race, Violence, and Justice in the Post–World War II South.* Chapel Hill: University of North Carolina Press, 1999.

Oliver, Melvin L., and Thomas M. Shapiro. *Black Wealth, White Wealth: A New Perspective on Racial Inequality.* New York: Routledge, 2006.

Olson, Keith W. "The Astonishing Story: Veterans Make Good on the Nation's Promise." *Educational Record* 75, no 4 (Fall 1994).

———. *The G.I. Bill, the Veterans, and the Colleges.* Lexington: University Press of Kentucky, 1974.

Onkst, David H. "'First a Negro . . . Incidentally a Veteran': Black World War Two Veterans and the G.I. Bill of Rights in the Deep South, 1944–1948." *Journal of Social History* 31, no. 3 (Spring 1998): 517–43.

Oostdijk, Diederik, and Markha G. Valenta, eds. *Tales of the Great American Victory: World War II in Politics and Poetics.* Amsterdam: Vrije University Press, 2006.

Orthwine, Rudolf. "Victory in Europe Brings Soldier Rehabilitation to the Fore," *Dance* 19, no. 6 (June 1945).

Overton, Grace Sloan. *Marriage in War and Peace, a Book for Parents and Counselors of Youth.* New York: Abingdon-Cokesbury Press, 1945.

Palmer, R. R., Bell Irvin Wiley, and William R. Keast. *The Procurement and Training of Ground Combat Troops.* 1948. Washington, D.C.: Center of Military History, U.S. Army, 1991.

Parker, Christopher S. *Fighting for Democracy: Black Veterans and the Struggle Against White Supremacy in the Postwar South.* Princeton, N.J.: Princeton University Press, 2009.

Paster, Samuel, and Saul Holtzman. "Experiences with Insulin and Electroshock Treatment in an Army Hospital." *Journal of Nervous and Mental Disease* 105, no. 4 (1947): 382–96.

———. "A Study of One Thousand Psychotic Veterans Treated with Insulin and Electric Shock." *American Journal of Psychiatry* 105 (1949): 811–14.

Pavalko, Eliza K., and Glen H. Elder Jr. "World War II and Divorce: A Life-Course Perspective." *American Journal of Sociology* 95, no. 5 (March 1990): 1213–34.

Payne, Charles M. *I've Got the Light of Freedom: The Organizing Tradition and the Mississippi Freedom Struggle*. 2nd ed. Berkeley: University of California Press, 2007.

Perea, Juan F. "Doctrines of Delusion: How the History of the G.I. Bill and Other Inconvenient Truths Undermine the Supreme Court's Affirmative Action Jurisprudence." *University of Pittsburgh Law Review* 75, no. 4 (2015): 583–651.

Perry, Susan. "Female Veterans: Their Fight Is Not Over." *Graduate Woman* 73, no. 3 (1980).

Petry, Ann. *Country Place*. 1947. Evanston, Ill.: Northwestern University Press, 2019.

Pfau, Ann Elizabeth. *Miss Yourlovin: GIs, Gender, and Domesticity During World War II*. New York: Columbia University Press, 2013.

Plumb, Betsy Loren. "How the War Lasts: World War II Veterans, Postwar Life, and Masculinity in America." PhD diss., University of Buffalo, 2017.

Pogue, Forrest C. *The Supreme Command*. Washington, D.C.: Center of Military History, U.S. Army, 1989.

Pols, Hans. "Waking Up to Shell Shock." *Endeavor* 30, no. 4 (Nov. 2006): 144–49.

———. "War Neurosis, Adjustment Problems in Veterans, and an Ill Nation: The Disciplinary Project of American Psychiatry During and After World War II." *Osiris* 22, no. 1 (2007): 72–92.

Porter, Lewis. *John Coltrane: His Life and Music*. Ann Arbor: University of Michigan Press, 1999.

Powell, Josephine. *Tito Puente: When the Drums Are Dreaming*. Bloomington, Ind.: AuthorHouse, 2007.

Pratt, George K. *Soldier to Civilian: Problems of Readjustment*. New York: Whittlesey House, 1944.

Preis, Art. *Labor's Giant Step*. New York: Pathfinder Press, 1972.

President's Commission on Veterans' Pensions. Omar Bradley, Chairman. *A Report on Veterans Benefits in the United States. Staff Report No. IX, Part A: Readjustment Benefits: General Survey and Appraisal*. Sept. 11, 1956; *Part B: Readjustment Benefits: Education and Training, and Employment and Unemployment; Part C: Veterans' Loan Guaranty and Direct Loan Benefits*. Washington, D.C.: GPO, 1956.

———. *Veterans' Benefits in the United States. Findings and Recommendations*. Washington, D.C.: GPO, 1956.

———. *Veterans in Our Society: Data on the Conditions of Military Service and on the Status of the Veteran. Staff Report No. IV.* Washington, D.C.: GPO, 1956.

Pressman, Jack David. *Last Resort: Psychosurgery and the Limits of Medicine.* New York: Cambridge University Press, 1998.

Pyle, Ernie. *Brave Men.* New York: Henry Holt, 1944.

———. *Ernie's War: The Best of Ernie Pyle's World War II Dispatches.* Edited by David Nichols. New York: Random House, 1986.

Rabinowitz, Paula. *American Pulp: How Paperbacks Brought Modernism to Main Street.* Princeton, N.J.: Princeton University Press, 2014.

Raines, Howell. *My Soul Is Rested: Movement Days in the Deep South Remembered.* New York: G. P. Putnam's Sons, 1983.

Rice, Rolundus. *Hosea Williams: A Lifetime of Defiance and Protest.* Columbia: University of South Carolina Press, 2021.

Rivas-Rodriguez, Maggie, ed. *Mexican Americans & World War II.* Austin: University of Texas Press, 2005.

Roberts, Mary Louise. *What Soldiers Do: Sex and the American GI in World War II France.* Chicago: University of Chicago Press, 2013.

Robinette, C. Dennis, Zdenek Hrubec, and Joseph F. Fraumeni Jr. "Chronic Alcoholism and Subsequent Mortality in World War II Veterans." *American Journal of Epidemiology* 109, no. 6 (June 1979): 687–700.

Robinson, Jackie, and Alfred Duckett. *I Never Had It Made.* New York: Putnam, 1972.

Roeder, George H., Jr. *The Censored War: American Visual Experience During World War II.* New Haven, Conn.: Yale University Press, 1993.

Rooney, Andrew A. *My War.* 1995. New York: PublicAffairs, 2000.

Roosevelt, Eleanor. *My Day: The Best of Eleanor Roosevelt's Acclaimed Newspaper Columns, 1936–1962.* Edited by David Emblidge. New York: Da Capo Press, 2001.

Rosales, Steven. "Fighting the Peace at Home: Mexican American Veterans and the 1944 GI Bill of Rights." *Pacific Historical Review* 80, no. 4 (2011): 597–627.

Rose, Kenneth D. *Myth and the Greatest Generation: A Social History of Americans in World War II.* New York: Routledge, 2008.

Rosen, Jules. "The Persistence of Traumatic Memories in World War II Prisoners of War." *Journal of the American Geriatrics Society* 57, no. 12 (Dec. 2009): 2346–47.

Rosenman, Samuel I. *Working with Roosevelt.* New York: Da Capo Press, 1972.

Rosner, Albert. "Neuropsychiatric Casualties from Guadalcanal: Persistent Symptoms in Three Cases." *American Journal of Medical Sciences* 207, no. 6 (June 1944): 770–76.

Ross, Davis R. B. *Preparing for Ulysses*. New York: Columbia University Press, 1969.

Rothstein, Richard. *The Color of Law: A Forgotten History of How Our Government Segregated America*. New York: Liveright, 2018.

Rubio, Philip F. *There's Always Work at the Post Office: African American Postal Workers and the Fight for Jobs, Justice, and Equality*. Chapel Hill: University of North Carolina Press, 2010.

Ruppenthal, Roland G. *Logistical Support of the Armies*. 1959. Washington, D.C.: Center of Military History, U.S. Army, 1995.

Ruvolo, Francesca. "American Soldiers and Italian Women: The Sexual Economy of Occupied Naples, 1943–1945." Master's thesis, Rutgers University–Newark, 2016.

Salinger, Margaret Ann. *Dream Catcher: A Memoir*. New York: Washington Square Press, 2000.

Samet, Elizabeth D. *Looking for the Good War: American Amnesia and the Violent Pursuit of Happiness*. New York: Farrar, Straus and Giroux, 2021.

Satterfield, Archie. *The Home Front: An Oral History of the War Years in America, 1941–1945*. New York: Playboy Press, 1981.

Saveth, Edward N. "Education." *American Jewish Yearbook* 51 (1950).

Saxe, Robert Francis. *Settling Down: World War II Veterans' Challenge to the Postwar Consensus*. New York: Palgrave Macmillan, 2007.

Schrijvers, Peter. *The Crash of Ruin: American Combat Soldiers in Europe During World War II*. Basingstoke, U.K.: Macmillan, 1998.

Scott, Wilbur J. "PTSD in DSM-III: A Case in the Politics of Diagnosis and Disease." *Social Problems* 37, no. 3 (Aug. 1990): 294–310.

Scranton, Roy. *Total Mobilization: World War II and American Literature*. Chicago: University of Chicago Press, 2019.

Selective Service System. *Dependency Deferment*. Special Monograph No. 8. Washington, D.C.: U.S. Government Printing Office, 1947.

———. *Physical Examination of Selective Service Registrants*. Special Monograph No. 15. Washington, D.C.: GPO, 1947.

———. *Selective Service as the Tide of War Turns: The Third Report, 1943–1944*. Washington, D.C.: GPO, 1945.

———. *Selective Service and Victory: The 4th Report, 1944–1945, with a Supplement for 1946–7*. Washington, D.C.: GPO, 1948.

Sevareid, Eric. *Not So Wild a Dream*. 1946. New York: Atheneum, 1978.

Sewell, George Alexander, and Margaret L. Dwight. *Mississippi Black History Makers*. Rev. ed. Jackson: University Press of Mississippi, 1984.

Shapiro, Harvey, ed. *Poets of World War II*. New York: Library of America, 2003.

Sharp, Bert Marvin. "'Bring the Boys Home': Demobilization of the United States Armed Forces After World War II." PhD diss., Michigan State University, 1976.

Shay, Jonathan. *Odysseus in America: Combat Trauma and the Trials of Homecoming*. New York: Scribner, 2002.

Shepard, Stephen B. *Salinger's Soul*. New York: Post Hill Press, 2024.

Shermer, Elizabeth Tandy. *Indentured Students: How Government-Guaranteed Loans Left Generations Drowning in College Debt*. Cambridge, Mass.: Belknap Press of Harvard University Press, 2021.

Sherrod, Robert Lee. *Tarawa: The Story of a Battle*. New York: Duell, Sloan and Pearce, 1944.

Sherry, Michael S. *In the Shadow of War: The United States Since the 1930's*. New Haven, Conn.: Yale University Press, 1995.

Sherwin, Martin J. *A World Destroyed: Hiroshima and Its Legacies*. 3rd ed. Stanford, Calif.: Stanford University Press, 2003.

Shields, Charles J. *And So It Goes: Kurt Vonnegut, a Life*. New York: Henry Holt, 2011.

Shuker-Haines, Timothy Maxwell. "Home Is the Hunter: Representations of Returning World War II Veterans and the Reconstruction of Masculinity, 1944–1951." PhD diss., University of Michigan, 1994.

Shukert, Elfrieda Berthiaume, and Barbara Smith Scibetta. *The War Brides of World War II*. Novato, Calif.: Presidio Press, 1988.

Simon, Arthur R. *Stuyvesant Town, U.S.A.: Pattern for Two Americas*. New York: New York University Press, 1970.

Simpson, Louis, "Soldier's Heart." *Hudson Review* 49, no. 4 (Winter 1997): 541–52.

Slawenski, Kenneth. *J. D. Salinger: A Life*. New York: Random House, 2010.

Sledge, E. B. *China Marine*. New York: Oxford University Press, 2002.

———. *With the Old Breed at Peleliu and Okinawa*. 1981. New York: Ballantine, 2007.

BIBLIOGRAPHY

Sloan, Stephen, Lois E. Myers, and Michelle Holland, eds. *Tattooed on My Soul: Texas Veterans Remember World War II*. College Station: Texas A&M University Press, 2015.

Smith, Richard Cándida. *Utopia and Dissent: Art, Poetry, and Politics in California*. Berkeley: University of California Press, 1995.

Smith, Clarence McKittrick. *The Medical Department: Hospitalization and Evacuation, Zone of Interior*. 1956. Washington, D.C.: Center of Military History, U.S. Army, 1989.

Smith, E. Rogers. "Neuroses Resulting from Combat." *American Journal of Psychiatry* 100, no. 1 (July 1943): 94–97.

Smith, Mapheus. "Populational Characteristics of American Servicemen in World War II." *Scientific Monthly* 65, no. 3 (Sept. 1947): 246–52.

Sparrow, John C. *History of Personnel Demobilization in the United States Army*. Washington, D.C.: Department of the Army, 1952.

Speed, Nancy, Brian Engdahl, Joseph Schwartz, and Raina Eberly. "Posttraumatic Stress Disorder as a Consequence of the POW Experience." *Journal of Nervous and Mental Disease* 177, no. 3 (1989): 147–53.

Spencer, Carl A. "State and Local Housing Programs After World War II." *Monthly Labor Review* 69, no. 5 (1949): 499–502.

Spencer, Michael T. "Jazz Education at the Westlake College of Music, 1945–61." *Journal of Historical Research in Music Education* 35, no. 1 (Oct. 2013): 50–65.

Spillane, Mickey. *I, the Jury*. New York: Signet, 1975.

Stancil, Stewart Alan. "After the War Is Over." *Student BMJ*, no. 340 (2010).

Starr, Paul. *The Social Transformation of American Medicine*. Rev. ed. New York: Basic Books, 2017.

Steinbeck, John. *Once There Was a War*. 1958. New York: Penguin Books, 1977.

Stockford, Donald, and Alice P. Carmody. *1980 Supplement to "Alcoholism and Problem Drinking, 1970–1975: A Statistical Analysis of VA Hospital Patients."* Washington, D.C.: Statistical Policy and Research Service, Office of Reports & Statistics, Veterans Administration, 1982.

Stolz, Lois Meek, et al. *Father Relations of War-Born Children: The Effect of Postwar Adjustment of Fathers on the Behavior and Personality of First Children Born While the Fathers Were at War*. Stanford, Calif.: Stanford University Press, 1954.

Stouffer, Samuel A., et al. *Adjustment During Army Life*. Vol. 1 of *The American Soldier*. Princeton, N.J.: Princeton University Press, 1949.

———. *Combat and Its Aftermath*. Vol. 2 of *The American Soldier*. Princeton, N.J.: Princeton University Press, 1949.

Sweeney, Michael S. *Secrets of Victory: The Office of Censorship and the American Press and Radio in World War II*. Chapel Hill: University of North Carolina Press, 2001.

Takei, Hiroshi. "The Unexpected Consequence of Government Manipulation: Racial Disturbances at Chicago's Public Housing for Veterans in the 1940s." *Journal of American and Canadian Studies*, no. 31 (2013): 49–77.

Terkel, Studs. *"The Good War": An Oral History of World War Two*. New York: New Press, 1984.

Tregaskis, Richard. *Guadalcanal Diary*. 1943. New York: Modern Library, 2000.

Turner, Sarah, and John Bound. "Closing the Gap or Widening the Divide: The Effects of the G.I. Bill and World War II on the Educational Outcomes of Black Americans." *Journal of Economic History* 63 (March 2003): 145–77.

Tuttle, William M., Jr. *"Daddy's Gone to War": The Second World War in the Lives of America's Children*. New York: Oxford University Press, 1993.

Tye, Larry. *Demagogue: The Life and Long Shadow of Senator Joe McCarthy*. Boston: Houghton Mifflin Harcourt, 2020.

Tygiel, Jules. *Extra Bases: Reflections on Jackie Robinson, Race, and Baseball History*. Lincoln: University of Nebraska Press, 2002.

Tyler, Robert L. "The American Veterans Committee: Out of a Hot War and into the Cold." *American Quarterly* 18, no. 3 (Autumn 1966): 419–36.

U.S. Army. Medical Department. *Medical Statistics in World War II*. Washington, D.C.: Office of the Surgeon General, Department of the Army, 1975.

U.S. Army. Office of the Comptroller, Program Review & Analysis Division, Office of the Adjutant General. *Army Battle Casualties and Nonbattle Deaths in World War II: Final Report 7 December 1941–31 December 1946*. Washington, D.C.: Department of the Army, 1953.

U.S. Army. Surgeon General's Office. *Neuropsychiatry in World War II*. Vol. 1, *Zone of Interior*. Washington, D.C.: Office of the Surgeon General, Department of the Army, 1966.

———. *Neuropsychiatry in World War II*. Vol. 2, *Overseas Theaters*. Washington, D.C.: Office of the Surgeon General, Department of the Army, 1973.

———. *Preventive Medicine in World War II*. Vol. 3, *Personal Health Measures and*

BIBLIOGRAPHY

Immunization. Washington, D.C.: Office of the Surgeon General, Department of the Army, 1955.

———. *Preventive Medicine in World War II.* Vol. 5, *Communicable Diseases Transmitted Through Contact or by Unknown Means.* Washington, D.C.: Office of the Surgeon General, Department of the Army, 1960.

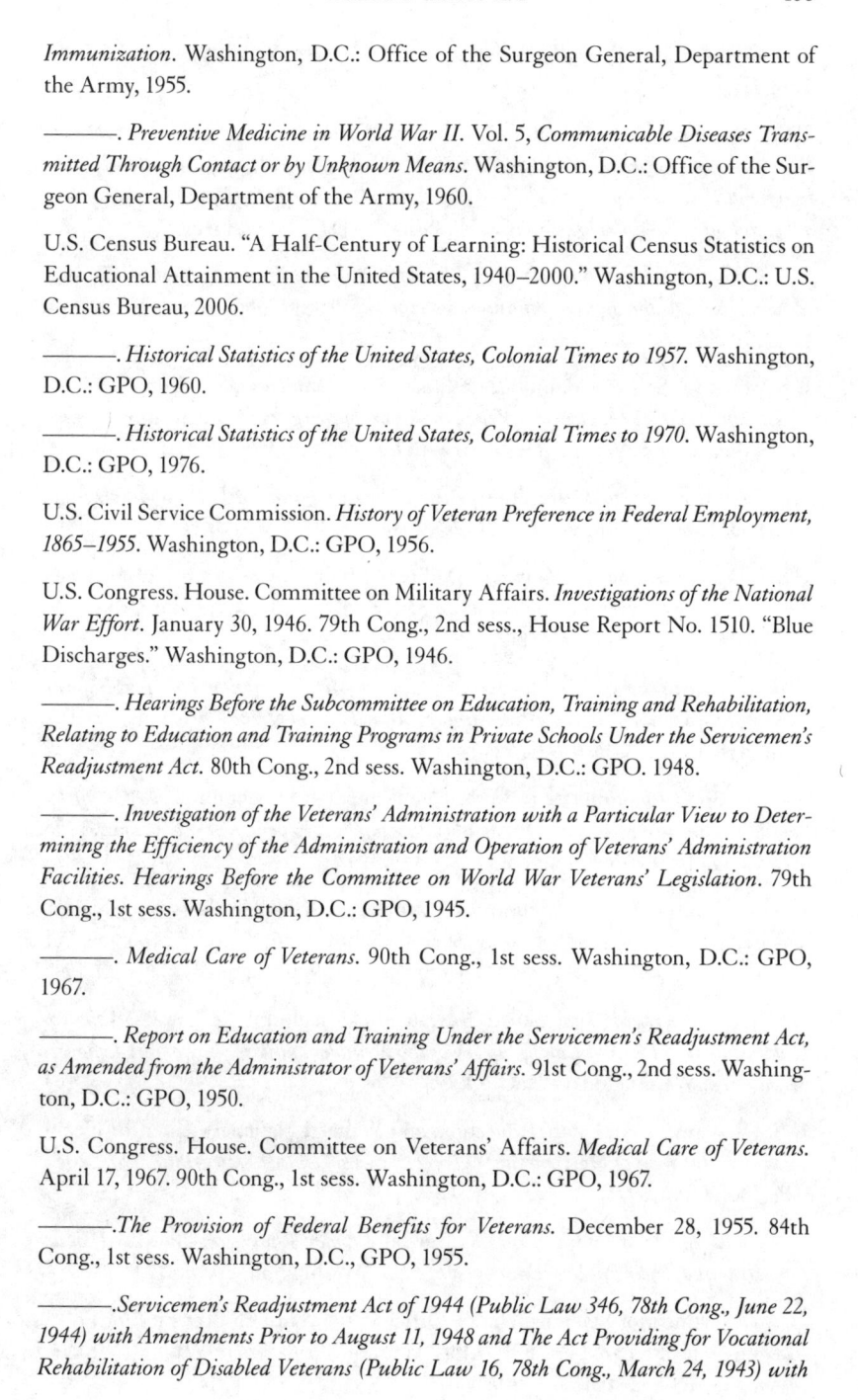

U.S. Census Bureau. "A Half-Century of Learning: Historical Census Statistics on Educational Attainment in the United States, 1940–2000." Washington, D.C.: U.S. Census Bureau, 2006.

———. *Historical Statistics of the United States, Colonial Times to 1957.* Washington, D.C.: GPO, 1960.

———. *Historical Statistics of the United States, Colonial Times to 1970.* Washington, D.C.: GPO, 1976.

U.S. Civil Service Commission. *History of Veteran Preference in Federal Employment, 1865–1955.* Washington, D.C.: GPO, 1956.

U.S. Congress. House. Committee on Military Affairs. *Investigations of the National War Effort.* January 30, 1946. 79th Cong., 2nd sess., House Report No. 1510. "Blue Discharges." Washington, D.C.: GPO, 1946.

———. *Hearings Before the Subcommittee on Education, Training and Rehabilitation, Relating to Education and Training Programs in Private Schools Under the Servicemen's Readjustment Act.* 80th Cong., 2nd sess. Washington, D.C.: GPO. 1948.

———. *Investigation of the Veterans' Administration with a Particular View to Determining the Efficiency of the Administration and Operation of Veterans' Administration Facilities. Hearings Before the Committee on World War Veterans' Legislation.* 79th Cong., 1st sess. Washington, D.C.: GPO, 1945.

———. *Medical Care of Veterans.* 90th Cong., 1st sess. Washington, D.C.: GPO, 1967.

———. *Report on Education and Training Under the Servicemen's Readjustment Act, as Amended from the Administrator of Veterans' Affairs.* 91st Cong., 2nd sess. Washington, D.C.: GPO, 1950.

U.S. Congress. House. Committee on Veterans' Affairs. *Medical Care of Veterans.* April 17, 1967. 90th Cong., 1st sess. Washington, D.C.: GPO, 1967.

———.*The Provision of Federal Benefits for Veterans.* December 28, 1955. 84th Cong., 1st sess. Washington, D.C., GPO, 1955.

———.*Servicemen's Readjustment Act of 1944 (Public Law 346, 78th Cong., June 22, 1944) with Amendments Prior to August 11, 1948 and The Act Providing for Vocational Rehabilitation of Disabled Veterans (Public Law 16, 78th Cong., March 24, 1943)* with

Amendments Prior to August 11, 1948. August 25, 1948. Washington, D.C.: GPO, 1948.

U.S. Congress. House. Committee on World War Veterans' Legislation. *Hearings Before the Committee on World War Veterans' Legislation on H.R. 7661 and H.R. 7662 to Amend Certain Laws and Veterans' Regulations to Provide for Rehabilitation of Disabled Veterans.* 77th Cong., 2nd sess. Washington, D.C.: GPO, 1942.

U.S. Congress. Joint Committee on Housing. *Study and Investigation of Housing: Hearings Before the Joint Committee on Housing.* 80th Cong. Washington, D.C.: GPO, 1948.

U.S. Congress. Senate. Committee on Finance, *Amendments to the Servicemen's Readjustment Act of 1944. Hearings Before a Subcommittee of the Committee on Finance.* 79th Cong, 1st sess. Washington, D.C.: GPO, 1945.

U.S. Congress. Senate. Committee of the Judiciary. *Crime of Lynching.* Hearings, Jan., Feb. 1948. Washington, D.C.: GPO, 1948.

U.S. Congress, Senate. Committee on Military Affairs. *Demobilization of the Armed Forces: Hearings Before the Committee on Military Affairs,* Jan. 15, 1946. 79th Cong., 1st and 2nd sess. Washington, DC: GPO, 1946.

———. Committee on Military Affairs. *Married Men Exemption: Hearings Before a Subcommittee of the Committee on Military Affairs . . . on S. 763.* 78th Cong. 1st sess. Washington, D.C.: GPO, 1943.

———. Special Committee to Investigate Campaign Expenditures. *Report of the Special Committee to Investigate Senatorial Campaign Expenditures, 1946,* Jan. 1946. 80th Cong., 1st sess. Washington, D.C.: GPO, 1947.

———. Subcommittee on Housing and Urban Redevelopment. "Postwar Economic Policy and Planning: Report to the Special Committee on Postwar Economic Policy and Planning," Aug. 1, 1945. 79th Cong., 1st sess. Washington, D.C.: GPO, 1945.

U.S. Department of Agriculture. Bureau of Agricultural Economics. *Veterans' Readjustment to Civilian Life: A Survey of the Attitudes and Experiences of Discharged Servicemen.* Washington, D.C.: GPO, 1945.

U.S. Department of Health, Education, and Welfare. National Center for Health Statistics. *100 Years of Marriage and Divorce Statistics, United States, 1867–1967.* Rockville, Md.: GPO, 1973.

U.S. Department of Labor. Women's Bureau. *Women Workers in Ten War Production Areas and Their Postwar Employment Plans.* Washington, D.C.: GPO, 1946.

U.S. Department of Veterans Affairs. Office of the Assistant Secretary for Policy, Planning, and Preparedness (OPP&P). "American Prisoners of War (POWS) and Missing in Action (MIAs)." April 2006.

---. "Legislative History of the VA Home Loan Guaranty Program." Updated Aug. 23, 2006.

U.S. Housing and Home Finance Agency. *The Housing of Negro Veterans: Their Housing Plans and Living Arrangements in 32 Areas.* Washington, D.C.: Housing and Home Finance Agency, 1948.

U.S. National Housing Agency. Federal Housing Administration. Veterans' Emergency Housing Program. *Rental Housing for Veterans.* Washington, D.C.: GPO, 1946.

---. Federal Housing Administration. *Underwriting Manual.* Washington, D.C.: Federal Housing Administration, 1947.

U.S. Office of War Mobilization and Reconversion. *First Report to the President, the Senate, and the House of Representatives.* Jan. 1, 1945.

---. *From War to Peace: A Challenge.* Washington, D.C.: Office of War Mobilization and Reconversion, 1945.

---. *Sixth Report to the President, the Senate, and the House of Representatives.* April 1, 1946.

U.S. Veterans Administration. *Survey of Aging Veterans: A Study of the Means, Resources, and Future Expectations of Veterans Aged 55 and Over.* Louis Harris and Associates, Dec. 1983.

U.S. War Department. *Helpful Hints to Those Who Have Lost Limbs.* Washington, D.C.: GPO, 1944.

---. *War Department Technical Manual, TM 12-235: Enlisted Personnel: Discharge and Release from Active Duty.* Washington, D.C.: GPO, 1945.

---. *You're on Your Way Home.* War Department Pamphlet no. 21-26. Washington, D.C.: GPO, 1945.

Vacha, Keith. *Quiet Fire: Memoirs of Older Gay Men.* Edited by Cassie Damewood. Trumansburg, N.Y.: Crossing Press, 1985.

Vagts, Alfred. "Battle and Other Combatant Casualties in the Second World War, II." *Journal of Politics* 7, no. 4 (Nov. 1945): 411–38.

Valenstein, Elliott S. "The History of Lobotomy: A Cautionary Tale." *Michigan Quarterly Review* 27, no. 3 (1988): 417–38.

Van Ells, Mark D. *To Hear Only Thunder Again: America's World War II Veterans Come Home.* Lanham, Md.: Lexington Books, 2001.

Veterans Emergency Housing Program. *Report to the President from Wilson W. Wyatt, Housing Expediter. Feb. 7, 1946.* Washington, D.C.: GPO, 1946.

"Veterans Return to the Nation's Factories." *Monthly Labor Review* 63, no. 6 (Dec. 1946): 928–29.

Von Hoffman, Alexander. "A Study in Contradictions: The Origins and Legacy of the Housing Act of 1949." *Housing Policy Debate* 11, no. 2 (Jan. 2000): 299–326.

Vonnegut, Kurt. *Letters*. Edited by Dan Wakefield. New York: Delacorte Press, 2012.

———. *Love, Kurt: The Vonnegut Love Letters, 1941–1945*. Edited by Edith Vonnegut. New York: Random House, 2020.

———. *Slaughterhouse-Five: Or the Children's Crusade*. 1969. New York: Dial Press, 2009.

Waller, Willard Walter. *The Veteran Comes Back*. New York: Dryden Press, 1944.

Ward, Jason Morgan. *Defending White Democracy: The Making of a Segregationist Movement and the Remaking of Racial Politics, 1936–1965*. Chapel Hill: University of North Carolina Press, 2011.

Wardlow, Chester. *The Transportation Corps: Movements, Training, and Supply*. Washington, D.C.: Office of the Chief of Military History, Department of the Army, 1956.

Wecter, Dixon. *When Johnny Comes Marching Home*. Boston: Houghton Mifflin, 1944.

Weinberg, Gerhard L. *A World at Arms: A Global History of World War II*. 2nd ed. New York: Cambridge University Press, 2005.

Weir, Margaret, Ann Shola Orloff, and Theda Skocpol, eds. *The Politics of Social Policy in the United States*. Princeton, N.J.: Princeton University Press, 1988.

Wertheim, Albert. *Staging the War*. Bloomington: Indiana University Press, 2004.

Westbrook, Robert B. "I Want a Girl, Just Like the Girl That Married Harry James." *American Quarterly* 42, no. 4 (Dec. 1990): 587–614.

White, Walter. *A Man Called White: The Autobiography of Walter White*. New York: Viking, 1948.

Wiley, Bell Irvin. *The Training of Negro Troops*. Washington, D.C.: GPO, 1946.

Willett, John. "Erwin Piscator: New York and the Dramatic Workshop, 1939–1951." *Performing Arts Journal* 2, no. 3 (Winter, 1978): 3–16.

Williams, Michael Vinson. *Medgar Evers: Mississippi Martyr*. Fayetteville: University of Arkansas Press, 2011.

Williams, Tennessee. *The Selected Letters of Tennessee Williams*. Vol. 2, *1945–1957*.

Edited by Albert J. Devlin and Nancy Marie Patterson Tischler. New York: New Directions, 2004.

Wilson, Sloan. *The Man in the Gray Flannel Suit*. New York: Simon & Schuster, 1955.

Wingo, Josette Dermody. *Mother Was a Gunner's Mate: World War II in the Waves*. Annapolis, Md.: Naval Institute Press, 1994.

Wise, James E., and Anne Collier Rehill. *Stars in Blue: Movie Actors in America's Sea Services*. Annapolis, Md.: Naval Institute Press, 1997.

Wolgin, Philip E., and Irene Bloemraad. "'Our Gratitude to Our Soldiers': Military Spouses, Family Re-unification, and Postwar Immigration Reform." *Journal of Interdisciplinary History* 41, no. 1 (2010): 27–60.

Woodbury, Coleman. "Objectives and Accomplishments of the Veterans Emergency Housing Program." *American Economic Review* 37, no. 2 (May 1947): 508–23.

Woods, Louis Lee, II. "Almost 'No Negro Veteran . . . Could Get a Loan': African Americans, the GI Bill, and the NAACP Campaign Against Residential Segregation, 1917–1960." *Journal of African American History* 98, no. 3 (2013): 392–417.

Wright, James. *Those Who Have Borne the Battle: A History of America's Wars and Those Who Fought Them*. New York: PublicAffairs, 2012.

Yank editors. *The Best from "Yank, the Army Weekly."* New York: E. P. Dutton, 1945.

Young, Alan. *The Harmony of Illusions: Inventing Post-traumatic Stress Disorder*. Princeton, N.J.: Princeton University Press, 1995.

Zeiger, Susan. *Entangling Alliances: Foreign War Brides and American Soldiers in the Twentieth Century*. New York: New York University Press, 2010.

Ziemke, Earl F. *The U.S. Army in the Occupation of Germany, 1944–1946*. 1975. Washington, D.C.: Center of Military History, U.S. Army, 1990.

Zipp, Samuel. *Manhattan Projects: The Rise and Fall of Urban Renewal in Cold War New York*. New York: Oxford University Press, 2012.

Index

Italicized page numbers indicate material in photographs or illustrations.

Abernethy, Thomas, 104–5, 310
Acadia (hospital ship), 14–16
Act of Violence (movie), 198
acting schools/actors, 328–30
Advisory Committee on Negro Troop Policy, War Department, 69
Africa, xii, 8, 15, 88, 156
Afro-American, The, 53, 68, 112, 116, 230, 312, 335
Alaska, xii, 63, 128
alcohol consumption, 41, 52
   military public relations and, 44–45
   and PTSD sufferers, 374, 378–81, 384
   of returning vets, xi, 46–47, 157, 173, 177–83, 204, 209, 368–69
   at war's end, 46, 123–25
   while in service, xi, 44–47, 58, 109, 114, 134, 143, 179–80
Alcorn A&M, 300
Alien Registration Act, 1940, 20
Allen, Willis, 95–96
Allord, Lorraine, 285–86
Ambrose, Stephen, 180
American Academy of Dramatic Arts (N.Y.C.), 330
American Civil Liberties Union, 348
American Council on Race Relations, 234–35
American Crusade to End Lynching, 232
American Journal of Psychiatry, The, 9
American Legion, 104, 243, 258, 383
   and "Bill of Rights for GI Joe and GI Jane," 99–102
   FDR's speech at, 94
   on foreign-born war wives, 131–32
   housing crisis and, 268–69, 271
   and striking vets, 278
American Legion Magazine, The, 152
American Negro Theater (ANT), 329–30
American Psychiatric Association (APA), 7, 375–76
American Pulp (Rabinowitz), 196
American Soldier, The (Stouffer), 339
American South, 312
   Black vets' exodus from, xv, 157–58
   Black vets seek jobs in, 282–84
   Blacks denied GI Bill benefits in, xvi–xvii, 102, 265–66
   and "blue-discharged" vets, 162
   colleges in, 300–304
   congressmen of, xvi, 104–5, 225, 233, 241, 244–45, 301, 315
   efforts to maintain racial status quo in, 66–67, 72, 160, 225, 238–39, 245
   Jim Crow discrimination in, 63, 65–67, 158, 224–30
   job-training programs in, 318–19, 321
   mob violence in, 228–34
   vocational schools in, 314–16
   White vets in, 277
   See also Jim Crow; segregation; White supremacy
American Theatre Wing Professional School (N.Y.C.), 330–31
American Veteran Back Home, The (Havighurst), 86, 203, 264
American Veterans Committee, 258, 270
Anderson, James, 319
Anderson, Maxwell, 199
Andrews, Dana, 195, 200, 214, 288

INDEX

Angell, Mrs. James Rowland, 322
antidiscrimination campaigns and laws, 284, 296, 308, 344
Archuleta, Benerito Seferino, 122
Ardent, Clarence, 264
Argenzio, Joseph, 255–56
Argosy, 196
Armstead, Bryson C., 302
Army Research Branch, xviii, 70, 134, 157, 248
Army Specialized Training Program (ASTP), 19–20, 80
art schools/artists, xvi, 322–25, 328, 335–36
Art Students League (N.Y.C.), 324–25
Arthur Murray Studios, 334
Asia, xii, 64, 85, 129–30
Asian war brides, 132, 220–21, 354
Athens, Tennessee, 245–46
Atherton, Warren, 99, 101
athletes, professional, 288–89
Atlanta Constitution, The, 17, 115, 130, 254
atomic bombs, 40, 118–23, 128
Audie Murphy Research Foundation, 378
Austin American-Statesman, 242
Australia, 3, 7–8, 45, 54, 69, 87, 212, 220–21, 336
automobile shortage, 152, 154
AWOL troops, 55, 114–16, 198

Baca, Dennis, 151–52
Bach, John, 46–47
Back Home (Mauldin), 154, 195
Baird, John, 187
Baker, Betty, 154
Baldwin, Hanson, 119–20
Band of Brothers (Ambrose)
Band of Brothers (miniseries), 180, 378
Bankhead, John, 66
Banking and Currency Committee (Senate), 269–71
banks, xvii, 263–66, 271, 340–44
Barden, Graham, 94
Barnett, Robert, 333
Barr, Mary, 208
Bartelt, James, 118, 121–22
Bataan (movie), 34, 39, 65
Battle of Midway, The (movie), 32–33
Battle of the Bulge, 70, 80, 151, 378
Beane, Gerald, 52
Bearden, Romare, 336
Belafonte, Harry, 329–30
Bennett, Tony, 331
Bernstein, Walter, 149

Berry, John, 284, 300–301
Best Years, 1945–1950, The (Goulden), 214–15
Best Years of Our Lives, The (movie), 91, 195, 214, 287
Better Homes & Gardens, 86, 92
Biden, Joseph, 233, 366
Bilbo, Theodore, 227
"Bill of Rights for GI Joe and GI Jane," 99–102
"Bill of Rights for the Disadvantaged," 358–59
Black, Timuel, 68, 112
black market, 50–51
"Black Panther" Tank Battalion, 69–70
Black press, 212, 312
  on Black GIs, 60, 64, 66–68, 73
  calls for integration of military, 60
  on Columbia, Tennessee, "race riot," 229
  on discrimination, 66–67, 97, 110–11, 160
  on violence against Blacks, 230
  war reports in, xviii
  See also specific newspaper titles
Black veterans, 153, 267
  denied civil rights, xv, 239
  disability benefits and, 96–97
  education of, 104, 300–302, 321, 335–36
  employable skills of, 282–84
  exodus from the South, 157–58
  and fight for civil rights, 231–34, 236–39, 249
  and GI Bill benefits, xv–xvii, 97, 111, 159–60, 164, 284
  homeownership of, 344–49, 360–63
  and housing loans, xvii, 264–66, 349
  and job assistance, 282–85
  and Levittown, 342–46
  menial jobs for, xvi, 282–84, 314–19, 329
  seek good jobs, 234–38, 315
  and Stuyvesant Town, 347–49
  unemployment benefits and, 100–102
  and vocational school, 312, 314–19
  Whites' attacks on, xv, 224–39
  See also voting: Black veterans
Blacks in armed forces, 49
  assigned occupation duty, 71–72
  barred from combat, 60, 63, 65, 69, 111
  discharge point system and, 111–12
  in infantry combat units, 69–73, 80
  and marrying White women, 54, 221–22
  morale of, 64–65, 112–13
  number mobilized, xv, 239
  off-duty activities of, 65–66, 68
  and racial status quo, 72–73

INDEX 463

and relationships with local women, 49, 53, 58
  segregation of, 59–62, 65, 110–11
  in service units, 61–65, 69, 111–12, 282, 303
  training of, 61, 65–68, 70
  in war films, 34, 64–65
Blain, Daniel, 188
Blandford, John, 257, 259
blast injuries, 8, 26, 185–86
Blithe, Albert, 180
Blue Book, 196
Blue Dahlia, The (movie), 214
Blue Star Mothers, 131
Bogart, Humphrey, 44, 198–99
Bohannon, Horace, 225, 234, 316, 318
Boldt, O'Brien, 261
Bolté, Charles, 193, 283
Bond, Pat, 57–58, 159
Bonder, W. A., 315
"Bonus Army," 93–94, 103
Boomerang (movie), 200
Borgnine, Ernest, 331–32
Boston, 132, 151
  gay and lesbian vets in, 158–59
  housing rally in, 268–69
  suburban developments in, 343
  vets study in, 97, 327
  at war's end, 107, 123–24
Boston Globe, The, 38, 123–24, 280
Bougainville Island, 41, 70
Bourke-White, Margaret, 298
Bowker, Benjamin, 14, 194
Boyd, Jack, 280
Braceland, Francis, 164
Bradley, Betty and John, 177
Bradley, Omar, 78, 80, 278, 356, 368
Brando, Marlon, 91, 199–200
Bratton, John, 189–91
Brave Men (Pyle), 28
Brazier, Wesley, 321
Brick Foxhole, The (Brooks), 199
Bridgforth, Carolyn, 109, 122
Bring Back Daddy Clubs, xiii, 131, 140
British troops, 8, 11
Broadway productions, xviii, 199–200, 328
Brooke, Edward, 66, 156, 158
Brooks, Raymond, 242
Brotherton, Marcus, 180–81
Brown, Edgar, 111
Brubeck, Dave, 80, 326–27
Brukman, Jack, 175
Buchwald, Art, 334–35
Buffalo Soldiers, 69

Bullock, Georgia P., 261
Burdine, Alpha and Carlis, 28
burial benefits for veterans, 353–54
Burnett, Eugene, 344–45
Burns, John Horne, 49–50
Bush, George W., 366
Bussel, Norman, 381–82

California School of Fine Arts, 324–25
California State Sheriffs' Association, 193
Camelon, Dave, 103–4
Camp Lucky Strike, 110, 112, 115
Campbell, J. C., 136
Campbell, John D., 134–35
Canafax, Wilson, 176–77
Capital Press Club, 68
Capra, Frank, 30, 65, 286–87
Carlisle, Bill, 254
Carpenter, Tyler, 56
Carson, Gordon, 180
cartoons, xviii, *1*, *12*, 28, 30–33, 39, 109, *133*, *145*, *167*, *180*, *193*, *204*, *219*, *235*, *251*, *262*, *281*, *351*, *361*
Cassius, Samuel R., 164
Catch-22 (Heller), 299
CBS Radio, 120, 139, 206
censorship, 11, 20
  of letters, 22–23
  of movies, 32–34
  of press photographs, 24, 36–37
  of war correspondents, 24–26, 50, 75
Chandler, Albert "Happy," 129
Chandler, Raymond, 214
Chicago, 149–50, 158, 205, 215, 241
  Bring Back Daddy Clubs in, 131
  gay and lesbian vets in, 158–59
  housing shortage in, 267–68
  racial violence in, 267
  suburban developments in, 343
  vets' education in, 295–96, 303, 312–13
Chicago Daily Tribune, 5, 15, 52, 213
Chicago Defender, The, 102, 111–13, 222
Child Study Association, 205
Childers, Mildred, 210–11
Childers, Thomas, 115, 210–11, 382–83
children, 22, 116, 202, 306
  in broken families, 223
  foreign-born, xii, 53, 131–32, 211–12, 221–22
  and prostitution, 49–50
  and returning fathers, xiv, 87, 172, 215–20
  in war films, 33
  and working mothers, 83–84
Childs, Marquis, 259

China, 51, 120, 129, 221, 237
Chipman, Clayton, 177–78
Chouinard Art Institute (Los Angeles), 324–25
Christian Science Monitor, The, 14, 78, 137, 275
Churchill, Winston, 74, 80
Ciardi, John, 175
cigarette camps, 110–13, 115
cigarette smoking, 26, 49, 51, 84
    and cigarettes distributed by military, 43–44, 370
    of returning vets, 157, 173, 370
    of servicemen/women, 41, 43–44, 46–47, 58, 370
CIO News, The, 277
civil rights leaders/movement, 72, 231–33, 236–39
civil service preference for vets, 354–55
Clark, Bennett Champ, 95, 100, 102, 161, 323
Clinton, Bill, 359–60, 366
clothing shortages, xiii, 152–54
Clyburn, James, 363
colleges/universities, 357
    and Black vets, xvii, 300–304, 308
    and gender inequities, 304–8, 360
    and GI Bill benefits, xv–xvi, 291–309, 337, 339
    historically Black, 300–303, 314
    postwar changes in, 307–9
    and racial inequities, 360
    segregation in, xvii
    women admitted to, xvii, 302–7, 309
Collier's, 260–61, 313, 340
Coltrane, John, 326
Columbia, Tennessee, "race riot," 227–29
Columbia University, 186, 294, 296, 300
combat fatigue, xi, 12–13, 76, 79–80, 178, 182, 375
Committee on Military Affairs (House), 139–40, 162
Committee on Military Affairs (Senate), 62–63
Committee on Veterans' Affairs (House), 363
Committee on World War Veterans' Legislation (House), 310
Conant, James, 297
concentration camps, 39, 176–77, 376, 380
condoms, distributed by military, 47–49
Congress of Industrial Organizations (CIO), 132–33, 277–79, 320
Connally, Tom, 233
Conner, Douglas, 158
Connor, Eugene "Bull," 227

Conserving Marriage and the Family (Groves), 86
cooking schools, 322, 335
Cooper, Frankie, 208, 210
Cordier, George, 216
Cornell University, 19, 296, 305
Cotten, Joseph, 90–91
counterintelligence corps (CIC), 80, 107, 135
Country Place (Petry), 214
court-martials, 53, 67, 160–61
Cox, Eugene "Goober," 233
Crawford, E. A., 265
crime wave, veterans, 193–94, 200–201
Crosby, Bing, 29
Crossfire (movie), 199
Culinary Institute of America, 322
Culman, Irene Stokes, 206
Cummings, Theodore "Ted," 4
Curtain Rises (Reynolds), 28
Curtis, Tony, 328–29

Daddy's Gone to War (Tuttle), 215
Dahlberg, Melvin, 378
dance schools/programs, xvi, 330–34
Davis, Ben, 323
Davis, Benjamin O., 112–13
Davis, David Brion, 71–72
Davis, Ossie, 156–57, 179–80
D-Day, 13, 43, 151, 176, 178
    anniversaries of, 366, 376–77
    Black GIs' role in, 63, 73
    human cost of, 75–78
    news/reports of, 74–77
De Nike, Barbara, 216–17
Dead Reckoning (movie), 198
Decision: The Conflicts of Harry S. Truman (documentary), 133
Dedmon, Jesse, Jr., 97, 164, 316
Dee, Ruby, 179–80
DeKoning, Big Bill, 342
demobilization of troops, 98, 101, 192, 337
    demands to speed it up, xiii, 134–40
    final steps in, 142–50
    and letter-writing campaign, 130–31, 139
    the press on, 130, 136–38
    point system for, 108–12
    protests against slow pace of, xiii, 108–9, 112–13, 117–18, 128–140, 143
    War Department's plans for, 77–78, 128–30
    See also transportation home
Democratic Party, 77, 104–105, 233, 243, 245, 247–48, 358
Dempsey, David, 190–91

Dempsey, Dorothy, 306
Dewey, Thomas E., 77–78, 308
Dieffenwierth, Dorothy, 373–74
DiMaggio, Joe, 288–89
Dippo, William, 177
Disabled American Veterans, 270
disabled veterans, 218
　alcoholism and, 368–69
　amputees, 10–11, 14, 16, 90, 95–96, 106, 213, 368
　benefits for, 94–99
　disability discharges of, xii, 3, 96, 368
　pensions for, xv, 13, 355, 368
　and preference for civil service jobs, 354
　rehabilitation programs for, 94–97, 357
　number of, 98–99, 367–68
Disabled Veterans' Rehabilitation Act, 354
discharges, xiii, 117–18, 138
　of Black GIs, 111–13, 159–60, 164
　blue, xvii, 55–57, 159–65
　disability, 3, 8, 12–14, 98–99
　and discharge pay, 147–49
　dishonorable, 57–58, 161–62, 200
　of fathers, 129, 131, 140
　final steps in, 144–50
　and homosexuals, 161–62
　honorable, 67, 79, 149, 159, 162, 164
　point system for, 108–12
　for psychiatric disorders, 79, 169
　reduction in, 136–37
　review process for, 163–64
diseases
　alcohol and, 45–47, 369
　of returning vets, 43, 90, 146, 148, 152, 165, 367
　smoking and, 43–44, 370
　venereal, 48–51, 85, 114, 148
　while in combat, 4–6, 12, 18, 109, 380
Ditterline, Hollace "Red," 378–79
divorce, xiv, 140, 202–7, 211–15, 223, 261, 340, 382
Divorce (movie), 203–5
Doing Battle: The Making of a Skeptic (Fussell), 174
Dole, Bob, 44, 96, 367–68
domiciliary care, 353–54, 356
Dondero, Don, 183
Donut Dollies, 357
Dorsey, George and Mae, 229–30
Dorsey, Joseph R., 347–48
Douglas, Paul, 241–42
Dowling, Monroe D., 347–48
draft, the, xvii, 150–51

4-Fs and, 87, 172, 209
　and Black Americans, 61–62
　exemptions from, 43, 80, 87, 241
　fathers' exemption from, 18–20, 62–63
　and Japanese Americans, 59–60
Dramatic Workshop at the New School (N.Y.C.), 328–30
DSM (*Diagnostic and Statistical Manual of Mental Disorders*), 375
DSM-II, 375–76
DSM-III, 376
Duckett, Alfred, 110–11
Duff, Norma, 220–21
Duff, Roy, 220–21, 274
Dumas, Alexander G., 173, 217
Dunn, Jack, 172–73

Eastland, John, 233
Easy Company, 180–81. *See also* Band of Brothers
Ecker, Frederick, 346–47
Eckstam, Eugene, 46, 51
economy
　conversion to peacetime, xv–xvi, 273, 275, 289–90, 337–39
　and GI Bill, xvi, 103, 105, 255, 337–39
　male-directed, 360–61
　postwar fears about, xiii, 103, 253, 338
education, 96, 98, 100, 245, 290
　abroad, 334–36
　of Black vets, 300–304, 335–36
　and blue discharges, 162–64
　democratizing of higher, 297, 307–8
　gender inequities in, xvii, 304–8, 360
　under the GI Bill, xv–xvii, 103–4, 236–38, 291–309, 336–37, 354, 356, 382
　local/state control over, 310–13
　racial inequities in, 360, 363
　vocational schools/programs for, 311–17
　See also job training; vocational education
Eisenhower, Dwight D., 24, 70, 74, 78–79, 115–16, 138–41, 287
Eisenstaedt, Alfred, 125–26
Elfenbein, Harold L., 152
Ellender, Allen, 260. *See also* Taft-Ellender-Wagner bill
Emmett Till Antilynching Act, 233
employment
　of Black vets, 234–38, 274, 282–85, 314–17
　and blue discharges, 162–64
　and discrimination against Black vets, 283–84
　gender inequities in, 285–86

employment (cont.)
  under the GI Bill, 103, 336, 339
  postwar layoffs and, xiii, 208, 253–55
  Public Law 16 and, 96–97
  of returning vets, xv–xvi, 248
  vets' anxiety over, 137, 144, 253, 286
  of vets at college, 294, 298–99, 307–8
  vets get old jobs back, 273–74, 353
  vets' high expectations for, 279–83
  of vets vs. nonvets, 360
  wartime skills and, 147, 279–80, *281*, 282–86, 289
  See also job counseling/placement; job training; vocational education; war industries; war wives
England, 88–89, 199, 210, 212
English war brides, 131–32, 221–22
enlisting, reasons for, 150–51
entertaining the troops, 15, 41–42, 327, 331, 333
Esser, George, 297
European theater, xii, 8, 45–46, 50–52
  American servicemen in, 3, 113–16, 378
  Black servicemen in, 63–64, 69–73, 112
  casualties in, 80–81
  demobilization protests in, 138
  and end of WWII, 76–77, 106–10, 112–15
  infantry redeployment from, 108–10, 114, 122–23
  occupying forces in, 130, 331, 334
  and psychiatric disorders, 79–80
  relations with local women in, 84–85, 210–13
Evers, Charles, 236
Evers, Medgar, 72–73, 236–37, 300–301
Evers, Myrlie, 236
expendability, feeling of, xviii, 5
eyewitness accounts, xvii–xviii, 25, 28–29, 75, 107

Faber, E. V., 215
factory work, 83, 274–75, 279, 339
Falstein, Louis, 145–47
families
  advice/counseling for, 205, 224
  broken, xiv, 140, 202, 222–23
  on college campuses, 294–95, 298–99
  housing crisis and, 264
  and infidelity, 87
  male-directed, xiv, 360–61
  and the returning vet, xiv, 201, 217–20
  violent vets and, 181, 218
farms/farmers, 43, 100, 103, 129, 282–83, 309, 321, 354–55, 361

Father Relations of War-Born Children (Stolz), 211, 217–20
Faubus, Orval, 135, 244, 247–48
FBI, 225, 230, 278, 373
Federal Housing Administration (FHA), 264, 266, 342–46, 362
Fiji, 6–8
Fine, Benjamin, 304–5
Fleming, Billy, 227–28
Folsom, Big Jim, 241, 244–45
Fonda, Henry, 32, 288
Ford, Gerald, 243–44
Ford, John, 31–33, 75
Forrestal, James V., 113
Fortune, 13, 152, 355–56
Fox Movietone News, 10, 30
Foy, Fred C., 43–44
France, 106, 129
  American servicemen in, 87, 113–16, 151
  Black troops in, 70, 72–73
  D-Day invasion of, 73, 75–77
  liberation of, 46
  sexual assaults in, 53
  See also specific cities
Frank, Stanley, 292, 294
Franklin, John Hope, 62
Freeman, Walter J., 189
Freudian treatment, 170–71
Fuentes, David, 319–20
Fuller, Eddie, 56
furloughs, 48, 54, 90, 108–10, 114–15, 120, 122, 211, 367
Fussell, Paul, 22, 44–45, 108–9, 174, 182–83

Galemb, Dorothy, 140
Gallery, The (Burns), 49–50
Gannett, Lewis, 27
Garcia, Willie and Elizabeth, 187–88
Gardner, Lewis, 76–77
Gardner, Mona, 208, 210
Garfield, John, 91
Garland, Joseph, 18
Gelman, David, 376–77
gender inequities, xvii, 105, 285–86, 304–8, 360–61
General Motors (GM), 136, 278
Gentry, Herbert, 335–36
George, Frank, 258
Germany, 114, 119, 173, 178, 193, 242
  American GIs in, 52, 59–60, 71–72, 116–17, 151, 338, 378
  army of, 9, 11, 17, 39
  and D-Day, 63, 74–77

INDEX

defeat/surrender of, 46, 106–10, 128, 176
fraternization with the enemy in, 116–17
musicians flee from, 327
occupying forces in, 128–29, 134–35, 138
and POWS, 115, 147, 285, 381–82
propaganda of, 30
resistance of, 76–80, 78
and war brides/war children, 54, 212
See also concentration camps
GI Bill
   amendments to, 292–93, 354
   art/music/theater schools rescued under, 322–34
   blue discharges and, 159–62, 165
   cost of, xv, 307, 355–56
   democratizes higher education, 297, 307–8
   employment provisions in, 279
   gender inequities in, 304–8, 360–61
   goals/purpose of, xv–xvii, 102–5, 293, 336–37, 354
   and homeownership, xvi–xvii, 104, 263–66, 341–44, 354, 362–63, 381
   local/state control over, xvi, 310–13, 315–18
   racial inequities in, xv–xvi, 300–304, 308, 344–49, 360–63
   and rights for the disadvantaged, 358–59
   vets' praise for, 293, 302, 320, 326–27
   vocational schools/job training and, 311–19
   See also education; job training; living allowances; mortgage guaranty program; readjustment allowances
GI Bride Clubs, 131
Glenn, Frank, 111
Glosson, Lonnie, 254
God Is My Co-pilot (Scott), 28
Going My Way (movie), 29
Gold, Michael, 115–16, 296, 382–83
Gold Star Mothers, 131
Goldwyn, Samuel, 287
Gooch, Ulysses Lee, 316–17
Good Housekeeping, 206
"Good War, The" (Terkel), 364–65
Goodman, George, 68
Gordon, Norman, 176, 383–84
Goulden, Joseph, 214–15
Granoff School of Music (Philadelphia), 326
Grapes of Wrath, The (movie), 31–32
Gray, Charles Harold, 306
Gray, J. Glenn, 47
Great Britain, 53–54, 68, 74–75, 87, 114, 129, 131, 221–22
Great Depression, 93, 103, 256, 364

"Greatest Generation" narratives, 142, 365
Greenberg, Hank, 289
Groves, Ernest, 86, 212
Guadalcanal, 3–9, 24–27, 39, 44, 91, 151
Guadalcanal Diary (Tregaskis), 27–28
Guam, 71, 85, 137, 328
Gudis, Anne, 88–89
Gunter, Marcus, 284, 321
Gunther, John, 231
Gutman, Jack, 256–57, 379

Haas, Lucien C., 258
Hackett, Shirley, 22–23, 82, 86, 209
Hahne, Dellie, 82–83
Hall, John, 56–57
Halloran, Ray "Hap," 380–81
Hargrove, Marion, 27–28
Harmon, Ernest, 72
Harper, Calvin B., 347–48
Harper's Bazaar, 172
Harper's Magazine, 87, 342
Harvard, 97, 296–97, 304, 348
Havighurst, Robert, 86, 256, 273
Hawaii/Hawaiians, 59–60, 137, 326. *See also* Pearl Harbor
Hayes, William, 283–84
Hayward, Louis, 38
Hearst, William Randolph, 99
Hearst News of the Day, 30
Hearst's International News Service, 24–25
Heath, William J., 153, 225–26, 314–15
Heck, Stanley, 213
Heller, Joseph, 299–300
Hellman, Lillian, 287
Helpful Hints to Those Who Have Lost Limbs (War Dept.), 10
Hemingway, Ernest, 169, 171
Hendrickson, Joe, 218
Hendrix, Hardine, 348–49
Hendrix, Wanda, 185–86
Henry, Aaron, 236–38
Henry, Tennyson, 222
Here Is Your War (Pyle), 28
Hersey, John, 25–28, 34, 39, 172, 243
Hewitt, Calvin, 151
Hicks, James L., 212–13
High Museum of Art (Atlanta), 323
high school, 300–301, 307, 315, 320–21
Hines, Frank, 10, 162, 187
Hinton, Harold, 246–47
Hiroshima, 118–20, 128
Hirsh, Joseph, 47, 182
Hitler, Adolf, 106, 113

INDEX

Hochschild, Fred, 273–74
Hoffman, Clare, 129
Homecoming GI (Rockwell), *155*, 156
homecoming narratives, 14–17
homeownership, 357
    billions of dollars for, 355
    gender inequities in, xvii, 360–61
    under the GI Bill, xvi–xvii, 104, 263–66, 341–44, 354, 362–63, 381
    racial inequities in, xvii, 266, 360–63
    See also housing, veterans; mortgage guaranty program
homosexuals in military, xvii, 44, 54–58, 158–64, 199, 264–65
Hoover, Herbert, 93–94
Hoover, J. Edgar, 225, 230
Hope, Bob, 27
hospital ships, 7–8, 13–17, 99, 357
hospitals
    costs of veterans' treatment in, 355–56
    evacuation, 9, 96, 99, 183
    homosexuals admitted to, 57, 161
    military, 169–72, 287, 292, 367–68, 381
    overseas, 12, 357
    See also VA hospitals
housing, veterans
    affordable, xiii, 267, 340–49
    and Black vets, 264–67, 344–49
    federal gov. and, 98, 260, 262–63, 266–72, 355
    loans for, xvii, 100, 103, 263–66, 271–72
    military structures for, 266, 294–95, 305
    prefab houses, 260, 262, 267, 295, 305, 341–42
    and same-sex couples, 264–65
    segregation in, xv, 344–49
    shortage of, xiii–xiv, *251*, 256–72, 340–41, 346–47
    state/city governments and, 266–67
    Washington, D.C. rally for, 270–71
    See also homeownership; mortgage guaranty program
Housing Act of 1949, 272
Houtz, Marie and Earl, 54
How Green Was My Valley (movie), 32
Howard, T. R. M., 236
Howard University, 158
Hughes, Dorothy, 197–98
Hughes, Langston, 71, 73
Hurd, Charles, 276, 281
Huston, John, 170–72
Hutchinson, Steve, 276

I, the Jury (movie), 197–98
I Never Left Home (Hope), 27
I'll Be Seeing You (movie), 90–91
In a Lonely Place (Hughes), 199
In a Lonely Place (movie), 199
India, 87, 154, 237
Inouye, Daniel, 367–68
Inside U.S.A. (Gunther), 231
intelligence units, 60, 80, 118, 135
Into the Valley (Hersey), 27–28
Italy, 26, 87, 338, 378, 384
    Allied invasion of, 9, 11–12, 17–18, 36, 49–50
    Black GIs in, 63, 69–70, 283
    and D-Day, 75
    Japanese Americans in, 59–60
    and neuropsychiatric disorders, 12
    prostitution in, 49–50
    Tuskegee Airmen in, 61
    war brides/war children in, 211–12, 222
It's a Wonderful Life (movie), 286–87
Iwo Jima, 82, 173, 177

Japan
    atomic bomb attack on, 118–23, 128
    occupying forces in, 57–58, 71, 128, 159, 333
    POWs in, 380–81
    racist portrayals of military, and, 39–40, 121, 197
    surrender of, 120–25, 128, 135, 143
    and war brides/war children, 54, 212
Japanese Americans, 40, 59–60
Javits, Jacob, 242, 244, 248, 267–70
Jenkins, Leon Frank, 7–8
Jewish servicemen, 19–20, 176, 220
    in movies, 34, 199
Jewish vets, 270, 296, 308, 328
    organizations, 296, 308, 345, 348
Jim Crow
    Black resistance to, 157, 224–30, 234, 238–39, 249
    Black servicemen and, 65–67, 72–73, 102, 113
    and Black vets' job search, 282–83
    and discrimination in housing, 348
    and menial jobs for Blacks, 316–17
    protection of, 102, 224–30, 238–39, 245, 348
job counseling/placement, xv, 100, 254, 279–85, 357
job training, 100, 228, 290, 308–9, 357
    abuses in vocational programs for, 311–19
    and Black vets, 237, 318–19
    gender inequities in, 360

INDEX

under the GI Bill, xvi, 103, 188, 291–93, 310–25, 337, 354
legitimate programs for, 319–25
Johnson, Campbell, 283
Johnson, Lyndon, 241–42
Joint Committee on Housing, 269–70
Jones, Clemon, 66, 230
Jones, James, 17, 35, 45–46
Jones, Jennifer, 211–12
Jones, John, 229
Jorgensen, Victor, 125, *126*
Josephs, Herman, 176
Juilliard (New York), 327

K Company, history of, 134–35
Kameny, Franklin E., 19, 55
Kazan, Elia, 199–200
Keen, Grace, 173, 217
Kelley, Richard, 280
Kelly, Ellsworth, 335
Kennedy, John F., 243–44, 248, 267–70, 367
Kennedy, Joseph, Jr., 243
Kennedy, Joy Windsor, 285
Kennedy Veterans Hospital (Memphis), 188
Kenner, Albert W., 50–51
Key Largo (movie), 198
King, Martin Luther, Jr., 238,
Bill of Rights for the Disadvantaged, 358–59
Kings Park State Hospital (Long Island), 178, 184
Kirk, Norman, 89–90
Kirksey, Henry, 158, 314
Kirstein, Lincoln, 134, 330–31
Kissinger, Henry, 19–20, 80, 135, 189, 296–97
Klausner, Marty, 162–63
Kleemann, Karl, 134
Kolb, Cheryl, 215–16
Korean War, 79, 272, 289, 370
Kowatch, Joseph E., 332
Kramer, Samuel, 88–89
Kupper, Herbert I., 172, 179, 192

La Follette, Robert, Jr., 94, 243
La Guardia, Fiorello, 259, 347
Ladd, Alan, 214
Ladies' Home Journal, 83, 189–90, 208, 210, 318
Lake, Veronica, 33, 214
Lanciotti, Joseph, 51
Laughridge, Jim, 187
Lawson, Ted W., 28
Le Havre, France, 110, 113–15, 138
Leckie, Robert, 4–5, 44

Lee, John C. H., 70
Lee, Robert Edson, 135
Leftridge, Allen, 111
Lehman, Milton, 146
Leinbaugh, Harold P., 134–35
Let There Be Light (movie), 170–72
Levitt, William, xvii, 341–46
Levittown (Long Island), 341–46, 349, 362
Levy, German, 321
Lewkowicz, Bella, 220
Lidz, Theodore, 6–8
Life magazine, 25–27, 36–37, 52, 74, 84–85, 89, 117, 123–26, 131, 153, 172, 202, 259, 297–98, 335–36
living allowances, GI Bill
amount of, 292, 298, 313–14
and arts/music/theater schools, 323–34
benefit the economy, 337, 339
civilians excluded from, 357
studying abroad with, 334–35
supplemented by jobs, 294, 298, 314
and vets' education, xvii, 296, 321, 336–37, 339
and vocational schools/programs, 313–18
loans, GI Bill
for businesses, xv, 100, 103, 162, 354–55
for farms, 100, 103, 354–55
See also mortgage guaranty program
Lodge, Henry Cabot, Jr., 241–42
Loeb, Charles H., 112
London, England, 54, 75, 131, 138, 171
Long Island, New York, 341–46, 349, 362
Look magazine, 26–27
López, John, 320
Los Angeles
art/dance/music schools in, 324–27, 333
gay and lesbian vets in, 158–59
servicemen stranded in, 150
VA clinics in, 184
vet housing in, 258, 346
vets seek jobs in, 280–81, 285
vocational programs in, 319–20
Los Angeles Times, 75, 124, 128, 258
Ludwig, Mrs. Al, 343
lynching, xv, 225, 228–34

MacArthur, Douglas, 79, 93
Mackey, Otis, 173
Maddox, Joseph H., 97
magazines, xii, 26–27, 36–40, 74, 84–87, 297, 308–9
on GI's fraternization with Germans, 117
on the home front, 87–90, 196, 356

INDEX

magazines (*cont.*)
   and off-duty troops, 41–42
   on PTSD sufferers, 183–84
   on vets as menaces, 246
   on vets at college, 297–98, 307–9
   wartime news in, 28, 31, 74
   for women, 27, 42, 205–8, 210
   See also specific titles
Magnuson, Warren, 241–42
Maharidge, Dale, 186–87, 366–67
Mahoney, Charles A., 137
Mailer, Norman, 174, 335
Maisel, Albert Q., 313, 317–18
Malcom, Roger and Dorothy, 229
Malveaux, Vincent, 234–35, 318–19
Man in the Gray Flannel Suit, The (movie), 211–12
Man in the Gray Flannel Suit, The (Wilson), 211–12
Manchester, William, 4–5, 195
Manila, 71, 136–38
manpower shortages, military, 18–20, 60–63, 69–71, 79–80, 139
"Manual on How to Treat the Disabled," *Life,* 89
Mare Island (San Francisco) naval hospital, 7
Marriage in War and Peace (Overton), 85
marriage, 58, 140
   and education, 292–95, 298–99, 306–8
   housing crisis and, 261, 264–65, 268–70
   and infidelity, 210–15
   interracial, 132, 220–22, 354
   Margaret Mead on, 87
   overseas, 53–54, 131–32, 220–22
   and returning vets, 202–7, 217, 339–40
   wives responsible for preserving, xiv, 205–10
   See also divorce; War Brides Act
Marsh, Robert, 180
Marshall, George C., 61, 66, 69, 78–79, 116–17, 136
Marshall, Thurgood, 345
Marshall Plan, 355
Martin, John Bartlow, 120
Martin, Ralph, 106, 280–81, 285
Mason General Hospital (Long Island), 170–71
Mathews, Tom, 216
Matthau, Walter, 329
Matthews, Herbert, 26
Mauldin, Bill, 213
   on army life, xi, xviii, 18, 108
   cartoons by, *1*, *12*, 28, *133*, *145*, *167*, *180*, *193*, *204*, *219*, *235*, *251*, *262*, *281*, *351*, *361*
   on vets, 154, 195

Mayer, Louis B., 288
McCarthy, Joseph, 241–43, 248, 269–71
McCloy, John, 60, 69
McDonald, Ross. *See* Spillane, Mickey
McGill, Ralph, 17
McGrath, Earl J., 291
McGraw Overseas Digest, 42
McGurn, Barrett, 118
McInerny, Nancy, 157, 265, 285
McKenzie, Marjorie, 224
McLaughlin, Phyllis, 178
McNutt, Paul, 94
McPherson, John, 163
Mead, Margaret, 87
medals, 108, 172, 226, 358, 385
medical care for vets, xv, 9, 12–15, 36, 48–49, 81, 91, 98, 103, 110, 277, 353–57, 367, 370–71. *See also* hospitals; VA hospitals
medical corps, 6–11, 13, 57, 379
medics, 64, 173, 176, 178, 255–56, 383
Meet McGonegal (documentary), 10
Meet Me in St. Louis (movie), 30
Meister, Sam, 153
Mellett, Lowell, 31, 64–65
Men, The (movie), 91
Mendonsa, George, 125, *126*, 127
Menninger, William, xii–xiii, 55, 92, 184
merchant marines, 241, 357
Metropolitan Life Insurance Company, 346–49
Mexican Americans, 285, 317
Mexico, 336
Meyerhof, Robert, 298–99
middle class, 238, 302, 360–62
Midway Atoll, attack on, 32
Miles, William Richard, 265–66
Milhaud, Darius, 326
military public relations officers (PROs), 5–6, 11, 23–25, 44–45, 143–44
Millar, Ken, 197–98
Miller, Merle, 56, 145–47
Miller, Robert C., 24–25
Mills College (Oakland), 326
Minch, Robert, 215
Mississippi Delta, 225
Moede, Leslie, 46
Moley, Raymond, 240
Montana Historical Society, 221
Montgomery, Robert, 197
Moore, Amzie, 236–37
Moore's Ford (Georgia), 229–30
Morgenthau, Henry, Jr., 118

INDEX

Morris, Frank D., 340
mortality rates, vets vs. nonvets, 369–70
mortgage guaranty program, GI Bill, xv, 262–66, 340–49, 354, 357
    cost of, 355
    gender inequities in, xvii, 264–65
    housing crisis and, 262–63, 271
    racial discrimination in, xvii, 264–66, 344–49, 362–63
Moser, Hanna M., 372
Moses, Robert, 267, 347
Motion Picture Production Code, 196
Moulton, Seth, 363
movies, xviii, 26, 39, 328, 374
    Black troops in, 64–65
    and D-Day invasion, 74–75
    on divorce, 203–5, 214
    focused on WWII, 28–40
    government sanctioned, 31–35, 39, 287
    grim realism in, xii, 33–34, 38–40, 75
    on infidelity, 211–15
    morale boosting, 31, 33
    and off-duty troops, 41–42, 66, 113–16
    postwar, 195–201, 214, 286–88
    propaganda in, 30–35
    on returning vets, 91, 214, 287
    on vets with psychiatric issues, 90–91, 170–72
    violent vets in, 194–201
    See also specific movie titles
MPs, 110–11, 113, 115–16
Mrs. Miniver (movie), 33
Murphy, Audie, 151, 185–86, 270, 378
Murphy, Henry, 235–36
music schools/musicians, xvi, 325–28, 335
Mussolini, Benito, 11, 36
mustering-out pay, 98, 100, 103, 149, 163
My War (Rooney), 364–65

NAACP, 113, 274, 296
    annual convention of, 261, 274, 318
    on blue discharges, 164
    and discrimination in education, 97, 302, 316, 318
    and discrimination in housing, 345, 348
    members of, 236–38
    mob violence committee of, 231–32
    and mortgage guarantees, 265–66
    Veterans Affairs Committee of, xviii, 97, 164
Nagasaki, 120–21
Naked and the Dead, The (Mailer), 174
Naples, Italy, 11, 18, 44, 49–50, 69

Nasaw, Joshua J., 181, 368
National Center for PTSD, 374
National Emergency Committee Against Mob Violence, 231–32
National Housing Acts, 355
National Housing Agency, 257
National Institute of Mental Health, 217
National Maritime Union (NMU), 132–33
National Negro Council, 111
National Resources Planning Board (NRPB), 97–98
Naval Discharge Review Board, 164
Navy Department, xviii, 23–24, 25, 36, 60
Nazis, 46, 52, 74, 107, 196, 198, 366
Negro Newspaper Publishers Association, 212–13
Negro Soldier, The (movie), 65
neuropsychiatric disorders (NP)
    medical corps unprepared for, 6–9, 13
    symptoms of, 7–9, 79–80, 172–73, 184–86
    treatment for, 6–9, 12–14, 90–92, 103, 169–73, 184–88
    See also psychiatric disorders
neuropsychiatric disorders, servicemen diagnosed with
    discharge of xii, 8, 12–14
    number of, xii–xiii, 13, 191
    homecoming of, 14–17, 21, 90–92
    on hospital ships, 15–16
    pensions for, 368
    removed from front lines, 76–80
New Deal, xvi, 31, 94–95, 98, 104, 240, 243, 254, 260, 353
New Guinea, 36, 197, 215, 226
New Republic, The, 98, 145, 280–81
New York City, 132, 216, 232, 256, 259
    art/dance/drama schools in, 324–25, 328–34
    gay and lesbian vets in, 158–59
    GIs disembark at, 144–45
    Harlem, 233, 347, 358
    vet housing in, 267, 346–49
    at war's end, 124–25, *126*
New York Herald Tribune, 15, 27, 36, 119, 144, 242
New York Times Forum, The, 306
New York Times Magazine, The, 10
New York Times, The, 26–27, 34, 36, 75, 88, 109–10, 113–14, 119–20, 124–25, 130, 136, 150, 157, 196, 213, 246–47, 259, 265, 270, 276, 281, 285–86, 304–5, 359, 384
New Yorker, The, 27, 42, 149, 183–84

INDEX

New Zealand, 3, 7–8
newspapers, 99, 212–13, 242
   on the atomic bomb, 119–20
   on celebrations at war's end, 123–27
   focus on White troops, 64, 73
   on home front, 87–89, 356
   on housing crisis, 258–59
   and military censors, 20–21, 75
   on vets as menaces, 194–95, 246
   on restless servicemen, 113–14
   war news in, 5, 24–28, 40, 74–77
   on the wounded, 9–10, 14–17
   See also war correspondents; *specific titles*
newsreels, 10, 15, 93
   focus on White troops, 73
   on GIs and women overseas, 84–85, 87
   on the home front, 87, 356
   propaganda on, 30–31
   on vets at college, 307–9
   war news in, xii, 5–6, 30–33, 37, 40, 75, 84
Newsweek, 27, 42, 153, 376–77
Nial, Thomas M., 254
Nicholson, Marguerite, 67
Nidasio, Luigiana, 222
Nijinska, Bronislava, 333
Niles, David, 231, 233
Nimitz, Chester, 32
92nd Infantry Division (Buffalo Soldiers), 69
Nixon, Pat, 124, 244, 257
Nixon, Richard, 124, 243–44, 248, 257, 271
No Boats, No Votes, Get Us Home clubs, 136
Normandy, 43, 46, 77, 79, 110, 366
North Africa, 3, 8–9, 12, 45, 61, 64, 128, 151, 187, 283, 327
Nuremberg, Germany, 171, 285

Obama, Barack, 366
occupation duty/troops, xiii, 71–72, 108, 128–31, 134–35, 138, 331, 334
O'Dwyer, William, 241–42
off-duty activities, 41–44, 46, 55, 65–66, 68, 113
Office of Defense Transportation, 13, 150
Office of the Surgeon General, xviii, 45, 48–49, 55, 79, 89–90, 92
Office of War Information (OWI), 9–10, 31, 34, 36, 64–65, 151
Office of War Mobilization and Reconversion, xviii, 253, 255, 338, 356
O'Hara, Frank, 156, 369
Ohio State, 295, 299
Okinawa, Japan, 85, 106–7, 109, 118, 121–22, 186–87

Oliver, Adrian L., 319
100th Infantry Battalion, 59–60
One Soldier's Story (Dole), 44
Operation Magic Carpet, 143–44
Orthwine, Rudolf, 332–33
Ostroff, Ray, 220
Ottley, Roi, 221–22
Overton, Grace Sloan, 85
Owens, Robert, 335

Pace, Gladys, 160
Pacific theater, xii, 3, 36
   Black troops in, 63–64, 70–71, 112
   documented by filmmaker, 32
   final WWII battles in, 106–9, 117–18, 122
   and neuropsychiatric disorders, 8, 12, 15
   relations with local women in, 51, 85
   relocation to, 77–78, 107–9
   troops marooned in, 134, 137
Palmasani, Frank, 186
parents, vets live with, 155–57, 162–63, 177, 256–57, 261, 328–32, 343
Paris, France, 68, 138, 169
   American servicemen in, 114–16
   American vets' study in, 334–36
   liberation of, 77, 84
   war correspondents in, 56, 84
Patman, Wright, 257
Patterson, Robert P., 117–18, 130, 137, 140
Patton, George S., Jr., 24
Peabody, George, 218
peacetime
   armed forces of, 60, 128–29, 138–40
   transitioning to, 97–98, 103, 159–60, 338–39
   See also economy: conversion to peacetime
Pearl Harbor, xiv, 25, 39, 59, 62, 94, 98, 137, 151
Pearson, Drew, 138
Peck, Gregory, 211–12, 288
Percy Jones Army Hospital (Michigan), 292, 367–68
Petcher, Emma Belle, 28, 37
Petry, Ann, 214
Philippines, 46, 51, 63, 137, 151, 174, 215
Phillips, Michael, 372–74
Pickett, Roscoe Simmons, 300–301
Pittsburgh Courier, The, 111, 160, 162, 221–22, 224
Planned Parenthood, 206
Poage, William R., 311–12
poets/poetry, xvii–xviii, 42, 129, 156, 175, 178, 336

political office
   vets' campaign for, 240–48, 267, 269–70
politicians, serve in WWII, 240–48
Poor People's Campaign, 359
post exchanges (PX), 41–42, 303
post-traumatic stress disorder (PTSD), 90
   diagnosed later in life, 376–85
   as distinct diagnostic category in *DSM*, 375–76, 380
   lobotomies for, 188–89
   and POWS, 380–83
   shock therapy for, 178, 187–88
   suffering in silence with, 374–75, 379–80, 383, 385
   symptoms of, 8–9, 178–83, 186, 374–77, 381–83
   and TBI (traumatic brain injury), 8, 184–87
   treatment for, 184–88, 374–85
   undiagnosed/untreated, xi–xiii, 165, 187, 374–80
postwar culture, xvi, 195, 323–25
"Post-war Plans of Negro Soldiers" survey, 157
Potter, George, Jr., 180
Powell, Adam Clayton, Jr., 113
Powell, Junior H., 106
President's Commission on Veterans' Pensions, xviii, 279, 313, 336–37, 339
President's Committee on Civil Rights, 233
Preventive Medicine in World War II, 45
Pride of the Marines (movie), 91
prisoners of war (POWs), 39, 80, 110, 115, 117, 147, 285, 380–83
Problem Drinker, The (Hirsh), 47, 182
propaganda, 121, 210, 277
   in movies, 30–35, 65, 171
   on newsreels, 30–31
   and wartime victories, 35–36
prosthetic limbs, 10–11
prostitution, 48–51, 58, 85, 114–15
Protzman, Thomas B., 15–16
Pryor, Thomas M., 286–87
psychiatric disorders, 165
   high incidences of, xii–xiii, 13–14, 79–80
   lobotomies for, 371–74
   medical corps unprepared for, 6–9, 13
   news reports on, 13–16
   shock therapy for, 372–73
   suffering in silence with, 173, 374–75
   symptoms of, 172–73, 371
   treatment for, 371–74
   See also neuropsychiatric disorders; post-traumatic stress disorder (PTSD); psychoneurosis

Psychiatric Primer for the Veteran's Family and Friends, A (Dumas and Keen), 173
psychiatrists, 170–73, 184–85, 188, 192, 205, 210, 371
psychoneurosis, 7–8, 90, 103, 169–72, 182–87. *See also* neuropsychiatric disorders
psychotherapy, 185, 379
Public Law 10, 353–54
Public Law 16, 94–97
Public Law 293, 354–55
Public Law 475, 341
Publishers Weekly, 27
Puente, Tito, 327
Purifoy, Noah, 323–24
Pyle, Ernie, 11, 28, 43, 75–76, 365

Quirk, Thomas J., 144

Rabinowitz, Paula, 196
racial conflicts, 70–73, 110–11, 225, 229, 231, 267
racial discrimination
   of Black GIs, xvi, 53–54, 65–68, 72–73, 111–13, 116
   of Black vets, 97, 158–60, 164, 224–30, 264–67, 308
   blue discharges and, 159–60, 164
   in employment, xv, 282–85, 314–17
   in housing for vets, xv, 344–49, 362
   of returning vets, 235
   in schools/job training, 314–19
   and war wives, 354
radio programs, 118, 212, 306, 356
   armed forces, 87
   celebrity commentators on, 29
   focus on White troops, 64, 73
   home front relies on, 23–24, 28–29
   on neuropsychiatric vets, 90
   politician speeches on, 29, 139
   politicians' speeches on, 99
   on postwar marriages, 206
   war reports on, xviii, 5, 23, 28–31, 40, 75, 120
RAMPs (Recovered American Military Personnel), 110
Randall School (Hartford, CT), 332
Random House, 27
rank, privileges of, 134, 137
Rankin, John, 95, 98, 100–102, 275–76, 278, 310, 323
ration packs, 43–44
Rauschenberg, Robert, 323–24

INDEX

Ray, Raymond, 153
readjustment (unemployment) allowances, GI Bill, xv, 103, 254–56, 278, 290,
    under American Legion draft, 100–102
    and Black vets, xvi, 284
    effects on economy, 338–39
Reagan, Ronald, 366
Red Ball Express (Europe), 64
Red Cross, 43, 111, 135, 190, 221–22
    Donut Dollies and, 178
    Java Junctions of, 113–14
    and postwar marriages, 206–7
    volunteers denied benefits, 357
Redbook, 206
Reese, Lavon, 180–82
Regional Council of Negro Leadership, 236–38
Reims, France, 113–15, 135
Reno, Nevada, 202–3, 329
repatriation of servicemen overseas, 3, 96, 132, 135–36, 144
Republican Party, 240, 242–45, 247, 271–72, 358
Reynolds, Quentin, 28
Richards, Franklin, 345
Riddle, Clinton, 151
Ride the Pink Horse (Hughes), 197-8
Ride the Pink Horse (movie), 197–98
Riefenstahl, Leni, 30
Robeson, Paul, 232
Robinson, Jackie, 67
"Rockin' Chair Money," 254
Rockwell, Norman, 155–56
Rodriguez y Gonzalez, Amado "Pancho," 200
Rood, Marcia Reese, 181–82
Rooney, Andy, 364–65
Roosevelt, Eleanor, 107, 118, 120–21, 138
Roosevelt, Franklin D., 77–78, 139, 240–41, 356
    on Blacks in military, 60–61
    on censorship/propaganda, 36
    on D-Day invasion, 75
    death of, 118–19
    on equal opportunity, xvi
    establishes OWI, 31
    on films of Tarawa battle, 38
    "four freedoms" of, 151
    and "second bill of rights" (1944), 100–101
    on shortage of manpower, 80
    on social welfare benefits, 94–95
    on transition to peace, 97–98
    on vets' benefits, 94–95, 98–100
Roosevelt, Franklin D., Jr., 270

Russell, Eugene, Sr., 315
Russell, Richard, 132
Rutgers University, 295, 306
Ryan, Robert, 198–99

Salerno, Italy, 11, 36, 63
Salinger, J. D., 76–77, 107, 135, 169, 171, 174–76, 183–84
Salinger, Margaret, 77
San Francisco, 120, 132
    gay and lesbian vets in, 158–59
    GIs disembark at, 190
    servicemen in, 122–23, 150
    vet housing in, 259, 346
    vets' education in, 326, 333
    war brides disembark in, 221
Sanchez, Lena and Emiliano, 83
Saturday Evening Post, The, 26–27, 42, 146, 155, 194, 292, 294, 305
Schmid, Al, 91
Schmidt, Dana Adams, 113–15
Schueler, Jon, 323–24
Scott, Robert, 28
See Here, Private Hargrove (Hargrove), 27–28
segregation
    in armed forces, 59–62, 65–69, 113
    Black servicemen and, 65–67, 72–73, 102, 113
    and Black vets' job search, 282–83
    in cigarette camps, 110–11, 113
    and discrimination in housing, 348
    in education, xvii, 301–2
    in housing, xv, 344–49
    and menial jobs for Blacks, 316–17
    overseas, 68–72
    on public transport, 65–67, 225–27
    in the South, 65–69, 225–27, 230–31, 238, 301, 345
    in training camps, 65–68, 70
Selective Service System, xviii, 6, 18–20, 283
Selective Training and Service Act, 20, 235, 273–74, 353
Service Fathers' Release Association, 131
Servicemen's Readjustment Act, The, 104, 311
Sevareid, Eric, 29, 50
sexual
    assault, 52–54, 58, 71
    desires of GIs, 47–58, 85, 87, 109, 114–15
    desires of war wives, 86–89
    disease, 48–51, 71, 85, 114, 148
    double standards, 212
    dysfunction, 210–11
    relations in marriages, 209

shell shock, 12, 26, 182, 186, 248, 375
Sherrod, Robert, 28, 37–39
Short, Jack, 293
shortages/rationing, xiii, 36, 152–54
Shull, Lynwood, 226
Sicily, Italy, 9, 11–12, 61, 186, *204*
signal corps, 59, 283–84
Simpson, Louis, 178, 184
Since You Went Away (movie), 34
Sledge, Eugene, 106–7, 122, 177, 185, 384
Smith, E. Rogers, 7, 9
SNCC (Student Nonviolent Coordinating Committee), 237
Snipes, Maceo, 229
Snyder, John, 253, 255, 338
social reformism, 353
social welfare benefits, 94–95, 98, 104–5
Soldier from the War Returning (Childers), 115, 382–83
Solomon Islands, 7–8, 41–42, 151
Soutar, Arch, 194
Southern Christian Leadership Conference, 359
Southern Regional Council (SRC), xviii, 225, 234, 284, 302, 316, 318, 321
souvenir collecting, 143, 193, 200, 229
Soviet Union, 120, 173, 295, 365
Spillane, Mickey, 197–98
St. Augustine's College (Raleigh, NC), 302–3
Stancil, Stewart Alan, 379–80
Stanford University study. See *Father Relations of War-Born Children* (Stolz)
Stars and Stripes, The, xvii–xviii, 87, 135–36
Stassen, Harold, 240
State University of New York, 296
Stavisky, Sam, 247, 279–80
Steffens, Paul, 153
Steinbeck, John, 24, 27
Steinhauser, Frederic, 298
Stelle, John, 99
Stephenson, James and Gladys, 227–28
Stevenson, Eleanor, 206
Stewart, Jimmy, 286–88
Stewart, Ollie, 53, 68, 116
Stimson, Henry L., 61, 69, 78–79, 119
Stolz, Lois Meek, 211, 217–20
Stouffer, Samuel, 248–49, 253, 339
Stratton, William G., 241–42
Streetcar Named Desire, A (play), 199–200
strikes, nationwide, 274–79
Stuyvesant Town, 346–49
Styer, W. D., 137

suburban developments, xvii, 341–46, 362
Swarthmore College, 305, 384

Taft, Robert A., 260, 341
Taft-Ellender-Wagner bill, 260, 262, 267–72
Talmadge, Eugene, 226–27
Tarawa (Sherrod), 28, 37–39
Tarawa atoll, 37–39, 173
Tauchin, Joe, Jr., 276
Taylor, Toni, 206
Terkel, Studs, 83, 111, 181, 293, 364–65
theater schools/programs, xvi, 328–32
Thirty Seconds over Tokyo (Lawson), 28
This Is the Army (movie), 33
Thurmond, Strom, 241–42, 244–45
Time, 27, 37–38, 42, 84, 136, 246, 294, 296, 300
Tittle, Marilyn, 181
Toye, Joe, 181
training camps, 65–68, 82–83, 369
transportation home, 129, 139, *167*
  of Black GIs, 112–13
  lack of ships for, xiii, 110, 136, 138
  ships/vessels for, 13, 78, 132–33, 143–44, 150
  via plane/railroad, 13, 143, 149–50
  and "war bride ships," 220–21
  See also hospital ships
traumatic brain injuries (TBIs), 184–87
Travelers Aid Society (Chicago), 149–50
Travis, Dempsey, 303
Tregaskis, Richard, 24–25, 27–28
Tritz, Roman, 372–73
Triumph of the Will (Riefenstahl), 30
Truckline Café (movie), 199
Truman, Harry S., 140
  and antilynching legislation, 230–33
  on demobilization, 130, 132–33, 138
  on dropping atomic bomb, 118–19
  "Fair Deal" of, 355–56
  housing crisis and, 253, 259–60, 262–63, 271–72, 341
  on job placement for vets, 273
  signs Public Law 293, 354–55
Trump, Donald, 366
Tunisia Campaign, 8, 194
Tuskegee Airmen, 61, 112–13
Tuttle, William M., 215

unemployment, xiii, 77, 338
  crisis, 255, 281, 313, 337
  effect of GI Bill benefits on, xv–xvi
  readjustment allowances, xv, 98, 100–103, 162–63, 254, 313–14, 357

uniforms, xv, 148, 152–54, 225–26, 244, 248, 278, 280, 358
unions, 132–33, 275–79, 320, 330, 342, 345
United Mine Workers (UAW), 275
United Parents of Veterans, 131
United Press Service, 24–25
United States Employment Service (USES), 255, 279–83, 285–86, 318–19
University of Chicago, 86, 179, 203, 264, 273, 298
University of Illinois, 19, 295, 296, 305
University of Iowa, 298–99
University of Michigan, 295, 299
University of Southern California, 299–300
University of Wisconsin, 295, 299
unmarried veterans, 203, 264–65, 285, 292
U.S. Army, 18–20
  Black GIs in, 62, 69–73
  breakdown of discipline in postwar, 134–35
  casualties in, 76–77
  and discharge eligibility, 108
  draft into, 150–51
  on homosexuals, 161
  integration in, 70–72
  politicians enlist in, 241
  racial discrimination in, 63, 65–68
  Research Branch of, xviii, 70, 134, 157, 248
  service units of, 60–65, 69, 111–12, 282–83
  surveys of vets' experiences in, 142–43
  White supremacy in, 66–67, 160
U.S. Army Air Force, 60, 175, 199, 218, 286–87, 329
U.S. Congress, 20, 363
  on abuses in vocational schools/programs, 311–12, 315
  and the GI Bill, xv–xvii, 292–93, 296, 306, 323
  and housing, 257–60, 262–63, 267–72, 295, 341, 355
  and vets as candidates for office, 241–44, 247
  and vets' benefits, 279, 356
U.S. Department of Agriculture, 14, 238
U.S. Marine Corps, 151, 216, 218
  Blacks in, 62, 64
  on Guadalcanal, 3–9
  neuropsychiatric disorders and, 6–9, 185, 186–88
  politicians enlist in, 241
  women in, 285–86
U.S. Navy
  Blacks in, 61–62, 164, 227
  on blue-discharged vets, 163–64

enlisting in, 151, 156
on homosexuals, 161, 163–64
Operation Magic Carpet of, 143–44
politicians enlist in, 240–42
and psychiatric disorders, 184
retirement board of, 367
segregation in, 113
vets, 216, 243, 278
U.S. Steel, 276, 278
USO, 29, 42
USS *Croatan*, 113
USS *Santee*, 327

VA hospitals, 3, 210, 226, 238
  and alcoholics, 369
  construction of, 99, 354–56
  electric shock therapy in, 187–88
  and the GI Bill, 103, 354
  lobotomies done in, 188–89, 372
  mental hygiene clinics of, 184, 371, 378–79
  and psychiatric disorders, 9, 103, 169–72, 187–89, 371–76
  and PTSD, 377–80, 383
Varns, Thomas, 255
V-E Day, 50–52, 61, 71, 106–7, 117, 125, 142, 152–53, 169, 182
Veasey, Millie Dunn, 302–3
Venereal Disease Control Division, 48–49
Veterans Administration (VA), xviii, 10, 173
  on blue discharges, 162–63
  Dept. of Medicine and Surgery of, 354–55
  and disability claims/pensions, 148, 368
  housing loans and, 263–66, 340–41, 344, 362–63
  and job counseling/placement, 163, 279, 284–86
  Neuropsychiatry Division of, 187–89
  opinion on tobacco use (1993), 370
  and vocational schools, 311–13
  See also VA hospitals
Veterans Administration's Office of General Counsel, 370
Veterans' Emergency Housing Program, 260, 262, 267
Veterans of Foreign Wars (VFW), 99, 179, 243, 258, 270, 278
Veterans' Preference Act, 354
Vietnam veterans, 79, 151, 365, 375–76
Villalobos, Robert Coronado, 317
Vinson, Fred, 253
V-J Day, 57, 128, 142, 274–75
V-Mail ("Victory Mail"), 23–24, 88–89

INDEX

vocational education, 100, 357
   abuses in, xvi, 311–19
   art schools/artists, xvi, 322–25, 328, 335–36
   Black vets in, 314–17, 321, 324
   for cooking, 322, 325
   for dance, xvi, 330, 332–34
   for flight training, 317–18
   GI Bill funding of, xv–xvi, 103, 310–25, 337, 339
   high attendance of, xvi, 308–9
   at high schools, 320–21
   for music, xvi, 325–28
   and postwar labor shortages, 321–22
   for theater, xvi, 328–32
vocational rehabilitation programs for disabled vets, 94–97, 354
Vonnegut, Kurt, 19, 80, 110, 115, 383
Voorhis, Jerry, 243
voting, 60, 271
   Black vets register for, 226–39
   poll taxes, 225, 245
   registration campaigns by Black activists, 234–37, 245
   by White vets, 239–49

WACs (Women's Army Corps), 43, 134
   Black women in, 62, 64, 67, 72, 160, 302
   and blue discharges, 163
   and GI Bill housing loans, 265
   lesbians in, 57, 159
   return home, 142, 144, 154, 157
   seek postwar education, 302–3
   seek postwar jobs, 285–86
   traumatic memories of, 178
Wagner, Robert, 260. *See also* Taft-Ellender-Wagner bill
Walker, Henry J., 312–13
Wall Street Journal, The, 372–73
Waller, Willard, 189
war bonds, 29, 33, 36
war brides, 53–54, 131–32, 220–21
War Brides Act, 131–32, 220, 354
war correspondents, 64, 78
   Black, 23, 110
   books by, 27–28
   censorship of, 24–26, 75
   on D-Day invasion, 74–77
   at the end of WWII, 106–9, 118
   on horrors of war, 25–27, 40
   on racial tension, 110–11
   role of, 23–28
   women, 10, 14, 23, 298
   See also specific names

War Department, xviii, 10, 19, 118, 137, 253
   on blue-discharged vets, 163–64
   demobilization plans of, 77–78, 128–30, 132
   demobilization point system of, 108–12
   on draft eligibility, 60, 80
   on homecoming of wounded, 14–17
   on homosexuals, 55, 161, 163–64
   patriotic homilies of, 151
   postal system of, 23–24
   psychoneurosis pamphlet of, 169–70
   on segregation of Black GIs, 60–61, 80
   soldier-marriage regulations of, 53–54
   on wartime victories, 36
war industries, xv–xvi, 83, 94, 98, 154, 157, 208, 353
War Shipping Administration, 132, 143–44
war wives, xii, 207–9, 283–84
   accompanying husbands to training camp, 82–83
   advice for, 189–90, 205–11, 224
   demand demobilization, xiii, 130–33, 139–40
   duties/roles of, 209
   forced to give up jobs, xiv, 82–84, 208–9
   foreign-born, 131–32, 220–22, 354
   infidelity of, 202, 212–15
   juvenile delinquency, blamed for, 8
   postwar roles, xiv, 208–10, 360–61
   sexual needs of, 86–89
   See also divorce; families; marriage
war workers, xiii, xvi, 36, 83, 253–54, 257, 273, 292, 356. *See also* war industries
Washington, D.C., 164, 270–71
Washington Post, The, 10, 119, 140, 153, 202–3, 247, 270–71, 279–80
Washington State, 222
WASPs (Women's Airforce Service Pilots), 286, 357
Watkins, Ulysses, 284
WAVEs (Women Accepted for Volunteer Emergency Service), 43, 72, 142, 178, 265, 274, 285–86, 335
wealth accumulation, 362
welfare state, for veterans, 94, 104, 353–63
Wenzel, John, 384–85
West Coast, 150, 257–58, 324
Wheeler, Burton, 62–63
White, Walter, 231–32, 345
White House Office of Management and Budget, 337
White supremacy, 66–67, 72, 160, 225, 238–39, 245
Williams, Hank, Jr., 254

INDEX

Williams, Hosea, 238
Williams, Ted, 289
Williams, Tennessee, 199–200
Willkie, Wendell, 60
Wilson, Sloan, 211
With the Marines at Tarawa (movie), 38–39
Wives in Waiting Club, 131
Wolcott, Jesse, 271
Woman's Day, 207
women, on home front, 82–92
   admitted to colleges, xvii, 304–7
   "Dear John" letters of, xiv, 88–89
   fear vets' bad habits, 58
   nurse the wounded, 89–92
   in postwar films/fiction, 196, 199
   postwar jobs of, 298
   and unfaithful husbands, 84–89, 210–13
   at war's end, 123–25, *126*, 127
   wartime duties/jobs of, xvi, 23, 88, 126, 306
women, in armed forces, xvi, 24, 35
   jobs/roles of, 285
   who are lesbians, xvii, 54–58
   See also WACs; WAVEs
women veterans, 157, 242
   denied benefits, xvii, 264–65, 357
   discriminated in education, 306–9
   discriminated in job search, 285–86
   postwar jobs of, 274, 285–86
Wood, Gilbert T., 15
Woodard, Isaac, 226
Woods, Sherby, 320–21

World War I, xii–xiii, 10–12, 60, 69, 93–94, 271, 338, 375
World War II
   celebrating end of, 107, 121–25, *126*, 127, 151–52, 172
   daily suffering during, 4–9, 17–18, 25, 27, 79
   duration of, xii–xiii
   and home-front complacency, 35–36
   human costs of, xii, 17, 20–21, 33–34, 37, 75–78, 80–81, 122, 173
   number of Americans in, xii, xv, 3, 239
   official reports of, 23–24
wounded, the, xviii, 18–19, 365
   homecoming of, xii, 3, 14–17, 21, 165
   medical care for, 3, 6, 9–11, 13
   POWs, 380
   those who cared for, 89–92, 178
   vast number of, 367–68
   See also disabled veterans
Wright, Teresa, 91, 214
Wyatt, Wilson, 260, 262, 341
Wyler, William, 33, 287

Yank: The Army Weekly, xviii, 16–17, 35, 56, 87–89, 106–9, 118, 138, 145, 163
Yoder, Robert M., 207
Yokohama, Japan, 137
YWCA, 206–7

Zeidler, Carl, 241–42
Zimmer, Greta, 125, *126*, 127